IRONCLADS AT WAR

IRONCLADS AT WAR

The Origin and Development of the Armored Warship, 1854-1891

Jack Greene
Alessandro Massignani

COMBINED PUBLISHING
Pennsylvania

PUBLISHER'S NOTE

The headquarters of Combined Publishing are located midway between Valley Forge and the Germantown battlefield, on the outskirts of Philadelphia. From its beginnings, our company has been steeped in the oldest traditions of American military history and publishing. Our historic surroundings help maintain our focus on military history and our books strive to uphold the standards of style, quality and durability first established by the earliest bookmakers of Germantown and Philadelphia so many years ago. Our famous monk-and-console logo reflects our commitment to the modern and yet historic enterprise of publishing.

We call ourselves Combined Publishing because we have always felt that our goals could only be achieved through a "combined" effort by authors, publishers and readers. We have always tried to maintain maximum communication between these three key players in the reading experience.

We are always interested in hearing from prospective authors about new books in our field. We also like to hear from our readers and invite you to contact us at our offices in Pennsylvania with any questions, comments or suggestions, or if you have difficulty finding our books at a local bookseller.

For information, address:
Combined Publishing
P.O. Box 307
Conshohocken, PA 19428
E-mail: combined@dca.net
Web: www.dca.net/combinedbooks
Orders: 1-800-4-1860-65

Library of Congress Cataloging-in-Publication Data
Greene, Jack.
　Ironclads at War : the origin and development of the armored warship, 1854-1891 / Jack Greene, Allessandro Massignani.
　　p.　　cm.
　Includes bibliographical references (p.　) and index.
　ISBN 0-938289-58-6
　　1. Naval history, modern—19th Century. 2. Armored vessels—History—19th century.
3. United States—History—Civil War, 1861-1865—Naval operations. 4. Armored vessels—United States—History—19th century. 5. United States—History, Naval—To 1900.
　I. Massignani, Alessandro. II. Title.
D362.G74　1998　　　　　　　　　　　　　　　　　　　　　　　97-47185
359.8'35—dc21　　　　　　　　　　　　　　　　　　　　　　　　CIP

Printed in the United States of America.
Maps by Beth Queman

Contents

Sidebars

Maps

Introduction

This tome is dedicated to the History Department of Whitman College and to Professor Andrea Curami.

Three themes will steam through this book and both entertain and enlighten you on the voyage.

First is the story of humanity's violence—so often man's violence—that is the story of *Ironclads at War*. The "guns and bugles" side of our yarn is one of heroic bravery, of close range broadsides, shellfire, ramming, torpedoes, and daring plans as well as disasters and disastrous leadership. We did not write this to be a dry discourse on battles won or lost, but wanted it to be an *adventure* in history. Humanity's ingenuity at war knows few bounds, and with the ironclad, it took many exotic and adventurous courses in its development.

Second, we want to weave the story of technological change throughout the story of the ironclads. From short range actions to greater and greater ranges for combat and evolving guns; to larger and more complex vessels and types; to new tactics and directions. We travel from a period of experiments and single examples to an accepted concept of a capital ship.

Third, we want to lightly touch on the national policies of the Great Powers and how their goals and desires affected the course of ironclad development in their respective nations. While the United Kingdom and France dominated this period at sea, they saw little in the way of naval combat and both, especially France after the disastrous land war of 1870-71, had their own specific naval needs. The position of third most powerful navy changed hands in this period. At one point it was the United States of America, at another time Italy, or Russia, or the Ottoman Empire, all vying to gain the fruits of naval power on the eve of Alfred Thayer Mahan's eye-opening writings on *The Influence of Seapower on History*.

This book is in part an attempt to update, in the light of new materials now available, H.W. Wilson's classic *Ironclads in Action*, first published in 1895 (though at times we wanted to retitle it *The Influence of Ironclads on History*). While certainly a worthwhile source, and well written, it contains errors of fact and areas of omission. Wilson later wrote a revised and updated book entitled *Battleships in War* which took the reader through World War I, that has recently been reprinted. While corrected after the original *Ironclads in Action* and including several of the actions he earlier passed over, it still contains many errors of fact.

We have tried to introduce several of the small ironclad operations that he ignored in his first book, like the exploits of the Danish *Rolf Krake*, or the Spanish Cartagena actions. We have also plumbed foreign sources to add new information for the English reader, especially about Lissa and the War of the Pacific. *Ironclads at War* is not just a rehash of ironclads in the American Civil War, but gives a world perspective to the revolution in naval technology which swept the last century from wooden ships-of-the-line to modern battleships.

While based largely on secondary sources, where confusion has arisen on tactical details in other books, we have used original sources to try to "set the story straight." Thus we try to clear up some of the missed aspects in the action between the *Monitor* and the *Merrimack* or the details of the ordnance used at the Battle of Lissa.

We discuss only in passing the many other aspects of naval combat that affected this period of history—with a few exceptions. Thus you will not find great coverage of the blockade runners, raiders, or river warfare of the American Civil War, the development of fortifications, the birth of the torpedo boat and the submarine, or other important aspects—except where it directly impacts on the ironclad. We do take this opportunity to acquaint readers with some actions that involved only wooden warships where it is an action that is not recounted in other easily accessible English language sources.

Readers should note that the amount of material on this period is daunting—and unbalanced. There are literally 400 works and 100 papers that discuss the *Monitor* and the *Merrimack,* while to find six works in English on the Chilean Civil War is quite an accomplishment and even in Spanish there are only a few dozen. Additionally, we have gone into detail on some actions, and skimmed over other battles for space and time reasons. So in this regard our work can not be considered definitive, but if we can spark interest in this incredible period of naval ferment, technology, and development, and maybe point some future historian down this path of study, than we have succeeded in our goal.

Special thanks for his help must go out to Andrew Smith for his timely assistance securing needed materials and his always helpful comments, including the contribution of his sidebar. He kept us from making errors of fact in several areas. And also to Beth Queman for her fine artwork and patience when asked to make yet one more change from the original!

Quotations from British Crown Copyright material appear by permission of the Controller of Her Majesty's Stationary Office.

We would like to thank the staff at Combined Publishing, and Chris Perello and the staff of *Command* magazine; Director Bob Holcombe of the Confederate Naval Museum; noted artillerist Dr. Spencer Tucker; the Curator of the Hampton Roads Museum, Joseph M. Judge; Richard M. Hatcher III, Historian for Fort Sumter National Monument; Dr. Peter Brook for assistance in researching the *Huascar* incident of 1877; Ms. Paola van der Meer for her kind patience with Dutch and French articles; Fabio Degli Esposti for procuring some documents on Cavalli and Lissa; and Dave Isby for his suggested corrections.

Our efforts were also aided by the staff of the Public Records Office, Kew, London; the British Library Newspaper Library, Colindale, London; Commander A. Holm of the Marinens Bibliotek, Copenhagen; John Montgomery of the Royal United Services Institute for Defence Studies, London, for promptly supplying copies of articles originally published in the Institute's *Journal;* Ann Hassinger and Mary Beth Straight of the U. S. Naval Institute for supplying copies of articles originally published in the Institute's *Proceedings;* David K. Brown, R.C.N.C., for advice on 19th century cruiser design; and Dr. Robert L. Scheina, Professor of History at the National Defense University, Fort McNair, Washington D.C., for his advice on sources for Peruvian naval history.

Also we would like to thank A.E. Sichterman of the Dutch museum ship *Schorpioen;* Vittorio Tagliabue and his photograph collection; the editor of the Japanese version of *Command* magazine, Yasushi Nakaguro, for help on the Japanese Civil War; Lynda Leahy for her help in obtaining articles from Northeastern University. Dr. Mike Bennighof also contributed a sidebar and helpful comments throughout on the Austrian navy and the Mobile campaign. Thanks to Captain Jaime Urdangarin of the Chilean Naval Mission for several photographs of the *Huascar* and his comments. Jose Luis Arcon Dominguez and especially Jose Lledo Calabuig for help on the Cartagena discussion. The fine computer artwork and comments by Daniel Dowdey enhanced our section on Charleston. Also P.C. Coker and his ship model work. We also thank the Wyles Civil War collection at UCSB and the staff at the South Bay Library who were helpful in getting us materials, the staff of the National Maritime Museum and especially David Hodge, the Archivio centrale dello stato at Rome, the Library of the University of London, Rian van Meeteren, Dana Lombardy, Jeff Kingston, Richard Pfost, Vance von Borries, Taran Stone, Amanda White, and Binky.

Of course, all errors are our own.

—Jack Greene, Baywood Park, California
—Alessandro Massignani, Valdagno, Vicenza

Warship Types

Ships-of-the-lines sometimes called liners, were the battleships of the era before the ironclad. There were three types of ship-of-the-line. One was the sailing ship-of-the-line which had the sail as its sole motive power. All American ships-of-the-line were of this type. The second type was a composite, or in French, the *vaisseau mixte*. It had both sail and screw steam power, but relied on the sail for most movement, reserving the steam engine for battle or if becalmed. The third type, which the French favored, was the *vaisseau a vapeur*, or steam battleship, which had sails solely as a secondary mode of movement.

Armored battleships are defined in this volume also as ironclads. The term *battleship* did not become common until the turn of the century. There are several types of ironclads.

The earliest are "broadside battery ironclads." Essentially this is a single gun deck ship that is armored and usually quite long, relying mainly on steam, but still retaining sail power. They had poor end on fire and were essentially old style warships with armor plate.

The "central battery ironclad," which first appeared in 1864, resembled the broadside battery ironclad, but had heavy guns concentrated amidships in a heavily armored central battery, often with some fore and aft fire ability. This was, according to Hovgaard, because "(the) increasing power of the gun required greater thickness of armor, but this could not be obtained without at the same time reducing the protected area, since it was not considered advisable to augment displacement, which in the (British) *Minotaur* already approached 11,000 tons." The Austrian-Hungarian *Tegetthoff*, French *Ocean*, Italian *Roma*, or British *Hercules* are good examples of this type. By 1880 the design was out of favor, and replaced by the standard "capital ship" design with turrets or barbettes.

The monitor type was a type of vessel that quickly developed following the Battle of Hampton Roads and employed the turret. A variant of this was the so called breastwork monitor that was essentially a ship with a turret mounted higher out of the water on a raised platform, and was the forerunner of the modern capital ship.

With the rapid increase in the size and power of guns, some individual guns exceeding 100 tons each and a bore of 17.7", the "central citadel ironclad" resulted, which concentrated thick armor amidships, around massive guns. The Italian *Duilio* is an example of this type. This type, combined with the breastwork monitor type evolved into the modern battleship.

Cruisers were unprotected, usually slightly faster, and armed with modern guns. Armored cruisers, or belted cruisers, were developed largely from Russian and French ideas and only slowly adopted by the British. They tended to be large and armored on the belt and main gun positions and often had great fuel endurance so they could act in distant seas. By the end of the ironclad era the protected cruiser was developed which had a curved armor deck, usually of steel, and 1-3 inches in thickness protecting the internal vitals of the warship.

Torpedo boats and torpedo gunboats were minor but influential warships that impacted the entire era of the ironclad. Torpedo boat destroyers, the forerunner of what we know as the destroyer, appear at the very end of the century.

References to the ORN are to the *Official Records of the Union and Confederate Navies in the War of the Rebellion.* We refer to Dahlgren and Rodman smoothbore guns in Roman numerals. Dahlgren rifled guns are referred to by weight of shell. When discussing money, we quote prices for that time period unless otherwise noted.

CHAPTER I

The First Modern Ironclads

*The senior officers did not understand the power of the instrument of war
they now controlled. And who could blame them? They were men of the
eighteenth century, not merely on the wrong side of a particular technical
revolution and unable to appreciate its significance, but men formed in
the era before great technical change had begun fundamentally to affect
the whole structure of the society in which they lived.*
—Basil Greenhill and Ann Giffard

*The steam ship-of-the-line was thus a passing phenomenon. They are gone
now, and have left only the memory of their elegant and stately forms; they
were the swan-song of the sailing navy.*
—Captain de Balincourt and Pierre le Conte

*We are now at the commencement of a new era in naval warfare, in
consequence of the introduction of steam as a propelling power for ships ....
This new power will necessarily modify, and, to a great extent, overturn,
the present tactics of war on the ocean.*
—General Sir Howard Douglas in his "On Naval Warfare with Steam"

A NEW AGE

The coming of the ironclad did not occur in a vacuum. Nor was the iron armor
on it the sole element that made it a monument to the age.

It was a combination of events that brought about the birth of this new type
of warship. Ironclads required several midwives, including the shell gun with all
of its destructive power; mechanical advances allowing men to handle and load
heavier and larger guns; steam power, especially in the form of the screw propeller;
and the technological growth, changes, and revolution that was all part of the
Industrial Revolution then sweeping Western Civilization. An undersea dimension to naval warfare was the evolution of torpedoes and mines and the introduction of the submarine, which stamped a new military face on this era.

Communications also radically altered naval warfare with the introduction of the telegraph and underwater sea cable carrying messages around the world. Electrical apparatus on board ships were introduced. All these forces affected the development of the ironclad.

For many centuries there had been a desire to protect ships from cannon fire. As early as 1557 Captain Jean de La Salle proposed the construction of a ship with thick "wooden walls" that would be artillery proof.

There were the early Korean experiments in 1592 by Admiral Yi-sun who designed a "tortoise-ship" that had iron plates layered on the sides and top deck to protect it from Japanese bullets and arrows, as well as fire because of the material used. This ship, which was also designed for ramming, led the inferior Korean fleet to a series of victories against the Japanese shortly before Japan turned inward and towards isolation.

Other less successful experiments continued. One of the best known later failures was the 1782 attack on Gibraltar by specially built Spanish batteries that tried to defeat the heated shot from the British fortress guns with pumps spraying water over their thickened wood and cork walls. This assault ended in bloody failure.

In the 1840s France and the United States especially carried on experiments with iron plating. This was largely fueled by the fear of the shell gun, perfected for ships by the French artillerist Henri-Joseph Paixhans—"... progressive ordnance officers had predicted the disastrous effect of shell-fire against wooden ships." Shell gun experiments had been tried before without great success. This was due to the necessity of having to light a fuse, put the shell into the gun, and then hoping the crew fired it in time so that it would not do more damage to their ship and crew than to the enemy's!

Paixhans' evolutionary contribution was the invention of a shell fuse that ignited when the gun was fired. The danger to the ship was removed and more accurate fuses allowed for more accurate and longer range fire. When a shell hit a wooden ship filled with combustibles, the potential combination of fire destroying the ship and large wooden and metal splinters ravaging the crews was greater than when a solid iron shot went through the wooden walls of a warship. Finally, even if the shell did not explode, it would still do damage akin to a shot.

Early experiments to defeat the shell gun failed in part due to the conservative naval hierarchy, and also for technical reasons. Iron by itself was not sufficient; it required a backing material—wood. It was a series of French experiments authorized by the Emperor Napoleon III on the eve of the Crimean War that resulted in a breakthrough, creating the armored, or ironclad, warship.

The Queen of the Seas of this period was still the ship-of-the-line, armed with 60 to 135 guns and firing virtually all from two broadsides—thus lacking much end on fire; a sailing vessel displaced an average of 4,000 tons and sometimes

6,000 tons. Steam had been introduced in some, but was essentially an auxiliary form of power to their main motive power—the sail. When mobilized it would take up to six months in wartime to create a fully efficient ship; which meant having enough trained sailors who could furl and unfurl the sails quickly and in good order.

One advantage of steam power was the ability to move when there was no wind. Another edge was that it gave an advantage in battle, when most of the ships of either the French or British fleets were still sail powered, let alone those of other nations of the world. Auxiliary steam power would allow a portion of the fleet to reinforce a threatened part of the line. It was almost a reserve capable of steaming, say, to the van of the line if the enemy was attempting to break that point of the line. This was a natural response and outgrowth from the evolution of sail tactics—not only did Admiral Horatio Nelson see the need to break the enemy line at Trafalgar, but the failed counter by the Franco-Spanish at that action was to have a reserve squadron reinforce the threatened portion of the line. Steam might be the card to make the concept of the reserve squadron work, or to break the enemy line in the first place.

A benchmark ship of this era was the French *Napoleon*. She was an expensive 90 gun steam ship-of-the-line designed by the brilliant Stanislas Charles Henri Laurent Dupuy de Lome. Laid down in 1848, and completed in 1850, when Dupuy de Lome was just turning 34 years old, she could steam at 13 knots, but due to the large amount of engine space, could only steam for ten days before coaling again. Steam power was not that unusual, as pointed out very well by C.I. Hamilton in his *Anglo-French Naval Rivalry 1840-1870*, but what was unusual lay in the fact that she relied upon steam as her *main* propulsion. While still masted, her engines were more powerful than a sail-steam mixed warship design. The sail-steam mixed design, favored by some powerful forces in the French and British navies, saw sail as the means to good cruising endurance and steam as auxiliary power for use when wind was not present, or in battle. A comparable French mixed design was the *Charlemagne* with a speed of nine knots under steam.

This reliance by the *Napoleon* on steam and her great speed gave her several advantages. She was in essence the "fast battleship" of her era, a design comparable to the 24 knot *Warspite* class of World War I or the 32.5 knot *Iowa* class of World War II. A ship like the *Napoleon* could run down or flee from any enemy ship and, strategically, operating in the Mediterranean, she could easily slip over to or back from France's new colony Algeria, both rapidly and dependably. *Guerre de Course*, or war on trade, was also envisioned as a possibility by her designer. A squadron of these vessels could even threaten Great Britain with amphibious invasion by protecting a fleet of fast steam transports, moving rapidly from port and loaded with troops and acting as a "steam-bridge." Carrying troops on board

The French revolutionary warship the Napoleon.

ships-of-the-line in the Black Sea during the Crimean War would be one of the functions of France's battlefleet, and could be duplicated by a squadron of this style warship. Potential in combat was great.

It was Major Delafield, in his famous report of 1860 after observing certain Crimean War operations, who reported to the Secretary of War of the United States, Jefferson Davis, that,

> The late European contest has shown how rapidly the continental powers could march to the coast and embark detachments of from ten to twenty thousand disciplined troops in steam transports, accommodating a thousand men each, with supplies for a voyage equal to crossing to our shores; ... leaving us at the mercy, in the first years of a conflict, of either of the naval and military powers of the Old World.

Another factor in France's acceptance of the *Napoleon*'s design was that while France knew Great Britain could outbuild her with her greater industrial strength, France, this time, was leading the way in a new naval innovation.

Her expense was a full one-third greater than a comparable 90 gunner of the mixed variety, which limited the quantity of this type that could be built. It was even greater than adding steampower to an existing sailing ship, which both Great Britain and France did. Such conversions of sailing ships-of-the-line to screw saved on timber, gave them auxiliary steam power as well as a decent speed under steam of six to nine knots, and was a lot less expensive. The largest drawback to conversions was that by putting a bulky engine with coal in an existing ship, its endurance was greatly reduced as the amount of food and supplies for the crew was limited, and she became a poorer sailer, or so called "crank."

The British responded directly to the *Napoleon* with a sail-steam mixed design ship built from the keel up with a more powerful engine than before. D. K. Brown has argued that British sail-steam mixed design, such as the 91 gun *Agamemnon*, which could steam at 11 knots, might have been a match for the *Napoleon*. Part of his argument lies in his assertion that the *Napoleon* in reality could not make 13 knots, French engines were poorly designed, and that the French trials gave better results than actual sea service would give. However the *Napoleon* did steam from Toulon, France, to Ajaccio, Corsica, "with a calm sea and with little or no wind (and) she kept up an average speed of 12.4 knots." While difficult to prove either way (and French historians do argue the point made by D.K. Brown), the key here is what a squadron of *Napoleons* could do. And if the British attempted to blockade the French coast, could they respond to the operations of four or eight such vessels operating under the command of an enterprising admiral? A powerful and fast force such as this, resolutely led, could strike deadly blows up and down the Mediterranean or against even the British Isles.

But not all was perfect with the *Napoleon,* a problem common in lead ships of a revolutionary design. She had a series of mechanical problems throughout her career. At the time of the diplomatic crisis between Turkey and Russia, which lead to the Crimean War, the French and British dispatched fleets to the Dardanelles. It was decided to steam both navies to the Turkish capital on the Bosphorus on 22 October 1853. Only two ships, each towing a ship-of-the-line, passed the Straits with an adverse current and wind that day. One was the most powerful paddlewheel French frigate present and the other was the *Napoleon*. The *Napoleon* severely strained her engines in passing up the Bosphorus, news carefully suppressed. But the French had humiliated the British in front of their eyes, as none of the British warships could pass up the Straits.

The French certainly recognized her ability and after a short period of analyzing the results of operating the *Napoleon,* they laid down (or in one case radically converted) nine such improved fast battleships, in 1853-54. One, the *Bretagne,* carried 131 guns. The British answered with one ship design of this type, the *Conqueror* of 101 guns in 1853. Sleepy nations, such as the United States of America or Imperial Russia, simply watched from the sidelines and experimented on a much smaller and more limited scale. At this point in history there were only two naval superpowers in the world.

What the *Napoleon* represents is the first modern battleship. Here was a ship that made full use of the new technology of the industrial age and from her roots would come eventually the modern capital ship. It is noteworthy that the *Gloire,* the first modern ironclad warship, also designed by Dupuy de Lome, would also have a speed of 13 knots.

THE CRIMEAN WAR

Thus it may be said that sails and wood went out, and steam and iron came in, in 1855.
> —Wm. Laird Clowes

Before the War the French and British navies had energetically begun the transition from sail to steam, from wood to iron and steel and from solid shot to shell fire. The Russian navy had not.
> — Aurele Joseph Violette

At the commencement of the Crimean war, Napoleon III was not slow to apprehend that any attempt to attack either Cronstadt or Sevastopol with unarmored ships was doomed to failure, and the more so because the channels in front of those towns were of small depth, and the heavy ships were obliged to remain a considerable distance from the shore.
> —Lord Brassey

A great deal of new material has been published on the Crimean War in the last few years. Scholarship on the war has been exciting, and at times controversial. The war was played out primarily in the area of the Black Sea, though an important (and ultimately the decisive) theater was in the Baltic Sea. In addition, there were minor operations in the White Sea and along the Russian Pacific coast.

At the combat level, the Crimean war was one of the oddest ever fought in the modern era. It began between two rivals who had fought each other on numerous occasions, the Russian Empire of the Tsar and the Ottoman Empire of the Sultan. But the Turks quickly gained powerful allies, the United Kingdom and Imperial France. Now the most powerful protagonists, as the Turks proved to be quite weak, were the allied Great Powers who shared no common frontier with Russia, and in many ways transformed it into a war between the whale and the elephant. Russia with her powerful land armies had to move her forces slowly over poor roads or by river to the theaters of war that the Allied powers could rapidly arrive at by sail or steam.

The Allied naval leaders, especially the British ones, expected some great naval victory such as at Trafalgar or Navarino. Instead there would be no great victory at sea, but a victory that was still gained through naval power. It was a form of naval power that few at the time fully grasped or understood.

While the third strongest in the world at the time, the Russian Navy could be quickly dismissed because of its technological inferiority. It possessed some fine and powerful sailing ships-of-the-line. Six of these easily destroyed a Turkish fleet at Sinope, but the Russian fleet had barely adopted the use of steam into her fleet.

In the course of the war only three Russian ship-of-the-line would have steam engines, inferior ones at that, and none were ready when the war began. Russia was so short handed in engineers, that she had to turn during the war to the railroads to supply personnel for the ships. In 1855 the tsar's government ordered the main Russian Baltic battlefleet not to prepare for possible combat, as it was thought that they would be too heavily outnumbered and could not counter the Allied technological edge.

Nor was the fleet as well trained and prepared as the Allied fleet. An aide-de-camp to the tsar reported on an inspection of the Baltic Fleet in the early 1850s, in which two cannon burst during practice, that "… the Admirals acknowledged that the crews were very unpracticed, especially in regard to sail handling." This lack of practice was due in part to the Russian winters that clogged the eastern Baltic with ice for much of the year.

In one area the Russians were more advanced than the Allies, an area in which the Russian navy remained the expert for many years—mine warfare. Originally, all underwater weapons were called torpedoes, named for the electric ray fish. That name comes from Latin to "render numb."

As early as 1853 Russia had a minelaying vessel. The Russians used three types of mines in this war to complement their defensive positions. One was an electrically activated mine, with power supplied from the shore, which exploded when a ship came in contact with it. Another was an electrical mine which was fired from the shore. The third type was a chemical mine that was anchored just below the surface of the water. When a glass vial was broken, it released sulfuric acid into a mixture of sugar and chlorate of potassium that caused a heat flash which triggered the mine to explode. It was known by the name of its inventor, the Russian philosopher and chemist Professor Jacobi, as the Jacobi Mine.

The British referred to the mines as "infernal machines," but they had little effect. Several that did explode did minimal damage due to their charges being too small. One story of these new machines is worth retelling. Vice-Admiral Seymour had one of these mines brought on deck after it was taken up from the water. He showed it to some fellow officers. "They all played with it; … and on the poop had the officers round it examining it… Some of the officers remarked of the danger of it going off, and Admiral Seymour who claimed to 'know all about it' said, 'Oh no. This is the way it would go off,' and shoved the slide in with his finger … . It instantly exploded, knocking down everyone around it." Several were seriously injured, including the Admiral, who lost partial sight in one eye.

Two early experimenters were the Americans Robert Fulton and David Bushnell. Robert Fulton referred to them as "torpedo mines" to differentiate between land based "mines" used during sieges and self-acting mines placed under water. Fulton was working on his devices as early as 1801 for the French. It would be later, with the invention of the "automobile torpedo," or moving mine, that the names would finally get sorted out. By the end of the century *mines* would be stationary while *torpedoes* would be what was originally an automobile torpedo.

Finally, the Russians built one submarine of German design. Wilhelm Bauer went to Russia, after showing a model of his proposed design to Queen Victoria and other members of her government in 1852, and received a contract to build the *Seeteufel.* Completed after the war, it conducted about 100 successful tests before sinking due to crew error.

The Allied French and British fleets had a variety of ships. All had sailing ships-of-the-line present in the war; the French sent most of theirs to the Baltic, while the British used primarily steam ships there. Paddle-wheel warships as well as mixed steam and sail and ships-of-the-line relying mainly on steam made for quite a conglomerate of warships. Admiral Astley Cooper Key remarked at Queen Victoria's July 1853 review of the Western Squadron (made up of a mixed bag of warships) that "Without doubt—just because the ships were there—it was to the Naval Officers present the most natural and appropriate thing in the world that the Fleet should be composed of sailing ships, screw ships and paddle ships. The belief that sailing ships were to go, and that paddle ships were almost gone, would have been impossible to inculcate."

With it came another problem which a former officer, Admiral C.R. Moorson, summed up quite well in a letter to Captain Sir Baldwin Walker, then holding the important post of Surveyor of the Navy and determined the type of warships to be built, "But who is the Commander now prepared to handle such a collective mess—a steam fleet? Where is the system of tactics by means of which the squadron are to be moved with the rapidity and precision that each ship is capable of?" These questions would take on real meaning, especially in the Baltic, where the elderly British commander Vice-Admiral Sir Charles Napier, who was conservative in the first place and not a charismatic leader of fellow warriors, simply did not take advantage of his steam capability and of the abundant coal available to him. On 28 June 1854, Captain Henry Keppel wrote "Our movements have been dilatory in the extreme. Our steam power with unlimited supply of coal has not been made use of ...."

THE BATTLE OF KINBURN

The introduction of the long gun to fire shells horizontally, both for land and sea service, with a tendency to increase the calibers, ... may now be considered the settled policy and practice of all the military powers of Europe.
    —Major Delafield's first line in his Official Report, after his visit to Europe
with a military commission from the United States in 1854-1856

Take it for granted the floating (ironclad) batteries have become elements in amphibious warfare, so the sooner you set about having as many good ones as the French the better it will be for you.
   —Sir Edmund Lyons to the British First Sea Lord

Perhaps the most valuable lesson of the war of 1854-55 was the importance to a naval power of being able promptly to utilize the newest and most formidable inventions that have been produced by the ingenuity of man. The lesson, unfortunately, has not been thoroughly learnt by Great Britain, even to this day. The war, however, led directly or indirectly to many naval reforms, including the introduction of continuous service for seamen, the building of ironclads, and the development of the power of the gun.
   —Wm. Laird Clowes, writing in 1901

The course of the war in the Black Sea focused mainly on the Crimean Peninsula. The Russians had opened the war with Turkey by destroying a small Turkish-Egyptian squadron made up of four frigates and seven corvettes, with a fleet of six ships-of-the-line, two frigates, and three small steamers at Sinope. Shellfire from Russian 60 pounder shell guns had been very destructive, causing many fires, and the Turks lost 3,000 men and all but one ship (the paddle frigate *Taif* commanded by a British captain). This was the first action where shell guns had been decisive, with the Turks fielding but two out of 236 guns against the Russian total of 76 shell guns out of a total of 372 guns. Paixhans shortly after the battle penned a pamphlet that appeared in the *Moniteur Universal* on 21 February 1854 pointing out the deadly effect of the shell gun.

Earlier there were some minor naval actions involving shell fire. The Russians used shell guns in 1788 against the Turks, while the Paixhans gun was first employed in combat in 1838 at Vera Cruz in Mexico. It was again employed in the Turco-Egyptian War of 1839-40. The best-known early use in battle was in 1849 between the Danish ship-of-the-line *Christian VIII* and Prussian shore batteries, at the battle of Eckernfjorde. The *Christian VIII* was destroyed in that action but the main cause of her loss was red-hot shot (round shot heated in a furnace and then carefully loaded) fired from the shore batteries. Shell guns had been present, but they played a secondary role in that action, though sometimes incorrectly credited with the loss of the *Christian VIII*.

But Sinope was the catalyst that brought the Allied Great Powers into the war against Russia. There was a fear of Russian strength, and the Allies thought a truce had been broken by Russia's action (there was no truce).

In 1854 the Allies mounted a landing near Sevastopol, the chief Russian naval port in the Black Sea, located on the Crimean Peninsula, with the intent to quickly seize and destroy the fleet and naval port facilities there. Instead it turned into a long two-year siege with great losses, mostly due to disease, though in the end the Russian fleet was scuttled and the port destroyed.

Ironically, as the Allied fleet (the British contingent primarily sailing ships) crossed the Black Sea, it was terribly vulnerable to attack as the French ships-of-the-line were crammed with upwards of 1,800 to 2,000 soldiers per ship, making them almost unworkable in combat. Coupled with the allied need to cover several *hundred* transports in convoy, the smaller Russian sailing fleet might have struck a blow that would have set back the Allied effort by a full year.

With the end of the terrible siege, the Allies looked to other means to apply pressure and bring Russia to the peace table. Several possible campaigns were bandied about, but Napoleon III, who had committed by far the most troops to the Black Sea, decided on the smallest blow against the Russians, as fall drifted towards winter. This blow would be directed against Fort Kinburn, where a revolutionary new weapon would first see combat.

It was after the destruction of the Turkish fleet by the Russians (with their French designed shell guns being the decisive weapon), that Emperor Napoleon III realized that his ships-of-the-line would be ineffective against the Russian coastal fortresses. The "effectiveness of shell fire in the battle ... was readily understood by such a student of artillery as Louis Napoleon" and was the catalyst for the Emperor to order his designers to begin work on ironclad steam batteries. He was aware of both the French experiments with armor in the 1840s, and of a proposed design using 90mm of armor plate along the waterline and amidships over the engine room of a French ship-of-the-line. Napoleon, an artillerist in his own right, feared the power of the shell gun and thought, correctly, that cladding a ship in iron would protect it from the effects. With powerful steam batteries of shallow draft, Napoleon felt he had the answer for Russian defeat. The French Navy saw two main purposes for these new vessels. One was to aid in conducting sieges and the other to defend a coast. So work began.

With a spur from Napoleon, the French design team went to work on producing a steam-powered floating battery with shallow draft that would carry large guns and be protected against shot and shell by iron plating. Initially the ships were designed for use against Kronstadt in the Baltic, but were later ordered in 1855 to the Black Sea. This was due to two reasons. First, the winter of 1854/55 in the Crimea was terrible, as Sevastopol had not fallen and the Allied troops suffered badly from disease and incompetence. Secondly, if the armored floating batteries were to go to the Baltic to reduce Kronstadt, there would be no Allied army to occupy it as all reinforcements were needed to successfully conclude the Crimean fighting.

The experiments with iron in 1854 concluded with the realization that iron by itself would crack and break apart, though it would stop the first round. But by using a substantial wood backing, the combination of the two was invincible

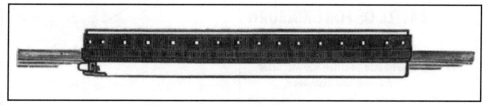

British schematic of French steambattery, as used in the Crimea.

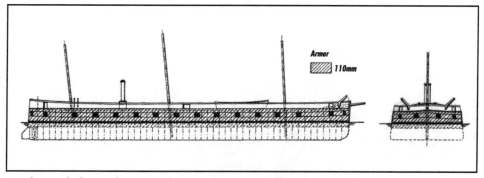

French ironclad steambatteries of the Tonnante *class. The ship had 15 mm of deck armor.*

against the weapons of the day. By July of 1854 the construction of five batteries with 100mm (4 inches) of iron plate was well under way. Three were to proceed to the Black Sea upon completion, while two others were laid up for the proposed 1856 campaign in the Baltic.

The French, in an unusual show of comradely spirit, contacted the British Admiralty in August and informed them of their advances. They sent all relevant test data possible to them and assisted the British in building their batteries. But both nations' ironclad steam batteries would prove to be poor sailers.

The British laid down five batteries, of which one was destroyed in a fire while under construction. Of the four completed, two, the *Glatton* and the *Meteor,* left for the Black Sea and the other two were laid up for the proposed 1856 campaign in the Baltic. The British batteries were slightly faster and more maneuverable than the French batteries, armed with two fewer guns, but arrived too late to take part in the Battle of Kinburn.

Major Delafield included some quite detailed drawings and a discussion of the building of the British ironclad steam batteries that he was able to examine in his report. He reported these vessels as stubby little ships of 172 foot length and 43 foot beam. The deck strength was increased "by covering (it) three feet deep with sandbags." Interestingly enough he incorrectly wrote that the iron plate was 4.5 inches thick, instead of the actual 4 inches. Delafield reported on experiments carried out in 1854 at Portsmouth that had shown that the armor carried on wood backing was proof against all shell guns and smaller guns firing shot. However, a 68 pounder at 400 yards with a 16 pound powder charge and firing a wrought

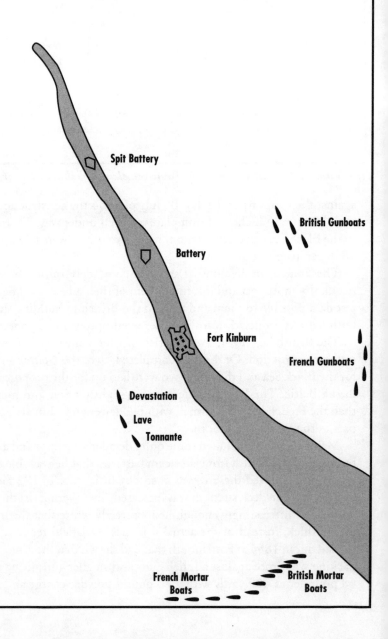

BATTLE OF FORT KINBURN
Initial Allied attack about 10.30
17 October, 1855. Gunboats
moved into position shown after
Russian fire slackened.

Otchakof

Pt. Otchakof

Spit Battery

British Gunboats

Battery

Fort Kinburn

French Gunboats

Devastation

Lave

Tonnante

French Mortar
Boats

British Mortar
Boats

iron shot "penetrated the plates" and the 6-7 inch wood backing. Cast iron shot from the same gun, as pointed out by Baxter, "cracked the plates and started the bolts."

In late July and early August 1855 the French dispatched three of their new armored steam batteries, the *Lave, Devastation,* and *Tonnante,* to the Black Sea. These steam batteries displaced 1,575 tons, were 170 feet long, had 38 feet of beam, and a draft of 8.5 feet. Their belts, and those of the British ships, are sometimes given as 4.5 inches, but they were 4 inches. They carried sixteen 50 pounders that could be fought from one broadside. Armored with wrought iron that extended below the waterline, they could steam at 3.5 to 4 knots. One of the three had an "improvised armored conning tower" (the British Rear-Admiral Edmund Lyons called it a "safe guard"). They were ugly "…excessively hot and ill-ventilated, hard to steer, and inferior in speed to the similar British ironclads." They were towed by three French warships to the Black Sea and arrived in late September. On the eve of the battle there was some thought given to placing sandbags up and down the deck for deck armor but it was decided against. The use of sand for protection will come up again in the story of the ironclad.

Kinburn lies between Odessa and the Crimean Peninsula and guards the delta of the Bug and Dnieper rivers. The important port of Nicolaiev lay on the Bug. Before the construction of railroads, these two rivers were the main arteries for transportation in southern Russia.

The actual fortifications were manned by 1,500 troops under Major General Kokonovitch in three positions. The main stone fort had 50 guns (some sources give 60) with some of the guns in casemates. There were two additional sand batteries mounting 10 and 11 guns. No large guns were present, the biggest being the standard Russian cast iron long 24 pounder. An additional battery covering the Dnieper Bay at Otchakof played little part in the coming battle.

The action against Kinburn opened with the Allied fleet of ten ships-of-the-line (six were British), with 17 British frigates and sloops, three French corvettes, 11 mortar vessels (five French and six British), 22 gunboats (12 French and 10 British), ten transports loaded with 8,000 Allied troops, and some minor craft heading to Kinburn after a feint at Odessa. The force was under the French Vice-Admiral Armand-Joseph Bruat and British Rear-Admiral Edmund Lyons (later British Ambassador to Washington at the start of the American Civil War). They arrived off Kinburn on 14 October 1855.

The water off Kinburn was surveyed before the battle, soundings taken, and it was confirmed that the ships-of-the-line could approach within 1200 yards of the forts—leaving two feet of water under their deep drafts. The action opened with five English and four French gunboats scooting to the rear of the forts on the night of 14 October, suffering some ineffective fire from both Kinburn and Otchakof, and landing of 8,000 troops under the future French Marshal Bazaine

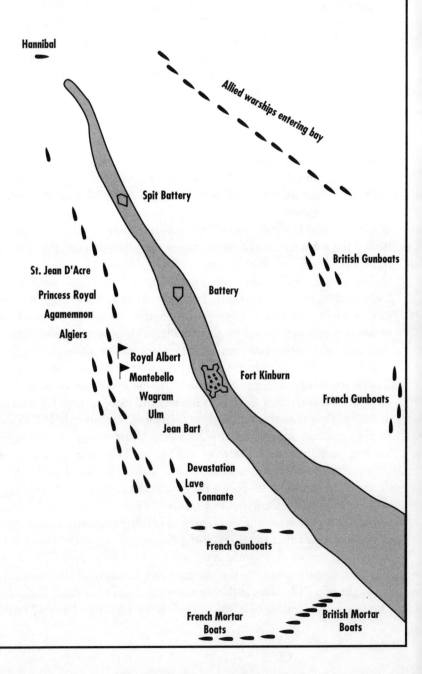

BATTLE OF FORT KINBURN
Allied attack at 12.50,17 October, 1855.
Final coup de grace. Named vessels are
ship of the line.

Otchakof

Pt. Otchakof

Hannibal

Allied warships entering bay

Spit Battery

British Gunboats

St. Jean D'Acre

Princess Royal

Agamemnon

Algiers

Battery

Royal Albert

Montebello

Wagram

Ulm

Jean Bart

Fort Kinburn

French Gunboats

Devastation

Lave

Tonnante

French Gunboats

French Mortar
Boats

British Mortar
Boats

at the head of the spit of the land on 15 October. The Russian garrison was now completely cut off and surrounded.

The three French steam batteries, with picked crews for this operation, stowed all their minor rigging and the funnel was lowered for the action. Earlier, Ensign de Raffin of the *Devastation* had taken a small boat in and placed three buoys for the three steam batteries, and was fired on by the fort for this daring act.

The battle opened on 17 October with the French steam batteries moving into position between 08:45 and 09:30. The original plan called for closing to within 600 meters, but instead the *Devastation* anchored 877 meters away, the *Lave* at 975, and the *Tonnante* at 1,150 meters from the Russian fort. The *Devastation* opened fire first at 09:06, followed shortly by the others. The advantage of anchoring was that it allowed for a more stable firing platform for accurate fire. Mortar boats also opened long range support fire 2,800 yards to the south on the forts. All guns and crews fought from the bearing broadside and a most destructive fire was opened on the fort.

The steam batteries fought for four hours, firing 3,177 shot and shells into the Russian fortifications, and when the Russian fire slackened in late morning, the gunboats to the rear joined in. Their fire certainly contributed to the Allied victory.

At 12:50 HMS *Hannibal*, 91 guns, took up position at the end of the spit to cover the passage of the French corvettes and British frigates into the bay. The *Hannibal* quickly silenced the spit battery. The frigates and corvettes heading into the bay were in position and firing at 13:30, just before Fort Kinburn surrendered.

However, the main fleet *did* get into heavy action, moving forward into firing position just past noon. HMS *Princess Royal* closed to within 650 yards of the middle battery at 12:30. Over the next hour, behind her and further out, at ranges upwards of 1,600 yards from the forts, were three British ships-of-the-line and four French liners, while one British liner, HMS *St. Jean d'Acre*, took up position on the bow of the *Princess Royal*. These ships, each about 250 yards from the next one, opened a heavy fire. In 45 minutes the HMS *Agamemnon* alone fired 500 rounds, while frigates supporting the ships-of-the-line fired 200 to 300 each.

Sources vary, but apparently the Russian fire ceased at 13:50 and the Allies halted their fire at 14:10. The Russian flagstaff had been shot away, and the fort and batteries were in ruins; the Russians had lost 45 killed and 130 wounded. Terms were arranged by 15:00 that afternoon and the Allies took possession of the fortifications.

James P. Baxter sums up the Russian fire on the *Devastation*, the hardest hit and closest of the three French ironclads,

> Twenty-nine shot rattled off her four-inch armor and thirty-five plowed furrows in her deck of heavy oak. One shell, however, entered the battery through the imperfectly protected main hatch, and two more through the ports, killing two men and wounding thirteen others.

The other two were hit over 60 times each, but only the *Tonnante* suffered nine wounded. The *Princess Royal* suffered two wounded, the only other Allied losses that day.

One classic witness of the Kinburn bombardment was Sir William Howard Russell (knighted in 1897), correspondent of the London *Times*. He wrote shortly after the event a lengthy article that reflected the spirit of the age and showed this as the watershed event of the period—until the battle of the *Monitor* and the *Merrimack* overshadowed it.

> The floating batteries of the French opened with a magnificent crash at 9:30 a.m. and one in particular distinguished itself for the regularity, precision, and weight of fire throughout the day.
>
> The Russians replied with alacrity, and the batteries must have been put to a severe test for the water was splashed into pillars by shot all over them.
>
> The success of the experiment (iron-cased batteries) is complete. They were anchored only 800 yards from the Russian batteries. The shot of the enemy at that short range had no effect upon them; the balls hopped back off their sides without leaving any impression save such as a pistol ball makes on the target in a shooting gallery.
>
> The shot could be heard distinctly striking the sides of the battery with a sharp smack, and then could be seen flying back, striking the water at various angles, according to the direction they took, till they dropped exhausted.
>
> On one battery the dents of 63 shot are visible against the plates of one side, not counting the marks of other which have glanced along the decks or struck the edges of the bulwarks; yet, all the damage that has been done to that vessel has been the starting of three rivets.

Lyon's flag captain wrote, in describing the effect of the Russian fire on the French ironclad, that "shells broke against them like glass." and the French batteries were "perfect." The French Vice-Admiral Bruat wrote afterwards to Admiral Francois Alphonse Hamelin, French Minister of Marine,

> I attribute the prompt victory that we have obtained, in the first place to completely surrounding the fort by land and sea; in the second, to the fire of the floating batteries which had already opened perceptible breaches in the ramparts and whose aim, directed with remarkable precision, was able to knock down the solidest walls. Everyone awaits the use of these formidable machines of war, ...

Dutch historian Anthonie van Dijk later said that "The three French batteries, ... which came into action, proved their worth beyond any doubt." Franklin Wallin would say on iron plating of ships that "It had been a speculative question, but after Kinburn it was a conspicuous necessity."

Clearly the French steam batteries won this action and were the tip of the spear that delivered the Russian fortifications into the hands of the Allies. The other warships helped, but their role was clearly secondary. If a formidable naval force, as planned, had steamed for the Baltic in 1856 to attempt the Russian fortress at Kronstadt, the plan called for the French and British steam batteries to open the way for the remainder of the fleet to deliver the *coup de grace*.

These same three French batteries would mobilize again for the war with Austria in Italy in 1859 and arrived at Venice on the day Austria and France declared an armistice. They saw no further action after this.

A SEAGOING IRONCLAD

… it is not surprising that the French were generally successful in keeping technically ahead of the British.
 —Dr. Theodore Ropp

We are not able to fool ourselves any longer. We must make it plain to ourselves that we are weak… restore the fleet—a fleet that must depart from the archaic forms of the past.
 —General-Admiral Konstantin Nikolaevich, written in 1857

It is easy for academics more than one hundred years after an event to argue about this or that detail, but what one must remember is the impact of the event at the time. Just as America would shortly be engulfed in "*Monitor* Fever" after the Battle of Hampton Roads, so too the Battle of Kinburn had a major impact on naval policies.

Great Britain immediately ordered four more of these batteries while France would lay down from 1859 to 1862 three classes with a total of 11 ironclad steam batteries, none with a speed over eight knots. Russia would build 15 ironclad rafts based on a plan proposed in 1855 and have the rafts all completed by May of 1856. These consisted of flat boats held together by transverse beams and then planked over. On the deck were four 80-pounders behind a wall of iron that had sheets laid first horizontally, and then a layer laid vertically, just as the CSS *Virginia* would receive her armor in 1861-62. The rafts were towed, having no power themselves, and were to be used for harbor or river defense.

From this event at Kinburn was born the first ironclad race between Great Britain and France that lasted until the Franco-Prussian War of 1870-71. France would build both a seagoing fleet and a coastal defense fleet. The latter would be initially made up of steam batteries, but she would also later embrace iron rams based on American and Battle of Lissa experiences. Britain would respond in kind but not with a well-thought-out plan for building a world battlefleet. It was one of the few times in her naval history when she found herself constantly responding to some other power's lead, until Imperial France began to run out of time and money in the late 1860s. It drove the Prince Consort, a thoughtful man, to write to Foreign Secretary Lord John Russell, "It is a perfect disgrace to our country, and particularly to our Admiralty, that we can do no more than hobble after the French, turning up our noses proudly at their experiments and improvements, and, when they are established as sound, getting horribly frightened, and trying by wasting money to catch up lost time, and all the while running serious risk of our security."

Also from this war would come thoroughgoing Russian reforms under the new reformist tsar, Alexander II. The Russian navy, headed by Alexander's brother General-Admiral Konstantin Nikolaevich, decentralized the navy, introduced naval reforms, and embraced new technology so as not to fall further behind in Europe. Steam was adopted fully into the Russian fleet after the war. By 1860 Russia had nine converted steam ships-of-the-line built or building. The year 1864 saw her adopt the new rifled built-up guns such as those manufactured by Armstrong in Great Britain.

These reforms reflected the spirit of Alexander II, the tsar who would free the serfs. These reforms also reflected the new age. Forced impressment of sailors could no longer suffice, though it was not totally abandoned. Instead trained personnel were needed, either foreigners or "free labor," hand in hand with promotion of the Industrial Revolution.

As pointed out by Jacob W. Kipp in his article "Das Russische Marineministerium und die Einfuehrung der Panzerschiffe," there was one other important bit of fallout. The industrialization of Russia was spurred. Russians recognized that buying machine parts or warships from potentially hostile nations was not good policy. The Ministry deliberately began a policy of boosting and supporting domestic industry in the building of warships. Shipyards and shipbuilding efforts were concentrated at Kronstadt and St. Petersburg. The future state naval gun company of Obuchov (sometimes given as "Obuchoff") began as a private manufacturer at the instigation of the naval ministry. All this occurred on the eve of the 1860s Russian railroad construction boom, fed by the initial naval construction effort. Part of Russia's limitations immediately after the war were monetary. But this was helped in part by the Treaty of Peace since a fleet in the Black Sea was forbidden, the need to maintain a naval commitment in the Black Sea was eliminated with the stroke of a pen! Russia's goals were reasonable, and often misunderstood by historians and politicians alike. She did not create a navy equal to that of France or Great Britain, but would accept a position as third largest naval power behind those two countries. In 1860 Russia spent about 21,000,000 rubles on her navy while the British and French spent the equivalent of 50,000,000 rubles each. Additionally her fleet was "stronger than an alliance of all second class naval powers." Russia would maintain a fleet to protect the Baltic, and a small Mediterranean squadron to protect Christians from the

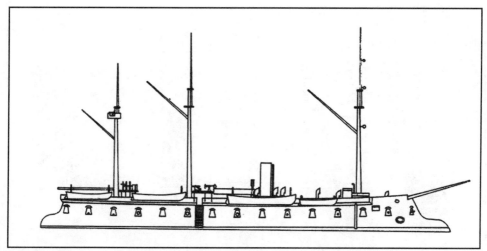

The first Russian ironclad, the Prevenetz, *British built.*

"… fanaticism of the Moslems." According to Kipp's research, she also wanted a navy that could be "in alliance with" either France or Great Britain. She needed a navy that "… can act decisively against the fleets of neighboring secondary powers and on the other hand can inspire in the great powers such respect that will force them to seek either an alliance with Russia or her neutrality in their wars among themselves." Finally, a sizable portion of her fleet was dispatched for service in the Pacific.

These post Crimean War problems came to a head in 1859 and brought about another change in Russia's naval building policy. In 1860 her budget had no new moneys for ships-of-the-line but instead contained money for ships designed for a *guerre de course*. A strategy of commerce raiding involved less for expenditure and reflected the reality of Russia's strength vis-a-vis France or Great Britain. Judging by the subsequent future successes of the *Alabama* and her consorts in hurting a major seapower, this seems to have been a good choice at the time. It certainly raised the ante if France or Great Britain were to go to war with Imperial Russia in the 1860s.

Andrew Lambert, in his *Battleships in Transition,* has argued that "Kinburn has always been considered the proving ground of the armored warship. However it was of more significance to contemporary observers, along with Sveaborg, as a demonstration that a well-handled combination of vessels could overcome major fortifications." Both Lambert and Admiral R. Custance in *The Ship of the Line in Battle* have argued that the ship-of-the-line alone might have been sufficient to bring victory. This probably is true. But the key point is that it was perceived that it was the ironclads that achieved victory.

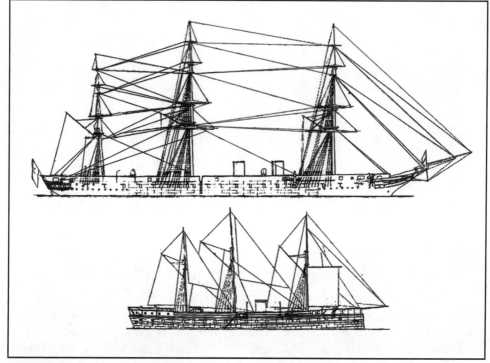

HMS Warrior *and the French* Gloire.

Admiral F.A. Hamelin commented in 1857 that "If war had not broken out in 1854, one would perhaps still be discussing today the utility of a sailing navy compared to a steam navy ... the hostilities were hardly declared when already the opinion of the few became the opinion of a majority."

So the transition was nearing completion. Steam would dominate the navies from this point on and no firm argument against it could be made, and the ironclad vessel was now in play. The next step was to combine the two in a true steam ironclad warship, and not an underpowered floating battery.

It would be France that would carry the naval revolution a step further with a seagoing ironclad ship. The main pushes for the death of the wooden ship-of-the-line were experiments with a new rifled gun at Lorient in 1855-56. These experiments showed that even a small ship armed with rifled shell guns *could* defeat a large ship-of-the-line. Thus the French government ordered on 17 January 1857 the halting of all work on ships-of-the-line (not February as given in some sources). While work would continue on ships already being built or converted, the decision had been made.

Armor was the only logical answer to the power of the rifled shell gun. So a design was called for that would give a ship 13 knots of speed (so she could choose her range), an armor belt that extended 4 or 5 feet below the waterline, a main gun deck at least seven feet above the water, a stern designed to protect the screw and full sail power for long range cruising. The Emperor himself pushed hard for the introduction of this new type of ship and had six ordered in 1858, the first being the *Gloire*. A spur ram was added to the *Magenta* and *Solferino* laid down in 1859, which also had the distinction of being the only two-decked ironclads. Of the first four French ironclads, one was the *Couronne* with an *iron* hull. She was authorized in 1858, well before the starting of HMS *Warrior*. But she cost almost 1,300,000 *more* francs than the *Gloire*, largely due to her hull being of iron, and this was a large factor in limiting the construction of more iron-hulled French ironclads.

Great Britain would reply by starting HMS *Warrior* and *Black Prince*, and shortly after this, two smaller broadside ironclads, the *Defence* and the *Resistance*. The *Warrior* can be seen today at Portsmouth, England, as a magnificently restored museum ship.

The first two British ships were larger than the *Gloire*, and were built entirely of iron, which allowed them to stay in service much longer than the French ship. Their armament was a bit better, with the 68 pounders capable of hurting the French ships at greater range than vice-versa. The British also felt that their powder and their iron and engines were superior to the French, which in part was true. (As an aside, the British felt that their powder was superior to all others, and may have been. The Americans were a close second, and close to the British in rapidity of fire, while the French, apparently, trailed both of those powers in quality of powder and rapidity of fire.)

The iron hulls did give one other big advantage in that they could be subdivided into watertight compartments, while wood hulled ships could not be subdivided. This is one reason why wooden ships tended to be completely armored on the belt, which also helped to prevent fires. The early British ironclads, unlike the French ships, were not armored on the ends and their rudders were particularly vulnerable. The *Warrior* and *Black Prince* were deliberately designed with a speed of 14 knots so that they could choose the range at which to fight.

All of the first four British ironclads could lower themselves by flooding some of their compartments to present smaller targets, and give additional protection to their exposed rudders, while slowing their speed. This trend in British design for compartmentalization of the hull to protect a ship from sinking quickly from underwater damage would culminate in HMS *Inflexible*, designed in the 1870s. She was designed with her central portion and turrets heavily armored, but with her ends having numerous compartments, and using coal and cork to give added protection in many of these compartments. Virtually half of her hull was unarmored. The *Inflexible* also housed four massive 80 ton 16" muzzle-loading rifles in two turrets!

Early British steam battery, the Thunder, *under sail.*

Thus the *Warrior* and *Black Prince* carried less armor over their length than the French ships and so could have their ends (bow and stern) riddled with shot and shell without sinking. Due to their extreme length they were less handy than the French ironclads, and they faced a French navy that gave its "officers the most advanced scientific training in Europe." Further, the French were busily building ten identical ironclads in the early 60s armored with 5.9 inches of iron plate. A squadron like this would have an advantage over the hodgepodge of designs that Great Britain would turn out in these early years, many with different types of guns, and all with different speeds and endurance at sea. If ably handled, the French, if war had come about, would have given a good account of themselves.

The backwardness of the British shipbuilding industry was such that Stanley Sandler wrote, "Throughout the period of the introduction of the ironclad there was no school of naval architecture in Britain. Because of such official anti-scientific bias, aspiring naval designers were compelled to go to the palatial *Ecole Polytechnique* in France for their scientific education." It would not be until 1864 that Great Britain had a naval architectural school. Until then it was assumed one learned by doing and copying previous designs and the other fellow.

But attention was diverted away from Europe for the next few years as a terrible war raged on the North American continent.

Forts and Guns in the Crimean War

No sailor could ever be such a born ass as to attack forts with ships.
—**Admiral Horatio Nelson**

From the dawn of artillery involvement in naval combat, ranges were relatively short. Half pistol shot or pistol shot (50 yards) were not unusual ranges, though close, and long musket shot of 200 or 300 yards for a battle was common. One of the significant changes brought on with the improvement in guns and fortifications in the 1800's was that battle ranges began to increase and new combat techniques were developed.

This was most dramatically seen in the bombardment of Russian forts in the Crimean War. As late as 1815, at the bombardment of Algiers, Lord Exmouth had fought at ranges as close as 50 yards with his large warships (the harbor there was particularly deep close to the forts). Mortar boats, then known as bomb vessels, were also used at Algiers, but at a much greater range of 2,000 yards.

Yet during the bombardment of Sevastopol on 17 October 1854, no ship-of-the-line approached closer than 750 yards while others were as far out as 2,000 yards, in part due to the depth of water and also because the operation was only a diversion for a major land operation. The Allies employed over 1,000 guns in the naval bombardment. It was felt at the time that to bring about a decisive action against the large Russian stone forts, the range would have to be 500 yards or less and that only the 68 pounders would be effective in such an action.

Additional factors affected this action. One was the knowledge that Russian gunpowder was inferior (often due to dampness) to the Allied powder, and low quality brittle iron was used in the manufacture of Russian guns. Also, the Allies had more powerful guns, which gave them a decided advantage in long range actions, though at this range much of the fire against the Russian fortifications was ineffective. But the Allied wooden warships rightly feared the power of shell guns that the Russians did have.

Further, the Russians relied, as they did throughout the 19th century, on smaller guns. They preferred the small guns as they were easier to handle. So their largest standard gun was a 36 pounder which fired a ball that actually weighed 32 pounds, 7.5 ounces. Finally, the distance from the firing guns gave the wooden hulls of the Allied ships-of-the-line additional protection as the Russian shot lost penetration power due to the long flight of the round.

The Allied ships (including two Turkish ships-of-the-line) were anchored for this action because of the severe losses due to cholera and the number of men ashore—there were not enough men remaining to operate both guns and sails. Another interesting aspect of this action was the use of pivot guns by some of the warships, usually mounted on the centerline and capable of being trained to either broadside. They were generally larger guns with a greater range than most of the remainder of the armament and at Sevastopol one of the first guns to fire was the pivot gun on HMS *Agamemnon*. Allied losses were not substantial and this has led some to argue, for example D.K. Brown in *Marine & Technique au XIXe Siecle*, that possibly shell fire against warships has been overrated. Yes, it was still hard to *sink* a wooden ship which had a great deal of natural buoyancy, but shells could still inflict many personnel losses, and the results of the 8 March 1862 action between the *Virginia* and the Union wooden squadron tends to support the effectiveness of shell fire.

The bombardment of Sveaborg in the Baltic in 1855 during the Crimean War carried gunnery developments further. The Allied fleet, under Rear-Admiral Richard Saunders Dundas, carried out the bombardment in the second year of the war. It was primarily conducted by mortar boats and gunboats. The latter were specialty vessels armed with long range shell guns. The bombardment itself was fought at distances of no less than 2,000 yards, with the mortar vessels firing from 3,300 yards out. The role of ships-of-the-line was simply to hold each end of the line and was secondary to the main attack. These ranges were much greater than those the sailing fleets of the last century had fought at.

This concept was developed in part by a paper written by Captain B.J. Sulivan. In it he discounted an attack on the Russian naval base of Sveaborg, or Kronstadt (protecting St. Petersburg) by ships-of-the-line by stating that "Such an attempt would only end in our defeat, and the destruction of many of our ships." He went on to propose a long range attack as was carried out on Sveaborg by using "... every mortar and long gun that can be brought to bear." Ships-of-the-line would only be brought up close to finish off the fortress after adequate bombardment from the mortars, 68 pounders (having an 8" diameter), 10" shell guns, and 8⁵/₈" Lancaster guns (which had a tendency to malfunction and would eventually be withdrawn). The Lancaster gun fired a slightly elliptical cylinder which is why the Lancaster is sometimes listed as an 8" gun as the shape of the shot varied between 8" and 8⁵/₈". Its wrought iron shell weighed about 100 pounds. The French contribution included screw gunboats usually armed with between two and four 6.5" shell guns each.

Also, it had been common in the past during the bombardment of a fort for the bombarding fleet to anchor. At Sveaborg, all were kept in motion, so as to distract the Russian gunners' aim. Still, it should be noted that the Russian Rear-Admiral Matyushkin inspected Sveaborg in late 1854 and noted its weaknesses. He commented that it had been "neglected for 40 years" and "materially and in the art of using our artillery we belong to the last century." He went on to say that if the Allies attacked that "very few of our projectiles will reach the enemy, but on our side a good deal will be burned and destroyed."

Gun Comparisons in the Crimean War Period (Shell Guns)				
	Gun Size	Gun Weight	Charge Weight	Shell Weight
American	8"	6300	9	51
British	8"	6500	10	51
French	80 pdr	7100	7.75	61.5
British	10"	8400	12	87
American	10"	8600	10	104
American	IX"	9000	10	72.5
Weights are in pounds. The IX" is a Dahlgren.				

There was genuine Allied respect for the Russian fortifications, the approximately 1,000 mines laid, as well as the realization that with increased ranges of guns, there was no reason to come closer than one had to and risk damage to your fleet. It should be noted that Finnish granite used in Russian fortresses was superior in hardness to the material available at Sevastopol.

Plus there was another player available which would reappear in the American Civil War. The mortar boat. The British employed mortar boats during this bombardment, though the newer guns did have a tendency to split open (as opposed to bursting). By the end of the war the British were experimenting with 36" mortars.

The bombardment took place on 9 and 10 August 1855. Loss of life was light, but the interior of the fortress was destroyed by fires and explosions of some of the fortress's magazines. It climaxed with a three hour evening bombardment by British rockets from about 30 small warships, causing "new conflagrations and increasing the old ones." However, the fortress did not yield and its defense "prevented the entrance of the enemy's fleet into the harbor." The Allies had to withdraw as the mortars were literally splitting open and ammunition was running low. Some of the officers wanted to attack and burn nearby Helsinki, but this was not done.

Thus we see the Allied fleets in attacking Sevastopol and Sveaborg failed to completely reduce the positions, though the attack on Sevastopol was simply a diversion. A second attack against either port was not chanced.

This line of thought culminated in the planned assault on Kronstadt which did not take place, but the threat of which, however, brought an end of the war. The plan called for a combination of long-range gunboats (often using rifled ordnance), mortar boats, and British and French ironclad steam batteries such as those that had reduced Kinburn. Sulivan, in his paper, recognized the value of these new ironclads and recommended their employment in any attempt against Kronstadt. He also knew that any purely naval attack against Kronstadt would be one of destruction, as an Allied army, which did not exist in that theater, would be required to occupy that fortress and St. Petersburg which lay behind it.

By 1855, the Russian government, recognizing the weakness of their smaller coastal fortresses, had abandoned many of them along the Finnish coast. They also began development of a "monster gun" for coast defense. A 13" smoothbore, it was 16.5 feet long, weighed 22 tons, and threw a 340 pound shot with a charge of nearly 80 pounds. This gun was being developed to stop the Allied attack, but was too late for the planned assault. Now the Russian government, with the results of the Battle of Kinburn before them, was faced with the knowledge that Kronstadt was threatened with a force that they could not resist. This would become the key to drive them to seek peace.

It was this threat to Kronstadt, and in turn to St. Petersburg which it protected, and the inability of the tsar's government to counter this threat, combined with the possibility of Austria or Sweden (Sweden would join only if Austria did) declaring war on the side of the Allies, that brought about the end of the Crimean War. It was not the partial fall of a distant fortress on the Crimean Peninsula and the destruction of the Russian Black Sea fleet.

The whale, ultimately, this time, had prevailed against the elephant.

This entire theme of longer and longer ranges combined with larger and larger guns bombarding a fortress would grow and remain apparent throughout the era of the ironclad. Its countermeasure would be increasing the range of the coastal defense batteries and other defenses such as mines (which are of limited use in deep water), torpedoes, rams, and obstructions placed at a harbor's entrance.

All the European nationalities recognized the changed rules of combat and responded as best they could. The Turks developed a 10'-1"–long 11" coastal gun, while the Austrians began work on a 9.4" coast defense gun. According to Major Delafield writing in 1856, "All Europe had adopted (large guns) for land and sea service." It would be his conclusion that to protect a seaport or position, defenses would have to keep the range of the enemy guns at least 7,000 yards away from the object to be protected. Even as he wrote, Antwerp and Copenhagen were in the process of building fortifications with that exact conclusion in mind. However, Delafield's conclusion would be short lived. The British would be shortly arming the *Warrior* with guns that could fire 9,000 yards and the *Swamp Angel* at Charleston would lob shells into that town at a range of almost 8,000 yards in 1863. A theme for the future of the gun, the fort, and the ironclad was longer and longer gun ranges.

CHAPTER II

The Monitor and the Merrimack

A new navy cannot be built in a day, no matter how necessary reconstruction becomes because of a revolutionary invention. Until the new navy is built the existing fleet continues to play its intended role upon the seas. One swallow does not make a summer, nor does one Napoleon, one Merrimac, or one Dreadnought provide a force before which whole navies must retire.
—Bernard Brodie

...if the Confederate Navy could not destroy the Lincolnian cordon, everything was lost. The difficulty was that there was no Confederate Navy.
—Burton J. Hendrick in *Statesmen of the Lost Cause*

It has been said that the Crimean War was the first modern naval war and the last of the old-fashioned land wars. The American Civil War was certainly the first modern land war, and brought naval developments to new heights, all being pushed by the engine of the Industrial Revolution that generated the new technology of this modern age. Steam moved land armies by railroads, as well as warships from theater to theater, often according to orders delivered by telegraph or cable, while inventors tinkered away at all sorts of new advances. It was this race between rival new technologies that propelled the arms race at an unprecedented pace. So the American Civil War continued the development of naval warfare as it interacted with the first modern land war.

It was also a war that fully developed amphibious operations into their modern form. While the British had some experience with this in previous wars, the marriage between the army and the navy had been tentative at best. Franco-British operations in the Crimean war had brought home the fact that the war would not be decided by a modern-day Trafalgar (and *some* in the naval hierarchies of the world realized that), but by the ability to field an army in a foreign land and supply it from the sea. It can be argued that the American amphibious developments in the American Civil War came to full fruition in American amphibious operations in World War II. It was the seizure of Southern port after Southern port that broke the Confederacy.

One of the most difficult eras in a nation's history has to be when a civil war occurs. In America's history, it was the bloodiest war fought, and shaped America as no war had since the American Revolution. The American Civil War is certainly a type of war America wanted to avoid. A nightmare war of brother against brother—father against son. Each person had his own reason for choosing sides, and for each it was a difficult decision.

The war at sea has a special place too. If one does not accept fate as the only hand that guides the course of nations, then the war at sea in the early ironclad period leads to many possible outcomes. The *what-ifs* of history abound.

The role of seapower is sometimes slighted in studies of this war. Yet it may be said that the Confederacy lost the war when she lost the war at sea, and she might have won it if she had won the war at sea. If the blockade had been broken, supplies to sustain the Confederate war effort would have been more plentiful. If she had held on to New Orleans to build a better and stronger ironclad squadron, could she have lifted the blockade of the entire Gulf? Would powerful European intervention have been likely if the seas off Southern ports had been more contested and fought over by ironclad squadrons?

BUILDING THE CSN

At the beginning the fact that sailing vessels were soon to be laid aside was still far from general recognition, especially among officers of conservative tendencies; the three great weapons of to-day, the rifled gun, the ram, and the torpedo, were almost unknown in the service; and iron armor was still an experiment.
—Professor James Russell Soley, writing in 1883

The raw materials base of the Southern economy could not support the industrial superstructure, and this basic weakness contributed mightily to the ultimate collapse of the Confederate nation.
—Charles B. Dew in *Ironmaker to the Confederacy*

Stephen R. Mallory, formerly U.S. Senator from Florida, and now Secretary of the Navy for the Confederate States, was considered by some to be the most knowledgeable civilian on naval matters in 1860. He had headed the Senate's Naval Affairs Committee before the war for seven years, and, what is more important, had kept abreast of naval developments in Europe. This led him to two conclusions that guided the Confederacy's course at sea for the entire war.

One was that the South could not outbuild the North. The second was that she must build ironclad warships.

Unfortunately for the South she had lost an important opportunity that might have changed the course of the war at the very start. It points to the need for the South to have acted quickly and decisively at the start of this major historical confrontation. According to David Hollett, Jefferson Davis was offered ten British East Indian warships on the eve of the war. The British East India Company was being liquidated with the end of the Indian Mutiny and the assumption of British direct rule of India. Ten warships were offered and Messrs. Fraser, Trenholm & Company, a company sympathetic to the Confederacy, accepted the option for a nominal price. General P.G.T. Beauregard, one of the two commanders at the First Battle of Bull Run, urged President Davis to take up this option which the South could have easily afforded. What ten steam-powered wooden warships, several with iron hulls, could have accomplished against the Union navy—a small and scattered force in 1861—*if* such a force could have been quickly armed, manned, and kept as a united squadron, is difficult to guess. It would certainly have delayed the Union's initial naval efforts, allowing for more military supplies to reach the Confederacy's ports. Or such a force might even have crushed in detail the Union fleet... .

As the facilities did not exist in the South at the start of the war to compete with the numerous shipbuilding yards of the North, with her advanced industrialization, it was only from a source outside the Confederacy that a large or modern force could arrive. The South was primarily an agricultural region, and this was one of the root causes of the war in the first place. An example of this is that she only had 500,000 tons of merchant shipping compared to the North's 5,539,812 tons at the start of the war.

In 1860 the South had only 11 large iron mills: five in Virginia (the most important being the J.R. Anderson and Company, better known by its older name of Tredegar Iron Works at Richmond), three in South Carolina, two in Tennessee, and one in Georgia. At the start of the war none of these foundries could produce 2–inch rolled iron plate, which is stronger than two 1–inch plates laminated together, such as was used for the *Monitor's* turret. By 1863 the Confederates would have Tredegar, Scofield & Markham Iron Works at Atlanta (later known as the Atlanta Rolling Mill), and the Shelby Iron Company in Columbiana, Alabama capable of rolling 2–inch plate. However, in 1863 the lack of iron was crucial and delayed Confederate naval projects, which combined with her transportation problems and the Union's seizure of key Confederate cities and territory to doom her national war effort. In the case of the *Virginia II,* her hull was ready in May of 1863, but lack of raw iron meant that Tredegar could not supply plate to her, and she was delayed nearly a year before being completed.

Tredegar was the single most important industrial firm in the South. The Tredegar Iron Works employed about 1,000 men, free and slave, at the foundry early in the war with the number falling to about "400-500 by late 1864." The proportion of slave to free labor increased as the war continued. It produced not only iron and armor plates for the navy, but also all manner of artillery pieces, machinery and boilers for ships, sea and land explosive mines, gun carriages, rolling stock and locomotives. To complete one large gun took 400-500 hours of labor.

In 1860 one-sixth of all raw iron produced in the United States came from the South, if one included Kentucky and Maryland. While all southern states had iron ore, except for Louisiana, Mississippi, and Florida, the South had to depend on the large deposits in Alabama and northern Georgia for her war effort. With Federal advances, the raw iron produced in Alabama became the single most important source available to the Confederacy. Once produced, it often had to be shipped long distances to be utilized.

There was one other major source of iron used in the course of the war—the rails from the railroads. The South literally ate her infrastructure to supply the war effort, but by the end of 1862 she could not rely on this source anymore, as all stockpiled rail was used up, and her vital railroads were all that was left. Also, as the war continued, the old rails needed to be replaced, which became more and more difficult. The combination of lack of pig iron and shortages of coal to fuel the furnaces forced Tredegar Iron Works to operate at one-third capacity for four years of the war. The war witnessed at *least* ten Confederate ironclads being "destroyed on the stocks" while awaiting their armor plate. Such shortages meant that the Confederacy would *never* have a full blown war economy.

Guns, especially the famous Brooke rifled ordnance designed by John Mercer Brooke, were manufactured in Charlotte (North Carolina), Atlanta, Selma (Alabama—known in 1863 as the Selma Naval Gun Foundry), and Richmond. Tredegar, again, was the largest producer, manufacturing 1,099 guns in the course of the war, of which 473 were heavy naval guns (some sources list 431). As Raimondo Luraghi wrote in *Marinai del Sud (Sailors of the South),*

> The other plant, the Bellona Foundry, was placed in a quiet corner of the country, along the right bend of the river which bathes Richmond. Today it is still a peaceful countryside: only a few wretched walls, one piece of machinery to cast guns, an unfinished artillery piece to speak to one of this tremendous story of war; but at that time the plant was feverish with activity. It succeeded in casting during the conflict about 135 heavy guns, being second, among private enterprises, only to Tredegar.

The Selma Naval Gun Foundry built 102 guns to hold the third position. The Selma plant could produce, with labor shortages and varying quality of iron, about one gun a week. Certain key parts such as the carriage, elevating screws, and bands were manufactured in Atlanta and Charlotte, then shipped. Selma produced an average of 16 to 20 shells a day for the guns, and hit a high in the second half of the war of 30 a day.

An armory was attempted in Norfolk and three in New Orleans, but little was manufactured and the early capture of those two ports hurt the Confederate cause. Charlotte did receive much of the manufacturing equipment when Norfolk fell. Late in the war an ordnance plant was built at Fayetteville (with materials salvaged from the fall of Atlanta), but it was destroyed by Sherman's march through the Carolinas.

Tredegar built 136 Brooke rifles in the course of the war and at Selma 55 of these rifles were built. The 7" rifle was the predominate type—only one 8" and one 11" rifle appear to have been manufactured, and both at Selma. Some manufactured guns were not accepted, which creates some discrepancies between various sources. The 6.4" came in two patterns, and the 7" in three. These different patterns involved the addition of more bands on the piece which in turn allowed for heavier charges and less chance of the gun accidentally bursting. A heavy extra-banded 7" gun would later be mounted on the *CSS Richmond,* stationed on Virginia's James River, on 26 November 1862 and used a 25 pound charge throwing a 140 pound iron bolt. It broke through 8 inches of armor, laminated in 2 inch thick plates, to where the wood backing was visible. This points out that John Brooke could design a gun that could defeat the armor of the *Monitor,* but with the few opportunities that arose, a Brooke gun did not sink or disable a monitor type warship in the course of the war.

Brooke also designed smoothbore guns, 10" and 11" in size. One triple banded 11" smoothbore designed near the end of the war for close action combat weighed 28,000 pounds and fired a spherical shot weighing 190 pounds propelled by a 40 pound charge. Guns of these types were designed to fight large wooden ships, of which the Union navy had plenty. They followed the design direction of Rear-Admiral John A. Dahlgren's large XI" and XV" guns.

The South was also short of gunpowder, and what it had was often inferior to the Union powder. Some powder mills, such as the powder work at Columbia, South Carolina, in the course of the war had "been conducted with singular skill and with commensurate results" for specialty tasks such as for naval combat. In the South drives for getting chamber pot "materials" as a source of saltpeter were common and led to a joke about "did you do your duty for the Confederacy this morning?" Flannel to bag cartridges was also in short supply, and this led to clothing drives to gather up old skirts and "ladies' woolen undergarments." Some of the demands of this war are hard to fathom more than a century later!

Another area of weakness was the ability to build engines for the ships. The South for the most part used engines from existing ships, but it should be noted that these engines were supposed to be replaced in many cases when better engines became available. This did not happen because the Union's blockade had a strangling effect. The engines needed and the materials for them could have come from Europe, but for the blockade. It was also this blockade combined with amphibious operations that would seize strategic point after strategic point early in the war. As Confederate positions fell on the coast, the facilities along with the partially completed ships that could be moved went inland. This relocation of vital industries and movement of ships under construction meant further delays.

Additionally, the South began to suffer from labor difficulties by early 1862. Many skilled workers joined the army, while others were later drafted. The need for skilled workers to build and operate warships grew worse as the war lengthened. Ironically, as pointed out by William N. Still, Jr., the South "—used Negro labor extensively, both skilled and unskilled, in its many establishments."

It can be argued that with the early fall of New Orleans, Norfolk, and Memphis with their rich naval facilities so early in the war, that the South's naval effort had its back broken. Adding the fact that the small naval facility at Pensacola was never usable with the Union in control of the mouth of the harbor at Fort Pickens, her only real hope to turn the tide was for European built ironclads or European intervention. Short of a spectacular Confederate land victory and the seizure of some prize such as Washington or Philadelphia to break the Union's will, it would have taken a naval victory or outside intervention to win Southern independence. And all the time the Northern blockade grew tighter and tighter. Material prices continued to rise, with the most dramatic increases coming in the second half of the war.

But Secretary of the Navy Mallory did not give up. With the outbreak of war he ordered the construction of five ironclads to break the blockade. The later ironclads were designed to protect ports and rivers.

With a total naval budget in the course of the war of $107,000,000 (compared to the Confederate army's budget of $2,065,000,000) 150 warships were ordered, of which over half were completed or converted. Nor must it be forgotten that the South had unlimited supplies of timber, often green as opposed to aged timber, but satisfactory for its intended use.

In trying to persuade the Confederate Congress to build ironclads, Mallory first quoted William Howard Russell, correspondent of the London *Times,* at length on the naval situation then existing between Great Britain and France and their ironclad rivalry. Russell wrote and was quoted by Mallory as saying:

> In 1857 France determined upon the construction of 10 ironclad ships; vessels that should not only possess in a superior degree the speed and seaworthy qualities of the finest ships afloat, but upon whose impenetrable armor the missiles of naval warfare should fall as harmlessly as a distaff upon a coat of mail.
>
> The first of this class of ships was launched and made her first cruise last summer and her extraordinary qualities have attracted the attention of the naval world.

Russell went on to describe the *Gloire* and noted that France had been stimulated to complete 10 ironclads as rapidly as possible. He then stated that:

The power of such a fleet, carrying 300 rifled 50-pounders, can hardly be estimated; but it seems to be admitted that there is no sea castle, fort, or defensive work in the British Channel that it could not demolish with comparative impunity. Eight inch solid shot can not penetrate their sides at a greater distance than 200 yards, while at double this distance their guns are capable of breaching and leveling the heaviest walls of granite known to England's channel defenses.

To meet this terrific power it is already suggested that iron-cased forts and artillery of 15, 20, and even 30 inches bore, must be supplied, and this very suggestion admits the present superiority of ships over forts.

While Russell's fear of 30" diameter guns was never realized, the race was on between bigger guns and thicker armor even at this early stage of this rivalry between guns and armor. His comments about the helplessness of forts would see mixed results before the fortifications of Charleston and Wilmington—and Lissa Island during the Seven Weeks War.

Russell discussed costs, primarily, that a new six-gun ironclad ton for ton was more expensive than a wooden 40-gun steam frigate, but with smaller crews, the extra costs would equal out over the course of five years. He concluded by saying, "And to this we may fairly add the further consideration that the wooden frigate entails upon the country the obligation to pension, for deaths and disabilities among a crew of 600 men, in a highly destructible ship; whereas the ironclad vessel, while nearly indestructible herself, would afford almost immunity to her crew of but about 150 men."

Mallory used Russell's account of the value of the ironclad to support his call before the Confederate Congress for such vessels, as well as a letter of 6 May 1861 from Lieutenant John Brooke, urging the purchase of an ironclad from France. Mallory then went on in his 8 May 1861 epistle to the Confederate Committee on Naval Affairs that:

I regard the possession of an iron-armored ship as a matter of the first necessity. Such a vessel at this time could traverse the entire coast of the United States, prevent all blockades, and encounter, with fair prospect of success, their entire Navy.

If to cope with them upon the sea we follow their example and build wooden ships, we shall have to construct several at one time; for one or two ships would fall an easy prey to her comparatively numerous steam frigates. But inequality of numbers may be compensated by invulnerability; and thus not only does economy but naval success dictate the wisdom and expediency of fighting with iron against wood, without regard to first cost.

Naval engagements between wooden frigates, as they are now built and armed, will prove to be the forlorn hopes of the sea, simply contests in which the question, not of victory, but of who shall go to the bottom first, is to be solved.

Should the committee deem it expedient to begin at once the construction of such a ship, not a moment should be lost.

The Confederate Congress supported his conclusions and after some delay, Mallory was authorized to proceed with construction of ironclads. Mallory also received an appropriation of $2,000,000 to purchase an ironclad abroad, most likely in France, though this effort would never fully succeed. Note, too, that he draws attention to the saving of expense over the long term and that it would give the Confederacy a leg up at naval warfare vis-a-vis the North.

Mallory did not stand alone in his view of iron plating warships. This was not a concept where only a select few realized the potential of this new technology. It was well known within the military and naval establishments. At Charleston, South Carolina, there were two projects undertaken that would be the first use of iron plating in the American Civil War.

One was the Floating Battery designed by a Captain John Hamilton, CSN. It was a barge covered with iron rails on a timber backing 40 feet wide and 80 feet long with a draft of about eight feet. It carried four guns: two 42 pounders and two 32 pounders. The rails were arranged so that one set was inward, and the other set outward (or upside down) so the outer surface was somewhat smooth. It was weighted so heavily to the firing side that a counterbalance of sandbags and a small hospital building were added. Unlike the steam floating batteries used in the Crimean War, this one had no motive power and had to be towed, but was quickly built in a few weeks at the cost of $12,000.

Apparently, based on one Federal report, some Southern troops were fearful of serving on board her—christening her "The Slaughter Pen," but she would be towed to a position near the west end of Sullivan Island, behind a rock breakwater which protected her waterline from ricochet rounds. From that position she fired 470 shots at a range of about 2100 yards. Captain J.G. Foster, the Union engineer officer in Fort Sumter, wrote later that this battery was hit several times and that it resisted "all the shot (32-pounders) which had struck it, with the exception of one, which had passed through the narrow angular slope just below the roof." Union Captain James Chester wrote that fire was directed at the Floating Battery from Sumter and that "the gunnery made excellent practice but shot was seen to bounce off its sides like peas. After battering it for about an hour and a half, no visible effect had been produced... it was evident that throwing 32 pounder shot at it, at a mile range, was a waste of iron,... so fire was transferred." Lieutenant Joseph Yates, commander of the battery later wrote that the armor was pierced several times.

It would later serve as a defensive work on Vincent Creek next to Fort Wagner, best known for the assault of the Afro-American 54th Massachusetts as portrayed in the movie *Glory*. It deteriorated quickly there due to its unseasoned wood.

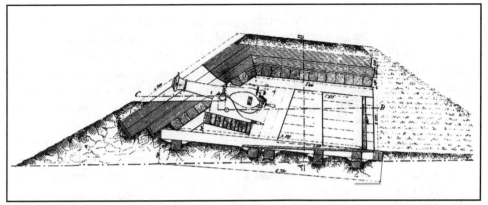

Cavalli's concept for an iron-protected coast battery which predated the American Civil War. This concept was utilized in the bombardment of Fort Sumter.

Also, there was the so called "Iron Battery" commanded by Major P. F. Stevens, Superintendent of the Citadel Academy, Charleston, at Cummings Point. It was armed with three 8" Columbiads—an early American shell gun design which combined features of the "gun, howitzer, and mortar." It was protected with inclined armor. It also had the outside armor heavily greased. This was to allow the shot to skid off the plate. Stevens commanded the battery and began its construction in January 1861. Captain J.G. Foster reported on February 5 1861 that "the idea of covering the bomb-proof with iron and giving it an inclination is no doubt derived from the Sardinian method for forming the sides of a man-of-war, so as to deflect the shot."

Italian artillerist Giovanni Cavalli was the father of the "Sardinian" method. While visiting Sweden in 1845-46, Cavalli developed with a Swedish officer a successful, but inefficient breech-loading rifled gun that fired oblong shells. He wrote just after the Crimean War concerning the design of an armored seagoing vessel, and what is more important, on the use of inclined armor. It should be noted that in February of 1861 Great Britain was in the process of building iron sheathed forts at Spithead, their main naval base in the Channel, so here again is evidence that the American military was abreast of European events and were mimicking them.

Against the Cummings Point Iron Battery, shot bounced off "like peas upon a trencher" and damaged only a port shutter on it. The Iron Battery fired 243 times on Fort Sumter. As James Baxter later wrote, "Sloping armor, so often advocated in the previous half century, had proved its value for the first time on American soil. Inclined sides became the characteristic feature of Confederate ironclads."

Finally there is one other interesting piece of evidence on the influence of Fort Sumter and the course of the war. The South had received as a gift from Charleston-owned Messrs. Fraser, Trenholm & Company in Great Britain a muzzle-loading Blakely 3.5" bore rifled gun that fired a small 12 pound oblong shot (it has been described as firing a "bolt" shot). The rifling gave the shot a high muzzle velocity, higher than the smoothbores used in the attack, and while small, it penetrated 20 inches into a masonry wall. Thus the South had forcibly recognized the value of the rifled gun from this point on to the end of the war. The Union would follow behind her lead, but surpass her with a greater ability to manufacture guns.

So all the ingredients for the future naval war in America were present at Fort Sumter: the early use of ironclad batteries, allowing for protected firing of large ordnance, and the use of rifled ordnance, whose ability to penetrate armor plating would improve as the war ran its course. It was these ingredients that the discerning Confederate Secretary of the Navy would see and use in the course of the war.

It must not be forgotten that wooden ships were still the main weapon throughout the war for maintaining the blockade (combined with the logistics to support it), but the ironclad was now destined to be the spearpoint.

THE BUILDING OF THE RIVALS

We have material enough to build a Navy of iron-plated ships.
    —*The Richmond Daily Enquirer*, 22 April 1861, on the fall of Gosport
    Navy Yard (Norfolk) to the Confederacy

The Secretary and myself had conversed upon the subject of protecting ships with ironclading very frequently, and at last I proposed to him a plan. That was about early in June, 1861, just after the Secretary came here from Montgomery
    —Lt. Brooke in testimony to the Confederate House of Representatives
    on 26 February, 1863

The Confederacy commissioned about one-fifth of the officers from the pre-1860 United States Navy (727 naval officers was the highest number employed at one time by the South in the course of the war). One of these men was Lieutenant John M. Brooke. He would design the CSS *Virginia,* or as known by many, the *Merrimack* (often spelled *Merrimac).* Among his many duties in the course of the war, most of which were with ordnance after the construction of the *Virginia,* he helped select the official naval uniform, personally designing the CSN button.

The *Merrimack* itself was burned, when the U.S. Navy yard at Gosport was abandoned on the night of 21 April 1861. Ordered in 1854, in part due to the Crimean War, she was commissioned in 1856. The wooden *Merrimack* was a screw frigate displacing 4,636 tons—equal in weight to a 74 gun ship-of-the-line. The old measurement of 3,200 tons, often given to the CSS *Virginia* and

An artist's concept of the Virginia.

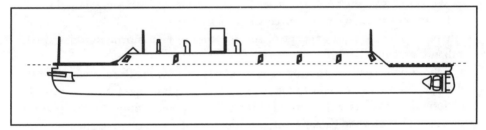

CSS Steam Frigate Virginia, *based on a drawing from the Maury papers.*

Merrimack, is using an archaic form of displacement. Armed with forty guns, this class of large frigate had a speed under steam of only 10.5 knots. Some thought well of this class because they carried the large IX" Dahlgren shell guns. The British Navy built two classes of frigates specifically to oppose these large ships, and felt that they came out ahead with smaller guns that fired more rapidly at a larger target. This points to the large American frigates of the War of 1812 that did quite well against their British opponents. It should be noted that the backward American navy saw the engines as purely auxiliary, primarily for use during a headwind, and not the main form of propulsion, as on the French *Napoleon.*

As a scuttled ship, burned to avoid being captured with the fall of the Gosport Navy Yard near Norfolk, Virginia, she would still have a future. She had sunk so rapidly, as some "of the workmen in the navy-yard scuttled and sank her, thus putting out the flames," that her machinery was not severely damaged. This allowed her hulk to be raised with the engines damaged from sea water, but capable of future use.

The design followed in the transformation of the scuttled *Merrimack* into the *Virginia* is disputed by some and claimed by others, primarily naval constructor John L. Porter. Porter built several U.S. naval vessels before the war, including the

Colorado and the *Pensacola*. He apparently had a prewar model of a casemate vessel, but without the extended ends, and suggested an ironclad vessel to Russia in the mid-1840s. While both Porter and Brooke worked on the construction of the *Virginia,* they did not get along. Porter later designed most of the Confederate ironclads.

Another claimant to the design of the original *Virginia* was E.C. Murray, builder of the CSS *Louisiana* at New Orleans. In testimony given before the Confederate House of Representatives, which in August 1862 was investigating the fall of New Orleans, Murray, a shipbuilder for 20 years, claimed to have submitted an ironclad design in April of 1861 in Montgomery, Alabama. He went on to state that, "I furnished the plan of the *Merrimack*, though, by some jeremy diddling, it is attributed to Lieutenant Brooke."

We submit that the muddied water of the paternity of the design of the *Virginia* is due in part to the fact that success has many fathers and failure is an orphan. But perhaps the design concept of the *Virginia* in fact is primarily due to the Italian Giovanni Cavalli?

The known facts are that by June of 1861, Lieutenant Brooke was working closely with Secretary Mallory, and submitted a rough design for the *Virginia* on 19 June that Mallory approved. He originally proposed using 3 inches of armor over 24 inches of wood backing, but the thickness of the plating was later increased to 4 inches due to gunnery tests at Jamestown Island. These tests were conducted by, among others, Lieutenant Thomas Catesby ap Roger Jones, an ordnance expert in his own right and later temporary commander of the *Virginia.* (The "ap" is "son of" in the Celtic language, which reflects Jones' Welsh blood.)

George M. Brooke, Jr., the biographer of John Brooke, notes while discussing the paternity of the design of the *Virginia,* that John Brooke *only* claimed the extended bow and stern as original and unique from any *existing naval design or concept,* which was true for the time. The extended ends "— augmented speed and flotation," were good for ramming and allowed more room for the crew.

Brooke was also well travelled and was one of the brightest stars in the pre-war naval establishment. Union Admiral David Porter later claimed he regretted losing only two men who went south to join the Confederacy—Brooke and Jones. While much later in the war, Brooke would write on 11 January 1864, to Commodore Samuel Barron CSN in Great Britain, that it "— renders it extremely important that one of the naval officers abroad should be directed to procure for this office such information on these points (European guns and ironclads) as may be required to enable us to apply our means to the best advantage. A supply of standard works embracing all branches of art and manufactures connected with the construction of guns, projectiles, fuses, powder, timberwork, mining, etc., is much needed." So Brooke certainly recognized the value of naval literature from around the world.

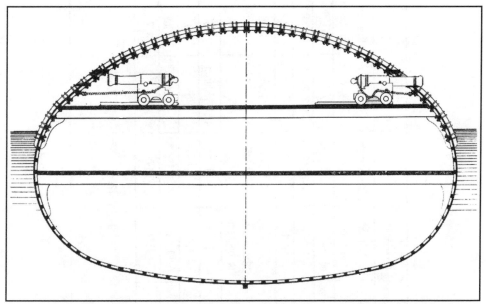

Cross section of Cavalli's proposed ironclad. Note that his proposal called for breechloaders.

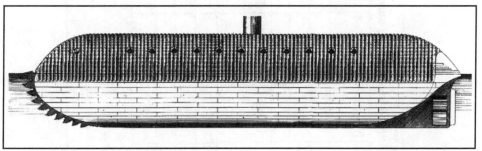

Cavalli's pre-American Civil War design for an armored steampowered ram, armed with rifled guns.

This is especially true in light of General Cavalli's ironclad, proposed before the American Civil War in 1856 for the Sardinian, later Italian, navy, which is mentioned in James Baxter's classic study entitled *The Introduction of the Ironclad Warship*. Cavalli actually proposed two ships, one of 1,600 tons and the other of 2,400 tons, the former with 24 guns and the latter with 36 guns. Relying solely on steam power they would also have a ram. Baxter does not supply a diagram of the ship designs in question, but in the 1988 article in *Rivista Marittima* by Ferruccio Botti, entitled "La 'Nave Invulnerabile' e le teorie del Generale Cavalli" (the 'Invulnerable Ship'—the theories of General Cavalli), Botti produces a diagram of the proposed 24-gun ironclad. This originally appeared in Cavalli's

Armored Steam Batteries and Early Seagoing Ironclads

	British Glatton	British Aetna	British Erebus	French Lave	French Saigon	French Gloire	British Warrior	Confederate Virginia	Union Monitor	Russian Pervenetz
Length	172'6"	157'10"	186'	170'	152'3"	255'6"	420'	279'4"	172'	221'9"
Draught	8'8"	6'	8'10"	8'6"	8'8"	27'10"	26'	22'4"	10'6"	14'9"
Beam	14'7"	16'	15'6"	—	46'1"	55'9"	58'4"	38'6"	41'6"	53'
Armament	14-68pdrs	16-68pdrs	16-68pdrs	16-50pdrs	12 6.4" RML	36 6.4" RML	10-110 BL; 26-68pdrs; 4-70pdrs BL	2-7"RML; 6-6.4" RML; 6-9"SB	2-11"SB	36 SB*
Armor belt	4"	4"	4"	4"	4.7 - 4.3"	4.7 - 4.3"	4.5"	4"	4.5", 9" turret	4.5"
Speed (knots)	4.5-5.5	4.5-5.5	5.5	3.5	7	13	14	4.0-7.0	6	9
Year laid down	1854	1855	1855	1854	1859	1858	1859	1861	1861	1862
Tonnage	1469-1538	1588	1973	1575	1508	5630	9137	3200	987	3277

RML = rifled muzzle loader BL = breechloader SB = smooth-bore
Note the 68 pounder (pdr) is a smoothbore

* = all 68pdrs(?) or 24 68pdrs & 10 36pdrs

Memoire sur divers perfectionnements militaires (Paris, 1856). Professor Luraghi also discusses this as a possible source for the design of the *Virginia*. We also know from the bombardment of Fort Sumter that Cavalli is associated with the use of inclined armor plate.

One can see that the jump from the French and British armored steam batteries to the Cavalli design is much further than the jump from the Cavalli design to the *Virginia*. The latter two share steam power as the sole propulsion system, a ram, inclined armor, the desire to employ rifled cannon, and similar displacements.

Cavalli was known to the American military community because his ideas were used during the bombardment of Fort Sumter, but we do not know who in the American naval community saw Cavalli's proposed ironclad design. However it takes only a small leap of faith to realize that some farsighted naval officers were reading what was published in Europe.

Donald L. Canney in *The Old Steam Navy, the Ironclads* notes that the American navy did not send naval observers to the Crimean War, though the army did. The three-man U.S. Army Commission was led by Major Richard Delafield and included Captain George B. McClellan. Canney goes on to write that "I have scoured large numbers of naval documents of the era immediately after Kinburn, including the Area File for the Mediterranean, and found scarcely a mention of the conflict and no reference to the floating batteries themselves (used at Kinburn). Any significant reaction among the naval hierarchy would have made some ripple through general correspondence."

However, Delafield wrote of his experiences, published in 1860, that "The failure of the combined fleets to produce any overpowering effects upon the harbor defenses of the Russians in the Black Sea and the Baltic, in 1854-55, induced France and England to use their greatest exertions to devise the means of destroying the sea-coast casemated defenses of their enemy." R.W. Daly in his *How the Merrimac Won* goes on to point out that the Delafield team noted the bombardment of the Kinburn forts in detail and,

> With carte blanche courteously extended to them, these gentlemen examined the British improvements after the war. Among other items, they made a copy of (British plans for an armored steam battery) to include in the last volume of their joint report, which was printed and sold at public expense, thus putting practical knowledge of the ironclad principle into the hands of anyone who cared to study it.

As the Civil War approached, then, naval architects North and South had authoritative knowledge about ironclads.

It should be noted too, that McClellan would later command during the Peninsula Campaign and he had unique and practical first hand experience with ironclads before the Civil War. It is also interesting to note that in Delafield's report the French and British ironclad steam batteries were proof against 8" and 10" shell guns, as well as smaller ordnance, but that at 400 yards range "the 8 and 10-inch solid shot will pass through the 4½-inch iron plates, or break the fastening. This single fact should cause us to renew our investigation in the armament of sea-coast batteries with the 8 and 10-inch (shell gun)... to the end that we abandon all further manufacture of such a gun, as a dangerous economy." With this in mind, we can see how Rodman was already developing a XV" for the army, the American service in charge of coastal defense, on the eve of war.

Also, we know that the famous bridge builder and well-known civil engineer Charles Ellet, Jr., visited Europe and proposed steam rams for the Russian fleet at Sevastopol during the Crimean War. He returned to the United States and was instrumental in building steam rams on the Mississippi River system early in the war for the Union. Admiral Dahlgren wrote *Shells and Shell Guns* in 1857 (which was read on both sides of the Atlantic) and included a section devoted to the Crimean War. Dahlgren also "monitored European developments by habitually collecting data from European newspapers, reports of American naval officers abroad, and correspondence with European ordnance experts." As for Secretary Mallory, he was "re-elected to the Senate in 1857, (and) he kept an eye on foreign (ironclad) progress." His work before the war on the Senate's Naval Affairs Committee and European newspapers kept him aware of stories of the new ironclad rage sweeping Europe, especially in France and Great Britain. In 1863 Rear Admiral Samuel F. Du Pont, who failed in the first naval assault against Charleston, refers in his papers to both the attack on Sevastopol on 17 October 1854, and a proposed assault against Kronstadt, as reasons for his fears for success in his attack.

Lieutenant Frank M. Bennett in his 1900 publication, *The Monitor and the Navy Under Steam*, stated concerning the pre-American Civil War period that, "Congress had permitted but little advance in naval material, resting passive while foreign nations experimented with guns, armor, and machinery, and were slowly changing their ideas of war-ships. Our naval experts, however, were watching the results of foreign experiments, and stood ready to apply the knowledge so gained when the need came."

Further, the United States had in fits and starts, starting in 1842 through the mid-1850's, been working on, and Congress had been appropriating large sums of money for, the so-called *Stevens Battery*, which was never completed. This was an early ironclad experiment of 4,683 tons and had a "central casemate whose inclined sides and ends were plated with 6 3/4" of iron." By the end of 1861 it had been decided not to complete it in part due to its deep draft.

So, while the United States Navy may have been unaware of the impact of the Crimean War *at the time of the war,* they were aware of its ramifications later during the period of 1856-1860. General Cavalli's ideas were certainly studied worldwide as he was already considered to be an expert on artillery, and this, combined with John Brooke's admission that the only original idea on the *Virginia* was the extended decks fore and aft leads one to conclude that the grandfather, if not the father, of the basic Confederate ironclad design used most during the American Civil War, must be Cavalli.

The construction of the *Virginia* officially began on 11 July 1861. She required 732 tons of iron (some of it from rails stripped from the B&O rail lines by Stonewall Jackson), which slowly arrived. Some iron plating took four weeks to move from Richmond to Norfolk due to lack of railroad flatcars. For six months up to 1500 men worked on her, and she was crewed by 320 men and 30 officers. Her ram was three feet of cast iron weighing 1500 pounds. Her iron belt extended downward about three feet from her deck to protect her hull and was supposed to extend further. However, at the time of the battle it was not complete. The most vulnerable point was her poorly protected propeller and rudder.

Her bow and stern sections were each 50 feet long, and her casemate was 180 feet long with 4 hatchways on her roof. The casemate was too narrow to place guns on either broadside directly across from each other, so they were staggered across the respective broadsides. The wooden casemate sides were of pine and oak and inclined at 36 degrees. Each iron plate was eight inches wide and was greased to help the enemy rounds to slide off when they hit. It was dark inside, so lanterns were hung during ship operations for light.

Opinions about her probable success were mixed, and Captain Charles MacIntosh (later commander of the *Louisiana,* who died in Farragut's victory at New Orleans) said to her Acting Engineer H. Ashton Ramsay, just before leaving, "Good-bye, Ramsay, I shall never see you again. She will prove your coffin."

Her speed is a debatable point. Heading down the Elizabeth River with the flow of the river current, she may have made "eight or nine knots." At the start of the first day of the battle in Hampton Roads, a top speed of six knots has been reported (seven before ballast was added), but with the riddling of her smokestack and loss of her ram bow, speed appears to have decreased to around four or five knots. There is no question that her turning radius was immense: she took half an hour to complete a turn!

Her two 7" Brooke rifles were designed as pivot guns, weighed 7.5 tons, and threw a 110 pound shell or a shot of 120 pounds. She had two broadside 6.4" Brooke rifles weighing 4.5 tons and firing a 65 pound shell or a shot of 80 pounds. Brooke designed an elongated shot that could be fired red hot against wooden ships, and used the Englishman Joseph Whitworth's 1858 design to develop a flat head bolt to punch through armor. Brooke also advocated large guns and "— demanded for the Confederate navy the maximum fire power feasible." She also carried six IX" Dahlgren smoothbores. Two smoothbores nearest the furnaces, the weakest guns in her armament, were supplied with solid shot with extra windage (for furnace heated shot). Except for the hot shot, there was no other solid shot on board. The Brooke rifles, due to delays and not intent, were supplied only with shells.

If additional resources had been given to build the *Virginia* she would have been completed much earlier. Just waiting to receive all her shells and 18,000 pounds of gunpowder took excessive time and effort, and work was slow in spite of complaints by her officers to Richmond.

The *Virginia* was not the best warship. At her launching she was a full three feet too high out of the water and ballast had to be added to lower her unarmored waterline. After her historic engagement, she proceeded on five occasions out of Norfolk to Hampton, a distance of only ten miles, and her engines broke down twice. John Porter discussed with her commander on one occasion that in his opinion the *Virginia* could not take to the open seas and "— such were the radical defects of her engines as greatly to retard and interfere with operations even in the smooth waters of Elizabeth City (river) and Hampton Roads."

Also on board was a 54 man contingent of Confederate Marines under Captain Reuben T. Thom. On the James River Squadron gunboats *Jamestown* and *Patrick Henry* were 20 and 24 more marines respectively.

So what was the Union Navy doing to counter this threat?

In July of 1861 Gideon Welles, Secretary of the Navy, recommended to Congress that a board of naval officers be appointed to make recommendations on ironclads, the so called "Ironclad Board." This was initially due to the ironclads under construction in Europe, but also due to the report of the slave Mary Louvestre, who was owned by a Norfolk ship chandler. She secretly copied the plans of the *Virginia*, escaped to Washington with the plans, and convinced Welles of their authenticity. Slaves, often called "contraband," escaping north would bring intelligence over the next few months, including a group who arrived on 28 January 1862 and reported that "the *Merrimack* was taken out of dock yesterday" and gave a very informative picture of the overall Confederate situation at Norfolk.

The Ironclad Board that was established to consider plans for an ironclad was appointed on 8 August 1861, but did not meet until 5 September. After two weeks, three plans were accepted. The *New Ironsides* and the *Galena* were easily accepted, though the former especially would take some time to build. It was the last one, the *Monitor*, that is of most interest. The Ironclad Board had some ideas that were viewed as quaint in Europe. For example, the Board felt that ironclads would never serve at sea, as they would be insufficient in speed, and wooden ships could always choose their gunnery range, yet both the seagoing *Gloire* and *Warrior* could outsteam virtually any Federal warship. Politics entered into the Federal program, and only after some discussions, compromises, and deals between

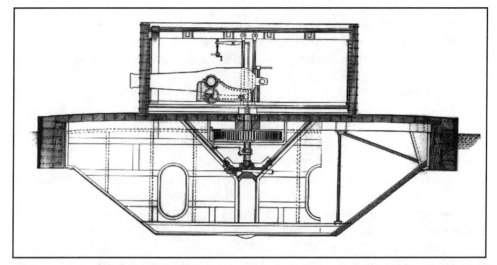

A cross section of the Monitor *'s turret.*

various Republican senators, lobbyists, and the Secretary of the Navy, were appropriations finally authorized.

The construction of the *Monitor* has to be understood in terms of the period. It was revolutionary in concept, though several of the concepts were actually common—especially in Sweden where Ericsson grew up. For example, the design was reminiscent of rafts used to move lumber. Some naval officers were concerned about firing the large guns in the confined space, but Ericsson was familiar with Swedish army operations and knew that like firing from huts, with the muzzles on the outside of the turret, the blast and sound would be minimal. Forty-seven patentable inventions were on board the *Monitor.* But the key point is that the Ironclad Board, at the urging of President Lincoln, had made a leap of faith. They knew that what they were approving was revolutionary, and that if it did not work, they would receive part of the blame; while if successful, Ericsson would receive the rewards. Many, for example, later referred to his vessel after the Battle of Hampton Roads as the *Ericsson.* Gustavus Fox, Assistant Secretary to the Navy, and a powerful influence on Gideon Welles throughout the war, later stated that he "never fully believed in armored vessels until I saw this battle" which he observed from the shore. He went on to say that "I know that the country is principally indebted for the construction of this vessel to President Lincoln...." So, in part, it can be argued that President Lincoln's oft-told story of the girl who put her leg in the stocking and said "there is something here," to help urge the Ironclad Board to accept this radical design, had a decisive effect on the history of the United States of America.

At this time Great Britain and France were able to roll plates 4.5 inches thick. It was the thickness of the plate combined with the wood backing, as D.K. Brown has pointed out, which deadened the tensile shock that would stop the shearing of the bolts holding the armor plate in place. This is why iron plate could not be used by itself.

Plates of this thickness were superior to the laminated plates on the *Monitor* by a factor of about 2 to 3—so six 1 inch laminated plates are almost the equivalent to about one 4 inch rolled plate. The *Monitor's* turret was armored with eight 1 inch plates, except in the area of the gun ports, which had 9 inches of armor plate. One of Lieutenant John L. Worden's concerns, as commander of the *Monitor*, was that "if a projectile struck the turret at an acute angle, it was expected to glance off without doing damage. But what would happen if it was fired in a straight line to the center of the turret, which in that case would receive the whole force of the blow? It might break off the bolt-heads on the interior, which, flying across, would kill the men at the guns; it might disarrange the revolving mechanism, and then we would be wholly disabled." Flying bolts from direct hits would later occur in battle, especially during the assault on Charleston in 1863, but were not a problem at the Battle of Hampton Roads.

The Dahlgren guns on the Monitor and later vessels are of considerable interest. They were originally designed as heavy cast iron smoothbore muzzle-loading shell guns and shaped like a soda bottle—jokes about its shape were made throughout the history of the use of the Dahlgren gun. Its distinctive shape did help protect the crew if the gun failed. Dahlgren's theory was to throw the shell with the minimum force needed the longest distance so the shell would explode with maximum blast. This was the idea behind the IX" and XI" Dahlgren, and later the XV" Dahlgren. The XIII" and XX" were designed to be Confederate ironclad killers—the XIII" fired a 280 pound shot propelled by 70 pounds of gunpowder. In contrast, the larger 440 pound XV" shot used 50 pounds of powder as the standard charge.

Dahlgren guns were designed to "rack" the enemy ironclad and not pierce the armor. The shot would be such a mass with enough force behind it that it would break up the armor and fastenings and then allow the next round to pass through. Rifled ordnance acted on the principal of piercing. While against thin armored Confederate ironclads, the concept of racking the enemy might work, as armor thickness grew in thickness and strength, Dahlgren's ideas were bypassed. Ultimately Dahlgren pursued a dead end.

Because of the failure of the "Peacemaker," the powder charge was kept to a minimum—too minimum. In a 1906 interview Captain Louis N. Stodder, the last surviving officer of the *Monitor*, made some interesting comments about the two XI" Dahlgrens, originally designed for firing shells at wooden ships. He said, "We had orders to use only 15 pounds of common black powder for discharging a 165 pound solid shot. For the same calibre of gun they now use from 250 to

500 pounds of powder, and the effect of one of our shot might have been compared in a way to that of a big rubber ball thrown by hand, such little penetrative possibility was there when fired against solid iron."

The *Monitor* was to be commanded by Lieutenant John L. Worden. His second officer was Lieutenant Samuel Dana Greene, whose station was in the turret. Third in command was Lieutenant Alban C. Stimers, who had served on board the old *Merrimack*.

But when was the *Virginia* going to appear? The waiting had become lengthy. The *Minnesota's* captain Gersom J. van Brunt had written on 28 February that "The *Merrimack* is still invisible to us, but reports say she is ready to come out. I sincerely wish she would; I am quite tired of hearing of her." The little *Dragon*, an armed tug with two guns, had been detailed by the Union to creep in each night towards Sewell's Point to learn what it could and also had been involved in picking up individuals who wanted to go north, under a flag of truce, off Confederate signal boats. It was on 1 March 1862 that in one of these meetings, the engineer of the Confederate signal boat was asked about the "old *Merrimack*." The Confederate replied, "Oh, she's all right.... You look out, she may be out in about a week."

THE BATTLE

There had been so many rumors about the Merrimac that some of the National officers had become skeptical of her prowess, and anticipated little trouble from her.
        —Edgar S. MaClay

When the battle ended, the Merrimac and her consorts had won a remarkable victory against great numerical odds, and were in complete control of the situation.
        —Lieutenant F.M. Bennett

At about 12:30 on 8 March 1862, the quartermaster of the *Congress* turned to one of the officers and said, "I wish you would take the glass and have a look over there, sir. I believe *that thing* is a-comin' down at last." Several Union ships noted three steamers coming down the Elizabeth River, which flows from Norfolk. The *Congress* dispatched the gunboat *Zouave* to determine who the new visitors were. As MaClay later wrote, "when the *Zouave* had proceeded about two miles on her mission her officers saw what looked to them like the roof of a large barn belching forth smoke from a chimney, and they were somewhat mystified as what it could be." Another observer said she was looking "like a house submerged to the eaves, borne onward by a flood."

Because of her deep draft, she had to come out with the tide rising. The *Virginia* had planned to come out on the evening of 6 March but five pilots had said this was too difficult at night. Certainly the fate of the wooden Union squadron would have been much worse if this had occurred.

Also present and observing the action was the French paddlewheel dispatch vessel (Aviso) *Gassendi,* launched in 1840. She is sometimes given as a frigate, but was much smaller and her commander gave one of the most concise after-action accounts of these two momentous days. The *Gassendi* reported sighting the *Virginia* at about 12:40 hours, looking like a "barracks roof, surmounted by a large funnel"—and noted that the Union warning gun actually was not fired for another 15 minutes. That was from the 625 ton *Mount Vernon* that was lying with her engine disabled under the guns of Fort Monroe. The little *Zouave* also claims this honor, and did shortly thereafter also fire a shot—firing a total of about six shots from her 30 pounder rifled Parrott at the *Virginia* before being recalled. She would fire throughout the action and suffered enough damage in the battle to be towed into Fort Monroe by the end of the day.

The French commander goes on to say that the *Virginia,* "after several evolutions, executed doubtless to assure herself of the good working of her machinery," and a pause, began to stand down on the Federal ships *Congress* and *Cumberland.* The temptation to move now against the Federal fleet was too much for the slave owning Marylander Confederate commander, Commodore Franklin Buchanan. Two Confederate gunboats, the little *Beaufort* and *Raleigh,* hung back at the entrance of the Elizabeth River to observe the actions of the remainder of the Federal fleet stationed to the east of their position, closer to the sea, and then steamed off to rejoin the *Virginia.* The *Beaufort* came alongside at almost 13:00 and gave a line to the *Virginia* until cast off at 13:30, to help her turn and move along in the shallow waters.

The Confederate squadron had as an overall commander Commodore Buchanan, who was also acting captain of the *Virginia.* Jones was the Executive Officer and in charge of the gun deck. Ramsay was third in command, and ironically enough had also served on the old *Merrimack* as the second engineer under Stimer, now of the *Monitor.* Buchanan's orders from Mallory were, "The *Virginia* is a novelty in naval construction, is untried, and her powers unknown, and the department will not give specific orders as to her attack upon the enemy. Her powers as a ram are regarded as very formidable, and it is hoped you may be able to test them." Buchanan had taken Ramsay aside before the action as they steamed down the Elizabeth River and asked, "what would happen to your engines and boilers if there should be a collision?" Ramsay replied that they were "braced tight." Buchanan had also communicated to Captain John Randolph Tucker of the Confederate James River Squadron that "my first object (is) to destroy the

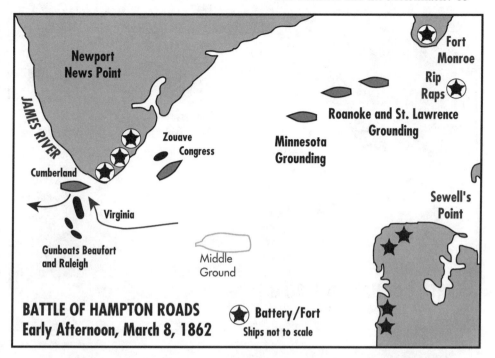

**Newport
News Point**

JAMES RIVER

Cumberland

Virginia

**Gunboats Beaufort
and Raleigh**

Zouave
Congress

Minnesota
Grounding

Middle
Ground

**Roanoke and St. Lawrence
Grounding**

**Fort
Monroe**

Rip
Raps

**Sewell's
Point**

**BATTLE OF HAMPTON ROADS
Early Afternoon, March 8, 1862**

⭐ **Battery/Fort**

Ships not to scale

frigates *Congress* and *Cumberland,* if possible, and then turn my attention to the destruction of the battery on shore and the gunboats."

The batteries he referred to were the guns at Newport News. Buchanan had wanted to co-operate with the plodding Major General John Bankhead Magruder on shore in an attack on those guns at Newport News, but Magruder had been unable to oblige—partly due to questioning the ability of the *Virginia* to help a land attack. Buchanan wanted to show what she and the Confederate Navy could do. Ironically, the elderly General John E. Wool, commanding Fort Monroe, was aware of the first plan and McClellan ordered that Newport News be evacuated on news of the action of 8 March, but rescinded the order after the *Monitor* and *Virginia* battle of the 9th. Buchanan also ordered his "No. 1" signal to be "Sink before you surrender."

As the *Virginia* approached the enemy Federal fleet, Buchanan addressed the crew. Combining two different accounts, he said something like, "Sailors, in a few minutes you will have the long-looked-for opportunity of showing your devotion to our cause. Remember that you are about to strike for your country and your homes. You must not be content with only doing your duty, but do *more than your duty!* Those ships (pointing to the Union warships) must be taken, and you shall not complain that I do not take you close enough. Go to your guns!"

The Federal fleet consisted of the 50-gun frigate *Congress* and the 24-gun sloop *Cumberland.* Both were anchored and about "a gunshot away" from each other,

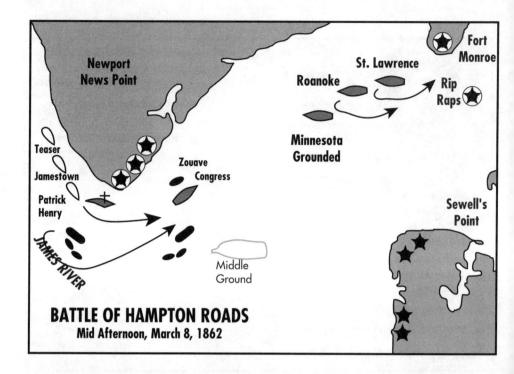

BATTLE OF HAMPTON ROADS
Mid Afternoon, March 8, 1862

the *Cumberland* closer and "about 800 yards" from shore, and both relied solely on sail power. The *Cumberland* could not be seen from Fort Monroe nor the *Gassendi*. The sailing ship *Congress* was armed with forty 32-pounders and ten 8" shell guns, the latter comparable to a British 68 pounder smoothbore. The *Cumberland,* originally a frigate but rebuilt (razed or razeed) in the 1850's as a sloop, was armed with twenty-two 9" smoothbore shell guns (also capable of firing an 80 pound shot—but as with all shell guns, at a low velocity), one 10" as a pivot gun and one rifled 70 pounder Dahlgren as the other pivot gun. The *Cumberland* had the unusual honor of being the first temperance warship in the U.S. Navy, largely due to the effort of Andrew Hull Foote, who would go on to honor, glory, and death in the fighting on the Mississippi. Her temperate crew in the 1840s was one of the best in the Mediterranean squadron at sport.

The original Union plan called for one of the small gunboats or tugs to ram the rudder of the *Virginia.* Also discussed was the use of the tugboats *Zouave* and *Dragon* to maneuver the *Congress* and *Cumberland* by towing, since the two large Federal ships were both sailing warships. In the course of the battle this tactic did not unfold. Commander William Smith of the *Congress* earlier had written that "I have not yet devised any plan to defend us against the *Merrimack,* unless it be with hard knocks." There seems to have been a lack of planning and anticipation for this combat, though the North knew for months that the *Virginia* was building. Why this was so is hard to say, except that few realized before the event *what* the *Virginia* was capable of. As Admiral Porter later said of the events of 8 March 1862, "many things which ought to have been done were left undone."

Also present, and to the east, was the screw frigate *Minnesota,* which had been in constant readiness for combat for the past month, the partially disabled steam frigate *Roanoke* (Her main shaft had been broken for the past four months. The delay on repairs was due to the war orders flooding manufacturers—her main shaft was difficult for suppliers to fix in peacetime let alone in these tumultuous times and so she had to rely on her sails and tugs), and the recently arrived sailing frigate *St. Lawrence,* due to replace the *Cumberland* on her duty. In addition to this there were two small six-gun ships and 10 gunboats, six converted ferryboats, and several army tugs—which gave their services to the U.S. Navy throughout 8 and 9 of March—and numerous Union transports. One question that has always been asked, is why did the Federal fleet consist of so many sailing ships present at this watershed event? The Union knew the *Virginia* was being readied. It was clearly a major lapse to have relied on so many sailing warships, two of the closest lying at anchor.

During the battle the *Minnesota* slowly moved towards the action, passing the Rip Raps, which had a Federal army battery, at about 14:00 and with a speed of about six to eight knots. The *Roanoke,* with the aid of three tugs, also was moving in the same direction, but all these vessels had to fight the current. The paddle-wheel gunboat *Whitehall* (four guns; two rifled 30 pounders and two 32 pounders) and the screw gunboat *Mystic* (five guns, four 32 pounders and one 24 pounder) did bear down on Newport News, but took only a small role in the fighting that day, withdrawing with the *Roanoke* later in the afternoon at 16:10. After the battle the *Whitehall* caught on fire on the 10th and became a total loss.

As these ships passed Sewell Point, the Confederate battery there fired at long range, about 2500 yards, with little effect, though the Union ships did return fire, the *Roanoke's* 10" pivot shell gun falling short. Also, the Confederate shores were lined with much of the populace of Norfolk and the surrounding areas as they witnessed "— a spectacle performed before them."

At about 14:30 the *Minnesota* ran aground about half way towards the battle. Both Sewell's battery (which contained the only XI" Rodman in the Confederacy, several IX", and some smaller guns, giving a total of 33) and the Confederate gunboats kept her under light fire during the course of the battle. This was followed by the *Roanoke* and *St. Lawrence* grounding slightly and both quickly coming off. As the afternoon wore on, the *Roanoke,* the *Mystic,* and *St. Lawrence,* reversed course, leaving the *Minnesota* aground, and anchored near Fort Monroe by the late afternoon. It was largely due to the groundings and the ineffective defense of the *Cumberland* and *Congress* against the *Virginia* that caused them to retire under the guns of Fort Monroe.

According to MaClay, the grounding of the *Minnesota* was the act of a pilot who had secretly sworn allegiance to the Confederacy but continued to serve on Federal vessels. Confederate Secretary of the Navy Mallory later stated that "— the stranding of that ship was in obedience to instruction from the office in Richmond, where information of the disaster was received in one hour and fifteen minutes after its occurrence." Whatever the true cause, a lack of seamanship was displayed by the Federal navy this day in an arena that the Navy had lived in for almost 100 years.

As the *Virginia* came on, first the *Cumberland* and then the *Congress* opened fire with their pivot guns, followed by fire from the shore batteries. Though hits were scored, no damage was done. An officer on the *Congress* remarked that shots "glanced off her forward casemate like a drop of water from a duck's back." The first Confederate shot came "exactly at" 14:00 from the *Beaufort*, commanded by Lieutenant William H. Parker, that fired a 32 pounder rifle shell at the *Congress*. Buchanan than made a signal to his squadron for "close action."

The *Virginia* at first did not reply to the Union fire, until just past 14:00, at an easy range of about 300 yards, she fired her bow Brooke 7" pivot gun on the *Cumberland*. It hit squarely and the explosion killed nine marines manning the aft pivot gun. As the *Virginia* steamed by the *Congress,* she fired a broadside into her as a way of saying hello.

Both the *Congress* and the *Cumberland* now fired full broadsides with no effect. Ironically, on board the *Congress* was Paymaster McKean Buchanan, brother to Franklin Buchanan. An officer of the *Congress* remarked that "our shot had apparently no effect upon her, but the result of her broadside on our ship was simply terrible." The pilot on board said that the shells from the *Cumberland* bounced off the *Virginia* "like India-rubber balls."

Earlier Buchanan had determined that the best guns on the Union vessels were those on board the *Cumberland,* so he had decided to "make right at her and ram her" while his ship was fresh and undamaged. The *Virginia* approached the *Cumberland's* starboard bow and was taken under fire by the *Cumberland's* bow pivot and forward guns of the starboard battery. The *Virginia,* now about 300 yards off, opened up and began the killing and destruction in earnest with between 10 and 15 minutes of sustained gunfire. One of the next shells from that same forward pivot gun hit and killed 15 men of a 16-man gun crew.

The *Cumberland* tried to work her springs and so bring more of her battery into play. This was a common maneuver for anchored ships dating back from the War of 1812 and earlier, but she could not accomplish it. She also tried to move guns around on deck to bring them to bear on the *Virginia*, which had taken up an advantageous raking position. As the *Cumberland* struggled to bring as many of her guns to bear, the crew closest to the action was the portion of the crew suffering the greatest number of losses, making any effective reply to the *Virginia*'s fire even less likely.

The Cumberland also had a wooden boom set up around her made of mast spars, and several of her small boats were in the water aft of her stern and to the leeside of the battle. The boom was to defend her against "infernal machines and fire craft." But it offered no defense against the *Virginia*'s iron beak as she kept heading straight on for the Cumberland, and rammed her amidships. Hitting the Cumberland amidships at about 5-6 knots, the Virginia buried her ram deep in the starboard side. "The shock was scarcely felt in the ironclad, but in the Cumberland it was terrific. The ship heeled over to port and trembled as if she had struck a rock under full sail, while the iron prow of the *Merrimack* [*Virginia*] crushed through her side and left a yawning chasm." She then fired her bow pivot directly into the Cumberland. The open ram hole was large enough to drive a small carriage through. The wave created by the blow caused a return wave to curl up over the bow gunport of the Virginia. As the Virginia reversed engines and attempted to pull out, it was noted that her ram was caught in the Cumberland. She began pivoting with the tidal current, turning partly parallel with the Cumberland. There was some fear that she would be dragged down with the sinking Cumberland, but her ram broke off, saving the Virginia from a watery grave.

There is some debate as to whether the *Virginia* rammed the *Cumberland* a second time. An officer on board the *Cumberland,* Thomas O. Selfridge, states that she did, towards the end of the action when the *Cumberland* was clearly sinking, as do several other sources. Selfridge later wrote that "It was a glancing blow, given at low speed, but it gave me the opportunity of delivering some telling blows from my battery." Confederate accounts do not tell of a second ramming. However, if she was rammed a second time it was not as effective as the first blow, and not at the *Virginia*'s best speed.

Tactically what happened at this point, and as best as we can reconcile various sometimes contradictory accounts, is as follow:. The *Virginia* had her port battery exposed to the greatest number of guns on the *Cumberland.* The *Cumberland's* crew had increased powder charges from 10 to 13 pounds and throughout this phase of maneuvering on the part of the *Virginia* delivered three good point-blank broadsides as the *Virginia* reversed engines to withdraw her ram and then slowly turned to expose her starboard battery. These broadsides from the *Cumberland* were delivered at ranges between 20 feet and 100 yards. When Buchanan called on the *Cumberland* to surrender, acting commander Lieutenant George Upham Morris shouted back, "Never, I'll sink alongside."

As the *Virginia* withdrew her ram a port IX" gun had its muzzle shot off, killing one man, and wounding several. Then as she turned, a second IX" on the "after starboard side" lost its muzzle. One of the two had been loaded and run out when this occurred and the muzzle hit caused the gun to fire. The two IX" guns that had lost their muzzles continued firing, which was dangerous in one case as the muzzle was so short that flames licked the wood backing of the casemate when fired. Fire was suspended when the danger was realized to be too great, and thus they would not be used in the action of the 9th with the *Monitor.*

It was during this phase of the action, the hottest action of the day, that more losses were suffered on both sides. Several men on the *Virginia* were stunned when they leaned against the casemate as a shot hit the outside plating, and Marine sharpshooters in the rigging of the *Cumberland* were also at work, so Jones ordered his men to stay away from the gunports. Another round "cut her anchor chain, which whipped inboard to..." kill and maim. One Confederate sailor jumped in front of the pivot gun to sponge it down when a round from the Union ship cut him in half. The heat and flame from the *Cumberland*'s guns actually sizzled the grease on the *Virginia*'s casemate. The cannon firing and burning grease made the interior of the casemate so dense from smoke that "we could hardly breath." One Confederate seaman turned to another working a gun in the smoke, and the heat, and the smell of battle, and said, "Jack, don't this seem like hell?" to which the reply came back of "It certainly does, and I think we'll be there in a few minutes!"

The *Virginia* drew off, lying off the port bow of the *Cumberland* and between her and the *Congress,* and poured it on. For the next 40-45 minutes, the *Virginia* with her two little consorts fired on the sinking *Cumberland.* The *Cumberland*'s crew fought on throughout, even hoisting extra ammunition before the water gained the powder rooms and ruined the gunpowder. As MaClay later wrote, "more than a hundred of the crew very soon were killed or wounded, the cockpit was crowded, the decks were slippery with blood and were strewn with the dead and dying, while the in rushing waters and the rapid settling of the ship too plainly indicated that she would soon go to the bottom." Many of the wounded drowned that day in spite of the best efforts of her crew.

The lower battery was eventually flooded out, but the upper battery continued to fight on. Lieutenant Morris ran up the red flag of "No Quarter" and so announced to the world that the *Cumberland* would sink before she surrendered. Eventually she went down bow first with her "stern high in the air" leaving only a few ensigns visible at the tops of her masts. The Confederate Lieutenant John Taylor Wood said that "No ship was ever fought more gallantly." Of a crew of 376, there were 121 killed, wounded, or missing.

As the *Cumberland* was dying, the Confederate James River Squadron under the immediate command of Captain Tucker came boldly down from Day's battery. It had been anchored there all night as it allowed Tucker to observe any ships issuing forth from Norfolk. Tucker's squadron would have to run the Union batteries at Newport News, but it could hide there until it saw Buchanan's ships. This squadron consisted of the sidewheel ex-passenger ships *Patrick Henry, Thomas Jefferson* (but always referred to by both sides by its original name

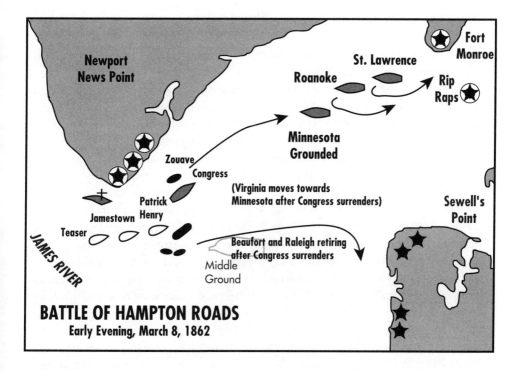

BATTLE OF HAMPTON ROADS
Early Evening, March 8, 1862

Jamestown), and the armed tugboat *Teaser.* The *Teaser* was commanded by William A. Webb, who would later command the ironclad CSS *Atlanta.*

The *Patrick Henry* had the distinction of being the first Confederate "ironclad" of the war. This 1,300 ton vessel was crewed by 150 men, and had the upper works removed, and mounted ten guns. Her armament was a 10" smoothbore shell pivot gun, a 64 pounder, six 8" shell guns, and two rifled 32 pounders. Tucker had 2 inches of iron plates fitted around the boiler and a 3 3/4 inch shield placed in front and to the rear of the engines to protect them from raking fire (sometimes given as 1 inch armor plate but according to Tucker's biographer this is in error). He had been in Virginia since the start of the war, and did not serve at the 7 February 1862 Battle of Roanoke. The *Jamestown* was less sturdy than the *Patrick Henry* and carried a lighter armament (two guns) and no armor.

Tucker knew there were three batteries at Newport News armed with about 18 guns. He decided to steam much closer in a line ahead (the *Patrick Henry* leading, next the *Jamestown,* and then the *Teaser)* and not at extreme Union gun range, thinking that the Union would have sited their guns for long range. He was right, as they fired at about 800 yards, over his head. The first two Union batteries fired over the racing Confederate ships with their "splendid gamecock appearance." The third battery corrected its range and scored several hits on Tucker's ship. Buchanan later wrote of Tucker's squadron, "They all came nobly into action, and were soon exposed to the heavy fire of shore batteries. Their escape was miracu-

lous, as they were under a galling fire of solid shot, shell, grape, and canister."
They arrived just after the *Cumberland* sank.

As Tucker took the *Patrick Henry* alongside the *Virginia* for orders he heard
Buchanan shout to him, "You have made a glorious run; use your own discretion,
do the enemy all the harm you can, and sink before surrendering."

The *Virginia* next turned her attention to the *Congress,* which had slipped her
cable and intentionally grounded herself with the help of the little *Zouave.* The
Zouave would be damaged in the course of the battle, suffer casualties, and later
be repaired at Baltimore after the action. The *Congress* had wanted to ground
parallel to the shore but her stern was somewhat exposed due in part to the tide.

The *Beaufort* closed with the *Congress,* followed by the *Raleigh,* and moved into
position on the starboard quarter of the grounded *Congress* where she could bring
guns to bear on the Confederates only with difficulty and her stern could be fired
on by the gunboats. Tucker's squadron now approached the *Congress* and was soon
engaged "in the thick of the fight" with her, the shore batteries, and even an
occasional shot at the *Minnesota.* The two Confederate sidewheelers had "forward
guns... engaging one enemy, (as) the after guns were firing at another!" The
Virginia took 35 minutes to complete a turn and had to move up towards the
James River to complete it, but in the process kept the *Congress* under long range
fire throughout. It was later reported these wooden gunboats were "firing upon
the unfortunate frigate with precision and severe effect."

The slow turning of the *Virginia* raised a cheer from the *Congress,* as they
thought she was leaving the action, but as she slowly swung around, and
approached, the *Congress* realized a different fate was destined for her. The *Virginia*
approached to within about 200 yards (there is some conflict as to the range at
this stage of the battle) and took up position off the stern of the *Congress* so as to
rake her. By 15:30 the *Virginia* was firing on *Congress* as well as the shore batteries.
The Confederate squadron's firing caused blood to run out of the scuppers "like
water on a wash-deck morning" and onto the *Zouave,* which lay alongside. By
16:40 the two stern guns of the *Congress* were disabled and the commander,
Lieutenant Joseph B. Smith, was dead from a piece of shell hitting him, so the
second in command surrendered the ship.

The *Virginia* ordered the *Beaufort* and *Raleigh* to go alongside the *Congress* and
"take the officers and wounded men prisoners, to permit the others to escape to
the shore, and then to burn the ship." The *Beaufort,* followed by the *Raleigh,* came
alongside the *Congress* and the process of surrendering the ship began with the
evacuation of some of the wounded onto the Confederate gunboats. However
this was interfered with when the Confederate gunboats came under field artillery
and small arms fire from Union soldiers on shore. This fire killed and wounded
several on board both gunboats and they were driven off. Lieutenant Parker
commanding the *Beaufort* had four balls pass through his clothing with one

slightly wounding him in the knee on the first volley from shore. The *Beaufort* and the *Raleigh* then began steaming towards Sewell Point to drop off the approximately 30 prisoners and the flag of the *Congress*, taken off before the rifle fire drove off the Confederate ships. Later the flag would be unrolled in front of Jefferson Davis, when it was "— found to be saturated with blood in several places." The *Beaufort* returned to the action early in the evening after being relieved of the prisoners, while the *Raleigh* retired to Norfolk for repairs (the carriage of her sole gun had been giving her difficulties in the action, and she had suffered from peppering from the shore).

The commander on the Union shore, General Joseph Mansfield, had seen the *Virginia* fire an occasional shell at the shore, one in fact hitting his personal tent and throwing splinters on him. He set up a light rifled artillery battery and two rifle companies to pepper the Confederate squadron and when told by an officer that the *Congress* had surrendered, he replied "I know the damned ship has surrendered, but we haven't." The commander of the *Beaufort* failed to signal Buchanan the reason for his withdrawal, and so the commodore was in the dark as to why the *Beaufort* had failed.

Buchanan then stated to Lieutenant Minor of the *Virginia* "that ship must be burned." Taking eight men with him, Minor started rowing a small boat towards the *Congress* while Buchanan ordered the *Teaser* to support Minor. When Minor was within about 250 yards of the *Congress*, small arms fire began hitting and Minor had to withdraw towards the *Teaser*.

Buchanan then signaled for the *Patrick Henry* to burn the *Congress*. As she approached, readying her ship's boats for boarding, several rounds hit, one on the boiler. Steam filled the ship, five men were scalded to death, and the *Patrick Henry* began to drift towards the enemy shore. On seeing this, the *Jamestown* bravely steamed forth, secured the *Patrick Henry* with a line, and towed her out of action. Partial repairs were effected and the *Patrick Henry* returned to action shortly against the *Minnesota* with half her engine power.

Buchanan at this point was livid with anger. With the retirement of the *Teaser* with Lieutenant Minor's party and now the *Patrick Henry*, Buchanan shouted, "Burn that damned ship." Buchanan now ordered Lieutenant Jones to "plug hot shot into her and don't leave her until she's afire. They must look after their own wounded, since they won't let us." The *Virginia* had set aside two of her 16 furnaces in the engine room for heating red hot shot. They took the shot and "rolled (them) into the flames on a grating, rolled out into iron buckets, hoisted to the gun-deck, and rolled into the guns, which had been prepared with wads of wet hemp. Then the gun would be touched off quickly and the shot sent on its errand of destruction."

The *Virginia* reversed engines, drew close to the stern of the *Congress* and poured the hot shot and shells into her, bringing about a general conflagration.

The *Congress* was "raked... fore and aft with hot shot and shell." It was after issuing this order that Buchanan grabbed a rifle and went up on deck to fire personally at the sharpshooters. This 61-year-old man received a "painful but not dangerous wound" in the fleshy part of the thigh from which he later recovered.

As the *Congress* burned, an enthralled audience watched from the Union and Southern shores, as well as from the ships. On board the *Virginia,* Ramsay wrote that,

> All the evening we stood on deck watching the brilliant display of the burning ship. Every part of her was on fire at the same time, the red-tongued flames running up shrouds, masts, and stays, and extending out to the yard-arms. She stood in bold relief against the black background, lighting up the Roads and reflecting her lurid lights on the bosom of the now placid and hushed waters. Every now and then the flames would reach one of the loaded cannon and a shell would hiss at random through the darkness.

That evening, shortly past midnight, with flames roaring through the ship, the magazine exploded "with a tremendous report" and the *Congress* was completely lost. Out of a crew of 434, there were 136 killed or wounded.

Young Joseph B. Smith on the *Congress* died early of a wound from an exploding shell. When his father heard that the *Congress* had surrendered he said "Then Joe is dead," knowing that his son would not have surrendered his ship.

The *Minnesota* was then approached, though with the tide ebbing, and her deep draft, the *Virginia* could not get closer than one mile, and so she scored but one hit. Her guns could not be elevated high enough due to the small gunports, which limited the ability of the *Virginia* to fire at long range. The return firing from the *Minnesota* had one ill effect, in that it drove the *Minnesota* further up on the mud bank where she was grounded. The *Jamestown* and *Patrick Henry* also engaged the *Minnesota,* firing at her bow and are credited with doing "the most damage in killing and wounding men."

The *Virginia* now retired towards Sewell Point, where the crew and men could watch the burning *Congress* in the distance. Her losses had been two killed, eight wounded, and two guns. Total Confederate losses were eight dead with 19 wounded.

THE ACTION OF 9 MARCH 1862

At 2:00 a.m. the iron battery Monitor, *Commander John L. Worden, which had arrived the previous evening at Hampton Roads, came alongside and reported for duty, and then all on board felt that we had a friend that would stand by us in our hour of trial.*

— **Captain G.J. Van Brunt of the USS *Minnesota***

The contest has been going on during most of the day between these two armored vessels, and most beautifully has the little Monitor sustained herself, showing herself capable of great endurance.
  —Captain John Marston of the USS *Roanoke*

Had the Virginia used solid shot instead of shells, or the Monitor full 30-50 lb. charges instead of only 15 lb. behind her 170-lb. shot, the result might have been different. As it was, there was long-drawn-out and resultless cannonade with the Monitor... and the Virginia.... Attempts to ram by both ships were frustrated by the use of the helm.
  —Oscar Parkes

As the *Monitor* arrived off Hampton Roads, Stodder says in his interview that,

> we arrived in the mouth of the Chesapeake late in the afternoon of March 8 and heard firing when we were 20 miles distant from Hampton Roads. This we took to be the guns of Fortress Monroe at practice, and the powder boat from which we got our ammunition could give us no information. We did not realize what had happened until we got near enough to see the *Congress* burning. It was midnight when we dropped anchor alongside the *Minnesota*, which had run hard and fast aground in her efforts to escape from the *Merrimac* during the afternoon. None of us had any sleep since leaving Brooklyn, for we had no hammocks, and nobody slept that night.

Immediately upon hearing about the battle of the *Virginia* with the wooden Union squadron, Washington D.C. was thrown into a panic. There was fear within Lincoln's government that the *Virginia* could attack a defenseless Washington—Secretary of War Edwin Stanton feared the fall of Fort Monroe and the leveling of New York City or Boston, or at least the ransom of those two ports. It was Gideon Welles who pointed out that the *Virginia*'s deep draft would not allow her to reach Washington, and the *Monitor* had arrived to stop her.

It should be noted that Mallory had sent an order to Buchanan on 7 March "for (his) consideration (of an) attack on New York by the *Virginia*. Can the *Virginia* steam to New York and attack and burn the City?... Once in the bay she could shell and burn the city and the shipping.... Bankers would withdraw their capital from the city, the Brooklyn navy-yard and its magazines and all the lower part of the city would be destroyed, and such an event, by a single ship, would do more to achieve an immediate independence than would the results of many campaigns." This plan would prove impractical. As pointed out by Buchanan in a letter two days later to Mallory, he noted his untrained crew ("two-thirds of whom have never been seasick"), the fact that he would be under constant attack on his voyage north, and that New York Harbor was difficult to enter with a ship

Thomas Nast sketch of Monitor *and* Merrimack *battle.*

of his deep draft. He felt that the *Virginia* was best suited for work in the Norfolk area and taking an "opportunity to make a bold dash at some other point."

Though Captain Tucker had seniority, in a conference with the wounded Buchanan on the evening of the 8th, it was decided, probably due to Jones's experience, that Jones would remain in command of the *Virginia* and would direct the overall operation. The *Virginia* left her anchorage just before 08:00 on the 9th.

The Captain of the *Minnesota*, later reported at the start of the engagement, when he ordered the *Monitor* to stop the *Virginia*,

> She immediately ran down in my wake, right within the range of the *Merrimack*, completely covering my ship as far as was possible with her dimensions, and, much to my astonishment, laid herself right alongside of the *Merrimack*, and the contrast was that of a pigmy to a giant. Gun after gun was fired by the *Monitor*, which was returned with whole broadsides from the rebels with no more effect, apparently, than some many pebblestones thrown by a child.

The battle was fought for the most part at ranges between 30 and 300 yards, most often at 200 yards. The *Monitor* tried to concentrate her fire to break through with her shot, while the *Virginia* peppered her as much as possible. If the *Monitor* had been allowed to use 30 pound powder charges and hit repeatedly into the same area, it is almost certain, based on the later experience with fighting the *Atlanta*, that her armor would have been started or outright penetration could have been made. Large wooden splinters flying from the wood backing of the armor in the confined area of the *Virginia's* casemate would have ended the standoff between the two ironclads and would have forced the *Virginia's* withdrawal or surrender.

The *Monitor,* even with the then standard 15 pounds of powder, did break the iron plating in places. But her rounds did not penetrate the wood backing, nor did they cause splinters in the casemate.

Jones, acting commander of the *Virginia,* had decided to try "... to attack and ram her (the *Monitor),* and to keep vigorously at her until the contest was decided, and you left the impression upon my mind that the engagement could only end in the overthrow of either the enemy or ourselves." He also had on board Marines who would pepper the *Monitor* throughout the action.

Worden's plan called for a series of circles with the completion of each circle bringing the *Monitor* back close to the *Virginia* when the guns had reloaded. The *Virginia* could reload quicker than the *Monitor* so each time that Worden completed his loop, the *Virginia* would reply to the *Monitor's* two shots with six to eight of hers. It was one of the first hits by the *Virginia* that eased Worden's mind. A direct hit on the turret did not cause it to jam. In the history of turreted ships, jamming of the turret was a problem, but not this day.

It must be recalled that during this era the number of guns firing was a matter of importance. Much of the pre-war opposition to the Dahlgren style guns was that a ship that carried them carried fewer guns and they were slower firing. This was viewed as a major disadvantage, and in Great Britain was one reason why the *Merrimack* type steam frigate was viewed as a faulty design. It was also one reason why the naval review board for the design of the *Monitor* almost rejected her—too few guns and they were slow-firing. The effect of a powerful gun versus numerous guns was not fully recognized yet.

In the second loop the *Virginia* plowed the deck of the *Monitor* with a hit that did not penetrate. It was this hit that made Worden crawl through a gunport and go over to the deck hit while under small arms fire from the *Virginia.* He lay down on his stomach to examine the scar on the deck left by the *Virginia's* shell. Worden wrote later that "the hull was uninjured, except for a few splinters in the wood." This was the second area of concern he had about a weakness of his ship. It had passed that test.

It was during one of the circuits of the *Virginia,* that the *Monitor* landed two rounds in the area of a previous hit and Worden observed some of the *Virginia's* iron plates falling away.

After about two hours of inconclusive action the *Virginia* struck a sandbar and stuck hard. This allowed the *Monitor* to close and fire at short range, a range that the *Virginia* found difficult to depress her guns and at angles that were equally difficult to traverse the guns to fire in reply. The *Virginia* was now also in danger because she had consumed a large quantity of coal in the last two days of action and was riding higher out of the water—she had lost some of her "fighting trim." Her incomplete iron skirt around her edge where her deck met the water was becoming exposed. A shell fired between "wind and water" might have easily penetrated her and caused grave damage.

While stuck, the *Virginia's* Acting Engineer Ramsay was ordered to do what he could to get the *Virginia* off the sandbar. He later wrote that "we lashed down the safety valves, heaped quick burning combustibles into the already raging fires, and brought the boilers to a pressure that would have been unsafe under ordinary circumstances— we piled in oiled cotton waste, splints of wood, anything that would burn faster than coal...there was a perceptible movement—" and the *Virginia* was no longer aground.

The *Patrick Henry* occasionally fired at long range during the action, and when the *Virginia* grounded, signal flags from the *Virginia* were sighted. It was thought to read oddly "Disabled my propeller is." Tucker's second in command thought that if wooden ships engaged in combat with the ironclads that they would survive about fifteen minutes, but they had to help. So Tucker ordered the *Jamestown* to accompany his ship and move down to help the grounded *Virginia.* As they started out into "the arena" the *Virginia* broke loose and so they retired back to the edge of the battle to continue to watch the action.

It was after breaking loose from the sandbar, that the *Virginia* tried a new tactic—ramming. The *Virginia* did strike the *Monitor* once "about amidships" and it gave the little *Monitor* "a shock, pushed us around, and that was all the harm." Jones, probably due to the missing ram and weakened bow, ordered the engines to reverse too early and Lieutenant Ramsay reported feeling no jar at the time the two ships struck. The bow did leak more from the two ships touching, but this was easily handled by the ship's two large pumps. According to Lieutenant Greene, the two ships touched each other on four other occasions.

Ramming was difficult for the *Virginia* and would point out one of the fundamental problems with Confederate ironclads. The Confederate ships tended to be big, ungainly, and slow. It is difficult to ram if you are the slower and less maneuverable of the two fighting ships. Worden said of the attempt of the *Virginia* to ram that "ours being the smaller vessel, and more easily handled, I had no difficulty in avoiding her ram. I ran around her several times, planting our shot in what seemed to be the most vulnerable places." The South was somewhat mesmerized by the initial success of the *Virginia* against the *Cumberland.* But being a stationary target made the *Cumberland* easy to ram. The South also preferred the ram as it did not use valuable gunpowder, chronically short throughout the war.

The *Virginia* now was between the *Monitor* and the *Minnesota* and fired some shells at the *Minnesota,* to which the *Monitor* responded by steaming towards the

The Monitor*'s turret, showing the impact of Confederate shells.*

stern of the *Virginia* in an attempt to break off her propeller or rudder. She failed in this, but again took up position between the *Virginia* and the *Minnesota*. It was then that the *Virginia* scored her best success of the afternoon.

Jones had ordered concentration of fire on the pilot house. The stern 7" Brooke rifle "delivered a rifle pointed shell which dislodged the iron logs sheltering the *Monitor's* pilot house." Worden was temporarily blinded by the shell explosion at the opening of the pilot house, because he was looking out the "lookout crack," so the impact of the round knocked him senseless and the gunpowder from the charge permanently blackened one side of his face. He remained unconscious for some time, but when roused immediately asked, "Have I saved the *Minnesota*?" which the *Monitor* that day had done. Greene now assumed command of the *Monitor*.

It was in the temporary lull as the *Monitor* retired to change commands and prepare to return to the fray, that the *Virginia* turned her attention back to the *Minnesota*, which was still hard aground and running low on solid shot (she claimed after the action to have hit the *Virginia* with about 50 solid shots—a much too high figure). The *Minnesota* was so concerned about her fate, that she prepared herself for self-immolation so to avoid falling into Confederate hands. She ended the action with three dead and 16 wounded, and had fired 529 rounds in the two day battle.

The second shot from the forward Brooke gun at the *Minnesota* also scored a minor but surprise hit. It missed the *Minnesota* and hit the armed tug *Dragon*, exploding in her boiler and completely disabling her. She did not sink, as sometimes stated, but was later sent to Baltimore and repaired.

The *Monitor* fought the *Virginia* after the wounding of Worden. Greene continued the action firing amidships in an area that Worden had thought might have been weakened. After some time, Greene withdrew from the loop she had been following, so that the *Monitor* could "adjust a piece of machinery." The *Virginia* at this point decided to retire to Norfolk and began steaming in that direction. Greene was concerned about mines and was unfamiliar with the waters, so after firing a parting round, withdrew at about 12:30, towards the *Minnesota*.

The action was over, and history had been made.

The *Patrick Henry* on both days expended a total of 138 shells and 19 solid shot. The *Minnesota* was slightly damaged. The *Whitehall* suffered three dead and 16 wounded from the battle and on 10 March caught fire and completely burned. The *Dragon* and *Zouave* both required repairs at Baltimore. There were five more Union wounded outside the losses on the *Congress* and *Cumberland*.

The little *Monitor* had expended 41 cast iron solid shot in the engagement and had been hit about 23 times with the most damaging scars being conical in shape and likely from the Brooke rifles. Three such rounds punched in between 2¹/₂" and 4"—one of the first hits on the turret formed a perfect mold of the shell tip and did not start any rivets. "It stunned the two men who were nearest where the ball struck and that was all." The *Gassendi's* report ends with "The other shots which reached the *Monitor*, and were for the most part round, did not appear to me to have produced a very great effect, those especially which struck the sides perpendicularly. Two, however, struck the side at the edge of the deck, lifting and tearing it, causing the iron plates to give way, and breaking three of them. The others only produced insignificant effects."

Of the hits on the *Virginia*, one broke the 4 inches of iron plate and displaced several feet of it, but did not penetrate the wood backing. In "two or three instances where shots had been placed close together, the wood backing was forced inward several inches." It was reported to Richmond that "— the shield was never pierced; though it was evident that two shots striking in the same place would have made a large hole through everything." It was later noted that the XI" could safely fire with 30 pound or even 50 pound charges—such heavy charges would have probably defeated the *Virginia.*

For Jones's part, he had decided that the stiff fight the *Monitor* put up required him to take on a load of solid shot, have the ram prow replaced, have the two damaged port guns replaced, have the gunport shutters installed, and get her iron belt completed. In the two day battle the *Virginia* had been hit 97 times, discounting any hits on the lost smokestack and ram.

REACTION

The confrontation at Hampton Roads may have been a draw; but the Northern fleet had been saved. The South may have resurrected the old hull of the Merrimac *with skillful improvisation, but she did not have the iron resources or the naval shipyards to out-produce the North in ironclads. More and better* Monitors *were on the way and would soon be in service, and the whole growing Northern industrial complex stood ready to challenge any power in an ironclad race. These thoughts had two effects; one, to make Southern independence seem less likely and the other, to make any form of foreign intervention much too hazardous a venture.*
—Lynn M. Case and Warren F. Spencer

The action of the (9 March 1862), and the performance, power, and capabilities of the Monitor, *must effect a radical change in naval warfare.*
—letter of 15 March 1862 to Lieutenant John L. Worden from Gideon Welles

To our Dear and Honered Captain
DEAR SIR These few lines is from your own Crew of the Monitor with there Kindest Love to there Honered Captain Hoping to God that they will have the pleasure of Welcoming you Back to us again Soon... we have got your Pilot house fixed and all Ready for you when you get well again... we are Waiting very Patiently to engage our Antagonist if we could only get a chance to do so the last time she came out we thought we would have the Pleasure of Sinking her But we all got Disapointed for we did not one Shot and the Norfolk papers Says we are Coward in the Monitor and all we want is a chance to Shew them where it lies with you for our Captain we can teach them who is cowards...
We remain untill Death your Affectionate Crew.

—The Monitor Boys (sic)

After the ocean spray settled from the battle, there were two reactions. One reaction was worldwide: the national and international focus on ironclads that now extended down to the mass of the reading public. The Union reaction was the need to create tactical ploys that could handle the continued threat of the *Virginia* while the counterpoint for the South was to build more ironclads like her.

The first news reports in the North told of a Federal victory. The *New York Times* wrote that it was both "an escape and a triumph." The arrival of the *Monitor* at the moment it did was called "Divine interference," "Providential occurrence," "hand of God," and other like sentiments. In the South, the *Virginia* was also hailed as a victor. Harrison A. Trexler would write of the two day battle that, "Naval experts of Europe had believed that wooden ships were doomed before these duels were fought, but the results of these two days overwhelmingly convinced the public of the fact."

The Battle of Hampton Roads brought on a virulent case of "*Monitor* Fever" that would not abate until their failure before Charleston in April of 1863. The first result was the *Passaic* Class of ten improved *Monitor*s that would be the mainstay of Union operations on the coast, and which were laid down immediately after the battle incorporating some minor improvements (the primary two being the moving of the pilot house to the top of the turret and a change in the armament so one XV" Dahlgren could be housed alongside an XI").

One officer wrote Brooke after the action to say that "as to the wooden gunboats we are building, they are not worth a cent." The Confederate House of Representatives passed a resolution on 17 March 1862 stating that it was "— of the utmost importance that this government should construct with the least possible delay as many small ironclad rams as practicable,... " By 1 May 1862, Mallory had "sanctioned at least twelve new ironclads, either by contract or in navy yards."

In Europe, the reaction was immediate. As the First Lord of the Admiralty, the Duke of Somerset, stated in the House of Lords on 3 April 1862, "— it was already the undivided opinion of all experienced men that where wooden ships met iron ships the former could not live." William Still quotes the London *Times* writing "There is not now a ship in the English Navy, apart from (the ironclads *Warrior* and *Black Prince)* that it would not be madness to trust to an engagement with the little *Monitor*."

The U.S. Consul and Minister in Paris wrote, "The devastating visit of the *Merrimack* in Hampton Roads on the 9th and 10th (sic) settled the fate of wooden vessels of war forever within one hour after the news arrived. The revelations of that day will be much more expensive to the other maritime powers than the day's damage were to us, for every dockyard will be put to its last resources in plating everything that carries a gun." Napoleon III stated that "it is now settled that there is no navy in the world that can make head against ironclad vessels."

The official French newspaper *Moniteur* reported on 7 April 1862 that "— this question of armored vessels seems to be preoccupying one after the other all of the governments of Europe." Italy sent naval designers to the Union, Great Britain, and France to study what types of ironclads to build. The Austrian Empire sent two designers to the North as well. While approximately 100 ironclads were being built around the world *before* the Battle of Hampton Roads in various countries from Great Britain to Spain to Russia, the battle caught the imagination of the world and meant that the turret for warships would not be ignored. Much of this European effort would be ships with turrets, either of Ericsson's design or British Captain Cowper Coles's turret design.

Another result of the action between the *Monitor* and the *Virginia* was that nations *beyond* Europe began or considered ironclad programs. This meant that no longer could Great Britain or France keep their ironclads only in European waters, but they had to consider ironclads for overseas duty. Both nations in the coming years would construct ships specifically for this duty, usually so called second class battleships. Their main characteristics would be large coal endurance, at first combined with sail power, and slightly smaller size with smaller guns and thinner armor, with their first class ironclads usually reserved for European duty.

Buchanan would eventually recover from his wound, go on to be promoted to rear admiral, and would command the Confederate Mobile naval squadron. Tucker, captain of the *Patrick Henry,* would command the ironclad CSS *Chicora* of the Charleston naval squadron, and later become commander of the navy at Charleston.

Worden was later given command of *New Ironsides,* then a new monitor, and later made Rear-Admiral, and ended up the second President of the Naval Institute after the war. It is noteworthy that when during the battle Worden had gone out on deck to check to see if any damage had been done on the first deck hit, he was subjected to some small arms fire. The shots missed and upon getting back inside he remarked "The *Merrimack* couldn't sink us if we let her pound us for a month." But later, while Worden was recovering from his wound, President Lincoln came to visit him. Worden had then had an opportunity to reflect on the action, and noted to Lincoln that the *Monitor* was vulnerable; boarding was one fear he expressed.

This caused Lincoln to contact Secretary of the Navy Gideon Welles who issued an order on 10 March 1862. It read, "It is directed by the President that the *Monitor* be not too much exposed; that in no event shall any attempt be made to proceed with her unattended to Norfolk." To help against boarders, special hoses were issued to pump scalding water on any Confederates who gained the *Monitor*'s deck.

But how to destroy the *Virginia?*

In April, the Washington *Star* newspaper wrote, "Since the naval fight in Hampton Roads some 1,500 different schemes for sinking or otherwise disposing of the *Merrimac* have been offered to the Navy Department by Yankee inventors."

The Union navy decided to try to defeat the *Virginia* by employing a full squadron. The *Monitor, Minnesota,* four steamers (including the 14 knot 3360 ton, 331 foot long iron hulled paddlewheel *Vanderbilt*—a speedy transatlantic passenger ship) to be employed as rams, and other Union vessels were massed to deal with the *Virginia* if she appeared again. The *Vanderbilt* had been built by Cornelius Vanderbilt, the richest man in America at the time.

He was at first approached by the Secretary of War (who doubted the Navy's ability to handle this crisis) and asked how he himself would defeat the *Virginia.* He then journeyed from New York to Washington and made the rounds. Vanderbilt was asked by Lincoln "Can you stop this ironclad?" and he said he would clad the *Vanderbilt* in bales of cotton, and use her as a ram. When asked by Lincoln the cost for his ship, Vanderbilt answered "I will accept no money, I will give the vessel free of charge to the Government."

Also present was a small "armored" gunboat, the Coast Guard *Naugatuck.* She was built on the principle of the *Stevens Battery* by her builders. She could lower herself in the water, like the first British ironclads, by filling watertight tanks, thus making her a smaller target. This tactic was used from time to time in several ironclads of various powers over the next decade. Her forward 100 pounder rifled Parrott (sometimes incorrectly given as a 150 pounder) was behind a bulwark of "armor" consisting of 20 inches of cedar wood.

The *Virginia* was a bit improved too, by 7 April when she left drydock, with a two foot steel and iron ram replacing her lost one and the arrival of chilled wrought iron bolts for her Brooke rifles, only 20 of which had arrived by 28 March. She had added nine 12 pounder howitzers on her unprotected promenade, or roof of the casemate, for use in repelling boarders. She also had her belt extended further down the edge of the deck to cover more of the hull normally below the waterline. Still, during the 45 days she was commanded by Captain Josiah Tattnall, she spent all but 13 days in the dock or in the "hands of the navy yard."

On 11 April the *Virginia,* under Captain Tattnall, made an appearance with the *Patrick Henry, Jamestown, Beaufort,* and *Raleigh,* as well as two armed tugs. The plan was to engage the *Monitor* with the *Virginia* and while engaged, to encircle and attack the *Monitor* with the four named wooden ships under the command of Tucker. They were to board her and cover her vents with wet blankets "forcing the hot gases back into the ship. They would throw a sail over the pilothouse, blinding the ironclad." The men would then drive wedges in the space between the deck and the turret, thus jamming the turret. Finally turpentine would be poured into the *Monitor* and ignited!

The *Monitor* raised steam and the *Naugatuck* fired a long range rifled shot at the *Virginia,* but the Federal fleet refused to come out and engage the Confederate squadron—even when three Union transports were captured. Tattnall refused to come out too far into the roadstead and so neither fleet made the move that would have brought about a general engagement. Tattnall did confirm from the captured transport's crews that several of the Federal ships were there to ram the *Virginia,* and with their shallower drafts, they could maneuver in waters that the *Virginia* could not enter. *Monitor* Paymaster William Keeler would wrote that "I believe the (Navy) Department is going to build a big glass case to put us in for fear of harm coming to us."

The Confederates also planned to destroy the *Monitor* with a submarine, which went through several trials, but the weather did not allow her to make an attempt. On 8 May 1862 there was a minor skirmish when the *Virginia* appeared to chase off the Federal fleet, then bombarding now Union Sewell Point battery at ranges of three-fourths to one and one quarter miles. The Union fleet, including the *Monitor,* retired under the guns of Fort Monroe, hoping the *Virginia* would approach them, which she and her consorts did not.

The demise of the *Virginia* involved Major General George B. McClellan's Peninsula Campaign. McClellan had been forced in part by the presence of the *Virginia* to switch from an amphibious movement up the James and York rivers directly on Richmond, to a land bound, longer, and less daring advance from Fort Monroe towards Richmond. It could be argued that the *Virginia* by forcing McClellan to adopt a new route kept him from capturing Richmond in 1862. R. W. Daly states that though the *Virginia* "did not decisively defeat the *Monitor* in their battle, she won a greater victory: she defeated Lincoln and his government in their hopes of winning a short war."

However, the Federal army landed a force on the Norfolk side of the Chesapeake Bay and forced the abandonment of Norfolk. Plans were made to move the *Virginia* up the James River. Unfortunately there was a bar of 18 feet that the *Virginia* could only pass if lightened of her warlike capabilities and if the wind was from the east. As Norfolk was being abandoned, the winds were from the west for two days running. Facing a much superior Union naval force without her guns, the *Virginia* was left with no course but self-destruction, though her crew escaped after a 22 mile march. Lieutenant Jones was the last to leave the ship on 11 May 1862.

The loss of Norfolk was a heavy blow to Confederate seapower. Not only was the *Virginia* lost, but so too the valuable shipbuilding facilities offered by Gosport Naval Yard. At the time of its loss construction had just commenced on some shallow draft ironclads that would have been used to contest the inner sound waters of the North Carolina coast by passing through the Dismal Swamp Canal that existed between Virginia and that state. This loss, combined with the loss of

New Orleans were grievous blows. The fall of Norfolk may have been the greatest success of McClellan's Peninsula Campaign.

Later, with the *Virginia* threat eliminated, McClellan tried to switch his supply point to the more convenient landing at Bermuda Hundred on the James River. Another ironclad building at Norfolk at this time, the CSS *Richmond*, was towed up the James River and later completed.

In May of 1862 the Union advanced up the James River with the *Monitor* and a new flagship ironclad, the USS *Galena*. The *Galena* design was submitted by Cornelius S. Bushnell, a railroad tycoon, who had been instrumental in getting Ericsson to submit his *Monitor* design to the U.S. Navy. It was armored with 3 3/4 inches of iron plate on an inclined (about 45 degrees) or "tumble home" design. The armoring was built up, and not with two inch rolled plates, but was rather an involved process with plates resting on iron "chairs" and both looking a bit like railroad rails.

The *Galena* first silenced the small Confederate Day's Neck battery and later the battery at Hardin's Bluff. When arriving at Drewry's Bluff further up the James River, now armed with the guns from the *Patrick Henry* and the *Jamestown*, as well as others, and being 80 to 110 feet above the water, the *Galena* with a small Union squadron, attacked again. It was here that it was shown "that she is not shot-proof; balls came through, and many men were killed with fragments of her own iron." It appeared after the action, that she fought from 600 to 800 yards, that the "whole side of the ship appeared to be caved in" from the repeated hits. The *Galena* fired 238 times and was hit about fifty times with half the hits penetrating her. The *Naugatuck* was also present firing at a distance, but her gun burst after only 16 rounds.

In this action *Monitor* at first tried to move ahead of the *Galena*. However, it was quickly realized that she could not elevate her guns high enough to fire on the battery, so she withdrew behind the *Galena*, which also now meant that the *Galena* received the bulk of Confederate fire, especially after the *Galena* ran out of shells and had to use shot—it was then that the Confederate fire redoubled. The *Galena* later had her armor removed and was converted to a sloop.

Over the course of the next few years of the war, the Confederacy built a new ironclad squadron to help in protecting the approaches to Richmond by the James River. A few minor skirmishes were fought, and there was one attempt late in the war on the part of the Confederate squadron to surprise the Union naval forces, but the naval war in Virginia was essentially over. The James River squadron, combined with shore defenses, river obstructions, and mines (torpedoes) kept the Federal Navy from advancing to Richmond during the entire course of the war, until the city was abandoned by Lee's army in 1865.

Finally as a footnote, there was much concern on the part of the British and French to monitor American progress in the naval art of war. One British study showed that the XV" Dalghren, soon to be introduced into American service, could not penetrate the *Warrior's* armor at ranges greater than 500 yards and only at 500 yards if using steel shot and not cast iron. This was firing a 440 pound shot with a claimed charge of 60 pounds of powder.

The British felt that American (and French) iron and gunpowder were inferior to their manufacturing skills and credit 60 pounds of American powder equal to 50 pounds of British powder. The Americans felt that their powder and British powder were about equal and the French powder was inferior. It is important not to look at a particular size of gun or weight of shell and assume all are equal—for they seldom are. Also, it had been discovered by British experiments that wrought iron shot was more effective than cast iron for penetration and damage to an ironclad target by a ratio of 3:1.

The Peacemaker Story

The War of 1812 had proved to the navy the superiority of ships armed with heavy, long-range guns. In the war's aftermath, many American naval officers believed that the logical step was to arm much larger ships with a few heavy guns and to omit the many but largely ineffective smaller ones.
—Spencer C. Tucker

The Princeton catastrophe accelerated the introduction of science to American naval ordnance.
—Robert John Schneller

Naval ordnance in this period was not a static subject, but a developing and evolving science. The conservative United States Navy might have lagged in accepting and developing the ironclad after the bombardment of Kinburn in 1855 by French ironclads, but it had always been in the forefront of ordnance development.

Much of the initial development was wrapped up in the use of wrought iron rather than iron. Wrought iron was about twice the strength of cast iron but required welding, which made the guns produced potentially weak at the weld points. The advantage of wrought iron was that larger charges and larger shot and shell could be used.

However, it all came down to producing a reliable gun. Without reliability gun crews got skittish—always at the forefront of a crew's mind with a gun that has a reputation for being unreliable is the question "Will this be the time, when instead of firing, the gun will burst?" Naval officer John A. Dahlgren, the inventor of the Dahlgren gun, once remarked about gun accidents of this type that "The ill effects of such a catastrophe on the minds of a ship's crew may easily be imagined."

The marriage of a large reliable shell gun to a revolutionary screw steamship design is the story of the "Peacemaker" and USS *Princeton*.

The story begins with John Ericsson, who later designed the *Monitor*. In 1837 Ericsson first approached the British Admiralty with a small screw steamer of his design and ran a very successful experiment towing a barge with important British naval personnel, including the Senior Lord of the Admiralty. Though Ericsson thought it was a successful demonstration, the British Navy rejected his design because the Admiralty's representatives decided that it would be difficult to steer the vessel. Ericsson, incensed over this rejection, became involved with the American consul in Liverpool, Francis Ogden, who introduced him to Captain Robert Stockton. Thus began the long relationship between America and Ericsson.

Stockton was a well-heeled naval officer who was interested in the technological advances then beginning to sweep the naval profession. Stockton had been involved in gunnery experimentation, and while in England, on his own initiative, he had authorized purchase of a John Ericsson designed gun, which was delivered in 1841 to the United States. It was built in Liverpool at the Mersey Iron Works. It should be noted that even back then customs for war materials was not a sensitive item—the gun, which still needed to be bored out and trunnions mounted upon arrival in the United States, was shipped with papers calling it a "hydraulic tube" and was called by Ogden "a shaft."

Later in his career Stockton helped capture California in the Mexican-American War in a spirited little campaign and had a major river city in California's Central Valley named after him. Earlier, Stockton had become heavily involved in Democratic Party politics and supported the Harrison/Tyler ticket for the presidency.

The fruit of the Stockton-Ericsson relationship was in the form of the USS *Princeton*. It was a steam sloop using a screw designed by Ericsson and specifically built to carry two large guns on pivots. She was authorized, at Stockton's urging, by President Tyler's administration as an experimental vessel. She displaced 672 tons, could steam at 11 knots, and was the first purpose built screw steam warship, with the screw arrangement designed by Ericsson. Among her several innovations was the first use of fans to force air into the furnaces. Called "forced draught," this enabled a ship to achieve higher speeds and would be typically "full speed" by the end of the century. Ericsson would go on to use fans and blowers on the *Monitor,* though some said that while it helped for speed, it also was of less help for ventilation and more for moving the bad air and high temperatures throughout the ship.

The *Princeton's* armament in 1844 was two 12" wrought iron guns and twelve 42 pound carronades. She was commanded by Stockton. There were other interesting features that, as pointed out by Spencer Tucker, had "Stockton and Ericsson [making the] *Princeton* the most technologically advanced warship of her time." Stockton said in 1844 that she was "the cheapest, fastest, and most certain ship-of-war in the world."

The British navy at this time was busily *converting* a building ship into her first screw warship—HMS *Rattler,* but the United States Navy was the first to build a screw warship from keel up. So while the British may have been first in completing a screw warship, they were clearly lagging behind the American design concept.

The 12" Mersey Iron Works gun mounted on the *Princeton* was called the "Orator." It was later renamed "Oregon" because of the then current crisis in the Pacific Northwest between Great Britain and the United States over the Oregon Territory. It was capable of penetrating 4.5 inches of iron with a 225 pound shot with charges of up to 56 pounds of powder. But the "Oregon," and later the "Peacemaker," were essentially experimental guns and the charges used on these guns varied, as well as the mounting. The "Oregon" was at one point fired without benefit of recoil which may have induced some cracking on the gun.

But it is with this second gun, the "Peacemaker," that our story develops. This second gun, according to Spencer Tucker, " was rather hastily made, of hot-blast iron, forged by Ward and Company of New York and then bored and finished at the Phoenix Foundry under Ericsson's direction." At this time Ericsson gave no indication of doubting the integrity of this gun. It could have very much been a combination of excessive powder charges combined with inferior American technology of that period (though some held the opinion at the time that American iron was superior to British) which produced a gun that would fail dramatically.

On 28 February 1844 between 350 and 400 Washington notables, including President Tyler, members of his Cabinet and their families, came on board the *Princeton* to see a demonstration of her abilities. While steaming on the Potomac, her guns were fired several times. It should be noted that by this time both guns had been fired many times previous to this cruise, though the "Peacemaker," unlike the "Oregon," had not been given the full U.S. Navy proof firing course. The "Peacemaker" was fired twice with a 25 pound powder charge, throwing a 212 pound roundshot. It was on the third firing that the gun exploded. It broke into three pieces, two of which flew overboard, but the third chunk was thrown about 30 feet into the crowded deck. The Secretaries of State and Navy were both killed, along with six others. Nine were injured including Stockton and Senator Thomas Hart Benton. President Tyler was below deck at the time with a young lady who lost her father in the accident. He consoled her in her grief, and shortly after this accident married her.

The Board of Inquiry over this explosion concluded that the "Peacemaker's" iron was three-fourths the strength of the British built gun and that the welding was poor. It also recommended that "—the use of wrought iron guns of large calibre—" not be constructed until the technology was perfected.

A cloud settled over Ericsson over this accident, but largely due to professional jealousies. Stockton had deliberately taken the limelight over the successes of the *Princeton* and had left Ericsson out of that fair light (Stockton literally left Ericsson standing on a dock with his luggage as he steamed out of New York City on his way to Washington in the *Princeton*). Now at the Board of Inquiry, Ericsson refused to participate because of Stockton's insult, and by that act muddied his relationship with the United States Navy. He submitted a bill of $13,930 that was not paid, largely at Stockton's direction. A Court of Claims awarded him the full bill in 1857, but the money was never authorized nor payment made.

The outgrowth of this explosion would see powder charges not exceeding 15 pounds. This limitation remained until the battle between the *Monitor* and the *Virginia* in 1862, and would probably cause the draw between those two instead of an outright victory for the *Monitor*. It would also spur John Dahlgren, Army Lieutenant Thomas Rodman, and Robert Parrott of Parrott gun fame, to experiment carefully in the development of new ordnance on the eve of the American Civil War.

Industrial Espionage

Robert John J. Schneller in his *The Contentious Innovator: A Biography of Rear Admiral John A. Dahlgren* tells an interesting story about industrial espionage and the early Dahlgren gun designs. Just after the Crimean War concluded, Dahlgren had perfected the IX" and XI" shell guns. They were unique in design as well as appearance, with their distinctive soda bottle look and large size.

Dahlgren's guns were built at several foundries, with the best early ones being produced at the Tredegar Iron Works at Richmond. But one plant was run by Cyrus Alger in Boston, and known as "The South Boston Iron Company."

In May of 1855 a Colonel Cox of the British Royal Artillery visited the foundry and was impressed with the "Iron Leviathans" of Dahlgren then under construction. Henry Wise, later Captain Wise, Chief of the Bureau of Naval Ordnance, informed Dahlgren of the first visit and that Cox was quite inquisitive. Dahlgren wrote back and "told Wise to keep Cox and other European visitors in the dark about the dimensions of the guns."

Cox called again in June, and wanted to see the plans of the gun, which Wise at that time politely refused. Schneller writes,

> At one point Wise was called away to the machine shop, leaving Cox alone in the office. Wise returned to find him busily measuring the plans of the XI". At the end of the day, Wise took the Englishman out for drinks. He noticed notches on Cox's swagger stick, which he assumed were measurements taken from the plan. 'In the beguilement of Mint Juleps,' as he put it, Wise pared off the notches with a pen knife and cut others in their place. He thought it was the cutest thing he ever did.

Later the steam frigate *Merrimack* (and future ironclad CSS *Virginia*) while sailing to Europe in late 1856, and carrying several IX", created a stir in naval circles. It was noted that the British in particular "repeatedly attempted to ascertain their dimensions." This would culminate in 1857 with two of Dahlgren's guns being spotted at Woolwich Arsenal, the government-owned gun foundry in Great Britain. The culprit was probably the South Boston Iron Company and done to simply help fatten the bottom line. The United States government, at Dahlgren's urging, denied the South Boston Iron Company any more government work, until the American Civil War forced their employment in the war effort.

The Austrian Empire Connection

In the category of lost opportunities we have the story Professor Lawrence Sondhaus has unearthed concerning the relations between the Austrian Empire and the Confederacy. Sondhaus published his findings in the September 1987 issue of *MARINE–Gestern, Heute.*

Relations between the Austrian Empire and the North were poor during the war, partly due to the building of two ironclads in New York City for the Austrian rival, Italy. Relations were so good between Italy and the United States that Giuseppe Garibaldi was even considered as a Union general by Lincoln.

In 1862 the Confederate agent Louis Merton approached the Austrian government for a possible naval arms deal. Over the next few months into 1863 negotiations took place between Merton and Archduke Ferdinand Max, head of the Austrian navy and future Emperor of Mexico.

Merton in 1862 was interested in wooden warships, but by 1863 primarily ironclads. Max tried to interest the Confederacy in one older steam frigate (the 31 gun *Radetzky*), two 22 gun steam corvettes, and 23 smaller warships, many of them gunboats. Max wanted to keep his small ironclad fleet Austrian in case of war with the growing Italian ironclad fleet. Max also hoped to sell the older warships so he could use the money to buy more ironclads.

CSA Captain Caleb Huse, Confederate army purchasing agent in Europe, traveled to several countries to negotiate the purchase of the wooden warships. He was arrested for a short time in Stuttgart as he lacked proper travel documents.

Huse decided the asking prices were too high and the drafts of the larger vessels too deep to be of value in the Confederate naval service. Max, for his part, would not allow the building of ironclads for the Confederacy at any of the busy private or government owned Austrian shipyards.

The combination of defeats at Gettysburg and Vicksburg, along with worsening financial and diplomatic matters, led the Confederacy to try to sell ironclads they were building in French and British yards to Austria. Max was interested in the ones in Great Britain, specifically the two so-called Laird rams.

Max sent his chief engineer to study them. Laird's asking price was too high for Austria, and the deal was not completed. The two Laird rams ended up in the British Navy as the *Scorpion* and *Wivern* in 1864. Another broadside ironclad being built for the Confederacy was considered but rejected as it was wood hulled and Max wanted iron hulls for the Austrian fleet.

By 1864 contact between the Confederacy and the Austrian Empire was broken off. Merton was reduced to trying to buy armor plate from Turkey at this late stage in the war, but his efforts proved in vain. The *Radetzky* fought for Austria both at Helgoland in 1864 and Lissa in 1866.

CHAPTER III

The Fall of New Orleans

The major difficulties encountered by Southerners in developing this war industry include exploitation of essential raw materials; transportation of raw iron, plating, and other crucial items to the various naval facilities; the acquisition and retention of competent and adequate labor; the development of shipyards and related facilities; policies of the Confederate government, especially the military services and their overall effects on the shipbuilding industry as a whole on the one hand—and the course of the war on the other.
—William N. Still, Jr. in *Confederate Shipbuilding*

Rivers dominate the geography of the South.... Civil War history recalls... the economic significance of port and shipping to the Old South. As the major agricultural area of the United States, the states that became the Confederacy were closely linked to the world market for raw materials and agricultural products. Those products were shipped out of Southern ports; then manufactured goods, household goods, luxury items, and industrial raw materials were shipped back.
Maxine Turner

The first engagement involving armored ships in this war, if we discount the long range skirmishes fought by the *Patrick Henry* in the James River, and the action of the CSS *Manassas* at the head of the passes, would be Foote's action at Fort Henry with his "tinclads," an excellent example being the restored *Cairo* now housed at Vicksburg.

This tome will not address the river battles of Plum Point or Memphis or even the actions with the CSS *Arkansas*, as they tend to lend themselves to a separate study. What is important to note is that in the spring of 1862 limited naval resources were going to each end of the Mississippi River front—which weakened the Confederate stand at New Orleans.

American Civil War Period Ironclads

	Confederate Louisiana	Confederate Mississippi	Confederate North Carolina	British Devastation
Length	264'	260'	224' 6"	285'
Draught	?	12'6"	16' 3"	26' 8"
Beam	62'	58	42' 6"	62' 3"
Armament	2-7""RML; 3-9"; 4-8""; 7-32pdrs RML*	2-7" RML; 18 others	4-9" 12 ton RML	4-12 RML
Armor belt	4"	3.75"	4.5" belt, 10" turret"	12" belt & turret
Speed (knots)	4.5-5.5	14 (planned - much lower)	11.5	13.8
Year laid down	1861	1861	1861	1869
Tonnage	1400 #	1400#	2750	9330

* the 9" and 8" guns are shell guns

R = rifled   RML = rifled muzzle loader   BL = breechloader   SB = smooth-bore

R = rifled   Note the 68 pounder (pdr) is a smoothbore.

tonnage is quite likely higher, one source giving the Mississippi 4000 tons. Louisiana would probably be about 3000 tons.

The North Carolina is one of the Laird Rams.

We now turn our attention to what may have been the most decisive battle of the American Civil War. The South's largest city was the prize in this campaign and her loss would hurt both the South's long term industrial war strength as well as depriving her of two potentially powerful ironclads.

THE CONFEDERATE SHIPBUILDING EFFORT AT NEW ORLEANS

Secretary Mallory did a good job producing a small Confederate fleet which, at times, played an important role and might have played a decisive role—if events had played out differently. We have already seen one possible decisive event—the saga of the *Virginia*. A might-have-been that was one of the largest missed opportunities for the South in her struggle was the early loss of New Orleans.

The loss of New Orleans inspired, on 27 August 1862, the beginning of the "Report of Evidence Taken before a Joint Special Committee of Both Houses of the Confederate Congress to Investigate the Affairs of the Navy Department," and appears in the *ORN* as a lengthy proceeding. Much of it discusses in detail the state of the Confederate Navy at New Orleans and specifically the state of two ironclads started there, the CSS *Mississippi* and CSS *Louisiana*. The completion of these two ironclads was delayed by the late or non-arrival of certain key equipment, such as a special 9" diameter propeller shaft from Richmond for the CSS *Mississippi,* and the "nonreceipt of iron… from Atlanta," or engine elements for the *Louisiana.* The fundamental problem was that Confederate shipbuilding was a difficult proposition in an agricultural nation, already facing an increasingly effective blockade. It is often forgotten that with the silent presence of the blockade, even limited as it was in early 1862, meant shipment by sea was impossible and the strained and limited rail lines had to move vital goods.

The Confederacy's ironclad effort at New Orleans also suffered from labor problems. So often a democracy is faced with a daunting task of getting everyone in the nation to pull on the traces together to move an important task forward. In November of 1861, Mr. Murray, the builder of the *Louisiana,* had been working for only two or three weeks when the carpenters struck for higher wages,

> … and my men were compelled to knock off work and join in the strike. I asked my men to remain at work, and I would abide by whatever result followed; that if the wages were increased as a result of the strike to $4 or $5 a day, I would pay it. They kept on at work after this assurance was given. The next day forty of the strikers came up and threatened to throw the tools in the river if my men did not knock off— We had to knock off for about four or five days.

It is ironic that delays such as this, fueled by unenlightened self-interest, and as with the *Virginia*, delays due to lack of gunpowder, iron and other components, might have made a decisive difference in the war. As the old saw goes, "For the want of a nail the battle was lost."

Another factor affecting the delivery of these ironclads was the chaotic financial situation of the Confederacy, especially with funds coming from distant Richmond. Finally, there was a conflict between builders, commanders of the army and the navy on the scene, fear of Union gunboats coming from *up* river (part of the Confederate wooden "Mosquito Squadron" was dispatched north early in the campaign), and the lack of a decisive overall commander, such as Beauregard in his defense of Charleston harbor. Again, the conflict between State's Rights, a cardinal philosophical point of the Confederacy, and the Confederate federal government would influence the course of events.

It should be noted that one of Farragut's goals was to destroy these building ironclads. He wrote in his detailed report to Gideon Welles on 6 May that "I neglected to mention my having good information respecting their ironclad rams, which they were building. I sent Captain Lee up to seize the principal one, the CSS *Mississippi*, which was to be the terror of the seas, and no doubt would have been to a great extent, but she soon came floating by us all in flames, and passed down the river— others were building in Algiers (across from New Orleans),..."

The CSS *Mississippi* is an interesting design primarily because of her propulsion system—she was to use triple screws (three shafts—one in the center and one on either side) with three engines and sixteen boilers—moving her at a projected 14 knots. The design of her engines was such that, if completed as *planned*, her "— indicated horsepower (was) probably not exceeded at that time by any warship afloat." Considering the state of the Confederacy, it is unlikely the machinery supplied could produce this high speed, but her triple screws and good speed would have made her more maneuverable than most Confederate ironclads. Several authors, including Shelby Foote, have written about the CSS *Mississippi* as being a potential savior for the South and her cause. Charles Dufour in *The Night the War Was Lost* states that she, and the *Louisiana*, were the "two greatest warships in the world"—almost a super ship, but her potential abilities, while great, seem to be exaggerated. Certainly some current European ironclads would have been superior to her, even if she had made her designed speed.

Nor was the CSS *Mississippi* built in a technological vacuum. She benefited from the visit of one of the two Connecticut brothers building her; Nelson Tift had witnessed the three day firing tests carried out in Virginia in 1861 for the building of the *Virginia*. Also, Nelson Tift, though not a shipbuilder by trade, decided that the CSS *Mississippi* could be built with straight timbers where possible and thus employ carpenters who normally built homes. This markedly improved the efficiency of the shipbuilding process. The Tifts were strong believers in the Confederacy and took no compensation for their design work on the CSS *Mississippi*. Ironically, many slaves were employed in completing her and the *Louisiana*. By March of 1862 the Tifts, knowing that their ship was delayed, were doing what they could to help complete the *Louisiana*.

The CSS *Mississippi* would have had two guns forward and two aft, like the Crimean-War-built French ironclad steam batteries, and a broadside of eight guns on each side. Wooden backing would have been three feet thick. She also would have had a small fighting position from where her officers could command, and for sharpshooters to fire from on top of the casemate.

One of the more unusual "ironclads" at New Orleans and one of the earliest was the *Manassas*. She was a river towboat that, with private money, had been purchased and was secretly being converted. Her masts and superstructure were removed and she was lightly plated with iron. Sometimes shown as having a single stack, she had twin stacks and looked a bit like a high backed turtle. William Still wrote of her that she was "christened the *Manassas* after the Confederate victory in Virginia; she was alternately described as looking like a turtle or a long cigar. The New Orleans *True Delta* called her "something very like a whale." She was going to be a privateer but was seized by the Confederacy and her command was given to Lieutenant Alexander F. Warley. Her existence was known to the Union by mid-July.

She carried one awkwardly placed 32 pounder firing directly forward with a slow rate of fire. She was 143 feet long, with a ram bow, and was armored with 1 1/2 inches of armor on 12 inches of wood backing. Weighing only 387 tons, she had a speed of four to six or even 10 knots depending on river conditions and her tired old engines. At first glance the armor looked inadequate, but because it was a convex covering, shot tended to glance off her back instead of penetrating into her interior, and she was low in the water which made her hard to hit at close range—the Union ships could not depress their guns sufficiently to hit her. As noted by Chester G. Hearn, "the engine was provided with pumps for ejecting steam and scalding water from the boiler" to prevent enemy boarders from winning the deck.

She was christened in battle on 11 October 1861 when a Union blockade force of four ships, led by the large steam sloop *Richmond,* stationed themselves at the Head of the Passes. This was the point on the Mississippi River where the delta opened up to several passages and was no longer one mighty channel. The *Manassas* led the way, followed by three fire rafts towed by two tugs, and five small wooden gunboats—ships converted from civilian duty.

The Union fleet lay anchored with all four ships' bows pointing up river under the command of Captain John Pope. With the *Richmond* were a small sailing sloop the *Preble,* a converted merchant ship the *Water Witch,* and a sailing sloop the *Vincennes,* a 703-ton ship built in the 1820s. No picket boats were out and no fundamental arrangements were made for a possible night attack, though a Confederate gunboat had scouted their position and fired on them a few days earlier.

The *Manassas* passed the *Preble* and made for the *Richmond* which was in the act of coaling. The alarm was just being raised when the *Manassas* rammed the side of the *Richmond*. Unfortunately for the *Manassas,* the shock knocked her men to the deck, disabled one of her engines, caused one of her smokestacks to collapse, and broke off her ram as the blow had vibrated her "like an aspen." The *Manassas* tried to deliver another blow but could not. She was effectively out of action and soon struggling back up river, lodging on a mudbank for some time after the action, before safely returning to New Orleans and repairs.

The *Richmond* had a small hole knocked in her about two feet below the waterline, breaking three planks, and the coaling barge alongside had the lines tying her snapped so it drifted downstream. Returning gun fire was too high to hit.

The fire rafts were launched but ran onto shoals. The Confederate wooden warships did not arrive until close to daylight. All but the little *Water Witch* had withdrawn by then, and she was chased down to the bar. Here was where a real Union disaster might have occurred, as both the *Richmond* and the *Vincennes* had run aground on the bar in awkward positions. The *Vincennes,* with Commander Robert Handy galvanized largely by fear, was temporarily abandoned by his orders, (though he claimed he received such orders to do so from the *Richmond* and later had three seamen so testify). Handy shortly thereafter melodramatically appeared on the deck of the *Richmond* wrapped in the *Vincennes'* flag. Before abandoning ship a slow match had been lit to blow up her magazine. But the match had been cut after lighting (to literally fulfill the order, the quarter–gunner, realizing the stupidity of the order, had lit it and then cut the fuse), and she was regained by the Union forces, as the Confederate squadron withdrew without pressing their advantage. The Captain had also thrown his guns overboard, to "put the finishing touches on his career."

Little else transpired except the withdrawal of the Union squadron to the open sea and delight in the newspapers of New Orleans. Pope would soon ask to be relieved and Commander Handy's career was over.

But then a real commander arrived to conduct the affairs of the Union fleet. Rear-Admiral David Glasgow Farragut took command off Ship Island on 20 February. Farragut was a Tennessee born Union officer who had grown up in New Orleans and had his home before the war in Norfolk. With secession and his pronounced Unionist sentiments, and informed that things would not go well for him if he stayed, he moved his family to New York in April of 1861.

Just one example of Farragut's resourcefulness was his intelligence of the enemy. This was gained by exploiting the Confederate media of the day. Farragut had sent on shore on 5 March at Biloxi a raiding force to seize newspapers from the Post Office, dated up to 25 February, 1862. Here was a man who would do his duty.

The defenses facing him, other than the Confederate ironclads, were two forts built before the war. Fort Jackson and Fort St. Philip lay on either side of the Mississippi River. Armed with numerous smaller and older guns, they were adequate in combating wooden ships—while the ships were under the fort's guns. Just before the battle a few larger guns had also been mounted.

But the high spring waters of the Mississippi had flooded the forts. There was about a foot of standing water in portions of Fort Jackson, the stronger of the two forts. Both forts were wet and "living conditions in the fort were almost unbearable."

Additionally, a chain had been stretched across the river, with the idea that any approaching fleet would lay helpless there trying to force passage while the guns of the forts plied shot and shell amongst them. It proved to be too vulnerable to the waters of the river. Finally there were wooden gunboats, with exposed positions clad in cotton bales (thus becoming "cottonclads") for additional protection.

By 1 April 1862 Farragut had all but two of his fleet across the bar and was approaching New Orleans. On 19 April, the Union mortar boats opened fire. In the course of the war, the Federal Navy took delivery of over two hundred 13" mortars lobbing a 200 pound shell a maximum of 4,200 yards. They were then placed on mortar boats and used in several actions, mostly confined to the Gulf and Mississippi Rivers as they were not very good sea boats.

While the mortar itself had been known for many centuries, the mortar boat of the American Civil War had a direct relationship with the mortar boats used by the British in the Crimean War. Delafield, in his report of 1860 on that war, has a detailed description (including diagrams) of the mortar boats used by the British.

Also present were new "90-day gunboats," a name based on how long it was supposed to take for them to be constructed. While larger than the British and French gunboats used in the Crimean War, they were constructed on the same principle. Furnished with a large shell gun, they were steam powered single screw warships constructed rapidly. They were none too popular with the service as they were too slow to run away from a powerful enemy steamer and were poor sea boats. A captain of one wrote that, "what she needs is more beam, more speed, and greater stability."

The Confederate reply was to send the uncompleted *Louisiana* down on 20 April and moor her to the river bank near Fort St. Philip the next day. Work crews worked feverishly on her from the 21st to the 24th. Six of her guns were mounted. Her captain was Charles MacIntosh.

The Union mortar boats were not totally ineffective by any means. Fort Jackson had been taking a pounding and several guns had been dismounted and the "damage done to the masonry was not irreparable, but the quarters and citadel... were burned down and the magazine endangered." One of the plans broached at this time in regard to employing the *Louisiana* was to anchor her to the shore *below* Fort St. Philip. This would have allowed for fire to be brought down on the mortar boats, though with a ship with no ability to move except by tugs—this would have been a dangerous expedient. Such an exposed forward position would have laid the *Louisiana* open to a classic cutting out expedition by Union small boats filled with armed sailors and officers ready to swarm onto her deck at night and let her drift down to the waiting arms of the remainder of the fleet. MacIntosh was also concerned that a mortar hit on his ship would go straight through the bottom of the *Louisiana*. Ironclads of this period of all nations had little or no deck armor which made them vulnerable to plunging projectiles.

The Confederate forts did fire back at the Union fleet and at ranges of 3,000 and even 4,000 yards. Farragut moved some of his gunboats up river into extreme range of the forts to draw their fire so the mortar boats would not suffer the fort's fire. Some hits were scored and portions of the Union fleet had to shift positions due to the fire.

THE PASSING OF THE FORTS

The amazing thing about (American Civil War) naval engagements are the accounts of men firing eight-inch guns at each other from a range of eight feet.
—Shelby Foote

During the winter and early spring the largest and best appointed fleet that ever flew the U. S. flag was organized, and placed under the command of the boldest, ablest and most enterprising officer in that service.
—J. Thomas Scharf

A more desperate, a more magnificent dash was never made, the rush of our little fleet over the barriers, through a fleet of rams, ironclad gunboats, batteries, and fire ships, and under the concentrated fire of two powerful forts, where the passage between them is just 1,000 yards, is, beyond all peradventure, the most brilliant thing in the way of a naval fight ever performed. As for myself, I must confess that I never expected to get through.
—Captain of the *Brooklyn*

In preparing for the passing of the forts, Farragut called on all his officers to prepare the ships as best they could for the coming ordeal. He later wrote,

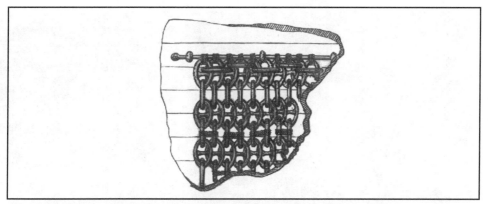

Section of chain armor placed on the side of the Brooklyn *to protect the boilers.*

Every vessel was as well prepared as the ingenuity of her commander and officers could suggest, both for the preservation of life and of the vessel, and, perhaps, there is not on record such a display of ingenuity as had been evinced in this little squadron. The first was by the engineer of the *Richmond,* Mr. Moore, by suggesting that the sheet cables be stopped up and down on the sides (of the ships) in the line with the engines, which was immediately adopted by all the vessels. Then each commander made his own arrangements for stopping the shot from penetrating the boilers or machinery that might come in forward or abaft (a raking shot), by hammocks, coal, bags of ashes, bags of sand, clothes-bags, and in fact, every device imaginable. The bulwarks were lined with hammocks by some, with splinter-net-tings made of ropes by others. Some rubbed their vessels over with mud, to make their ships less visible, and some whitewashed their decks [apparently only the *Richmond* whitewashed her deck], to make things more visible by night during the fight, all of which you will find mentioned in the reports of the commanders. In the afternoon I visited each ship, in order to know positively that each commander understood my orders for the attack, and to see that all was in readiness.

Additionally, Farragut, in his General Orders issued on 5 March, ordered his ships to mount as many guns fore and aft as possible to fight the Confederate warships in the confined waters of the Mississippi. Farragut also ordered that "no vessel must withdraw from battle under any circumstances without the consent of the flag-officer." He ended by saying that "hot and cold shot will no doubt be freely dealt to us, and there must be stout hearts and quick hands to extinguish the one and stop the holes of the other."

On 20 April, the obstruction across the river had been broken and a gap opened. Originally a chain, the heavy flows of the Mississippi kept up a growing pressure on it and had broken it by the first week in March. It had been strengthened with small craft chained together with their bows pointing up the river, but due to a daring raid just before the battle, combined with the high water, the obstructions now had a gap in them.

Passage of the Forts.

At 01:55 on 24 April 1862, Farragut hoisted the signal, two blood red lights from the top of the *Hartford's* mizzenmast. Ships began to weigh anchor and the attack was about to begin, but the response of several ships was slow.

The attack formation was in line ahead with seventeen steam warships. Farragut arranged his ships into three divisions. The First Division consisted of eight ships, two being somewhat powerful, the steam sloop *Pensacola* and the paddlewheeler USS *Mississippi*. Four 90-day gunboats and the *Oneida* and a converted ship, the *Varuna*, rounded out the division. The *Varuna*, after a valiant fight, would be the only Union vessel sunk when rammed by one of the Confederate cottonclads. The next division consisted of three uniform pre-war steam sloops, the flagship *Hartford*, followed by the *Brooklyn* commanded by Captain Thomas T. Craven, and the *Richmond*. The Third Division was made up of six weaker ships.

The weakest ships placed last suffered much damage as the fully roused Confederate gunners fired on them. Three were disabled and were unable to pass, the *Itasca, Kennebec,* and the *Winona.*

One of the factors that is sometimes forgotten in these naval actions, especially the early ones, is that the dead hand naval routine and a top heavy seniority system weighed down the North's efforts. There were a large number of elderly officers, most of whom were not vigorous enough for active commands at sea. Additionally, promotions had been slow over the previous thirty years, so junior officers

Brooklyn *and* Manassas.

were drained of initiative. J.R. Soley tells of a story that reflects this during the passing of the forts where "it is related one of the captains (it was Melancton Smith of the USS *Mississippi)* at the battle of New Orleans, a man of unquestioned courage, when he fell in with the *Manassas,* hailed ship after ship to obtain an order from the admiral to run her down. Nor was this an extreme case."

The First Division led the way and was received with heavy fire from the forts and was attacked by the Confederate cottonclads. Nor was the passage through the gap easy. There were delays and even some minor collisions in getting through the gap and past the forts. The smaller warships of the First Division pushed on ahead to engage the enemy steamers while the heavier ships engaged the guns of the forts. The *Pensacola,* after her captain had ordered his men to lie flat until they could bring their guns to bear, steamed deliberately and fired heavily on Ft. St. Philip and was supported by the slower USS *Mississippi.* The crew of the *Pensacola* and the gunners in the fort were close enough to exchange curses as well as gunfire.

The *Manassas* fought bravely but her limitations were obvious in this action. The *Manassas* appeared and made a dash first at the *Pensacola,* which avoided her ram, and so she then turned on the USS *Mississippi,* which had Lieutenant George Dewey (later the Admiral of Manila fame) at the helm.

A news correspondent on board shouted over to Dewey that there "is a queer-looking customer on our port bow." Dewey tried to run her down, which caused the *Mississippi* to avoid a perpendicular blow from the *Manassas.* The *Manassas* succeeded in striking her at an angle on the port side and firing her gun into her. "The effect on the ship at the time was to list her about one degree and cause a jar like that of taking the ground, but the blow, glancing, only gave a wound seven feet long and four inches deep, cutting off the heads of fifty copper bolts as clean as though done in a machine."

The *Manassas* next rammed the *Brooklyn.* The *Brooklyn* had early in the passing of the forts become entangled with the chain. After extricating herself, she continued up river when, as reported by Captain Craven,

> ...she was feebly butted by the celebrated ram *Manassas.* She came butting into our starboard gangway, first firing from her trapdoor when within about 10 feet of the ship, directly toward our smokestack, her shot entering about 5 feet above the water line and lodging in the sandbags which protected our steam drum.
>
> I had discovered this queer-looking gentleman while forcing my way over the barricade, lying close in to the bank, and when he made his appearance the second time I was so close to him that he had not an opportunity to get up his full speed, and his efforts to damage me were completely frustrated, our chain armor proving a perfect protection to our sides. He soon slid off and disappeared in the darkness a few moments thereafter, being all this while under a raking fire from Fort Jackson.

Just after the ramming, "a leadsman on the *Brooklyn* threw his lead at a couple of men standing in a scuttle just forward of the smokestack(s), knocking one of them overboard." The *Brooklyn* would suffer eight dead and 26 wounded in passing the forts and her subsequent combat with the Confederate wooden squadron.

The *Manassas* was also fired on by both Fort St. Philip and Fort Jackson, the latter scoring several hits and keeping her from descending the river and attacking the supporting Union mortar boats. She was also sighted by and fired on by up to six other Union warships.

The *Manassas,* after this pause, now followed several Union gunboats up river that were engaging and sinking a valiant cottonclad. Before the *Manassas* could save her she was turned on by the USS *Mississippi* which fired a broadside into her (or over her) but received little damage from her. However, she was forced to fire herself as her engines had become disabled and she was soon floating down river helplessly with the current.

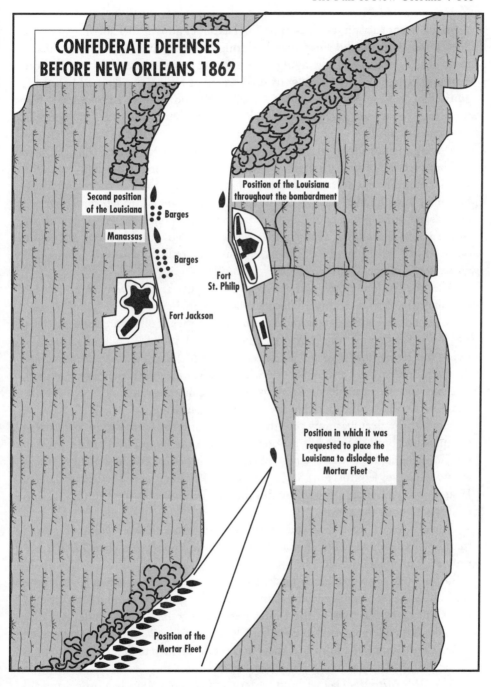

CONFEDERATE DEFENSES
BEFORE NEW ORLEANS 1862

Second position
of the Louisiana

Barges

Manassas

Barges

Fort
St. Philip

Fort Jackson

Position of the Louisiana
throughout the bombardment

Position in which it was
requested to place the
Louisiana to dislodge the
Mortar Fleet

Position of the
Mortar Fleet

In the heat of action the *Louisiana* "had used her guns against all of the Federal fleet as they passed, and every man had fought bravely and well… there she lay, with her little flag bravely flying, after having resisted every projectile from Admiral Farragut's fleet." The guns used were her bow and starboard broadside guns. Her bow guns were two IX" shell guns and one 7" Brooke rifle. Her starboard broadside guns were two 8" smooth bores and one 32 pounder converted to a rifle.

During the passing of the forts, a "large" Union warship fouled the *Louisiana* and her commander, MacIntosh, was in the act of throwing "a fire-ball" on to her when a cannon ball carried off both of his legs. He made the shore and a fort hospital but he quickly bled to death. The *Louisiana* fired into her but could not depress her guns low enough to fire a shot or shell through the enemy's bottom. In the action she was hit, among other rounds, by two, possibly three, XI" shells, one from the 90-day gunboat *Katahdin*. Some iron railroad plate was crushed but no serious damage was done to her.

After the battle the crew and workmen kept at her and she was able to put her machinery in order by 28 April. The plan was to steam her to Mobile. Unfortunately, the forts had surrendered, in part due to a mutiny of the cut off Confederate garrison, and it was felt that the best course of action was to destroy the Louisiana instead of trying the daring foray into and across the Gulf of Mexico. She was hauled out into the river and destroyed, and all but one of her officers were shortly thereafter captured. The fact that the Confederate Army, as with the Union, commanded coast defense batteries may have contributed to the loss of the Louisiana.

Most of the fleet was now past the two forts and the Confederate cottonclad steamers had been defeated. It is noteworthy that the Union ships and especially the Confederate forts fired too high in far too many cases. Possibly better training would have avoided this. Fort St. Philip fired 1,591 times in the action while Fort Jackson was well fought though under mortar fire as well as fire from the Union fleet throughout the action.

The sandbags and chains had proved their worth and several ships reported that they had stopped both shot and shell from doing more damage. Now it was time to consolidate the victory.

Oneida was considered an unlucky ship and would later be lost at sea after the war. On her first exposure to the Confederate fort guns she was hit and suffered losses but saved the crew of the Union gunboat *Varuna* that was sunk in action with the Confederate wooden gunboats. It was the *Oneida,* under Commander, later Rear-Admiral, S. Philip Lee, that Farragut dispatched to determine the status of the CSS *Mississippi*.

The CSS *Mississippi* lay without battery and power, and only a little armor in place, though her troublesome 9" main propeller shaft had arrived. An attempt was made to tow her north up the Mississippi River for completion, but sufficient tugs for the strong current running could not be procured. With the CSS *Mississippi* drifting down towards the Union fleet, there was no real course of action available. She was burned. The heartbroken Tift brothers would, even when arrested at Vicksburg due to their northern birth, continue to believe in "the cause" and would head to Savannah to convert the blockade runner *Fingal* into the *Atlanta*. It is interesting to note that the two most potentially powerful Confederate ironclads were designed by Yankees.

New Orleans was lost. It has been argued that this may have been the decisive battle of the Civil War. With the loss of New Orleans went many manufacturing capabilities. It, according to the Confederate ambassador there, may have dissuaded Napoleon III and Imperial France from intervening in the war on the side of the Confederacy. It cut off a major overseas shipping point and gave control of the lower Mississippi to the Federals. It also meant that the ambitious ironclads program at that city was snuffed out.

We know that the Union in 1862 had no ironclads to spare for the Gulf waters and it is quite possible that the CSS *Mississippi* and *Louisiana* might have dominated the waters of the Gulf of Mexico for a summer and a fall. The consequences of this may have been catastrophic for the Union. Union maritime operations in the Atlantic might have been paralyzed as they scrambled to regroup to stem this new threat in the Gulf. Mobile and New Orleans, possibly Galveston, and several small ports would have been open for trade. A move against Ft. Pickens at Pensacola might have been possible. Given aggressive commanders and decent weather, the South may indeed have won the war by gaining European intervention or increased supplies had they managed to stop Farragut and his fleet in April of 1862.

War with Europe: Intervention in the American Civil War

But the potential for (British) intervention remained high until late 1862
—Howard Jones from *Union in Peril*

In 1862, the threat of European intervention on the Confederate side seemed as real to Union officials as the threat posed by enemy ironclads.
—Robert John J. Schneller

It is readily evident to anyone who studies the statistics that the South, unaided, simply did not have the physical and material capacity to win the war, provided the North retained its determination to fight. Outside help, in the form of recognition, raising of the blockade, and material assistance, was absolutely necessary for the Confederacy to establish its independence of the Federal Union.
—Charles L. Dufour

The summer of 1862 saw a conflagration roaring through New York City, eating up block after block. Wall Street, the warehouses, the wharves, the naval yard, all were being consumed in a raging inferno. At this point the fire was unstoppable and soon the heart of the city would lie in ashes. Warning had been given, and so loss of life was minimal, but the blow was grievous in terms of money and industrial strength. Earlier the British squadron, led by ironclad steam batteries and ironclad frigates, supported by almost a dozen steam powered ships-of-the-line, had forced the harbor entrance and put to the torch the largest city of what was shortly to be the dismembered United States of America. The city continued to burn into the night as the British fleet steamed away, already preparing for their next blow. Confederate Secretary of the Navy Mallory's dream that he hoped could be accomplished with the CSS *Virginia* had been achieved by a powerful British squadron.

While neither the British nor the French intervened directly in the American Civil War, it was a possibility that was discussed on both sides of the Atlantic. The "Trent Affair" alone brought the Union and Great Britain to the brink of war. In late November 1861 the British government was busily arming and almost dispatched the Channel Fleet to American waters. War was only averted when Abraham Lincoln's government took a step back. Later in April 1862 Napoleon III was discussing the possibility of sending a joint Franco-British squadron to open up the so-called "paper" blockade of New Orleans.

Still, in any discussion of European intervention in what, as some call the "War of Northern Aggression," it must not be forgotten that for France or Great Britain, it would have meant coming to the aid of the "Rebellion of the Southern Slaveholders," a difficult political chasm to jump for many of their people. It is easy for today's apologists to say that the American Civil War was fought over States Rights, but in 1861 Confederate Vice President Alexander Stephens' "Cornerstone Speech" was known on *both* sides of the Atlantic. To have a nation based "upon the great truth that the Negro is not equal to the white man; that slavery, subordination to the superior race, is the natural and moral condition" was as outmoded then as it is today. Western Europe recognized this fact.

With that caveat, if war had come, how would it have been fought? The British, or a combined Franco-British, effort would have had two, possibly three courses of action open to it.

I

The first course would be an aggressive war at sea based around their powerful fleets and backed with lessons learned from the Crimean War.

The British or British Imperial key to all military thought on North America, as so well pointed out by Kenneth Bourne in *Britain and the Balance of Power in North America 1815-1908*, was that Canada would be difficult to defend. Her long border had little in the way of natural defenses. The militarily weak Sugar Islands of the West Indies, whose importance was much devalued after the wars of the 17th and 18th centuries, were exposed.

In 1858 the British had convened an interdepartmental Parliamentary committee which in 1860 issued the "Report of the Committee on Expense of Military Defences in the Colonies." One of the vital points this report made, acted on by the British Government in making their plans for imperial defense, was the need to have "strongholds." Great Britain would base her defense of Canada in a war against the United States on several key naval bases and employing her overwhelming naval power based around the steam-powered ship-of-the-line. The most important naval bases, or strongholds, would be Halifax and Bermuda, the latter especially had recently been upgraded and had received new fortifications. During the war Bermuda saw the ironclad steam battery HMS *Terror* stationed there. Additionally, the ports of Kingston, Jamaica and the Bahamas Islands were slated as bases for British operations. The Bahamas were viewed as important as they lay on the Florida channel and could be used for disputing the North's movement between the Atlantic and the Gulf of Mexico.

Esquimalt on Vancouver Island, British Columbia, served as a fortified base for a small British squadron operating from there. But this British squadron was much larger than the tiny American squadron operating on the West Coast.

The French basing situation would have been more difficult, but if they had not used British bases, they could have used their West Indian ports, or possibly Mexican or Confederate bases. The latter two possibilities suffered from lack of proper docking facilities but in time could have been improved and upgraded. Operations of steam powered fleets distant from bases had proven possible in the

Baltic operations of the Crimean War so distant basing was by no means an insurmountable barrier in 1862. The nature of the fleets used by both powers would not have been a navy that one might anticipate.

Using some of the few but new and powerful ironclad frigates like the *Gloire* or *Warrior* which were built for seagoing duty (though the latter had a draft too deep for use at Bermuda) would have been a possibility off the American coast. But in the summer of 1862 the British had only the *Warrior* and a smaller broadside ironclad, the *Defence,* commissioned, while the French had the *Gloire, Normandie, Invincible, Couronne*, and *Magenta*—all steam-powered frigates. None carried guns capable of penetrating a monitor's armor. Certainly all warship building programs of the European powers would have been accelerated in the event of war. It should be noted that the *Normandie* was the first ironclad to cross the Atlantic; she made her maiden voyage to Mexico and the West Indies in July of 1862, returning in April of 1863. This was clearly a move to support France's imperial policies in Mexico, and a defiant warning to the North that France was willing and able to back up her policies with force.

The *Warrior's* most powerful guns were ten Armstrong breech-loading 110 pounder or 7" rifles, and she had numerous smaller guns. The 7" rifle could not penetrate the armor of a *Monitor* but did have tremendous range—up to 9,000 yards. The Armstrong breech-loaders also had some technical problems that would bring about their removal from British warships in the near future. The French ships had the 6.4' breech-loader (they had replaced their earlier 6.4' rifle muzzle-loaders), which was even less effective than the British 110 pounder against armor, but was a more reliable gun. Nor did the numerous wooden ships of either fleet have any standard guns that were more powerful. However, all the ironclads were capable of 11 to 14 knots. It should be noted that in the event of war, some of the newer and larger gun designs still not in full production might have been mounted on pivots or in other special gun positions, or, as in the Crimean War, on gunboats in small numbers.

There is one other weapon that both European powers had which might have affected this equation. Both France and Great Britain had shallow draft steam powered ironclad batteries from the Crimean War period. France by the summer of 1862 could have fielded her original five, plus four new ones ready that fall and winter. Great Britain had eight, which individually were larger and superior during seagoing operations than the French batteries. Designed specifically to attack stone or masonry fortresses and operate in shallow water, several of these vessels from across the Atlantic could have been decisive in the reduction of New York or Boston, or in the shallow rivers and deltas of the South.

British experience during the Crimean War had been valuable. One lesson, of course, was the effect of armor—knowledge gained in the Black Sea operations.

The result of this experience was that all major nations of Europe were using ironcladding well before the Battle of Hampton Roads.

Second, the recently concluded Crimean War had embarrassed the British government, as the French naval officers were much more determined (and younger) than their British counterparts. It is possible that the British would have acted more vigorously in the prosecution of their war with America. However, it should be noted in this regard that the British thought that the French fleet was inferior in navigating and seamanship. As Andrew Lambert wrote, "Louis Napoleon increased the size of the fleet, but lacked the experienced seamen and officers for an effective fleet." Still French officers were more thoroughly trained in the sciences than their British counterparts.

Finally, long range gunfire, especially during the bombardment of the Russian port of Sveaborg on 9-10 August 1855 in the Baltic had resulted in the burning out of much of the town's arsenal with little in the way of losses to the Allies. Several small Russian-Finnish towns had also been put to the torch in 1855 by the Allied powers. Long range guns and the burning of America's great seaports could possibly have been the result if war had come. Admiral Farragut threatened to fire on the City of New Orleans after his victory in 1862 if the populace were not more co-operative, and America resorted to the weapon of pillage and fire in 1864 in Georgia and elsewhere, so war to the hilt was not an alien concept in this period.

But on the Atlantic and Gulf coasts, the French could field over 30 steam powered ships-of-the-line, while the British had over 60, and most had in excess of 80 guns each. Steam powered frigates and smaller craft were equally numerous. While only a portion could operate in American waters (the European balance of power required both nations to maintain sizable fleets at home), the steam powered ship-of-the-line gave the European powers an overwhelming advantage over the North.

Facing one or both of these powers was the Union navy in 1862, a navy that could offer little in the way of opposition. It had no steam powered ships-of-the-line and only a handful of older laid up sailing ships-of-the-line. With a few modern steam frigates and sloops that were capable of 8 to 11 knots, all slower than most of the British or French fleets, she had little to match the European powers' strength. The Union's hastily raised force of converted merchant ships and 90-day gunboats were fine for blockading the Confederacy, but would be worthless against a real Anglo-French seagoing warship—one designed from keel up for battle. Finally, many of her officers and men had only been recently mustered in and lacked proper training and experience.

Of the Union's monitors, which could not be considered sea-going but primarily designed for coastal work, there was the *Monitor* and the failed experimental ironclad *Galena*. The good but slow *New Ironsides* was completing for sea in August of 1862. Every other ironclad capable of defeating the wooden Anglo-French fleet was either under construction or not due for completion until the end of the year, or still on the drawing board. Additionally, without the historic spur of the Battle of Hampton Roads between the *Monitor* and the *Virginia*, the "*Monitor* Fever" that broke out after the Battle of Hampton Roads and the construction of the *Passaic* Class would have been less certain.

One may have a weapon, but how it is used depends on the spirit of the times and the men wielding the weapon. While war plans may be drawn up, one can only speculate on how those plans unfold. Still, there is evidence that war with the United States in 1862 would have been a vicious war. Prior to the Trent Affair, the powerful Colonial Secretary Henry Pelham, the Fifth Duke of Newcastle, spoke to Prime Minister Palmerston of the need to put Boston and New York City to the torch in the event of war. Admiral Sir Alexander Milne (an example of a British admiral sometimes lacking in vigor), commander on the North American Station, at this time thought that instead of burning a city such as New York, an embargo on trade or demand for a ransom for the city would be more appropriate than torching. But Milne did feel offensive actions would be required in a war with the Union and acting defensively would not bring victory. He also expressed the need to bring the hand of war down on the Atlantic coast and "— every place must be made to feel what war really is." Nor must it be forgotten that Washington D.C. had been burned before by a British army.

Milne envisioned a threefold blow against the Union. Operating primarily from Bermuda and the Spanish port of Havana, as well as smaller forces from Halifax and several island bases in the West Indies, he would have had about 60 steam powered ships mounting 1,273 guns. Though the Union had 264 ships by the end of 1861, it must be remembered that those 264 ships were for the most part converted merchant ships, others operated with just sail power, and most were of little value against a large warship with a well-trained crew.

As Bourne points out, Milne first intended to break the Northern blockade of the Confederacy. This would have been an easy matter. The Havana squadron, with at least one ship-of-the-line, would have moved against Pensacola, the main Union base in the Gulf, and might have encountered Admiral Farragut's force gathering for the New Orleans operation. With the advantage of speed and more power, the edge if battle had been joined would clearly lie with the British Navy. Isolated Union ships or small squadrons could have easily fallen victim to a swiftly advancing and greatly superior force.

Milne, with a nucleus of at least three ships-of-the-line, would have taken his Bermuda force to break the blockade of North Carolina and Virginia's coasts, cut off Fort Monroe, and possibly attempt to "harass the Union Capital." If McClellan had already moved his army for operations in the Peninsula Campaign, this could have resulted in a grand disaster for the Union operations. Suddenly cut off by a superior naval force and lacking adequate supplies, the possibility of a Union Yorktown in the spring or summer of 1862 would have been in the cards.

The First Lord of the Admiralty expected Milne to establish a base in the South to obtain coal and as a "base for further operations." However, joint operations with the Confederacy were not envisaged. The British felt that independent actions were easier to carry out than operations with an ally. However, if the war became extended, this attitude might very well have evolved into one of closer cooperation.

The second prong of Milne's plan was to blockade the Union's coast. Forty vessels would first be used to blockade the main ports, increasing to 60 to cover the minor ports as well. A close blockade would have been difficult as the war went on, and as Union monitors came down the way and entered the fray.

Finally, Milne was to sweep the seas of Union commerce. Orders were already issued for this when the Trent Affair ended on a peaceful note. The North's shipping would certainly have been driven from the seas.

The dividends to the South of European intervention would have been enormous. After breaking the blockade, supplies could easily arrive at Southern seaports, and that other valuable commodity would have then been available—time. Time gained would have been vital in completing several Southern ironclads such as the CSS *Mississippi* and CSS *Louisiana* at New Orleans. The *Virginia* would never have had to be burned at Norfolk. Open ports might have also allowed for additional armor plating, guns, and superior engines to be imported into the Confederacy for other ironclad projects.

The *ORN* in a lengthy excerpt from the "Joint Special Committee of Both Houses of the Confederate Congress" discusses in detail the state of the Confederate Navy at New Orleans and specifically the status of the two ironclads *Mississippi* and *Louisiana* and that their completion was largely dependent on a few key items. With no blockade, such key items could have moved or arrived easily and more safely.

Additionally, the Confederate armies could have benefited from the supply of better rifles and specialized items such as long range Whitworth or Blakely cannon. Ammunition and support equipment could have readily been imported. Historically the Union blockade constantly reduced, by capture at sea, supplies destined for the Confederate armies. Robert M. Browning, Jr., a scholar of the war, has stated that "the presence of a powerful (Union) navy had a tremendous cumulative effect on Confederate logistics." Intervention would have changed this equation.

Finally, war would have meant that the South's clandestine projects to obtain warships from British or French yards would no longer be illegal. More *Alabamas* could be built as funds were made available, as well as ironclads. However, it is likely the latter would have still ended up in the British or French navies in the

Allied war with the Union. It is common for a nation building warships for another country to take them over and complete them as their own when war threatens or breaks out.

Cotton and fine Virginia tobacco would then flow easily to Europe, and the cotton depression at the mills in Manchester and elsewhere would have ended. This in turn would have given capital for the South's war effort.

Thus we can see clearly that the lifting of the Union blockade would have helped invigorate all the industrial, military, and agricultural efforts of the Confederate States. The positive effects of this momentous change in the fortunes of war would continue to strengthen with each day of the continuing Allied intervention.

Ironically the Union weapons of retaliation at sea would have been, due to her striking naval inferiority, the very weapons used by the Confederacy: raiders, Union *Alabamas,* which would have wrought havoc on the sea-lanes of Great Britain and to a lesser degree of France. Construction of coast defense and later sea-going ironclads would have accelerated. Coastal fortifications would have sprung up and existing ones been strengthened, and all would require more men, resources, and money.

The longer the war continued, the more unlikely that the Union harbors could be razed with fire and brimstone, as each harbor would have had one or two *Monitors,* plenty of mines, and strengthened fortifications—taking resources away from the war against the Confederacy and Canada. The raiders could have been neutralized if the French and British adopted convoys, but there was deep historical resistance to the use of convoys. It should be noted that this threat of the Union raiders and ironclads weighed heavily on the British in the fall of 1862 and beyond for not intervening in the American Civil War.

II

The second major theater of war would be Canada.

The British thought they needed 100,000 militia and 10,000 regulars to defend Canada, with the regulars concentrated in Quebec and Montreal. They also needed fortifications and command of the Great Lakes. Major General Sir Patrick Macdougall, commander of British forces in Canada before the American Civil War "was quite aware, the real difficulty for the British in North America lay not so much in the character of the attacking force as in that of the territory to be defended." The frontier was 1,500 miles long and Macdougall said it was "everywhere vulnerable through its whole length." The British knew they would face a major Northern assault, but the size and character of the troops would be dependent on the war with the Confederacy. The British expected the Northern attack to be based on Albany, New York and to threaten both Montreal and Quebec, as well as Lake Ontario.

It should be noted that while Macdougall would not become as famous as Field Marshal Earl F.S. "Bobs" Roberts or Field Marshal Lord Garnet J. Wolseley, he was considered one of Britain's best generals, posted to an important post, and would later go on to be the first head of the Intelligence Branch of the War Office. Thomas G. Fergusson, a historian of British Military Intelligence, has written that Macdougall "was one of the leading theorists and intellectuals of the mid-nineteenth century British Army." So once again Canada, as in the two previous wars with the United States, had posted to it one of the better British leaders.

To aid in the defense of Canada, the British planned to seize control of the Great Lakes as well as maintain strong fortifications for the North to attack, while largely militia units harassed the flanks and rear of any enemy force advancing into Canada. However, it should be noted that in 1861-62 the British and Canadians were terribly deficient in troops, guns (just over half the militia were armed with rifles, the others with smoothbore muskets), artillery, fortifications, and training. If the North moved rapidly at the outbreak of war (especially in a winter campaign with the Canadian east to west river communications frozen over), the long Canadian border could have been deeply penetrated in several areas. But who would have commanded such an advance? A McClellan or a Grant?

There were discussions and some thought given to attacking Maine and trying to cut that state off from the rest of the Union, as it is situated somewhat on an isthmus. An overland drive on Portland combined with a coastal operation was a possibility. This would have required a large army, would have been a very difficult operation, and would not have been attempted straight away with the declaration of war.

To the credit of the British government in 1861-62, they did quickly prepare for a war with Lincoln's government, and dispatched thousands of winter equipped regulars to Canada. They were prepared to send more, which would have put a regular force of over 25,000 in Canada (over 17,000 were dispatched or stationed in Canada by the end of the crisis). While small compared to the forces of the Union, the South would still have occupied the vast majority of the North's effort. Finally, the British government recognized that the loss of Canada was quite possible. The intended outcome of such a war was one "not merely of defending Canada, but generally waging a successful war against the United States."

III

The third possible major effort mounted by the European powers would be direct aid to the South on land.

It would be possible for a corps of European troops to help the Confederates, along with additional war supplies. Most likely such a force would have to be largely French, as the British did not contemplate much in the way of military operations beyond possibly ejecting the Union forces from Port Royal on the South Carolina coast. Plans for such an intervention by the French are a subject that some future historian should address in English.

Based on the policies of Napoleon III in Mexico or Italy, one can envision an expeditionary force of two or three divisions operating with a Confederate army. A disciplined, well armed force, with uniform armament would have been a welcome addition to the Confederate army, possibly in Virginia, as it would be easier to supply and was viewed as the main theater of the war.

New Orleans also offered opportunities for an independent French effort. The French already had an army at Vera Cruz in March of 1862 (Spanish troops had occupied that port in December of 1861 and had withdrawn in March) and a small fleet operating in the Gulf of Mexico. With their historic ties with New Orleans and the early French explorations of the Mississippi, it is easy to see a French expeditionary army operating from a friendly New Orleans, or attempting to recapture it, if Farragut had already seized it.

So, while one may argue what might have occurred if war had come with Britain or France, one cannot argue that European intervention would have had little effect on the outcome of the Civil War. The war would have been much different, certainly longer, and the scars would not have been limited to just this continent.

The problems besetting Lincoln's government would have been immense as it faced war on three grand strategic fronts; the newly invigorated Confederate border, the Canadian front, and the oceans. Lincoln would have had other problems too. The Copperhead movement would not have melted away, especially with the possibility of an earlier wartime draft. The funding of the increased war effort and the lack of overseas supplies would have ratcheted up the ante for this Civil War to a new and higher level. Lincoln might also have faced increased Indian problems on the western frontier, and while minor, the Pacific would have witnessed at a bare minimum a blockade of Seattle, Portland, and San Francisco. "Peace" might have seen a united continent under the American battle flag from Nova Scotia and Hudson's Bay to the Mexican border. Or "Peace" might be a name for a truce on a militarized continent fragmented into several suspicious armed camps preparing daily for revenge or the next trial of strength. Winston Churchill penned a short story on the possibility of two armed camps in North America if the Confederacy had won the war.

Finally, there is one other twist to this scenario. The war might have spread to encompass most of Europe. Imperial Russia resented the defeat suffered in the Crimean War and might have taken this opportunity to redress her losses. Prussia might have launched an earlier war against (or with) Austria under her brilliant "Iron Chancellor" —Bismarck. Italy, too, might have taken the French preoccupation with America to move against Rome in 1863 instead of 1870. Whenever the Dogs of War are unleashed it is hard to predict whose yard they will eventually end up in.

The Reintroduction of the Ram

The sinking of the Cumberland by the Merrimac revived belief in the ram as a weapon to such an extent that very few vessels of war have been built since that day that have not been provided with an under-water projecting or ram bow.
    —F.M. Bennett, writing in 1900

The growth in the cost and dimensions of ironclad ships has been such, that we may well pause to consider whether we have been pursuing a policy in all respects satisfactory in the recent development of the fleet. Foreign opinion is almost unanimous that the ram must now be recognized as the primary and most deadly weapon of naval warfare. In an engagement with the ram there must a be decisive advantage in numbers. When the crash of the hostile lines has thrown the contending fleets into disarray, the squadron which has the most ships in reserve in the second line of attack will have a splendid opportunity of taking an adversary at a disadvantage in the act of turning— The shorter and smaller ship will have great advantages over the longer and heavier ship both for avoiding the ram and striking an adversary.
    —Sir Thomas Brassey in *The British Navy*, 1880

The tactic of ramming revived in the period of the ironclad. Ships would be equipped with ram prows up to the start of the 20th century and the introduction of the *Dreadnought,* or modern capital ship, in 1906. In 1868, the British Navy introduced written instructions for the ramming procedure, a practice which in that service was forbidden only in 1943.

In earlier centuries, ram tactics had died out as oared warships became obsolete and sailing warships came to the fore. A bowsprit projecting from the forecastle of a ship made ramming virtually ineffective and with the emphasis on broadside gunnery and line-ahead tactics, it made ramming improbable.

Even with the introduction of steam power and ironclads, ramming did not automatically dominate the arena of naval tactics. Ram tactics with the long broadside ships such as the *Warrior* or the *Achilles*, especially prevalent in the British Navy, were unlikely as they were not short and maneuverable and they could only turn slowly. Again, too, there was a reluctance on the part of the naval officer corps to adopt a "new" form of combat.

The American Civil War saw a real jump in the development of ram tactics, especially in confined waters such as the Mississippi River. Charles Ellet, Jr., before the Battle of Hampton Roads, found the army to be more receptive to his ideas than the navy about rams and ramming. After Hampton Roads he visited Fort Monroe to discover what preparations were taking place for fighting the *Virginia.* He wrote his wife on 18 March that "—the naval officials have decided whenever she comes out again, to go right at the *Merrimac* and run her down." He wrote shortly after that the navy was now more receptive to the ram and that "The demand for steam rams has suddenly become... great." Ellet was instrumental in building and commanding rams on the upper Mississippi and rendered a great service to the cause of the North.

At New Orleans, commander of the *Manassas* Lieutenant Warley later contended that if the Confederate cottonclad steamers had been used as rams to attack the Union fleet, more of it would have been forced to stay under the guns of the Confederate forts and possible destruction might have resulted. The South emphasized the use of the ram throughout that conflict.

Ironically the conservative Federal navy resisted the ram even after the American Civil War. Lieutenant Frank M. Bennett, writing at the turn of the century when warships were still being built with a ram, found it ironic that the American navy was slow in abandoning clipper bows on her wooden ships in the American Civil War and had not adopted the ram bow immediately. He wrote,

> This reluctance on the part of American naval officers and architects to give up an established form that had outlived its purpose is the more remarkable because it was our country that first suffered from the revival of the ram, and because at the very time American shipbuilders were constructing for the Italian government (two) war-vessels that were conspicuous for the prominence of their ram bows.

One of these two vessels, the *Re d'Italia,* built in New York City between 1861 and 1863, achieved fame after being sunk at the Battle of Lissa in 1866 by an Austrian ram bow. The outcome of Lissa caused navies to adopt the line abreast as a battle tactic to deliver the powerful weapon. As Stanley Sandler rightly points out, "the Battle of Lissa yielded apparently incontrovertible proof of the awful power of the ram."

In Europe the way had been paved, as usual, by France. As noted by Professor Baxter, there had been many suggestions for steam rams in the 1800s, many coming from the French. The Crimean War seemed to increase interest in the iron spur and it was the French *Magenta* class, begun in 1859, that was the first ironclad designed with a ram bow. Most ship designs acknowledged this tactic in the following years.

The Germans in the late 1870s felt the dominant weapon was still the gun. But a memorandum of the period stated that "Turning to the ram, it is an indisputable fact that the strongest ships, whether armored or unarmored, even those fitted with the most approved appliances which the science of construction has discovered, and subdivided into numerous compartments, would be disabled if rammed by an enemy on the broadside, at, or nearly at, right angles.... The decisive effect of a well-delivered blow with a ram is indeed indisputable."

In Russia, Admiral G.I. Butakov in his *New Principles of Steam Tactics* advocated the use of the ram and developed a system of having ships in contact while exercising ramming, but not so they damaged each other. In Austria, Admiral Tegetthoff stated that "the stem will decide future naval battles."

In Italy the battle of Lissa had a great impact. The commander of the ironclad *Principe Carignano* said that "for war only armored ships with strong bows" were needed. Commander Francesco Del Carretto of the ironclad *Maria Pia* stated that the warships should be "short, manageable, with two protected screws, with a strong bow... and protected helm (conning tower)."

In Britain, Edward Reed designs for handy central battery battleships revived the ram there. Several British warships, such as the *Glatton* and *Hotspur,* would be built that employed the ram as the main weapon of attack.

British Admiral Sir George Sartorius, chief British advocate of the ram, wrote in 1872 that,

> The most important requisite for the ram is speed. What can the strongest man do if his enemy can always avoid his blows? Such a vessel may have the charge of a convoy of transports, and they are met by an enemy, ram or otherwise, but very rapid and handy; she could get in amongst the convoy, without giving the slow and heavy protector the chance of getting a shot at the interloper. To use its prow of course is out of the question, and could such a ram escape destruction from the attack of two smaller but swifter rams? The efficient ram must have very great speed and great handiness. This is an important fact for us always to bear in mind.

Because of the lack of naval combat from 1867 to the 1890s, when the rate of fire of guns increased and the effective range of ordnance grew, it is hard to prove that the ram would have been an effective tactic in naval combat between ironclad fleets. David K. Brown and Philip Pugh in an article in *Warship 1990* argue that it was not.

By statistically categorizing ramming attempts and overall situations, for example lack of sea room for maneuver versus open waters, Brown and Pugh argue that ramming was relatively ineffective, *especially when one ship was engaging one ship and both could maneuver.* They present a strong mathematical argument on this point. They may be correct.

But one could argue that they overlook certain important points concerning ramming, and specifically during the period from after the Battle of Lissa to the 1880s. First, the increasingly heavier and fewer guns carried by warships of that period meant that the overall volume of gunfire dropped. The 17.7" rifles carried on some of the Italian battleships of the period took seven or eight minutes *with a well trained crew* to fire just once. One round every two minutes for smaller guns was not unusual. Whether a shot would hit its intended target was an entirely different matter.

Second, even if a ship was hit by gunfire, it is problematical that it would be hit in a vital spot, and that its armor would be penetrated. And simply hitting, as with a ram, would not necessarily bring about any decisive result. Virtually all the gunnery hits that occurred at the Battle of Lissa support this conclusion—many hits/little damage.

The chances of hitting with a few slow-firing guns with rudimentary fire control instruments leads one to suspect that any decisive battle would be fought at close ranges, such as in the American Civil War, the battle of Lissa, and in actions of the War of the Pacific. After the battle of Lissa, a common tactic adopted by navies of the period was the line abreast. This called for lines advancing on each other instead of steaming in line at relatively distant positions. Note too that when one or two lines are charging and the range is decreasing quickly, that fire may be less accurate because of the rapidly changing ranges.

It was recognized by some, such as Brassey and Sartorius, though, that if two swift and smaller rams attacked a single ship, the odds of successfully ramming increased substantially. This might be the largest error in Brown and Pugh's view—assuming ramming attacks in an isolated environment, instead of in the heat of a close ranged fleet action, possibly with a second line attacking immediately after the first has struck the enemy.

So, while ramming may have been statistically a long shot, so to speak, so was gunnery in this period. And by ramming a vessel with a lucky and well directed blow an enemy would be more likely to disable or sink it, than with a gun hit.

Equipping ships in this period with the ram made tactical sense and was a logical course of action. That it would be difficult to employ successfully, as Brown and Pugh point out, is also true.

CHAPTER IV

The Struggle for Charleston

...(the) fall of Charleston is the fall of Satan's kingdom.
—Assistant Secretary of the Navy Gustavus Fox

Since the fall of Fort Sumter, Northern public opinion, spurred on by the newspapers, kept up a constant clamor for Charleston's capture. The city was considered by many to be symbolically more important than Richmond. It was the birthplace of secession and heart of the rebellion.
—Stephen R. Wise in *Gate of Hell*

W e now return to the birthplace of secession, Charleston, South Carolina. During the first part of the war this was an important blockade running port. In addition, the Confederates built several ironclads at Charleston and two of them engaged in an action before the Union brought real pressure to bear on this busy harbor and symbol of rebellion and the Confederacy.

General P.G.T. Beauregard commanded the land forces at Charleston in September of 1862, while at the start of the siege the naval squadron built there was commanded by Commodore Duncan N. Ingraham. By November 1861 Ingraham was in command of naval construction at Charleston, and in overall command by March 1862. Ingraham, who had fought in the War of 1812, was considered to be too cautious and "a perfect old woman" by some of the younger officers.

The Confederate Navy first laid down the ironclad *Palmetto State* in the spring of 1862. The local State government had also begun tentative construction of a wooden gunboat at Charleston, but shifted construction to an ironclad when Mallory persuaded them of its value. So the state of South Carolina followed with the *Chicora*, near sister ship to the *Palmetto State*, and both of the so called Porter-designed *Richmond* class.

The *Chicora* was completed first, launched in August and sold by the state government to the Confederate government, with the proceeds being used to start a new ironclad, the *Charleston*, which would be armored with 6–inch thick iron

ANATOMY of an IRONCLAD

C.S.S. PALMETTO STATE

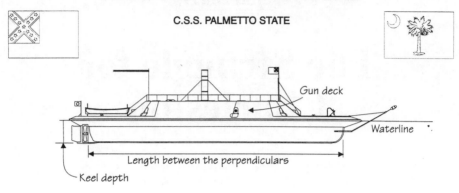

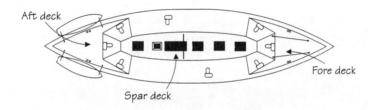

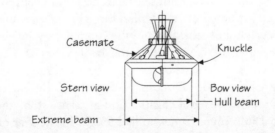

plating. The *Palmetto State* was launched in October and completed in the fall of 1862. She was known as the "Ladies' Gunboat" as the local Confederate ladies had raised some of the money for her construction. This method of funding for warships originally started at New Orleans and also occurred at Savannah, Richmond, and elsewhere. Confederate women's fund raisers such as "Gunboat Fairs" and "Gunboat Quilts" were part of the war effort throughout the conflict. In the case of the *Palmetto State*, 15% of the $200,000 price was raised by Confederate women. Both had thick iron plates laid in 7 inch wide, 20 foot long strips, backed by 22 inches of wood on which was fitted two inclined 2 inch thick plates. Two inches of armor was carried five feet below the waterline and on the deck. The

A muzzle loading Brooke 6.4" rifle at Norfolk naval yard. (Kent Queman)

Palmetto State, unlike all the other *Richmond* class, had her pilot house placed abaft the smoke stack.

Both ironclads were flat bottomed, given a ram bow, and were well built in private shipyards. Unlike the *Virginia,* their ends were not submerged. Both drew about 11 feet, were 34 feet wide, and 150 feet long. The *Chicora* was armed with four 32 pounder rifles, and two 9" shell pivot guns. The *Palmetto State* was armed with a 6.4" Brooke rifled gun forward, a 60 pounder rifled gun aft, and two 8" shell guns on the broadside. Some sources list her as having ten 7" rifles, but this appears never to have been the truth. Both were single screw. Speed in smooth water was about six knots, though the *Palmetto State* had reliable engines which on occasion could reach seven knots. Both vessels were painted a blue gray, or pale gray—known as "blockader's blue" to make them difficult to see at night. Due to the lack of paint in the Confederacy they "quickly became a rust brown." They were extremely hot in the summer months as they were poorly ventilated.

The Confederacy, when it took over Norfolk's Gosport naval yard, inherited 1,195 heavy guns, all smoothbore. This number varies, and some sources list up to 3,000 pieces; the 1,195 figure is from an inventory of the booty. Recognizing the value early on of rifled guns, the local ordnance expert, Captain Archibald B. Fairfax at Norfolk, converted many of the various six–hundred–and–thirty 32 pound smoothbores to rifles, and added a reinforcing iron hoop to the body of the gun. These retrofitted guns fired an elongated shell weighing 60 pounds. Some authorities consider this one of the best services performed by the Confederate ordnance department in the war.

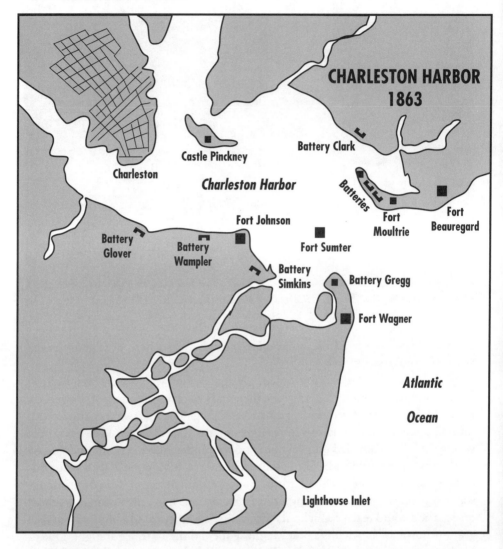

The ships were not designed for open sea work, but were harbor defense warships. The Charleston squadron was one of the best-manned Confederate squadrons, as the port had a fair number of seamen, including some foreign born, and at least three free Afro-Americans who signed on and served on board the *Chicora*.

The *Palmetto State* was commanded by Lieutenant Commander John Rutledge, from an old South Carolina family; also on board was Lieutenant Alexander F. Warley, who had been exchanged after being captured at New Orleans. The commander of the *Chicora* was "Handsome Jack" Tucker, late of the *Patrick Henry* and the actions in Virginia. Tucker relieved Ingraham of command at Charleston

Reconstruction of CSS Chicora. (P.C. Coker III)

later in the war and was very involved in much of the torpedo development at that port. Lieutenant Parker, late of the *Beaufort*, was executive officer of the *Palmetto State*.

Early on Friday, 30 January 1863, with the moon eleven days old, this squadron, poorly supported by the small Confederate wooden squadron, crossed the bar and made a dash at the Union wooden blockaders. The Union squadron numbered ten ships of which only three, the *Housatonic, Ottawa,* and *Unadilla,* were built from the keel up as warships. By 04:30 the ironclads had crossed the bar and were in the open sea. In the ensuing action it should be noted that the Union fleet reacted quickly, but it was not to attacking Confederate ironclads that they responded—they thought they were chasing blockade runners—instead of an invulnerable ironclads that they should be fleeing.

The *Palmetto State* had led the way with her port shutters closed so as not to emit any light "and the few battle-lanterns lit cast a pale, weird light on the gun-deck." She, and her consort, were burning poor soft coal which "left a huge black trail behind." She first engaged the small but speedy nine gun wooden gunboat *Mercedita*. The latter had just returned from chasing a blockade runner and was anchored when suddenly looming up in the dark was a new shape low in the water. The captain, Henry S. Stellwagen, had retired, and the officers of the deck first sighted the approaching ram. Captain Stellwagen later recalled, as recounted in Edward S. Miller's *Civil War Sea Battles,* that the deck officers called out "She has black smoke. Watch, man the guns, spring the rattle, call all hands to quarters!" The fact that she had black smoke was significant because clean light smoke for higher speeds was associated with blockade runners.

Stellwagen, after gaining the deck, called on his crew to "train your guns right on him and be ready to fire as soon as I order." Upon hailing the stranger, Captain Stellwagen at first received no answer. Stellwagen then ordered his crew to fire and shouted, "you will be into me." Only then did the *Palmetto State* reply, as it came back across the water "This is the Confederate steamer *Palmetto State!*" The *Palmetto State* then "plunged her ram deep into the quarter of the *Mercedita,* and fired from her bow-gun a shell which went through the enemy's boiler and exploded on the other side of the ship, tearing a great hole in her planking. Two men were killed by the shell and many more were scalded by the escaping steam." On deck, Stellwagen received several reports in rapid succession of "Shot through the boiler," "Fires put out by steam and water," "Shot through both boilers," "Gunner and one man killed," "Number of men fatally scalded," "Water over fire-room floor," "Vessel sinking fast." "The ram has cut us through at and below the water line on one side, and the shell has burst on the other about at the water's edge." The time from the *Mercedita's* first sighting the *Palmetto State* and being rammed was later reported as two minutes. Total losses on the *Mercedita* would be four dead and three wounded by the end of the action.

Without firing a shot because they could not depress the guns sufficiently, the captain of the *Mercedita* surrendered his vessel to the *Palmetto State.* A small boat came over to the *Palmetto State* and delay now followed delay as paroles were given and Ingraham was unsure as to what to do with the *Mercedita.* Possession was supposedly to be made by the Confederate wooden gunboats, but they did not put in an appearance. The *Mercedita* eventually steamed on to the Union base at Port Royal, with her men and officers still under parole, but yet a Union vessel. The men were exchanged later.

While the *Palmetto State* was thus engaged, the *Chicora* passed the *Palmetto State* with the *Palmetto State* on the *Chicora's* port and sighted a "schooner-rigged propeller (screw steamer)," which he fired on and then reported seeing afire. This was the 1,428 ton, 13 knot sidewheeler *Quaker City,* armed with nine guns—nothing larger than a 20 pound rifled Parrott. She was already alert and underway, having heard the firing from the *Palmetto State.* The second shell from the *Chicora* entered the ship, and while not disabling her, damaged her boiler and exploded in her engine room. Two other shells exploded quickly, having fuses that were too short. The *Quaker City* did reply to this attack, first firing her forward pivot Parrott and then two shots and two shells from her loaded broadside 32 pounders. She got off three more rounds before she speedily made off into the night to join the flagship, the *Housatonic.*

Next, the *Chicora* sighted the *Keystone State,* a 1,364 ton sidewheeler with an average speed of six knots, capable of just over nine knots for short bursts and in favorable weather. She had an armament of 10 light guns. Tucker took his ship in towards the *Keystone State,* and was sighted by her as he closed. The *Keystone State,* after her Captain William E. LeRoy had determined that a Confederate ironclad was approaching, slipped her cable to get underway, and "fired a gun" at her and to warn the fleet. The *Chicora* immediately fired her forward gun and two other rounds into the *Keystone State,* which started a fire in the forward hold. The *Keystone State* replied with her guns as they bore, and sighted the *Palmetto State* on her other quarter.

The *Keystone State* moved into shallow water, put out the fire, got "things in condition to attack the enemy," and "then turned around and under full steam proposed attempting to run down the ram." The *Chicora* saw her approach and one of her next ten hits knocked out one of her boilers, which scalded many of the men on board. At this point the *Keystone State* surrendered to the *Chicora.* However, before the *Chicora* could take possession, the *Keystone State* began to draw off from the slower *Chicora,* with just one sidewheel working, and began pulling away. Several urged Tucker to reopen fire, but Tucker, remembering his own experience on the *Patrick Henry* when her boiler was pierced at Hampton Roads, waited until too late to reopen. Tucker probably never dreamed that the captain of the *Keystone State* would be so dishonorable as to do what he was about to do. Several hundred yards from the *Chicora,* the *Keystone State* reraised her flag and reopened fire! She then made off into the night. The *Keystone State* lost 20 dead and 20 wounded in the engagement and would be towed to Port Royal for repairs. LeRoy would go on to command the *Ossipee* at Mobile and after the war would be the chief of staff to Farragut on his postwar trip to Europe.

The two Confederate ironclads, with the sun now fully up, proceeded out to sea about seven miles and were engaged at long range by several Union warships. Tucker later wrote of this stage of the battle while engaged with one ship that "... in spite of all our efforts, was unable to bring her to close quarters, owing to her superior steaming qualities." Seeing that no result could be gained, they both returned to the bar at 08:00 and finally crossed back into the harbor at 16:00. Parker wrote that the Confederate squadron could not capture a fast enemy ship because "we could not catch her." This inability of the Confederate ironclads to engage faster ships successfully manifested itself throughout the war time and again.

Tucker was outraged by the act of the *Keystone State,* especially in contrast to the *Mercedita,* whose officers conducted themselves as if they were paroled prisoners of war. It was compounded by the fact that shortly after the battle the Union squadron could not be seen from Charleston, even with vessels going out of the harbor. This, according to the rules of war at the time, meant that the port of Charleston was an "open" port and that the blockade was legally no longer in effect until it could be reapplied. The Union never recognized this condition.

As pointed out by Tucker's biographer David P. Werlich, "the raid of the Charleston gunboats was the only time during the war in which Confederate ironclads successfully engaged the enemy on the open seas." It is interesting to note that the Union gunboats did not have a coordinated plan to defend themselves from the ironclad rams. As so often with the U.S. Navy, it needs a defeat or a check before it learns from its errors and responds with the corrective measures.

After the action the *Keystone State* was rearmed twice in 1863, first with a Dahlgren 50 pounder rifle, and later with a 150 pounder, for defense against Confederate ironclads. This upgunning was not at all unusual (the *Quaker City* was soon carrying a 100 pounder rifled gun as well). A gun of this size might be capable of damaging a ship like the *Chicora.* It must be remembered, though, that placing a large heavy gun on a small ship not designed to carry it in the first place is a dangerous expedient. The weight makes a ship more difficult to operate in rough seas, and the simple firing of it may cause structural strain to the firing ship.

The ironclad *New Ironsides* was rushed from Port Royal to Charleston immediately after the attack. It has been incorrectly written elsewhere that she was present with the blockaders and refused action. She was at Port Royal at the time of the attack.

By 1863 an evolutionary step in naval gunnery and Union attacks on Southern forts had developed. It was noted earlier that at the start of the war the Confederacy embraced rifled ordnance more quickly than the Union which preferred large smoothbores such as the Dahlgren. Dahlgren recommended as late as December 1860 that ship's gun batteries not replace "... the present smooth-bore guns by rifled cannon of any kind." It would not be until the Battle of Fort Pulaski that this attitude on the North's part changed. Against the Confederate Fort Pulaski at Savannah, Georgia, the Union successfully employed Parrott 30 pounder rifled guns to force the masonry fort to surrender in April 1862.

An old 42 pound smoothbore could penetrate into a masonry fort about 8 inches at normal battle ranges. That same gun, rebored as a rifle, and firing an 84 pound elongated and pointed shot could now penetrate 26 inches into a masonry wall. So the gunnery evolution continued.

Nor was it valuable just against brick and mortar forts. It also was realized that "the power of the XV" gun as a breaching force against masonry is considerable, but against a work constructed of sandbags it has not the value of a XI" gun, and nothing like the power of a 100-pounder rifle for boring through the sand."

The XI" Dahlgren was preferred by many in the Union as it had a higher rate of fire than the XV", which could take up to five minutes to load and fire, while a XI" could fire about once every two to three minutes. The 150 rifled Parrott muzzle-loader carried on the *Patapsco* during the attack on Charleston fired at a rate of three times that of the XV" Dahlgren also carried in her turret. A breech-loading rifled 100 pounder could fire a round a minute in this period.

The problem with the Union breech-loaders, particularly the Parrott rifles, was that they tended to burst after a number of rounds. The Dahlgrens tended not to burst and were a particularly safe piece. It was for this reason, in large part, that the United States Navy after the American Civil War would readopt the smooth-bore Dahlgren as their official ordnance and reject the rifled gun.

It had already been recognized that different manufacturers produced better or worse plate and shot projectiles—not all were equal. The shape of the shell as well as the material it was made of had to be taken into consideration. It had been discovered by British experiments before the American Civil War that wrought iron shot was more effective than cast iron for penetration and damage to an ironclad target by a ratio of 3:1. Nathan Okun in *Warship International* summed up the development of armor and guns in this period quite well when he wrote,

> Soft homogeneous wrought iron, ... was the first metal armor to be used in warships. Incoming cast iron or wrought iron cannon balls and hollow explosive shells striking such armor would flatten out or shatter on impact even if the protective plates were relatively thin. Within a few years of its introduction, however, the effectiveness of wrought iron was severely challenged by the new elongated chilled cast iron projectiles fired from rifled guns. These so called "Palliser" or "Gruson" projectiles would still break up on impact, but only after their extremely hard noses had punched deeply into the plate or penetrated completely. Large caliber flat nose projectiles, known as *bolts*, could easily punch through thin or laminated wrought iron places, so that by the end of the U.S. Civil War even heavily armored ironclads were vulnerable again.

Sir William Palliser and Herr Gruson of Prussia invented, probably independently of each other, "chilled cast-iron projectiles" or chilled shot. The entire process of adopting rifled ordnance and abandoning smoothbore guns would take some time. To place it in perspective, it must be recalled that Great Britain did not formally adopt rifled muzzle-loading ordnance until 1864, both Austria and Italy in 1866 were still in the process of switching to rifled guns at the time of the Battle of Lissa, and the conservative United States navy after the war rejected rifled ordnance well after all other major powers had adopted it.

Earl W. Fornell notes British Captain Augustus Charles Hobart-Hampden, better known as Hobart Pasha, says he successfully ran the Union blockade as a private citizen 18 times. Hobart had commanded the gunboat HMS *Driver* in the Baltic during the Crimean War and while "on shore" awaiting appointment as a Post Captain to a British warship, had decided to embark on blockade running. Hobart was a quite interesting and adventuresome naval officer—even

Sideview of the interior of the turret of the monitor Passaic.

if he was an anachronistic leftover from a dying past.He proved to be a "bluff, bold, dashing, and somewhat dogged" character later in Turkey.

Hobart, in his book about blockade running entitled *Never Caught,* says that if the Southern forts had been armed with more long range artillery, forcing the Union vessels "… to keep a respectful distance…" that the blockade would have been less effective. Fornell correctly points out that a portion of the long-range Brooke and other type rifles were deployed along the rivers or in the inner defenses of Charleston or Mobile, and not on the outer defense positions. But the real question here is first getting *enough* of the required long-range artillery, which was not easy for the South, and then positioning it to allow the artillery fire to be effective. The Southern coast tends to have low lying land, and to build proper fortifications, without the Union interference, may have been impossible. Finally, the South had to think in terms of defense in depth. The failures at Fort Henry and Fort Donelson, and then at New Orleans, had allowed for deep penetrations by the Union flotillas up the Cumberland, Tennessee, and Mississippi Rivers. It can be argued that the South learned that bitter lesson in 1862 and knew better than to depend upon one strong point with no secondary fall back position. Powerful artillery was needed for these secondary or even tertiary positions.

There were three other skirmishes before the attempt against Charleston that caused some disquiet in the gathering Union fleet of ironclads. The *Montauk*

Interior of the monitor Montauk.

under Commander John L. Worden, with support from wooden warships, engaged Fort McAllister in Georgia on 27 January 1863. The goal of Admiral Samuel Du Pont was to test the new *Passaic* class monitor as well as to attempt to destroy the nearby sidewheeler blockade runner *Nashville,* which was being fitted out as a raider.

Range was long as obstructions and suspected torpedoes kept the *Montauk* from approaching too near. The new XV" (each turret of the *Passaic* class had usually one XV" and XI" Dahlgren) worked fine, but Du Pont did note to Gideon Welles that the rate of fire was so slow that Fort McAllister was in little danger. The *Montauk* was hit 13 times and suffered no real damage.

The next attack took place on 28 February 1863 when the *Montauk* engaged and destroyed the stranded *Nashville.* The *Nashville* had grounded the night before; Worden had noted this and so arranged to approach her in the morning. Again, supported by the wooden blockaders present, he closed within about 1200 yards and opened fire, while under fire from the fort. The effects of the shells were quickly seen. Fire on the *Nashville* began at 07:07, after anchoring. At 07:57 it was spreading, and she was totally engulfed by 08:35, after firing only about a dozen shells. By 09:35 she had blown up—another example of how effective shell fire could be.

As the *Montauk* dropped down the river after the action, she struck a torpedo that did some damage. It exploded under one of the boilers and caused a serious leak, but one that the pumps were able to handle. She was later beached and repaired on station.

The attack was repeated on 3 March 1863 when three monitors engaged Fort McAllister. They fired at about 1000 to 1200 yards range at the fort, near the line of obstructions. The Union commander was of the opinion that any attack would be ineffective due to the shallow waters, obstructions, and the range of the action.

One of the nine hits on the *Passaic* was by a 10" mortar shell filled with sand that hit her deck directly over a beam. The commander, Percival Drayton, was of the opinion that it would have passed entirely through the deck except for the presence of the beam. Inadequate deck protection was perceived as the major weakness of the monitors and of the *New Ironsides*.

The Union admiral and his captains recognized that this magical weapon, the monitor, had its limitations. Slow rate of fire and vulnerable decks were just two points of care when commanding one of these vessels.

THE FIRST ATTACK ON CHARLESTON

If we lose our Monitors we lose the whole coast.
—Rear-Admiral Du Pont

Up to this point of the war Admiral Samuel F. Du Pont had a very successful career. He had captured Port Royal, also called Hilton Head, early in the war; it was his command that had reduced Fort Pulaski; and he had enjoyed several other victories up and down the coast. Now he was about to attempt to capture one of the South's most important seaports and the birthplace of the rebellion with these new-fangled and revolutionary ship types—the ironclad. And his faith in these new ironclads was not complete.

Though his command was given the bulk of Union ironclads then built, he wrote on 27 March 1863 of the monitors that "Those monitors, wonderful as they are, by a sort of paradox, they must be led or towed as you would help a tottering child." Du Pont was worried about engaging a strongly fortified seaport with ships. He was well aware of the losses the Allied fleets had suffered before Sevastopol and felt that Admiral Napier had, correctly, refused to attack Kronstadt in 1854 because of its strong defenses.

He would be receiving the *New Ironsides*, which would have the honor of going down in history as one of the most shot at and most hit ironclads ever built—hit 193 times (the monitor *Montauk* may hold the record by being hit 214 times, but the little Brazilian *Alagoas* would be hit about 180 times in one action during the war with Paraguay), but suffering very little damage in her lifetime. This ship was the third ship accepted by the 1861 "Ironclad Board." It was also the most conventional of the three designs and in the words of one of her officers, "the personification of ugliness." The original advertisement for design submissions had requested proposals for "iron-clad steam vessels of war" built with wood or iron hulls that were shallow draught—ten to sixteen feet was the goal. It said "the smaller draught of water, compatible with other requisites, will be preferred," and that it be rigged with two masts. The *New Ironsides* was 230 feet long, displaced 3,500 tons, had an almost 16 foot draft, could steam at seven knots, and carried 14 XI" Dahlgrens and two 150 pounder muzzle-loading Parrott rifles. Fifty pounder Dahlgren rifles would later be added to her spar, or upper, deck (above the main gun deck).

She was built of green timbers and would have rotted away quickly after the war, if she had not caught fire and burned in 1866. The armor was attached in a "tongue and groove" method, with each plate being 4.5 inches thick and not laminated, as in the *Monitor*. The disadvantage of the tongue and groove method was that if a plate was damaged, the adjacent plates needed to be removed to fix the bad one and the tongue portion of the plate was liable to break from a solid hit.

Well documented by William Howard Roberts, the *New Ironsides* had four boilers each fed by six coal furnaces. This single screw ship was built fairly rapidly in Philadelphia at William Cramp & Sons, though the general contractor was Merrick and Sons. (Cramp would go on to build much of the new United States navy at the turn of the century.) It should be noted that the wage problems suffered by the Confederate navy at New Orleans were mirrored in the North. Wages for shipwrights at Philadelphia rose from $1.75 a day to $3.00 per day in a two month period during the early stages of the war.

Officially delivered to the navy on 10 August 1862, *New Ironsides* still had workmen on board. But this was a powerful Union ironclad. She was considered so powerful that Rear-Admiral L. M. Goldsborough at the time of her completion urged that she immediately join his squadron before the James River in Virginia. On 8 July 1862 he wrote "From all I gather and believe, the enemy is making every exertion to prepare the new *Merrimack (Richmond)* at Richmond, and she will doubtless be a very formidable vessel.... I would urgently suggest that the *Ironsides* be sent here as early as practicable. I have but little faith in the *Galena*, and regard the *Monitor* as exceedingly overrated in prowess."

For the battle of Charleston, the *New Ironsides* would strengthen her upper deck. The deck received 6000 sandbags resting on untanned animal hides. Also, her iron plates were greased to help make rounds skid off her sides—causing her to smell to high heaven.

CSS Chicora *and the CSS* Hunley.

The assault on Charleston was long discussed, expected, and prepared for by both sides. Du Pont's orders were to reduce Fort Sumter and he planned to do this by using eight ironclads. He intended to pass the fort and attack it from the north-west face, that is, from inside the harbor. It was weakest there and he would face fewer guns from Fort Sumter. Circumstances conspired to bring about failure.

One reason for Du Pont's defeat lay with the Confederate defenses. Essentially they had two lines of defense, the outer forts, and then a series of weaker batteries and forts inside the harbor. Fort Sumter, the main target of Du Pont's attack, alone had 85 artillery pieces and 7 mortars. According to Major John Johnson who served there and later wrote *The Defense of Charleston Harbor,* many of the guns were older (i.e., ineffective against ironclads), or did not bear, and there were only two 7" Brooke rifles, four X" Rodman shell guns, two IX" Dahlgrens, eight 8" shell guns and eight smaller rifled guns that could be effectively used from Fort Sumter in the forthcoming attack. The outer line had an additional 70 guns of various sizes that bore on the harbor entrance.

Beauregard had clearly planned to defend the cradle of secession vigorously. When he arrived he asked for heavy rifled guns and said he wanted to increase the defenses "to the greatest possible extent, as soon as practicable, in all possible ways." It should be noted that after the war he wrote that the City of Charleston and the state strongly supported the war effort, "though I was never able to procure the necessary amount of slave-labor required for work on the fortifications."

Only the Brooke at close range would have a chance to penetrate the heavy armor of the monitors. The *Chicora* and *Palmetto State* were stationed behind

Fort Sumter and were there to sally forth against a Union naval advance into the harbor. During the action they steamed slowly around in circles behind the fort.

Each ship had recently received an addition to her armament in the form of a "spar torpedo." This was, on the Charleston ironclads, according to Daniel Dowdey, a 90 pound rifle powder charge placed at the end of a 20 to 30 foot pole that could be raised or lowered. Some sources give the charge as 60 to 70 pounds. Lowering it would place it six feet below the water where it could be exploded on the side of an enemy ship to try sinking it. It would explode if a glass phial was broken, causing the fuse to ignite the powder. This apparatus was checked once every two weeks—a most unpleasant task as accidents could happen.

In addition to this there were obstructions and torpedoes (with 100 pounds of powder) placed in the waters around the entrance to the harbor, which shifted about with the currents and the tides. At the time of the ironclad attack on Charleston, none were present in the main harbor, but some had been placed in some of the local rivers and estuaries. These defenses were not as extensive nor as effective as believed by the Union commander, but psychologically, they had an adverse effect on Du Pont and all the Union commanders. Part of this fear was further fueled when the Confederacy strung a rope barrier across part of the harbor, kept in place by closely placed floating barrels. It is possible that a more aggressive advance by the Union ironclads might have broken into the inner harbor, possibly led by a ram or two in a night attack charging the obstructions. Beauregard later wrote that his greatest fear was that the Union ironclads would attack Fort Sumter at night. They would be difficult targets while Fort Sumter was an easy target even at night. He feared they would pass the forts at night and enter Charleston harbor.

But herein lies the story of the Union failure. Essentially they fell between two posts in their planning. One course suggested in a letter to Du Pont was to remain some distance from Fort Sumter. Captain John Rodgers, who was on board the lead monitor, the *Weehawken,* had read of recent British experiments that discussed ironclads in action against forts. In a letter written in October of 1862 to Du Pont, Rodgers recommends the ships be placed at "…a distance at which our projectiles will breach a fort while the fire of the fort will be useless against our ironclads, … " He cites these British experiments that had shown at 600 yards a large Whitworth gun, though not an Armstrong gun, had penetrated a target that represented either the *Warrior's* or the *New Ironsides'* armor plate and backing—but nothing could penetrate at about 1,500 yards.

Rodgers goes on to suggest that "I think that it will be safe to assume that at 1,200 or 1,300 yards our ironclads will be secure." He also suggested that the ships anchor as this would mean "… better aim, less danger from torpedoes." This would place Confederate guns firing from Fort Johnson and Fort Moultrie at an even greater distance and Fort Sumter could then be reduced at leisure.

Du Pont could have led from the front with the *New Ironsides* or possibly another monitor ironclad, and forced the harbor entrance. This course would have involved, and endangered, the ironclads in a vicious battle. Inside the harbor, the Confederate ironclads would certainly have attacked, along with all the guns of the inner harbor defenses. Du Pont noted that the *New Ironsides* was terrible at maneuvering and that inside the harbor it would run a high risk—but also represented "half my force." But the battle could have been decisive. With Charleston lying under the guns of the Union fleet, and many of the weak inner Confederate defense positions having light guns, such as 24 pounders, Charleston's surrender might have been forced, or the town could have been burned. Beauregard did plan to defend the city "street by street" if the Union fleet did successfully break in.

Instead Du Pont adopted a third course. He would close to between 600 and 800 yards with the ships steaming slowly—a tactic similar to that he had employed at the capture of Port Royal. The lead vessel would be the *Weehawken,* which had attached to her a particular invention of Ericsson's to "catch" torpedoes—an early attempt at mine sweeping which proved more a hindrance than a success. Instead of heading the line, he would take the center of the line to communicate more easily with the fleet, but due to her unwieldiness the *New Ironsides* would never close. (Part of the poor steaming on her part was due to the flood tide that was pushing her and the other ironclads towards the harbor obstructions and torpedoes.)

The *Weehawken* was to lead the attack just after noon, but was slow in getting started as her torpedo-sweeping device—her "Alligator" —was snagged with her anchor. The device was essentially a raft attached at her bow with hanging chains to detonate floating any stationary torpedoes. In reserve were five wooden warships to support the attack against Morris Island after Sumter was reduced.

Finally the advance began against the ebbing tide at about 13:45. The abortive battle commenced at 15:00 on 7 April 1863 with the Confederate batteries opening on the advancing Union ships. Fire was concentrated on the *Weehawken* as the lead ship and shortly after the action opened an apparent torpedo exploded near her throwing, up a column of water and "lifted the vessel a little." Most likely, this was not a torpedo but a large mortar shell from one of the Confederate forts exploding just beneath the surface. As the *Weehawken* approached the rope barrier, Rodgers noted that the "rows of casks (were) very near together" and "to the eye they appeared almost to touch one another, and there was more than one line of them." Rodgers made the "deliberate judgment" that he could not pass through this obstruction. This would hold up the advance of the line.

The Confederate rope obstructions were just that—ropes strung between casks. There were no torpedoes in this line. The "slack lines of rope (were) to entangle wheels and propellers." In addition, there was a 300 yard wide opening

Smokestack of the Weehawken, *showing battle damage.*

in the obstruction near Fort Sumter for use by blockade runners. At the time of the attack the *only torpedo* placed at the entrance of Charleston Harbor was the boiler torpedo discussed below.

If some think that Rodgers and the *Weehawken* were not brave enough in this endeavor, it should be noted that the *Weehawken* was hit at *least* 53 times. One shot penetrated the deck and caused a small leak. The "Alligator" had also caused some small bow leaks due to its banging on the hull, with its movements not corresponding to the movement of the *Weehawken,* except in a smooth sea. At one point her turret was jarred hard enough so as to cease operation for a short period of time. The storm of shot including "bolts, ball, rifled shells, and steel-pointed shot" combined with this thick rope obstruction, were too much for the Union force.

The *New Ironsides* was unhandy, and with the ebbing tide, the number of ships close by, and unfamiliar shoals, she moved slowly forward with hesitation. Twice to avoid grounding her pilot had to drop the anchor. The *Catskill* and *Nantucket* tried to pass the *New Ironsides* and collided lightly with her to add to her discomfort. In the short battle that day the *New Ironsides* would fire only eight times in the action, though she was hit about 50 times and suffered minor damage.

With the Union line disordered the ironclad USS *Keokuk* (Commander Alexander Rhind) passed the *New Ironsides,* and closed to within 550 yards of the fort. Rhind knew that his ship's draft was shallower than the other ironclads and took advantage of that by maneuvering his ship closer to Fort Sumter than any other that day. Unfortunately the Confederate batteries concentrated their fire on her and the *Keokuk's* system of armoring quickly proved a failure. She sank the next day due to the damage; some of the decisive hits had come from a Brooke rifle. She fired only three times, while being hit about 90 times and suffering 16 wounded. She was described as "one of the crop of inventions that sprang up after the successful performance of the *Monitor,* and was proved useless when put to the test of war." Brigadier General R.S. Ripley, the Confederate commander of the local Charleston garrison under Major General P.T. Beauregard, noted that removed from the wreck of the *Keokuk* were "two captured abolition ensigns."

That day the *Nahant* also distinguished herself under the command of Commander John Downes. (Namesake of the *Downes* destroyed in the spectacular fire and explosion at Pearl Harbor while in drydock next to the battleship *Pennsylvania.*) Downes gallantly followed the *Keokuk* to lend her support and came under intense fire from Fort Sumter and the batteries on Moultrie Island. He early on lost his quartermaster in the pilot house to a crushed skull from one hit. While ordering up a new quartermaster, he yelled to Acting Ensign Charles E. Clarke in charge of the XV" gun "you hav'n't hit anything yet!" Clarke "roared" back, "We ain't near enough, Captain Downes!" Downes reply was, "Not near enough! God Damn it, I'll put you near enough! Starboard your helm, Quartermaster!" and the *Nahant* closed the range further. She would fire that day 15 shot and shell from her two guns and would be hit 36 times in 40 minutes of "close action." She lost one dead, two severely wounded, and four lightly wounded, including Downes, struck by a 78 pound piece of iron that fell on his foot from a hit on the pilot house. The turret was jammed by one of the nine hits on it and 56 bolts on the turret alone were broken—some of these flying bolts caused the injuries on board.

It was only then that the entire Union squadron was engaged. Confederate Major John Johnson, Engineer at Charleston, present at the action, would later write of this moment that,

> The forts and batteries also were firing with more steadiness and combined effect than they had hitherto attained. Upward of one hundred of the heaviest cannon of all descriptions were flashing and thundering together, shooting their balls, their shells, and fiery bolts with deafening sound and shocks of powerful impact that surpassed all previous experience of war. The smoke of the battle, brightened by the sun into snowy clouds, seemed to the distant observer entirely to envelop the small objects on the water which were causing all the trouble. Only when the light breeze availed to lift or part and roll away slowly the heavy masses could a glimpse be had of the movements of the squadron. The water all around the fighting ships was seen on nearer view to be constantly cut, ploughed, and splashed with every

form of disturbance, from the light dip of the ricochet shot to the plunge of the point-blank missile, from the pattering of broken pieces of solid shot falling back from impenetrable turrets to the sudden spout of foam and jet of spray sent up by a chance mortar shell exploding just beneath the surface of the water. Sometimes from the same cause a waterspout raised near the fort would reach to a great height and throw its shower of descending spray upon the guns frowning over the parapet or in the act of discharging their own messengers of defiance.

Another interesting account of this action is by British Admiral P.H. Colomb, a long time student of naval warfare. He wrote later,

We hear the very old story of the whole expedition being in the hands of the pilots, and of their being unwilling to move till noon on the 7th of April. Then the ships weighed and proceeded along the shore of Morris Island led by the *Weehawken,* which had a most hampering and inconvenient torpedo-catching structure attached to her bows. It was intended that the ships should be in line ahead, and about 100 yards apart, but precise order was found to be difficult to maintain. By the time the head of the line had reached Fort Wagner, Forts Moultrie and Sumter, and all the batteries within range opened fire, and the orders had been not to return it until within easy range of Sumter. But a line of obstructions was observed between Sumter and Moultrie, which barred the further progress in that direction, ...

Various difficulties occurred in getting the ships into accurate positions against Sumter. Some ships got within 500 yards of the fort, others no nearer than 1,000. The fire of the monitors was found to be exasperatingly slow. It was difficult for the commanders, between their narrow outlook from the pilot-houses and the smoke, to see what they were doing. The ships were hampered by the tides and shoal water, and the space, which was artificially narrowed by the supposed obstructions. The machinery of the guns failed in unexpected quarters. Bolt-heads and nuts flew about the interior of the turrets and pilot-houses in showers. The mere concussion in the interior, due to blows of enemy's shot on the outside of the turrets, seem to have temporarily disabled the inmates.... .

None of the ironclads displayed large ensigns in the action, most likely so as not to provide marks for the Confederate gunners. Nearby were some tugboats to assist any disabled Union ironclads.

At the end, the *New Ironsides,* effectively out of the action, had anchored directly above an electric torpedo (an old boiler 18 feet long and three feet in diameter) which contained 3,000 pounds of powder (accounts vary, but this is as reported to Beauregard). It was fired twice by the land operator, but failed to explode, not because a wagon wheel ran over the electrical wire and cut it, as sometimes cited, but apparently due to its not being placed, as reported by Jones, where first planned and thus throwing off the adjustments on the electrical firing device. Another cause cited in the ORN is that one of the men who worked on it deliberately caused it to malfunction as it "was too bad to blow people up in that way; it was not Christian." Weapons such as these, even if not always successful, show the vigor and ingenuity of Charleston's defense.

Joseph Yates, now Lieutenant Colonel, who had commanded the ironclad floating battery during the bombardment of Fort Sumter, and fought in the siege of Charleston in 1863, considered "the Brooke gun decidedly the most efficient gun in use for operating against Iron-clad vessels." One Brooke rifle Yates worked with fired over 1700 rounds without failure in the course of the war. He had also introduced a device used in this action to help have the guns maintain training on their target ship while loading for the next shot.

Admiral Du Pont originally planned to attack again the next day, but after meeting with his captains, was dissuaded from trying the fortifications again. Du Pont later wrote in his official dispatch,

> No ships had been exposed to the severest fire of the enemy over forty minutes, and yet in this brief period, as the Department will perceive by the detailed reports of the commanding officers, five of the ironclads were wholly or partially disabled; disabled, too, as the obstructions could not be passed, in that which was most essential to our success—I mean in their armament, or power of inflicting injury by their guns ...
>
> I had hoped that the endurance of the ironclads would have enabled them to have borne any weight of fire to which they might have been exposed; but when I found that so large a portion of them was wholly or one-half disabled by less than an hour's engagement before attempting to remove (overcome) the obstructions or testing the power of the torpedoes, I am convinced that persistence in the attack would only result in the loss of the greater part of the ironclad fleet, and in leaving many of them inside the harbor to fall into the hands of the enemy.
>
> The slowness of our fire and our inability to occupy any battery that we might silence or to prevent its being restored under cover of night were difficulties of the gravest character.

A strictly naval attack was seen as no longer feasible at Charleston after this failure. Colomb goes on to say about Admiral Du Pont that, "... seems to have attributed his failure to the misapprehension of the nature of things, and not to any removable causes, and he was careful to lay down a subordinate part for the ships in any future attack (supporting the army). That is to say, that, in spite of the radical changes which had been made in the material, the Federals would have been wise to have taken past experience as their guide" and realize that ships fighting forts usually lose if at all evenly matched. This sense of expecting to fail comes through in a letter to his wife written on 8 April 1863 in which he writes "We have failed as I felt sure we would." After the war, several Confederates would state that the defenses of Charleston, especially in terms of mines, booms, and obstructions, were not as thorough as believed, and it was feared that the inner harbor was feebly armed and could have been forced by a more aggressive Union Navy.

The tactics of the Federal fleet had failed to achieve victory, but it goes beyond the range chosen or the method of attack. It was forgotten that, as Rear-Admiral Belknap (at the time first lieutenant on the *New Ironsides*) later wrote, "Tactical formations look pretty on paper, but in the melee and ever changing conditions of marine fighting, methodical positions and movements of ships cannot be maintained, a fact always borne in mind by the great sea officers of modern times,—Nelson and Farragut."

During this first bombardment, the forts fired 2,209 rounds and the ironclads 139 rounds (Wise's account states 154 rounds). About 19% of the fort's rounds hit (520), while the Union forces had a 50% rate of hitting, though their target was certainly larger than the individual ships. The Confederates were helped by preplaced range markers, since normal gunnery percentages for hits would have been closer to 10% than the 19% achieved. They had hurt the Union ironclads not by penetrating shots, but by pounding them and eventually loosening bolts and knocking machinery out of alignment.

Fort Sumter itself was hit directly 34 times with near misses or slight damage from about 20 other shells, of which real damage was accomplished by about 15 of those hits. One observer wrote later that the shell hits on the fort caused the "... massive walls, piers, and arches ... to tremble to their foundations." Fort Sumter employed 40 guns in the action and fired 810 times. Total losses from all forts were four dead and 10 wounded. This compared to the total losses of one dead and 22 wounded on the Union ships. John Johnson, later summed the action up by writing,

> ...it was rather a trial of strength than a sanguinary battle. Indeed, compared with the fighting of the iron-clad boats of Captain Eads's construction the year before on the Cumberland and the Tennessee Rivers, when at Fort Henry they were victorious and at Fort Donelson they were beaten, the attack on Fort Sumter was not made with the vigor or persistency that often distinguished the United States Navy, and particularly in forcing an entrance through torpedo obstructions into Mobile Bay the following year.

One of the interesting conclusions reached by Du Pont on the Confederate shot was their shape. Du Pont later wrote that, "the blunt-headed shots had proven much less effective than the round shot, not only in confining their injury to the indentation, made more distinctly than is the case with round shot, but the indentations themselves were less than those made by the spherical balls." Why this flies in the face of future developments, but may have been a fluke or in some way related to poor powder and manufacture of the bolts or poor observation on the part of the soon to be relieved Rear-Admiral Du Pont.

The Confederate naval squadron would be reinforced with two more ironclads, including the powerful *Columbia* with 6 inches of armor plate. But the work of the squadron was minor for the remainder of the war before being blown up by their crews in 1865 with the fall of Charleston from Sherman's army's imminent arrival. They did collectively fulfill the role of a fleet in being and may have delayed the fall of Mobile by keeping Union ironclads off Charleston throughout 1863 and 1864.

THE CAPTURE OF THE CSS ATLANTA

The possibilities of a XV-inch gun, fired at a range of two hundred yards, were matters that (the crew of the Atlanta) had no wish to investigate further.
—J.R. Soley in *The Blockade and the Cruisers*

Du Pont had one other important service to contribute before his relief for his failure to take Charleston. He had learned of the CSS *Atlanta* being built at Savannah and that it was ready for sea. He dispatched the monitors *Nahant* and *Weehawken* under Captain John Rodgers (from a family with a long naval lineage going back to the War of 1812 and the American Revolution).

The *Atlanta* was one of the best ironclads built by the South. She was under the command of William A. Webb, former commander of the *Teaser*. Webb was known as "a very reckless young officer" and had received his command as it was expected he would seek action with the *Atlanta*. His plan was to go down the river and engage the two Union monitors known to be there. Webb had a spar torpedo in place and wanted to try it on one of the Union monitors. He planned to return after the action and to wait for the smaller ironclad *Savannah* that was completing for sea.

Savannah was thought to have potential for a major impact on the war. Tattnall, now commanding the Savannah station, had wanted to take her and raid Port Royal between Charleston and Savannah which had been captured early in the war and now was a major supply base for the Federal fleet. If successful, it might have delayed the Union war effort in this theater for some time.

The Weehawken led the way up the channel, as she had the pilot on board, and in the short ensuing action the Nahant did not even fire her guns. As the Atlanta came down river with her firebrand captain she grounded slightly during the rising tide. She got off after about 15 minutes, but in shallow water she was unwieldy and did not answer the helm well . (This is a problem that occurred with the Virginia at Hampton Roads and the New Ironsides at Charleston.) Shortly thereafter she grounded again where she remained for the next hour and a half. The *Atlanta* opened fire on the *Nahant* at 04:55.

As the *Weehawken* approached, Rodgers was very deliberate. He withheld the *Weehawken's* fire until about 300 yards off and then fired but five times in fifteen minutes. The first shot broke through the *Atlanta's* casemate and killed one man and wounded 16. The second shot hit the pilot house, which added to the *Atlanta's* discomfort. As Rodgers later wrote, "the first shot took away her desire to fight, and the second destroyed her ability to do so." Two other hits did not hurt the *Atlanta,* while the fifth shot missed.

But it was enough. The *Atlanta* was firmly grounded and with her casemate compromised, surrendered to the monitors. The *Weehawken* had used a 400 pound cored (hollowed) shot to inflict the damage. Her solid shot was 440 pounds and the XV" Dahlgren shell weighed 330 pounds. Firing rules allowed for up to 60 pounds of powder but the gun could only be fired 20 times with charges of that size and preferably at an ironclad at 50 to 150 yards range.

It is noteworthy that subsequently the *Atlanta,* built in much the same manner as most Confederate ironclads, steamed up and down the Atlantic coast during the war under the Union flag, and would eventually be used in the James River operations at the end of the war. It leads to the conclusion that when the seas were moderate to smooth, Confederate ironclads might have been more of a threat to Union cities than is sometimes argued. After the war the *Atlanta* was sold to Haiti for $260,000 to be used in a civil war there. While on her delivery voyage to that country as the *Triumph* (also shown as *Triumfo),* she foundered. Included with the 120 hands on board were "two Haitian senators and several former U.S. naval officers and a large number of black men recruited in Philadelphia." She was lost off Cape Hatteras (some argue off the Delaware Capes) in mid-December of 1869.

THE SECOND ASSAULT

The Navy did not take the opportunity to force the port, limiting her actions to the port's siege.
　　—C. Jacobi in *Gerzogenen Geschuetze der Amerikaner*

The failed naval assault on Charleston proved to some that the monitor type vessel had too few guns to capture a heavily fortified position such as Charleston. However, most were pleased to learn that a few days at Port Royal, South Carolina, a Union base seized early in the war, was all that was needed to effect repairs and return most of the monitors to combat readiness off Charleston.

Du Pont, though, was out. He was too opposed to the monitors to continue in command. He was replaced first by Rear-Admiral Andrew H. Foote, who had distinguished himself in the early battles on the upper Mississippi, but had died on his way to take command, and so it fell to Rear-Admiral John A. Dahlgren, the inventor of the gun, to take command.

The initial campaign was to seize Morris Island and it was largely going to be an army affair. But for the assault on Fort Wagner (really a battery in design), the navy would give a hand. It is noteworthy that the Confederate garrison at this time, recently reduced by 10,000 men sent to North Carolina and Vicksburg, was largely from South Carolina. The total garrison at the time numbered 2,600 infantry, 550 cavalry, and 3,800 artillerists. A general strengthening of the defenses of Charleston by the Confederate engineering staff would be continuous throughout the rest of the war.

The South also now had two XI" guns of their own, as they had salvaged two from the sunken *Keokuk*. With it also came a coded signal book. The salvage operation is of some interest. The Federals and several Confederate engineers said that the guns were not salvageable from the wreck of the *Keokuk*. But in April and May the Confederates waited until a low calm tide at night when they had about two and a half hours a night to work at the removal of both guns from two separate turrets.

The first 16,000-pound gun was lifted out by block and tackle through a hole cut in the turret roof as the men stood waist deep in ocean water. It did not clear until sandbags were shifted and a fortunate wave lifted the gun out the final few inches. The second gun was easier to remove and the operation was completed after three weeks in May. The *Charleston Mercury* newspaper said, after the task had been completed (and not while it was in progress), "Enterprise, even with scant means, can accomplish much."

The Union ships only once fired on the working party; the covering *Chicora* returned long range fire, but the Union never realized what was transpiring and did not seriously interfere. Gideon Welles later wrote Du Pont, shortly before his removal from command, after learning of this Confederate operation from the *Charleston Mercury.* In a later letter, Secretary of the Navy Welles wrote, "The duty of destroying the *Keokuk* and preventing her guns from falling into the hands of the rebels devolved upon the commander in chief ... . The wreck and its important armament ought not to have been abandoned to the rebels, whose sleepless labors appear to have secured them a valuable prize."

Also during this two month period, according to *Lifeline of the Confederacy*, 17 blockade runners arrived at Charleston and 14 cleared the port. Of the latter, two were destroyed and one was captured. That this much activity could transpire while the port was under siege, between the time of two direct assaults, gives one a sense of what the blockade could and could not do and why the seizure of the ports was the only way to shut down the blockade runners.

The South was aware of the approaching second assault (sometimes called the "First Great Bombardment"), though unsure of the details of it. One method of detection was the use of an observation balloon near Port Royal that saw the gathered troop transports readying for an expedition.

The initial Union advances on Morris Island in early July were supported by several monitors firing shell, which aided greatly the advance of the Union army to the front of Fort Wagner. The men on the monitors suffered in the summer heat, and many of those below decks fainted from the heat. The ventilators were ineffective, and actually distributed smoke thoughout the ship. Crews received a special ration of ice, and an attempt was made to supplement their diets with whiskey—though this was quickly overturned by the navy's chief of the Bureau of Medicine and Surgery. He suggested strong coffee and early morning swims in the ocean instead.

With the threat growing, Beauregard suggested to Confederate commander John Randolph Tucker that the fleet sortie, armed with their spar torpedoes and attack the monitors. The sortie would have been made by the *Chicora, Palmetto State,* an unarmored *Charleston* that was to be used as a ram, the blockade runner *Juno,* and other small ships rounded up in the harbor. Tucker did not attempt this plan, due to his ship's low speed and that his ironclads had only 4 inches of plating. The monitors with their XV" guns would have most likely disabled them, as they had the *Atlanta.* Tucker's only hope for success would have been the element of surprise. Tucker had already proven his resourcefulness and daring at Hampton Roads, and later would prove daring in commanding the Peruvian fleet after the American Civil War, so, again, this was not a case of lack of spirit, but a judgment choice.

Resourcefulness in the defense was not lacking at Charleston. Several novel experiments with torpedoes and small ships armed with spar torpedoes were prepared for or attempted during the course of the war, including at one point the preparation of an attack of a spar torpedo boat *flotilla.* The attack with this force was called off due to the poor quality of the small boats to be used in the night attack. One of the few successful attempts culminated in the first successful submarine attack by the CSS *Hunley.* The *Hunley* sank after its successful attack and has been recently located. It may soon be raised and placed in a museum.

During the course of this second assault of July and August—the attack on Fort Wagner—Union ironclads, along with wooden gunboats making use of their large pivot guns, bombarded the Confederate defenses.

A major attack was planned for 18 July. It consisted of the flagship *Montauk* with Dahlgren on board, the *Catskill, Nantucket, Weehawken, Patapsco,* and the *New Ironsides.* As the *New Ironsides* approached Fort Wagner and Battery Gregg, the Confederates "poured a furious fire upon her." The *New Ironsides* dropped anchor about 1200 yards off Fort Wagner and opened a heavy fire. Her relatively

Battery Wagner as viewed from the main ship channel.

rapid fire with her XI" guns contrasted with the larger shell explosions from the monitor's XV" guns, which were much slower firing. Her belt armor was dented but her sandbagged deck gave quite good protection, only small leaks developed after a shell hit the deck.

She used an interesting tactic on 20 July, firing her guns "in rotation" to keep the gun crews of Fort Wagner down. That is, by maintaining a steady fire instead of broadsides, the Confederates could not work their guns for fear of heavy casualties. On the 24th, again using this tactic, she fired 464 times and was hit but five times. She could fire more rapidly than the monitors with her smaller guns, roomy dimensions and conventional gun mountings. Her maximum range was 2,000 yards.

General P.G.T. Beauregard, Confederate commander at Charleston, later wrote of the attack by the *New Ironsides*, that "her fire was delivered with more rapidity and accuracy, and she was the most effective engine employed in the reduction of Wagner." She would not be withdrawn from the siege until 1864.

It is interesting to note that Captain Belknap, who fought in the *New Ironsides* off Charleston, thought that two or three more ships like her, in lieu of the monitors, would have made the difference. They had a more rapid fire than the monitors, and he thought could suppress Confederate fire more readily. It should be noted that in her engagements she suffered no losses and only one bit of serious battle damage, though hit "by over 150 heavy projectiles." The only damage inflicted on her of any consequence was a spar torpedo attack at night, which failed, but caused some damage to her hull which in the summer of 1864 caused her return to the North for repairs and refitting.

One aspect about the Confederate reply often overlooked is that her ordnance was powered by *Confederate* gunpowder which with few exceptions as the war drew on, became more and more inferior to Union powder. The bottom line is that the Confederate industrial capability was not equal pound for pound with the Union as several authorities note.

Additionally, for reasons not fully understood, but most likely due to excessive tolerances in the rifling and the manufacture of elongated shot and bolts, ammunition did not fly straight on. The *Catskill* was hit about 60 times in one of her first engagements. The rifle bolts that struck were often at an angle or "striking sideways." So Captain Belknap remarked after the war in an article about *New Ironsides* approaching Fort Wagner. He wrote later that, "One morning, when the tide was exceptionally high, the commodore was fortunate enough to get the ship within nine hundred yards of the enemy, and she received 31 hits on that occasion, mostly from 10" shot, though once in a while struck by a rifle bolt. The round always made the most impression on the armor; the bolts rarely struck fairly on end, but generally sideways, and their supposed punching power never had verification in the experience of the *New Ironsides.*"

The land assault, portrayed in the 1989 movie *Glory,* failed with heavy losses, in spite of the ship and land artillery support. However, the Confederate garrison at Fort Wagner was relatively safe in their bombproofs and also received supporting fire from nearby Confederate batteries, including Fort Sumter.

During the continuing actions with the Union ironclads, the Confederates had one of their few outright gunnery successes. A 10" shot on the *Catskill* broke the inner lining and killed her captain and paymaster. These two dead, along with the quartermaster killed on the *Nahant,* were the only men killed on a monitor from gun fire in the entire American Civil War.

With the failure of the land assault combined with naval fire against Wagner, a regular approach using trenches and continuing artillery bombardment was the order of the day.

But then a new weapon arrived at Wilmington—two giant guns, made by Blakely. These were 12.75" breech-loading rifles weighing over 27 tons and over 16 feet long. They fired a 650 pound shot and 450 pound shell. They were shipped out with two iron carriages, 150 solid shot and 50 shells, and apparently, according to Hobart Pasha, lacking "proper instructions for loading." They were the largest guns used by the Confederacy. They were shipped down to Charleston, where, after the fourth discharge, one burst. This was due to the charge being left with no air next to it and the round. This was quite a novel arrangement at the time, and was also used by Lieutenant John M. Brooke in the design of his later Brooke rifles.

It was thought that if the charge had any air around it that it would strain the gun and lead to its bursting, but this was not true. So for years the navies of the world had been "ramming home charges" to prevent an air space between the charge and the back of the gun. Brooke, and apparently Alexander T. Blakely, the manufacturer of the Blakely, had both independently discovered this new principle which would lead to greater and greater guns and charges over the next 80 years.

Ironically neither Blakely was ever fired in anger, the second one remaining in the City Battery until it was destroyed when Charleston was abandoned. Apparently a piece of the battery when it exploded became part of an attic in a downtown house and remains there to this day.

Another weapon used was a large 8" Parrott gun set up deep in the swamps behind the coast to fire on Charleston. Called the "Swamp Angel," it fired into Charleston until it burst, causing little real damage but bringing home the concept, if not the full execution, of total war against the city. Hobart Pasha claimed to be in the town at the time of the bombardment and commented that the battery had been "placed by the enemy ... five miles from the town, and that day had opened fire for the first time. At that enormous range the shell occasionally burst over or fell into the city, doing, however, little damage."

Even before the fall of Morris Island, the Union army's artillery was firing on Fort Sumter from its land batteries. Fort Sumter was literally being demolished, beginning in August, 1863. The Union Navy aided this bombardment, especially on the night of 1 September, when six monitors took up a position at 700 to 1,500 yards and opened on the fort. With the cover of darkness and the reduced Confederate defenses, only the Confederate batteries on Sullivan island could react vigorously. The *New Ironsides* joined about two hours into the attack to fire from 1,500 yards out.

The ironclads were hit a total of 71 times. Fort Sumter, however, "had cause to remember this night-attack." Her magazine was threatened from several shell hits, and every casemate on both stories of the fort was breached on the side facing the assault. As Johnson later wrote, "the fort had now lost all offensive character." Shortly after this the siege of 58 days ended with the successful evacuation of Morris Island by the Confederates. Dahlgren followed this up with an attempt to take Sumter in a small boat attack at night that failed.

During the rest of 1863 Fort Sumter was constantly bombarded. This period is known as the Second Great Bombardment—of what was really little else than an armed outpost—no longer a formidable fort. Dahlgren considered naval attacks in October 1863, as well as in 1864, but decided against them. The siege continued but Charleston would never fall to the Navy. It would be the army advancing through Georgia and into South Carolina that would eventually bring about the fall of the birthplace of the war.

Anatomy of One Small Nation's Response: Dutch Treat

The transition of our former ships of the line into such floating batteries has turned out to be a deplorable waste of money.
  —Dutch States-General (parliament) in 1862

All Serviceable vessels must be armored.
  —The 1862 States-General Commission of Inquiry regarding the Navy

Understandable, perhaps, is the tendency to focus on either one's own navy's story and history, or else seize on some event, large or small but usually exciting, and study that, while ignoring other stories in the rich tapestry of naval history. Thus it has passed that when the word "ironclad" arises in a conversation, discussion is usually drawn to HMS *Warrior,* the *Monitor* and the *Merrimack,* or some other watershed event in history.

But the smaller European powers, who were not involved directly in any of the grand events unfolding in Europe and the world, still reacted to the new technology. It must be remembered that neither Europe, nor the world, was a peaceful place in these years. After the revolutionary activity of 1848-9, there followed the Crimean War; the Franco-Austrian War of 1859 fought in Italy; the Schleswig-Holstein, or Danish War, of 1864; the Seven Weeks War of 1866; the Franco-Prussian War of 1870-71; the Russo-Turkish War of 1877-78; as well as civil war in Japan, Spain, China, and the United States. South America was in flames with the Triple Alliance war with Paraguay, Spanish squadrons off Chile and Peru, and all culminating in the War of the Pacific—so it is no wonder that there was a naval buildup in the smaller nations of Europe.

But not all naval architects are brilliant or perfectly in tune with what the future will hold. So it was that in the Netherlands, at the start of the naval revolution, there was a man who would *not* leave his name alongside Ericsson or Dupuy de Lome. As described in *Voor Pampus,* this Dutch Director of Naval Construction was Lambertus Katharinus Turk. Turk was not alone in this era, as others, such as Cornelius S. Bushnell, the producer of the *Galena,* also designed failures.

Turk recognized the naval revolution brought about by the French and British armored steam batteries built for the Crimean War, and in 1857 he also recognized that the Dutch government would have little money for new ships. So he proposed taking one of the existing small Dutch ships-of-the-line, the *Koning der Neder-landen* (King of the Netherlands), and razing and converting her to the armored floating battery *Neptunus.*

The design of the *Neptunus* went through two phases. The first design was somewhat like the French and British ironclad steam batteries, though without steam power, and having a 4.5 inch armored belt, 3/4 inch armored deck, and 60

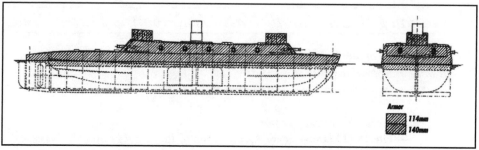

The steambattery De Ruyter, *the Netherlands version of the CSS* Virginia. *It was a failure as a design.*

pounders—comparable to the British 68 pounder. This was due in part to the Dutch acquiring copies of the plans of the British-built batteries—though *how* this was done is unclear! (It is hard to realize in the era of the CIA and KGB that in the last century if you arrived at a foreign shipyard in the name of *science* you were quite often made welcome. Science was then a new international religion for many and represented the enlightened mind at work.)

Turk also visited the French yards while the *Devastation* was being built and "prepared a very detailed report" on her. Both French and British designs on these early batteries were too heavy when fully loaded with ammunition and supplies and sat low in the water, so the Dutch did try to compensate for this in their designs.

The Dutch also looked at a seldom studied Austrian design for a floating battery. The Austrian navy had begun armor experimentation in 1859, in part due to the war with France and Cavour's Kingdom of Sardinia–Savoy. They designed an armored floating battery, the *Feuerspeier,* and armed her with sixteen 48 pounders. Also shielded by 4.5 inches of plate, she had the benefit of being armored all around including four fighting positions, or primitive conning towers, for officers to observe the action. Firing ports allowed for limited, but all around fire.

The problem that arose with the *Neptunus* and other Turk designed ships, several not started, was due to a design change. By the start of the 1860s it was decided, due to a lack of funds, that only the *ends* would be armored, but not the sides. An iron plate 4.5 inches thick was placed on the bow and the stern of the ships; the lower portions of the ships had two decks with three 60 pounders each. These lower portions of the ship's ends were protected by cells filled with sand. One wag said that the orders were that "in case of war a notice would be nailed to the ship's sides, informing the enemy that no firing at the sides of the battery was allowed!"

This final design had six smoothbore 60 pounders on the bow and stern, and twenty 3.9" (200cm) "heavy" shell guns on the broadside. Four of the 60 pounders

The Dutch armored ram Buffel. ("Prins Hendrik" Maritime Museum, Rotterdam)

could be trained on the broadsides. Fully loaded, she displaced 2200 tons. The *Neptunus* was commissioned in May of 1861 and was retired in 1876.

The experiment with sand continued throughout the era of the early ironclads. The French and British Crimean War steam batteries almost received sand bags on their decks. The Confederate Navy took the old sailing sloop *Germantown,* gained when Norfolk and the Gosport Navy Yard fell in 1861, removed her masts, cut her down, and had a "sand-filled bulkhead seven feet thick for a superstructure" placed with it "running around the ship." She had three pivot guns (one amidships and one on each end) and a broadside of four IX" shell guns. She was anchored at the head of the Elizabeth River as a floating battery. It was discussed assigning her a permanent tug boat to place on her leeside in battle so she could have some motive power if used to bombard Union forts in the Hampton Roads area. Later both the Union and the South used cotton bales, cables and sand bags to give extra protection to their ships in combat—*ersatz* armorplate.

The *Neptunus* was viewed by most as a failure as she was completing—and there were six other ships slated for conversion, roughly on her lines. The troubles were so numerous and extended from the lack of armor to structural problems encountered in the conversion that the Dutch parliament upon reviewing the *Neptunus* froze the salaries of the Naval Constructors for an entire year in punishment. Next, the Parliament in 1862 formed a committee to review the Netherlands naval policies and recommended the following: first, tiny armored

Dutch ironclad Schorpioen *as preserved at Middleburg, showing its armored ram.*

gunboats were to be built of shallow draft (two would be); second, slow but fully armored floating steam batteries were to be converted or built; and third, fast ironclad steam batteries for work in shallow Dutch waters were to be constructed. This policy was indifferently implemented before the next parliamentary review.

One ship ordered in 1863 reflected the uneven and uncertain building policies of this period. The Dutch were impressed with the *Virginia* and so ordered one of their frigates converted to a Confederate style ironclad. The *de Ruyter* was not commissioned until 1870, and while capable of ten knots, all the gunports had to be closed at speeds in excess of five knots in a moderate sea. An excessively hot ship, she was armed with fourteen 60 pounders behind 4.5 inches of armor. She was obsolete before commissioning and would be retired in 1874.

But Dutch policies were still uncertain and underfunded. This might have come to a head by itself, especially with the Schleswig-Holstein War between the Danes and Prussia allied with Austria taking place next door in 1864. But the town of Flushing had a shock that year, when one morning the populace awoke to find a "South American ironclad," most likely Brazilian, sitting in their harbor. She had taken refuge there during the night. The fact that the Dutch defenses took no notice of her arrival sent a message to the entire nation.

So the Dutch in 1864 had a new parliamentary commission that made sensible recommendations. Building on the 1862 committee, it was recommended that forts be built with guns that could penetrate 4.5 inches of armor at ranges of 2,000, or sometimes 1,000, meters. This was dependent in part on the narrow

The Schorpioen *under construction, showing the watertight compartments introduced during the ironclad era.*

waters being defended. Twin screwed ironclad rams capable of at least 10 knots of speed and armed with a few heavy guns in turrets were also recommended. Additionally the retention of privately owned fast steamers for "reconnaissance, despatches and if necessary for transport of troops" was proposed.

This would culminate in a series of rams built in British, French, as well as Dutch yards. The first one was designed by Lairds in Great Britain, with Turk's design input deliberately bypassed. Two exist today as museum ships in Rotterdam and Middleburg respectively—the *Buffel* and the French built *Schorpioen*. With the switch over that began in 1864-5 the Dutch navy would make another positive move by building warships with iron hulls. This lengthened the life of the ships. They were all propelled by twin screws, allowing for easy maneuvering in the narrow waters of the Netherlands, as well as her island colonies. The *Schorpioen* was armed with two 9" Armstrong rifled muzzle-loaders with 6 inches of iron armoring the turret, and made 12 knots.

These ironclad ram ships employed a turret designed by British Captain Cowper Coles. Coles developed his turret based on his Crimean War experience. He had noted that guns on a broadside warship, to have a wide traverse, required a wide gunport. A wide gunport allowed for enemy shot and shell to enter the ship, causing both damage and large crew losses. So he designed a turret, or "cupola" that moved on a turntable. This differed from Ericsson's design on the United States *Monitor* in that Coles' design used ball bearings on the outside edge of his turret, while Ericsson's was on a central spindle in the center of the turret.

First adopted by the Danish *Rolf Krake,* it proved fairly popular among some European powers and was employed several years afterwards. Unfortunately for Coles, he drowned on a ship of his design, the *Captain,* in 1870 in a storm off Spain. A design error resulted in the *Captain* being top heavy and having inadequate freeboard. (Its loss did bring about a serious and successful review of ship design policies in Great Britain.)

The Dutch also ordered the construction of several monitors similar to the United States designs with the Ericsson style turret. Over ten were built between 1868 and 1878, of which one was lost in bad weather in the North Sea. The Dutch also built two slightly larger ships for overseas duty, mostly in the Dutch East Indies. As pointed out by Rear Admiral Roger Morris in a recent article in the World Ship Society's *Warships,*

> Between 1867 and 1875 they had built two large and four smaller seagoing armored turret ships, and thirteen low-freeboard coast defence turret ships. Of these, one of the larger and one of the smaller seagoing turret ships and ten of the low-freeboard types were built by Dutch yards.

So these would be the basic types of ironclads in the Dutch navy for the coming years. Rams with a single or twin turret and single turreted monitors. Beyond a few minor colonial actions the Dutch navy would not see combat until World War II.

The Netherlands would also build several wooden cruisers in this period. One is still in existence and there is a move afoot to preserve her. This is the 120 man 853 ton *Bonaire.* She was armed with one 6" gun and three 4.7" guns as her main armament and made a speed of nine knots. Readers may contact her support fund by writing to: Comité tot behoud van de "Bonaire," Mr. G. Jonker, Singel 70, 9934 BX DELFZIJL, The Netherlands.

By 1880, J.W. King, Chief Engineer of the United States navy, said of the Dutch navy, "It is strong, however, chiefly for the purposes of coast defence, there being only two sea-going armored ships on the navy list ... (which) were built some time ago." But, as other smaller navies, the Netherlands had made the transition to the new ironclad age.

The Chattahoochee & Apalachicola River System

The naval operations in Florida waters during the war were not perhaps as brilliant and far-reaching in their character as those in some other parts of the Confederacy, but they are not without a vivid historical interest, and had a solid importance in connection with the whole plan of attack upon the Southern sea-coasts and sea-ports.
  —J. Thomas Scharf, in his *History of the Confederate States Navy*

East of Pensacola on the Florida panhandle is the river valley of the Chattahoochee and the Apalachicola. These rivers support the towns of Columbus, Columbia, and Chattahoochee, as well as many small towns up and down the river system. While not directly on the rivers, the coast town of St. Marks, Florida, and smaller nearby landings were blockade running ports, and nearby was Tallahassee, Florida, the state capital. A picture of naval activity in this relative backwater offers some insight into what the South was facing in her war with the Union.

Confederate naval effort took place everywhere up and down the Southern coast, including the construction of ironclads, and as pointed out in Maxine Turner's *Navy Gray;* this river system was no exception. Only 42 steam blockade runners ran in or out of the west Florida ports in the course of the war (the majority through St. Marks). The last ones made the run in early 1864, but the small inlets along the coast allowed, at least at the start of the war, small sailing schooners to also run the blockade and there was some limited small ship coastal trade that declined as the war progressed.

The problems endemic to the South's naval effort are mirrored on a small scale by the blockade of this river system, which was inaugurated on 11 June 1861 with the arrival of the first Union warship. Confederate defenses at this time were negligible, but their first move was "removing buoys and dismantling light-houses," which was a deterrent to a Union navy in waters that were literally uncharted in places. As the war continued more Union warships appeared off the coast as small Confederate batteries were erected on the coast and up river, along with the placing of obstructions in the river system.

At the start of the war, one of the Confederate naval stars, oceanographer Captain Matthew Fontaine Maury, advocated the construction of small wooden steam gunboats with rifled guns that would keep Confederate ports open by shear numbers and rifled ordnance. His ideas carried some sway and at the start of the war many wooden gunboats were laid down, until the ironclad swept them into the dustbin of history. They may have ended up there anyway, as personified by the career of the CSS *Chattahoochee*, a gunboat, in part, representing Maury's philosophy.

Begun at Columbus in October of 1861, it took 120 days to construct. The *Chattahoochee* was commissioned on 1 January 1863, but was not fully ready until 7 April 1863. It was monumental delays such as this that further doomed the Confederacy's hopes. She sank on 26 May 1863 when her boiler accidentally exploded, but was later raised and made operational. The remainder of her career was uneventful.

But, as elsewhere, the South was building ironclads on this river system to defend her waters or, possibly, break the blockade. But it would be a day late and a dollar short in the naval effort. The *Muscogee*, later renamed *Jackson*, was originally designed as a paddlewheel ironclad, but redesigned as a twin screw, 223 foot long casemated ironclad with 4 inches of iron plate. She had two 6.4" and three 7" Brooke rifles shipped to her in early 1865. She was begun in December of 1862 and was not quite complete when destroyed in April 1865, to avoid capture by approaching Union forces. Her remains are housed at the Confederate Naval Museum at Columbus, Georgia.

But she offered hope while under construction to the local populace. One Southern Belle after seeing the *Jackson* under construction wrote that "She will be formidable; will mount five heavy guns, each capable of whipping a fleet of Yankees. I will rest perfectly secure in knowing that 'The Pines' [her plantation] will never be molested by the enemy." The *Jackson's* troubled history involved delays on delivery of guns and materials, as well as a false launching in January of 1864, which required her being redesigned and rebuilt—this is when she became a twin screw ironclad.

Ironically, in a 28 January 1865 letter to Captain Thomas Catesby ap Roger Jones who commanded the Selma Naval Iron Works, it was proposed to build at Columbus a 175 foot, six foot draft *Monitor* style vessel armed with 11" guns—to be completed in 1866. Jones considered this a good idea, but it was not to come to fruition. Even to the end, there was a desire to keep the navy, and the cause, alive and not to give up until the Union army arrived at the proverbial front door.

CHAPTER V

Mobile & Wilmington
The Closing of the Last Major Confederate Ports

Mobile, New Orleans, Vicksburg must, unless their lessons are hereafter reversed, teach us that forts have of themselves little power to stop a fleet passing them.
—P.H. Colomb

No incident entitled to historical notice marked this cessation of the commerce of Mobile (at the outbreak of war), and from this date until Farragut's attack the port and town passed through three years of closure to marine intercourse, broken only as the low, long, swift ocean racers stole in under the guns of the sentinel fleet, with cargoes of arms, ammunition and stores, and out again with the cotton for which the great mills of Lancashire were waiting.
—J. Thomas Scharf

Well, Johnston, they got me again. You'll have to look out for her now; it is your fight.
—Admiral Franklin Buchanan to Commander J.D. Johnston of the CSS *Tennessee* after being wounded

The battle for Mobile was approaching. Mobile was by far the most important remaining Gulf port available to the Confederacy, and before the war was ranked second in the nation for the cotton trade, behind New Orleans. The Union army would not be taking it from the rear in 1864 due to lack of troops and the defeat of Nathaniel Banks' army in the Red River campaign. The Federal solution was to send Rear-Admiral Farragut with a powerful squadron to pass the forts and enter Mobile Bay. While this would not bring about the immediate surrender of the city of Mobile, it would end her role as a haven for blockade runners.

While the Union army could not help in a large way, it was decided that 1,500 troops could be sent to invest Fort Gaines on Dauphine Island, which was at the head of the harbor. The fleet would have to pass between that fort and the more powerful Fort Morgan, originally built as an old brick and mortar fortification, and maintained today as a national shrine. Then, with the fleet inside and outside of the bay and with an army at the rear of Fort Gaines, the surrender of Gaines and the strengthening of the Union stranglehold on the port would only be a matter of time.

On 3 August 1864 the troops landed and advanced on Fort Gaines. The troops in the fort replied, but all interest slackened on 5 August with the purposeful approach of Farragut's fleet.

The Confederacy had not been idle. Rear-Admiral Franklin Buchanan, who had recovered from his wound received at Hampton Roads, had been promoted to rear-admiral and dispatched to Mobile to command the naval forces there on 19 August 1862. For a man in his sixties, Buchanan was a dynamo of energy. He was in constant touch with the local builders and contractors working on additional ironclads and supplies for his squadron and for the defense of Mobile. (As a footnote, Buchanan's home in Maryland had been burned down in 1863, possibly by arson.)

Mobile had been preparing a defense of her region from the start of the war. She also had recognized early that additions to her naval position would aid in her defense. The first ironclad was a floating battery, the *Danube,* a small 980 ton ship seized in May 1861 and given four 42 pounders, and according to Arthur W. Bergeron Jr., was armored. In December 1861 the *Baltic* was taken in hand for conversion, armoring, the adding of a ram, and the placing of four guns on board. She would prove to be a complete failure and would have her armor removed in 1864 to help supply the building of *Nashville.* Another ironclad floating battery was the *Phoenix,* armed with six guns, but she was never completed. Two very slow (3-4 knot ships, which found it difficult to "stem the tide") and partially armored ironclad steam batteries would also be built, the *Tuscaloosa* and the *Huntsville.* They would finally get their machinery and be completed in the summer of 1863, with six guns planned for each. They received two Brooke 7" rifles, while additional guns supplied to them were two converted-to-rifle 32 pounders, two smoothbore 32 pounders, and two 42 pound smooth-bores; they were missing two additional guns. When later forced to retreat up river in April of 1865 with the fall of the city of Mobile, their engines proved so weak that they could not stem the river flow and were scuttled.

Finally, there were at least two Confederate army floating batteries, one of which was armored on one side with railroad ties and mounting two 10" guns, anchored near the City of Mobile's sea front. One of these was tested by the Confederate gunboat *Selma* that fired its guns at the battery's armor; the shells broke up without damaging the iron. It should be noted that not all of the army floating batteries used in the defense of this region were necessarily armored.

Again, a chronic complaint was lack of armor plate for several projects, which in turn meant fatal delays in the completion of powerful Confederate ironclads. The sidewheel *Nashville,* an ironclad longer than the *Tennessee,* and also armored with 6 inch iron plate, lay incomplete near Mobile at the time of the battle. Selma did send, according to W.W. Stephen, 53 Brooke rifles and large Brooke smooth-bores to Mobile. The type of shot had been improved upon in theory, but, as the letter below by Brooke indicates, the theory could not be put into practice. He wrote on 11 April 1864,

> Urgent applications have been received from generals commanding at Mobile and Wilmington for wrought-iron projectiles, and it is to be regretted that we have not at other establishments machinery adapted to their manufacture.
>
> It has long been considered important that the manufacture of steel projectiles, which are undoubtedly superior to those of wrought iron, should be carried on in the Confederacy, or that at least some of the processes employed abroad in the production of material better suited than simple cast or wrought iron for shot and shell to be employed against ironclads should be adopted, but with the limited amount of skilled labor at command, insufficient to supply the current demand for the ordinary munitions of war, it has not been possible to do so.

So yet again we see the South's technological backwardness and the inefficiency of harnessing all her resources to her war machine as a team dragging her down in her effort to win independence.

But she had accomplished some things. The Selma-built *Tennessee* was 209 feet long, 48 feet wide, with a draft of 14 feet and a ram spur exceeding two feet out from under her prow. She was considered by Alfred Thayer Mahan as "the most powerful ironclad built, from the keel up, by the Confederacy, and both the energy shown in overcoming difficulties and the workmanship put upon her were most creditable to her builders" for an ironclad that saw combat. The casemate was almost 79 feet long. Towed down to Mobile to take on her guns and armor she was armed with two 7" Brooke rifles fore and aft on pivots, and two 6.4" Brooke rifles on either broadside with 6 inches of armor on her forward sloping casemates and 5 inches on the remainder of her casemate with the plates being a combination of 2 inch and 1 inch thick plates (William Still states only 4 inches instead of 5 inches). Her gunport shutters were 5 inches thick. Her yellow pine backing was 25 inches thick. Her skirt at the waterline had 4 inches of armor and projected beyond her casemate, or shield, by ten feet. Her four boilers drove her at a top speed of six knots.

One area of poor design was the steering apparatus that was outside the armored casemate and exposed to enemy fire. Mahan would say of her two grave defects—lack of speed and exposed steering lines—that "she was therefore a ram

The Confederate ironclad Tennessee.

that could only by a favorable chance overtake her prey, and was likely at any moment to lose the power to direct her thrust." Unlike most Confederate ironclads by 1864, she was not armed with a spar torpedo.

With the *Tennessee* were three wooden gunboats with some thin iron plating around their boilers. The *Morgan* was armed with two 7" rifles and four 32 pounder smoothbores. The *Selma* was armed with three 8" shell guns and one old style 32 pounder "clumsily rifled and not reliable for close shooting." The *Gaines* was armed with one 8" shell gun and five 32 pounders. The combined crews of all four ships numbered 470 men. Fort Morgan had 640 troops garrisoning it, while Fort Gaines had 864 officers and men.

Fort Morgan was the main land adversary to the Union fleet and had between 45 and 60 guns in total (sources vary). The following guns could bear on the passing Federals:

7	X" Rodmans
3	8" shell guns
2	8" Blakely rifles
2	7" Brooke rifles
4	6.4" Brooke rifles
32	32 pounder smoothbore

Also present were sharpshooters. Twenty-seven more guns were placed in exterior batteries including a sea-facing "water battery" that contained four X" Rodmans, one 8" rifle, and two rifled 32 pounders and four 24 pounder smoothbores that had been rifled. Fort Gaines, which had little effect on the battle, housed three X" Rodmans, four 32 pounder rifles, and some smoothbore 32, 24, or even 18 pounders.

The other ironclads at the time of the battle were in various states of completion or condition. The *Baltic* was having her armor removed and was in the process of becoming a wooden gunboat. The *Tuscaloosa* and *Huntsville*, due to their slow speed, were not sent down to the harbor entrance to do battle with the Union fleet. They were considered to be less warships and more armored steam batteries due to their weak engines. Additionally, with only 4 inches of armor plate they would have been vulnerable to the Union's larger Dahlgrens.

Before the battle there had been one other incident of note. With the *Tennessee* being completed in May 1864, Buchanan considered taking the naval war to the enemy. When the *Tennessee* came down, she had to be first floated over a bar near the city of Mobile. He planned to load her quickly with coal and ammunition, attack the wooden blockading squadron that morning before the Union was aware of her presence, and then proceed on to Fort Pickens at Pensacola. He planned to use the *Baltic,* as well as three wooden steam gunboats in his attack. On 18 May he tried to put this daring plan into effect, but delays in getting the *Tennessee* over the bar and loaded with stores, as well as running aground, kept her from her raid. The nine blockading ships learned of the presence of the *Tennessee* and surprise was lost. After 21 May, between 13 to 18 blockaders were kept off the entrance to Mobile until the battle, and by 20 July 1864 the first Union ironclad, the *Manhattan,* arrived. The *Baltic* was shortly thereafter sent back to the City of Mobile to have her armor used for the *Nashville.*

Could Buchanan have succeeded in a dash against Pensacola?

Possibly. The guns at Fort Pickens were few and old for the most part, and Buchanan would at this stage have contended only with wooden ships, but plenty of them. Most likely, if resolutely led, the Union ships would have pounded the *Tennessee* into submission, but it was probably worth the attempt instead of waiting for the Union to mass several ironclads for their move at leisure against Mobile. It does point out the fact that while many authors comment or assume that neither the monitor design nor the Confederate casemated ships were considered "sea-going," they were capable of going to sea in calm or moderate waters. That their ability to survive in rough seas, a gale, or a hurricane was limited is another matter. It points out yet again that if the Confederacy had assigned a larger portion of their war effort to building ironclads quickly and early in the war, and had been more aggressive with the ones they built, they might have secured control of the waters off some of their major ports. We feel that this possible course of action and its potential repercussions are not fully appreciated by some writers on the American Civil War. Open seaports allowing free access to trade, even if temporary, thus encouraging foreign intervention on the side of the Confederacy, as well as the possible outright defeat of a portion of the Union fleet, would have adversely affected the Union will and ability to win ultimate victory. In turn, it would have been more likely that the Confederacy would have achieved her goal of independence.

Rear-Admiral Farragut was off for Mobile by early 1864 and wrote to the Navy Department that "without iron-clads, we should not be able to fight" the *Tennessee* and the completing *Nashville.* If forced to employ just wooden warships he would have to get "within one hundred or two hundred yards, so as to ram them or pour in a broadside." Four ironclads, in due course, were dispatched to Farragut, the first, the *Manhattan,* arriving on 18 July, and the *Tecumseh,* arriving on the day before the battle.

Farragut had recognized the importance of Mobile early on. As early as 8 July 1862 he had written to Gideon Welles of his desire to take Mobile "after Vicksburg falls" which, of course, delayed his project. But now the project was moving forward.

In preparing for the battle, the Union fleet had regularly visited Pensacola. The sail area of the warships had been reduced, with topsails and several spars being landed. Steam was recognized as the main motive power. Farragut did not want portions of masts to fall in battle and block the guns. He also ordered that the ships be protected by what other means were available. "On the outside of each vessel, in the wake of her engines and boilers, chain cables were ranged fore and aft, and inside, sand bags were placed, from stem to stern, and from the berth to the spar deck; and, in short, every contrivance that Yankee ingenuity could suggest was resorted to for the protection of the vessels and their crews from shot and shell, from splinters and falling spars."

In passing the forts, Farragut used steam warships. What he also did was reminiscent of the Allied fleet at Sevastopol on 17 October 1854, and a tactic he had first employed when passing Port Hudson in March of 1863. At Sevastopol the Allied fleet was sail, paddle, and screw, so the Allied admirals arranged to have many of their ship-of-the-lines lashed next to a small screw or paddle warship. So for example, the 120 gun sailing ship-of-the-line *Britannia* had as an escort the 16 gun paddlewheel warship *Furious,* or the 120 gun French *Friedland* with the 20 gun steam warship *Vauban.* This allowed for the Allied ships to have some assured capability of movement while undertaking the dangerous bombardment of Sevastopol.

At Mobile the Union wooden fleet was arranged with small ships on the outboard sides, nearest to distant Fort Gaines, while the larger wooden ships were closest to Fort Morgan. The old ironclad *Galena* was present, lashed to the unlucky *Oneida.* However the *Galena's* armor had been removed and she was now a sloop of war. Many of the small boats were either landed or towed in the water on the lee side of the ships away from Fort Morgan except for the "little *Loyall,* the admiral's steam barge, which, with its saucy howitzer in the bows, was making its way into rebeldom unaided." (The *Loyall* is sometimes given as the *Loyal* but was named for Farragut's son.) Farragut's plan called for releasing the smaller warships after passing the forts to pursue and capture, or destroy, the wooden Confederate warships.

Leading the wooden warships was the *Brooklyn* because she could fire four guns ahead (known as chase guns), and had an attached apparatus for sweeping the torpedoes. Farragut had originally wanted to lead the line, instead of taking the

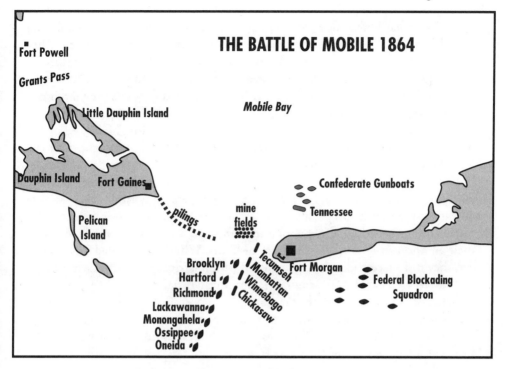

THE BATTLE OF MOBILE 1864

Fort Powell

Grants Pass

Little Dauphin Island

Mobile Bay

Dauphin Island   Fort Gaines

Pelican
Island

pilings

mine
fields

Confederate Gunboats

Tennessee

Tecumseh
Manhattan
Winnebago
Chickasaw

Fort Morgan

Federal Blockading
Squadron

Brooklyn
Hartford
Richmond
Lackawanna
Monongahela
Ossippee
Oneida

second position back, but was persuaded by his captains to let the *Brooklyn* lead as, Farragut later wrote, "they urged it upon me because, in their judgment, the flag-ship ought not to be too much exposed. This I believe to be an error; for, apart from the fact that exposure is one of the penalties of rank in the navy, it will always be the aim of the enemy to destroy the flag-ship, and such attempt was very persistently made, but Providence did not permit it to be successful." Farragut later thought that by not leading the attacking line, it resulted in the fleet remaining under the fort's guns for an additional 30 minutes.

The *Hartford* was once again Farragut's flagship. It is interesting to note that using steam alone this "modern" sloop could run at only eight knots, while under sail and steam she could manage a slow 11 knots' speed. She carried for this action 18 IX" Dahlgrens, two 100 Parrott rifles, and one 32 pounder Parrott. The largest and best ships were at the head of the line with the four monitors arranged in a separate line parallel to and closer to Fort Morgan.

Farragut insisted upon having the guns of his fleet traverse as much as possible forward to bring fire on the enemy as soon as possible. One story has an officer in charge complaining that " ... if it's fired in that position, it's liable to blow away the main chains." Farragut replied, "Well, blow them away, then! Any way to get a shot in first thing!"

The wooden Union fleet was kept as far from Fort Morgan as possible and would actually sail outside the channel and over the line of torpedoes. This, naturally, made firing from Fort Morgan less accurate as the range increased.

The passage to be used by the Federal fleet was determined by watching the blockade runners enter the harbor. One had run in that very morning. So it was obvious where obstructions and mines were.

The four monitors were arranged with the *Tecumseh* leading, followed by the *Manhattan, Winnebago,* and the *Chickasaw.* The latter two were light draft (six feet) double turreted monitors built originally for river work. Designed by James B. Eads, they were members of the *Milwaukee* class. They were 220 feet long and 56 feet wide and each turret housed two XI" Dahlgrens, and had four screws, two on each quarter, due to the shallow waters of the Mississippi river country. The turret was protected by 8 inches of armor and had 3 inches of armor protecting their pilothouses; they could steam at nine knots. While not designed for the open sea, they did successfully join Farragut off Mobil, arriving via New Orleans.

The *Tecumseh* and *Manhattan* were improved *Passaics* of the *Canonicus* class. Capable of about eight knots, they carried two XV" Dahlgrens each in a single turret and were much better armored than the two Eads monitors, ... but had a 12' draft. Deck armor was 1.5 inches thick while the turret armor was reduced from the 11 inches in the *Passaic* to 10 inches.

As the fleet approached, Captain Percival Drayton of the flagship *Hartford* ordered his quartermaster to tie Admiral Farragut to the rigging, a position Farragut had taken to better observe the passing of the forts. Farragut was not "lashed" to the ship's rigging, but the piece of lead line being passed from one shroud over his middle and tied to another shroud, almost like a waist belt. Drayton was in part assigned to the *Hartford* due to his experience as former captain of the monitor *Passaic.*

The "morning was a beautiful one, the sea smooth, and the sky unclouded." A light breeze was blowing towards Fort Morgan from the fleet so the fleet's smoke would obscure the enemy's fire. At daybreak the quartermaster of the *Tennessee* came "down the ladder, rousing us up with his gruff voice, saying: 'Admiral, the officer of the deck bids me report that the enemy's fleet is under way.' Jumping up, still half asleep, we came on deck, and sure enough, there was the enemy." By 06:30 the Federal fleet was closing on the forts. The lead monitor *Tecumseh* opened fire with two shots from her turret at the fort at 06:47. She then loaded with steel bolts and held her fire, to be ready to fire on the *Tennessee.*

The *Brooklyn* opened the action for the wooden ships by firing two 100 pounder bow "chasers" at the fort a little past 07:00, with the fort's guns replying at 07:06. The entire mouth of the channel was about 2,000 yards wide opposite Fort Morgan but the obstructions (piles) and a triple line of approximately 180 torpedoes had narrowed this opening considerably to between 400 and 500 yards.

Battle of Mobile Bay.

Nine large electrical mines such as the boiler mines used at Charleston were built or building but none had yet been deployed.

The use of mines at Mobile was almost an afterthought. It was not until one of her local commanders had witnessed the success of this weapon in the Confederate defense of Vicksburg in 1863 that work began in earnest with them at Mobile. But, though started late, eventually they would be strewn throughout the harbor and river systems and by the "war's end, the torpedoes at Mobile had accounted for the sinking of ten enemy vessels."

The *Tennessee* and her small wooden consorts came out from behind the fort at 06:00 and opened fire from a raking position on the advancing Union fleet, with their port batteries bearing when the action became general. The wooden gunboats continued to fall back in front of the *Hartford,* firing into her and the rest of the wooden Union line constantly. Ranges varied from 700 to 1,000 yards, and, as the wooden gunboats fell back, they relied on their stern guns to maintain fire on the Union. Buchanan gave an order to the captain of the *Tennessee* at the start of the battle to "Get under way, Captain Johnston; head for the leading vessel of the enemy, and fight each one as they pass." Buchanan intended that the *Tennessee* steam towards the lead ship, the *Tecumseh,* and ordered the forward 7" pivot gun "not to fire until the vessels are in actual contact." Earlier, now Commander Thomas Catesby ap Roger Jones, who was in charge of the Selma Gun Foundry, had written to Buchanan on 10 May, that in an engagement with monitors, to "aim at the base of their turrets." Jones went on to write to Buchanan that "I rather apprehend you will not be able to catch the wooden vessels. The ironclads you will find tough customers."

The larger Union ships were beginning to silence the fort as they came up with their numerous guns and the use of grape shot and shells that disabled the crews or kept them from their guns. So it was going well for the advancing Federal fleet when disaster struck about 07:40.

The *Tecumseh* had turned to the west past a red buoy and thus *through* the torpedo line to attack the closing *Tennessee* when an explosion was heard and felt. The *Tecumseh* was seen to lurch and almost immediately sink. Of a crew of 112, only three officers and 17 men survived this sudden disaster. She had struck a torpedo that worked. At the time she was slightly to the right of the *Brooklyn* and 300 yards ahead of her.

An often told story is that her captain, Commander Tunis A. Craven (not the same Craven who had commanded the *Brooklyn* at the Battle of New Orleans), met the pilot at the pilot house hatchway at the instant of the explosion. Craven stepped back, and said to the pilot, "After you, pilot." The pilot survived by gaining the turret below and jumping out of a gunport while Craven went down with his ship. An officer on the *Tennessee* wrote later, "she had her bottom blown out by a torpedo and went down like a shot." The *Tecumseh* in her hurry to come to grips with the *Tennessee* had been dramatically sunk "in less than twenty-five seconds after the explosion."

The *Brooklyn* now stalled the advance. She mistook some floating debris ("a row of suspicious-looking buoys was discovered directly under her bows"), apparently empty shell boxes for torpedoes, and reversed engines. When the captain of the *Brooklyn* shouted this warning to Farragut as the *Hartford* came alongside, he roared "Damn the Torpedoes! Jouett, full speed! Four Bells, Captain Drayton!" which in the colorful sea language of that profession means "Charge!" Chester Hearn correctly points out that in the deep sound of battle, it was hard to hear and even harder to recall later exactly what was said or even done. The media of the period may have aided in the creation of this myth. Hearn relates a story by Chief Engineer Thom Williamson who was apparently on deck when Farragut gave the order, "Go ahead!" Williamson asked, "Shall I ring four bells, sir?" Farragut was said to reply, "Four bells, eight bells, sixteen bells—damn it, I don't care how many bells you ring!" Farragut also ordered the rest of the fleet to "close order, " which would have the fleet concentrate in the passing of the forts into the inner bay.

The *Hartford* quickly passed the *Brooklyn* and led the line into Mobile Bay. Men could hear the mines scraping alongside and even the plungers, or trigger springs, going off. Milton F. Perry, who wrote the best study on Confederate mines to date, later stated that "no one knows why (more) mines did not explode, but evidence points to damp powder and frozen trigger springs as the cause." Another possible cause was that marine worms tended to cluster around the firing pins, impairing their action.

Before the battle, Farragut had sent out in "nightly reconnaissances" his flag-lieutenant who had determined where the torpedoes were. Farragut had thought that pushing through them might not be too dangerous as the torpedoes had been in the water quite some time. Now, in the present circumstances of being stalled under the guns of Fort Morgan in his advance, it was worth the gamble to forge through the lines of torpedoes.

The advantage of this advance was that it now brought more guns of the fleet to bear on the fort, the fire of the *Richmond* being particularly telling at a range varying between 300 and 150 yards. As Farragut later wrote, "from the moment I turned to the northwestward to clear the Middle Ground we were enabled to keep such a broadside fire upon the batteries at Fort Morgan that their guns did us comparatively little injury." The monitors, steaming slowly as in response to their orders to cover the wooden ships, stood near the fort to help draw fire and maintain fire on the fort as the wooden fleet passed within. By now the *Hartford* was in the lead of all the ships and some way ahead and by 08:20 the fleet was past Fort Morgan and the next stage of the battle was to begin.

By the time the rear of the line approached fire had slackened on Fort Morgan and the gunners had returned to their duty. Fire was heavy on the *Ossipee*. On board was the future captain of the battleship *Oregon*, Charles E. Clark (who would make a dramatic run with the *Oregon* from California to Cuba at the time of the Spanish American War). In his autobiography he says that two guns from the port battery were moved to the starboard side to bring more fire to bear on Fort Morgan. Also the *Ossipee's* escort ship, the gunboat *Itasca* began firing in the action on the port side towards Fort Gaines. The captain of the *Ossipee*, Captain LeRoy formerly of the *Keystone State*, called over to the captain of the *Itasca* to ask if his guns could reach Fort Gaines. The captain of the *Itasca* shouted back that "No, but I can add to the smoke and bother Fort Morgan for you."

The most damaged ship that passed the forts was the unlucky ship *Oneida* that had one boiler knocked out. She still had power, but was also assisted past the fort by the lashed *Galena*. Farragut now had his small ships chase the Confederate wooden gunboats. The *Hartford*, being so far out in the lead, by casting loose the *Metacomet* allowed her to get a jump on the chase of the Confederate wooden gunboats. The *Selma* was captured by the *Metacomet* after a short but stiff fight, the *Gaines* was hit below the waterline and shipping water was run ashore and burned near Fort Morgan, while the *Morgan* first escaped under the guns of Fort Morgan and later escaped to Mobile.

The *Morgan's* crew later would burn a stranded Union sidewheeler and former blockade runner, the *Philippi*, that had been abandoned by her crew due to the

CSS Tennessee *engages USS* Hartford *during the Battle of Mobile Bay.*

fire from Fort Morgan. The *Philippi,* a lightly built captured blockade runner, had tried to follow Farragut in after he passed the forts—an act of brave stupidity—and was the only other Union vessel lost that day.

The *Tennessee* had now moved after the *Hartford* in an attempt to ram her. In this she failed, but she fired a 7" forward pivot with a shell directly into the *Hartford* early in the action at a range of 200 yards. It tore a large hole in the *Hartford,* but not where intended. It hit *above* the waterline and not on it. Lieutenant A. D. Wharton, the division captain who personally changed the aim of the gun, and fired it, later wrote "I have often speculated since upon the effect of not having raised the breech of our bow-gun, and thus caused that shell to ricochet before striking the *Hartford.* I wish I had let the captain of the gun fire the piece himself." It might or might not have disabled or sunk the *Hartford,* but it raises once again the aspect of how one small change in fate brought about by the actions of one individual might have changed the course of history. The *Hartford* also "poured her whole port broadside against the ram, but the solid shot merely dented the side and bounded into the air."

The *Tennessee* now turned back towards the approaching remainder of the Union fleet. After exchanging fire with the lead wooden warships it was the turn of the *Monongahela.* She ran at full speed into the *Tennessee* and reported that "I struck her fair, and swinging around poured in a broadside of solid XI" shot which apparently had little effect upon her." The *Tennessee* swung around on the port side of the *Monongahela* with the lashed *Kennebec* alongside and fired into her, wounding five.

Buchanan and the *Tennessee* did well for some time, even if she missed ramming the Union vessels. She had fired broadsides into them that created a great amount of damage and losses. The *Tennessee* at this point of the battle was impervious to the enemy shot while she "… only suffered from the musketry fusillade into (her) ports as their shutters were swung open to allow of the guns being run out." By 0820 the *Hartford* had passed out of range of the forts and enemy ships and was anchored by 0835.

The *Tennessee* now retired under the guns of Fort Morgan to rest her crew with the Union fleet anchoring about four miles away in the bay. It was intensely hot in the *Tennessee* and some of the men ventured out on deck, while the scuttlebutt (water tank) was in great use. After observing the deck and determining that there was not great damage to the *Tennessee* (though her smokestack was riddled—it would be carried away by an XI" from the *Chickasaw* when the *Tennessee* made her second foray), Buchanan was determined to attack again. He was asked by one of his staff officers if he was "going into that fleet, Admiral?" to which he replied, "I am, sir!"

His orders to his captain were straightforward, "Follow them up, Johnston; we can't let them off that way." Buchanan might, with luck, have disabled or sunk some of the Union wooden warships. By attacking he would now have an opportunity to engage the Union ironclads. Finally, he might win through and gain Mobile, and from there carry on the defense of the city.

As the *Tennessee* began her advance at about 08:45, Farragut cut short the breakfast being served to his crews and ordered all ships to attack with the ram and with their heavy guns and at 08:55 signaled "Rebel ram coming up the bay toward us." Of the *Tennessee*'s attempted approach to ram the Federal ships, Farragut later wrote "In this engagement the *Tennessee* ran at our entire line of fourteen vessels, and yet never succeeded in striking one, but, on contrary, she was herself struck in succession by the *Monongahela*, the *Lackawanna*, the *Hartford*, and the *Ossipee*. All the injuries she inflicted were with her guns. As a ram she did us no harm whatever." This was due to her low speed and the inherent difficulty in ramming a ship that is underway.

As the *Tennessee* advanced, "the fleet closed in around her and in ten minutes time she was the center of an irregular circle, the periphery of which consisted of the hostile ships, she firing as rapidly as her guns could be handled, while on each side and for and aft she was pounded with shot and shell." At this point of the battle the *Monongahela* and then the *Lackawanna* rammed the *Tennessee* at an angle, causing some minor leaks. The *Monongahela* actually spun the *Tennessee* in her course, but the only substantial damage was the loss of the *Monongahela*'s own iron prow.

When the *Lackawanna* ran alongside the *Tennessee* after ramming her, Captain John B. Marchand wrote in his report,

> In running against the *Tennessee* we did her no perceptible injury except demoralizing the crew but our stem was cut and crushed far back of the plank ends. All the time I was standing on the bridge, and while alongside, looking into the ports of the *Tennessee,* one of the crew looking out, but standing at a distance from the port, hallooed out to me, 'You damned Yankee son of a bitch' which, being heard by the crew of the *Lackawanna,* redoubled their discharges of small arms into the rebel ports, and as some of them had not small arms in their possession, one of them threw a spitbox and another a hand holystone at the fellow.

Additionally, one of the *Tennessee's* shutters was smashed by a shot from the *Lackawanna.*

The *Hartford* also struck a slight blow, in part because the *Tennessee* sheered off at the last moment as they were both heading to ram bow on. Captain Drayton is reputed at this sheering off the *Tennessee* to have run forward to see if they were about to ram each other and shouted, "The cowardly rascal; he's afraid of a wooden ship!" This may have been discretion instead of a lack of valor, for if the two bows had met, the *Tennessee* might have plunged so deeply in that she might have been unable to extract her ram. There was no lack of bravery on either side on this day.

As the two flagships slid by each other, the *Tennessee* got off only one shell. Powder burns from the flash blackened the *Hartford's* side, while the *Hartford's* broadside merely bounced off the ironclad. "As the *Tennessee* left the *Hartford* she became the target of the entire fleet, and at last concentration of solid shot from so many guns began to tell." Shortly after that the *Hartford* and *Lackawanna* were steaming after the *Tennessee* when the two Union ships collided. The *Hartford* was damaged aloft from the collision, and suffered the "dismounting of two guns and raising the devil generally."

It was now that the Union ironclads entered the fray. They approached the *Tennessee* and began firing at her. Most of their shot was no more effective against the *Tennessee's* armor than the wooden warships were, but one shot was effective.

Commander J.W.A Nicholson in the *Manhattan,* using 60 pound charges, on three shots, hit the *Tennessee,* the only shots of the 53 hits that caused significant damage. One "had penetrated so far as to cause splinters to fly inboard, and the washers over the ends of the bolts wounded several men." The other two hits also caused splinters within the interior of the *Tennessee* but did not penetrate. The only gunnery success in this battle was with the heaviest charges. The history of the XV" Dalghren is one with essentially no failures—they later were used with 100 pound charges. The *Manhattan* could only fire one gun as the other had been disabled early in the action due to a gunnery vent accident.

Lieutenant Wharton had seen the approach of the *Manhattan* and later wrote,

The *Monongahela* was hardly clear of us when a hideous looking monster came creeping up on our port side, whose slowly revolving turret revealed the cavernous depths of a mammoth gun. "Stand clear of the port side!" I shouted. A moment later, a thundering report shook us all, while a blast of dense, sulphurous smoke covered our port-holes, and 440 pounds of iron, impelled by 60 pounds of powder, admitted daylight through our side where, before it struck us, there had been over two feet of solid wood, covered with five inches of solid iron. This was the only XV-inch shot that hit us fair. It did not come through; the inside netting caught the splinters, and there were no casualties from it. I was glad to find myself alive after that shot.

The *Chickasaw* had stayed on the *Tennessee's* stern firing away with her XI" Dahlgrens from her forward turret when one of her shots wounded Buchanan. What had occurred is this. One of the *Tennessee's* port shutters was stuck and four men were effecting repairs when a shot hit the shield and the concussion killed two of the men (one of whom had to be cleared up by having "the remains ... shoveled into buckets"), and a fragment of iron "fractured the large bone of the leg" of Buchanan.

The Confederate crew was so busy fighting that word was taken to the surgeon but he had to go up on the gun deck, locate the admiral by himself, and determine his condition. The surgeon asked, "Admiral, are you badly hurt?" Buchanan answered, "Don't know." He recovered from his wound and did not lose his leg.

The *Chickasaw* fired 52 XI" solid shot and Captain Johnston later said of her, "Damn him! he stuck to us like a leech; we could not get away from him. It was he who cut away the steering gear, jammed the stern port shutters, and wounded Admiral Buchanan." After the battle it was noted that many of the armor plates on the stern of the *Tennessee* were loosened around the bolts.

It was now that the fatal flaw in the *Tennessee's* design came home. Her outside wheel chains were disabled and shortly after that she lost all ability to steer. The Union ships took up advantageous positions and poured on their fire for upwards of 30 minutes to which the *Tennessee* could make no effective reply. At about 10:00 hours Johnston went out of the shield, took down the flag, and when the Union continued to fire, he went out again and put up a white flag. The *Ossipee* took possession of her for the fleet. By 10:10 the *Manhattan* had her in tow and the battle was over.

The Union lost 145 dead and 170 wounded, the vast majority on the *Tecumseh*. Buchanan's fleet lost 12 dead and 20 wounded, while Fort Morgan lost but one dead and three wounded. Two died on the *Tennessee* and nine were wounded. Several Union ships had been severely handled, the *Hartford* alone suffering 20 hits, three of which were kept from penetrating by her chain armor. The *Brooklyn* was hit 30 times, while the *Oneida* was nearly sunk. The *Tennessee*, while damaged, could be repaired in good time and was used by the Union navy later that month in a bombardment against Fort Morgan. She was decommissioned in 1865.

The Federal monitors, with the exception of the *Tecumseh,* were only slightly damaged. The *Winnebago* was hit 19 times with three hits inflicting enough damage on her deck (protected by only 1/2 inch of armor) to convince her captain that plunging fire would have damaged or sunk her. The *Chickasaw* was hit 11 times and had her funnel severed (which slowed her considerably; her engine room crew had responded by throwing flammables into her furnaces). One shot penetrated her deck in the area of the bow and started a small fire. She had expended 75 shells on Fort Morgan while the *Tennessee* had been fired on with four steel shot and 48 solid shot. The *Manhattan* was hit nine times and fired a total of 11 times.

Buchanan has been criticized for his second run at the Union fleet. In his defense, he later wrote,

> ... when all the Federal vessels had passed up and anchored four miles away, then I saw that a long siege was intended by the army and navy ... I determined then, having the example before me of the blowing up of the *Merrimac* in the James River by our own officers, without a fight, and by being caught in such a trap, I determined, by an unexpected dash into the fleet, to attack and do it all the damage in my power; to expend all my ammunition and what little coal I had on board, only six hours' steaming, and then, having done all I could with what resources I had, to retire under the guns of the fort, and being without motive power, thus to *lay* and assist in repulsing the attacks and assaults on the fort.

Farragut had stated earlier that if the *Tennessee* had stayed under the guns of Fort Morgan that he would have transferred to the *Manhattan* and attacked her that evening. So if Buchanan had not attacked a second time, he probably would have simply delayed the inevitable. Certainly Fort Morgan was poorly fought, especially in contrast to the defense of Charleston and Wilmington. The Confederate Army was in command of the sea defenses of Mobile—as at other ports, not the Navy.

Bergeron sums up the main reasons why Farragut won. He wrote, the "easy victory came primarily because of weaknesses in several elements of the Confederacy's coastal defense system." Additional ironclads, especially the *Nashville,* would have aided the struggle and the divided command was not a help in the defense of Mobile.

But the battle was over and the cork was in the bottle of the harbor of Mobile. By the end of August all three forts at the harbor entrance would have the Union flag waving over them.

Secretary Mallory later wrote after reviewing the reports on the battle that the enemy broadsides "were discharged upon the *Tennessee* at distances ranging from 3 to 30 yards" and that with the exception of one shot from the *Manhattan,* she resisted the attack well. Mallory felt that the inclined armor was the best arrangement possible for an ironclad and used Farragut's assessment after the action as support. Farragut had reported that "the *Tennessee* is in a state to do good service now." But Mobile was lost as a seaport to the Confederacy and would later be captured in 1865 from the landside.

There was one other Union success with the XV" Dahlgren. That was in a skirmish at Trent's Reach on the James River fought on January 24, 1865. The Confederate James River squadron had come down the river from Richmond and planned to pass the Union obstructions in the river and raid the Federal supply base at City Point on the 23rd.

Unfortunately their largest ironclad, the *Virginia II,* armored with six inches of plate, was stranded, forcing the cancellation of the raid. While waiting for the rising tide, the Confederate squadron came under fire from the shore and the wooden squadron attached to the Confederate ironclads suffered severe damage. As the tide was finally rising, the Union double turreted *Onondaga* arrived and fired on the *Virginia II.*

The *Onondaga* was armed with two XV" Dahlgrens and two 150 pounder rifles. The *Onondaga* was built by G.W. Quintard and was not a true Ericsson monitor. She could steam at seven knots and was 226 feet long. She was returned to the builder at the end of the war and later sold to France and served in the Franco-Prussian War of 1870-71. She was the only Union ironclad present due to the massive naval force that had gathered for the attack against Wilmington.

The *Onondaga* fired but seven times, hitting the *Virginia II* twice. One shot glanced off the *Virginia II,* but the other round hit the *Virginia II* squarely on the port broadside with a XV" shot which knocked "a clear hole through her armor and (crushed her) wood backing and sending a whirl along the gun-deck huge iron fragments and wooden splinters that killed (one and wounded two) of the crew. Luckily she was floated by the rising of the tide and moved out of the range of shot that would pierce any armor then placed on a ship."

Though the Confederate squadron still wanted to engage this lone Union ironclad with spar torpedoes and try "the effect of steel-pointed shot upon her turrets," their later move down the river to attack failed, when Union batteries opened up on the squadron and the pilot lost his nerve. Unable to steer further down the river, the squadron retired, eventually to be destroyed with the fall of Richmond later that year.

So, in the war between armor plate and the gun, by 1864-65 the gun was once again reasserting its strength over the plate—with a caveat. For any powerful gun to obtain its best performance it must be loaded with the best type of shot and must hit at the best possible angle against the armored side. Ideal conditions are seldom found in battle.

THE SAGA OF THE ALBEMARLE

After studying the early coastal campaigns, committees of Confederate engineers and ordnance experts emerged with a radical design for more-or-less standardized shallow-draft armored rams. These vessels would be cumbersome and slow, and they would sacrifice armament in favor of protection—each would carry only a pair of heavy-caliber rifled cannon. The theory was that these hulking ironclads could withstand dozens, maybe hundreds of hits, yet could disable the Yankee gunboats with a few powerful shells and then finish the job with their armored rams.
    —William R. Trotter from *Ironclads and Columbiads*

To check any Union counteroffensive was the Albemarle. While the frightening ironclad remained anchored at Plymouth, no enemy attempt to renew the invasion from the sea could be successful. Behind her iron plates the North Carolina coastal population was rather quiet. Moreover, the Confederate soldiers, engaged in the struggle against an overwhelming enemy on the Virginia Front were sure that no enemy coming from the sounds of Carolina could arrive at their backs.
    —Professor Raimondo Luraghi

While the *Albemarle* was a small inland waters type of ironclad, her battles are included here for their interest in ironclad combat against non-armored enemies and her eventual fate. Additionally, the existence of the shallow draught ironclad *Albemarle* forced the Union to modify operations in the North Carolina Sounds. One must consider what would have been the strategic implications of an 1863 or even 1864 thrust into central North Carolina, destroying the building Confederate ironclads and cutting off the Wilmington supply line to Lee's army in Virginia. Would the entire course of the war have ended faster and with fewer losses? But then the eastern Union army commanders never used sea power as decisively as they did on the Western rivers. McClellan did use it to press close to Richmond in 1862, while Grant, a western bred commander, would use seapower to supply his army during his decisive drive on Richmond and Petersburg.

In 1861-62, the Union had some of her early successes in seizing first Cape Hatteras and later various points, including the small coastal city of New Bern, and the Unionist town of Plymouth. These early losses caused the Confederacy to make a decision to develop a small two gun ironclad ram. Several were laid down at Norfolk, and if completed, could have passed through Dismal Swamp Canal to the North Carolina sounds. With the loss of Norfolk, the next ones would be started at several out of the way locations—hence the term "cornfield ironclad." Five were laid down in the North Carolina sounds, of which the *Albemarle* was the only one to be completed and see action.

One, the *Neuse,* never saw action (presently several pieces of her are on display at a naval museum at Kinston, North Carolina). The *Albemarle* would demonstrate the success of Secretary Mallory's policy of protecting the Confederate coast with small ironclads. The *Albemarle* was a 376 ton, 152 foot long ironclad with an eight foot draft, protected by 4 inches of armor. Each of the two 6.4" Brooke rifles had three gunports with shield coverings. They were pivoted so they could fire forward or aft, respectively, and on either broadside from one of three gunports. Speed varied between four to six knots, depending upon source and local currents.

Completed in 1864, she, along with the *Neuse,* was to be used in conjunction with the army in an attack against the Union fortified garrison at Plymouth and New Bern, North Carolina, as part of an overall plan to recapture the North Carolina sounds. Robert E. Lee detailed Pickett's and Hoke's divisions for use in the winter of 1863-64 for operation there in part due to the absence of any Union ironclads, and the vicinity of the Army of Northern Virginia.

However, neither the *Neuse* nor the *Albemarle* were ready in time. Hoke's division was to try at minimum to capture Plymouth. On 16 April 1864 all was in readiness. Hoke's first attack faltered, in part due to supporting Union gunboat fire, but the *Albemarle,* under Captain C.W. Cooke, was on her way to help.

The *Albemarle* had successfully passed Fort Gray, which had a 100 pounder Parrott rifle especially detailed to try its power against her, and another, Battery Worth, armed with a 200 pounder Parrott rifle, when two Union wooden gunboats came into view, the flagship of Commander C.W. Flusser, the *Miami,* accompanied by the *Southfield.* The *Miami* was a purpose built double-ender sidewheel gunboat, which allowed her to move in either direction without turning, ideal for narrow waters. The *Miami* was 730 tons, 208 feet long, and could make eight knots. She carried six IX", one 100 pounder Parrott rifle, and howitzer, while the converted ferryboat *Southfield* carried five IX", one 100 pounder Parrott rifle, and howitzer. The *Southfield* had been purchased into the service and was almost identical in size to the *Miami.*

Flusser had wind of the *Albemarle's* approach and had devised a plan. He had strung between his two ships rope hawsers (iron chains were unavailable). Early on 19 April, they approached, hoping to entangle the *Albemarle's* propellers in the ropes, disable her, and then pound her into submission. Cooke, spying their approach, ordered full speed, which with a favorable current gave her five knots, and swinging from the river bank, came at the two Union ships at an angle. The Union ships began firing as she approached, but inflicted no damage. Cooke crossed in front and between the two, damaging the port bow of the *Miami* and ramming full into the *Southfield's* starboard bow area, all in about two minutes, making " ... an opening large enough to carry her to the bottom in much less time than it takes to tell the story." Cooke reported that the "prow of the *Albemarle* extended about 10 feet into the sides of the *Southfield.* "

The *Southfield* and *Albemarle* were locked together, with the latter now going full astern. The *Albemarle* actually began to go down with the *Southfield* with water coming in the forward gunport. But when the *Southfield* touched the shallow river bottom, she shifted, freeing the *Albemarle* which bobbed like a cork back to the surface.

Meanwhile the *Miami* was busily firing on the *Albemarle*. Flusser was personally commanding the forward IX" gun crew that fired its third shell "at point blank range of probably about thirty feet" at the *Albemarle*. Striking the casemate, the shell rebounded and when overhead, exploded, a piece of it killing Flusser "by cutting his heart out" and wounding several of the crew.

The fact that rope hawsers had been used and not chains may have saved the *Miami,* as she might have been unable to get away quickly after the *Southfield* sank. The forward ones broke, while the aft ones were cut loose.

Both the *Miami* and *Albemarle* wanted to continue the fight, but after a few minutes of desultory firing, the *Miami* drew off and steamed east, accompanied by two other newly arrived and smaller Union gunboats. The *Albemarle* now proceeded to Plymouth.

Hoke had continued his attack on Plymouth, and now was aided by the *Albemarle* firing shells at the fortifications. By 10:00 on 20 April, the Union garrison had surrendered.

Meanwhile the United States Navy had sent reinforcements and a new commander, Captain Melancton Smith, who had served under Farragut at New Orleans, to rid the sounds of this new gray menace. Smith had been given special orders on dealing with the *Albemarle* from Acting Rear-Admiral S.P. Lee, commander of the North Atlantic Blockading Squadron. Lee ordered Smith to fire at the gunports and load his guns with "heavy charges ... and solid shot—and they should be so depressed as to fire as near a perpendicular line to the slope of the roof as practicable." A close ranged action with ramming was also recommended. Lee hoped that heavy gunfire would loosen the plates on the *Albemarle*. (This latter hope, to rack the enemy with repeated hits from large caliber shot, as opposed to penetrating shot, was a theory common to this period that simply did not play out in reality.)

Smith raised his flag on the double-ended gunboat *Mattabesett.* He decided, on 2 May, to advance in two columns on the *Albemarle* and issued his orders. The first, or right, column was led by the flagship, followed by the *Sassacus, Wyalusing,* and *Whitehead.* The *Miami,* now armed with a spar torpedo, led the second column, followed by the *Ceres, Commodore Hull,* and *Seymour.* Also included in the attack against the *Albemarle* was a fish seine to entangle the screws of the Confederate ironclad. While used in the ensuing action, it did not work.

The right hand column consisted of three sisterships—gunboats built for war. They displaced 1173 tons and had a mixed main armament of IX" Dahlgrens and 100 pounder rifled Parrotts. The *Miami* was the next largest warship, while the remaining craft were minor warships—the *Seymour* being but a tender.

On 5 May, the *Albemarle* was sighted approaching with two small wooden consorts. She was on her way to New Bern to help General Hoke in an attempt against that Union held town. One of the wooden consorts, the *Cotton Plant,* carried troops, while the small and lightly armed *Bombshell* was carrying supplies. The Union fleet quickly attacked and at 16:40 the *Albemarle* fired the first shot—which destroyed the flagship's launch.

The two Confederate wooden vessels were ordered to retire, and the *Cotton Plant* did. But the brave and foolish *Bombshell,* lightly armed with four small guns, decided to join the fray—or for some unknown reason did not immediately flee.

The Union ships tried to run by the *Albemarle,* though it was clearly a crowded field in those narrow waters. The *Albemarle* lost the end of her aft Brooke rifle from one enemy shot (it was later hit a second time). By then, not even 17:00, the three large Union gunboats had the *Albemarle* surrounded and were firing away at her. The smoke grew dense, both outside and inside the small ironclad's casemate.

The *Sassacus* looped off and, being peppered by the *Bombshell,* brought her under fire. The *Bombshell* was forced to surrender after three hits. With this accomplished, the captain, Commander Francis A. Roe, of the *Sassacus* saw that he had a clear run on the *Albemarle* and so ordered full speed. He gained speed as he approached and rammed the *Albemarle.* Roe wrote later that when he hit, the *Sassacus* was making "9 or 10 knots." Just before he struck the rear half of the *Albemarle,* where her casemate joined the deck, the *Albemarle* fired her damaged 6.4" point blank into the *Sassacus.* That shot passed clear through the *Sassacus,* going out the port side but doing little actual damage.

Nor did the ramming, at first, as Confederate ironclads were built with an iron knuckle around the edge of the ship at the waterline. The *Sassacus,* when she hit, rode almost on top of the knuckle and the *Albemarle* deck—she could not go *through* the knuckle. The bow of the *Sassacus* was damaged, as the knuckle "had sliced into the *Sassacus's* bow like a huge knife." It did force water into the *Albemarle's* aft broadside gunport, knocked Cooke to the ground, when Roe, rather smartly, kept the *Sassacus* driving forward with her engines, for up to "ten minutes," trying to force the *Albemarle* under.

Cooke maintained the forward movement of the *Albemarle.* Rifle and grenade fire between the two locked antagonists was heavy throughout. Roe attempted to throw charges of gunpowder down the stack of the *Albemarle.* Roe also managed

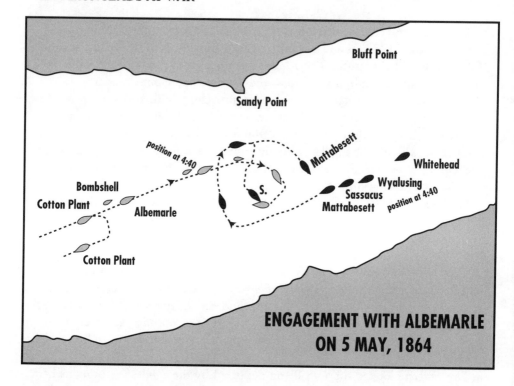

**ENGAGEMENT WITH ALBEMARLE
ON 5 MAY, 1864**

in the action to fire the 100 pounder Parrott rifles with solid shot at the *Albemarle* and they "flew into splinters upon her iron plates."

Finally Cooke freed the two vessels by taking advantage of the turning of the two locked warships and shifting his rudder in the opposite direction. As the two vessels swung parallel, he ordered the forward gun to be fired into the *Sassacus* which burst the boiler, scalding "all the men in the fire room, killing one coal handler instantly" and putting the *Sassacus* out of action. Cooke gathered about 25 men together for an attempted boarding action, but was frustrated in this effort due to Roe's perception of the situation and his ability to gather a larger defensive boarding party.

The *Sassacus* tried to withdraw slowly from the action, under fire from the *Albemarle* throughout. As she did so, other Union ships brought the *Albemarle* again under fire, having no fear of hitting the *Sassacus*. Inside the poorly ventilated oven-like casemate, smoke swirled and mixed with the heat, stench, sweat, and smells of sixty men, as they listened to shot and shell hitting their iron shield from all directions.

The *Miami* then attempted to place her spar torpedo under the *Albemarle* but failed to maneuver close enough. The captain of the *Miami* later wrote that "I used every endeavor to get at her, bow on, but the *Miami* proving herself so

The Sassacus *ramming the* Albemarle.

unwieldy and so very bad to steer, the enemy (who was probably well aware of my purpose) succeeded in keeping clear of us by going ahead and backing and turning." Under fire from the *Albemarle,* she had her rudder disabled by one shot.

By now it was nearing 18:00 and the firing on the *Albemarle* continued heavy. The concussion of shot and shell hits had "every man on board (bleeding) from the ears and nose." It was shortly after that Cooke ordered the *Albemarle* to retire. His smokestack was riddled and he was running out of coal, which meant his speed was beginning to drop. Wood from the interior of the ship was thrown into the furnaces, but air draft to fan the flames was almost nil. It was at this point that someone thought to throw bacon, ham and lard into the fires, and quickly there was a "blistering fire" and the *Albemarle* could steam for home. By 19:30 the action was over. One of the crew later wrote that "She was very hot inside. The men were nearly exhausted. She could not have held out an hour longer."

The *Albemarle* had fired 27 times in the action, and suffered no substantial damage—though she had lost five of her six gunport shutters—a common problem with Confederate ironclads. With 60 guns, the Union had fired 557 times and hit her 44 times. While the Union squadron had failed to capture or destroy the *Albemarle,* they had stopped her in her attempt to join with Hoke against New Bern, and had captured the little *Bombshell.* Hoke was shortly after shifted back to Virginia, while the *Albemarle* was detailed to defend Plymouth.

Cooke had to give up command due to his health in late June, and while stationed at Plymouth, was relieved by two commanders in succession, the third and final being Lieutenant Alexander F. Warley, formerly of the *Manassas.* As the

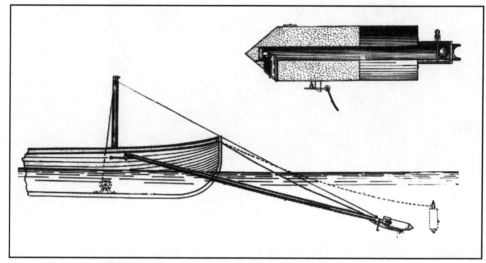

Cushing's launch and sideview of spar torpedo showing methods of working.

summer drifted into fall, the Union devised a plan to sink this troublesome little Confederate ironclad.

Union Lieutenant William B. Cushing was one of those dashing types who do poorly in peacetime but in wartime are indispensable. He had already led several daring raids in and around North Carolina and suggested a night attack with a steam launch armed with a spar torpedo.

Earlier, in April of 1864, the flagship of the North Atlantic Blockading Squadron, the *Minnesota,* had been attacked by the Confederate small steam launch *Squib,* armed with a spar torpedo. In a daring raid down the James River, the *Squib* had exploded its spar torpedo and inflicted some minor damage to Lee's flagship in a form of attack well known to the forces in this theater.

On the night of 27 October, Cushing moved quietly up river towards the *Albemarle* with his launch, accompanied by a small boat with armed men, a total of 28 volunteers. Carefully, he passed the wreck of the *Southfield* that was used from time to time as a Confederate sentry post. The Confederates had earlier learned of the presence of Cushing's launch and her armament and were on the lookout for her, but failed to adequately prepare for her attempt on the *Albemarle.*

Approaching the *Albemarle,* Cushing considered boarding and capturing her, but the barking dog of a dozing sentry on duty alerted the Confederates. He ordered the accompanying boat to retire and capture the enemy picket on the *Southfield.* The enemy on the *Albemarle* were quickly roused and several on the shore and the ship sighted Cushing's launch and the boat.

Cushing's men came under small arms fire, and Cushing, after firing a small boat howitzer to sweep the enemy in front of him as he approached, had his coat and shoe hit with rifle fire. As Cushing later said, "the enemy's fire was very severe, but a dose of canister, at short range, served to moderate their zeal and disturb their aim." Standing at the bow of the little launch, he drew up to the log boom protecting the *Albemarle*. Cushing then, while hearing the gun crew of one of the Brooke rifles preparing a blast of grapeshot, steadily worked the spar torpedo apparatus that required both hands. Finally it was in place and Cushing pulled the triggering device. As Elliot has written, "Two dreadful explosions occurred together. An immense wave of water erupted from beneath the hull engulfing the launch as it descended. Simultaneously Brooke's blast slammed everyone in the launch, though the grape passed just over their heads. The flame and hot air belching from the muzzle may have accounted for injuries to some of Cushing's men. The launch was flattened, swamped with water, and the crew devastated."

The *Albemarle* quickly sank with a hole "in her bottom big enough to drive a wagon in." She was quickly on the bottom and the South's last effective threat in these waters had vanished in the explosion of the torpedo.

Cushing would escape back to the Union squadron, alone of all the men in the launch, to be hailed a hero—Lincoln's commando.

FORT FISHER

The new fleet that assembled off the fort had the greatest firepower to that time in United States naval history, 627 guns in over sixty vessels.
—Professor Robert M. Browning, Jr.

The actions which closed these individual Confederate ports seldom receive more than a few sentences even in detailed histories of the war, yet while each might have seemed of only minor importance, the cumulative effect was strangulation.
—Jac Weller

The city of Wilmington was the busiest port for blockade running in the second half of the war, until it was closed by the Union assault on Fort Fisher in 1865. It was a difficult harbor to blockade. To give one a sense of its value, it meant that North Carolina troops, in part due to the fact that North Carolina's government ran state owned blockade runners, as well as the materials that flowed through that port, were the best equipped troops in the Confederacy.

The story of Confederate ironclads at Wilmington is a short and sad story. One, the *North Carolina*, because of her poor machinery, was used as a floating battery when completed in the spring of 1864. She was so full of rot from the beginning that worms ate her bottom out and she sank at her moorings in September of 1864. The *Raleigh*, a sister ship, had a complement of 188 men, was 150 feet long, armed with four 6" rifles, armored with 4 inches of iron with 22 inches of wood backing, and with a planned speed of six knots, but she was known to be "very slow." She was commissioned on 30 April 1864 under command of First Lieutenant Pembroke Jones, who had served under Captain Tattnall during the attack on Fort Pulaski near Savannah.

On 6 May 1864 the *Raleigh* sortied with a 64 ton torpedoboat, the *Equator,* and a small 300 ton gunboat, the *Yadkin.* This was at the time of the planned Confederate attack on New Bern, North Carolina, which began on the 5th. The *Raleigh* first moved down to the head of the bay in preparation to cross the bar and enter the open sea off Wilmington. She was observed by the Union gunboat *Mount Vernon,* but was ignored by her captain and no alarm was raised. At between 19:50 and 20:00, near sunset, the *Raleigh* headed out to sea, followed by her two consorts. The *Raleigh* was sighted by the converted merchant ship *Britannia,* which was armed with one 30 pounder Parrott rifle, two 12 pounder rifles, and two 24 pounder howitzers. This 12 knot sidewheeler set off signal flares and fired her large Parrott rifle, missing the *Raleigh.* The *Raleigh* then fired several rounds at about 600 yards range at the *Britannia,* and while close with two shots, missed with all. The *Britannia* turned, changing course three times, and moved away from the harbor entrance but closer to shore where she knew the deep draft *Raleigh* could not follow. However, apparently, the *Britannia* was still somewhat unsure of whom she fired on. The *Raleigh* gave chase but quickly lost her.

The *Raleigh* searched to the northeast until 23:45 when she encountered the 10 knot sidewheeler *Nansemond* (the *Britannia* and *Nansemond,* both credited with short bursts of higher speed, were built in 1862). She was armed with two 24 pounder howitzers and probably a 30 pounder Parrott rifle. The *Raleigh* charged the *Nansemond* and fired at 500 yards range, with no effect.

At daylight the entire wooden Federal fleet advanced and fired long range at the *Raleigh* which attempted to cross back into the harbor. While steaming in she grounded on the bar and with the fall of the tide "she broke her back." What could be salvaged was.

An important point here is that some authors have argued that the best role for the Confederate ironclads at Wilmington, Charleston, and Mobile, was to act as defensive gunboats in the harbors. This is probably a correct, albeit unromantic, view of their use because of their slow speed. Off Wilmington in September 1864, of the Union fleet of 26 ships, eight could steam at 12 knots or more, and were constantly getting maintenance at Norfolk in the late part of the war. A Confederate ironclad moving at four, five, or six knots, was simply inadequate for sinking ships, though they could chase them off. The need for speed on the part of the Union fleet was related to the need to catch the fast blockade runners, not engage the slow Confederate ironclads.

Rear-Admiral David "Black Dave" Porter, who would command the attempt against Wilmington, commented on the role of blockaders and blockade runners in his journal that "It was very much like a parcel of cats watching a big rat hole: the rat often running in when they are expecting him to run out and vice-versa. The advantage was all on the side of the blockade runners. They could always choose their time." The blockaders would maintain an outer ring of fast ships(12+ knot ships, often captured blockade runners) to chase down the blockade runners. They never could be sure when they approached an unknown ship, if it were friendly, a blockade runner, a ship like the Confederate raider CSS *Alabama* that captured the US gunboat *Hatteras* off Galveston, or if it were some other well-armed Confederate naval vessel. The blockaders "kept their guns ready for use on Confederate naval vessels and employed sharpshooters for the enemy's officers, captains, helmsmen, and loaders of guns."

One of the unusual artillery defenses developed by the South at Wilmington was the use of a "flying battery" of 2.75" British built rifles. They would be sent to an area needing help, usually near a grounded blockade runner that was being unloaded. Their long range fire discouraged closer Union attention. One Union wag wrote that they "carried a sting that discouraged close acquaintance."

Several plans were advanced for the capture of Wilmington earlier in the war, and the *Monitor*'s voyage south when she was lost off Cape Hatteras in a storm was so she could have been used in an assault on the port.

Wilmington had over 100 guns deployed in the defensive positions, the "Malakoff of the South," a reference to a strong Russian position during the Crimean War at Sevastopol. There was an 8" Blakely rifle and a 150 pound Armstrong rifle and at Fort Fisher they were particularly effective. The sea face of Fort Fisher was approximately 1300 yards long and mounted 24 heavy guns, while the spit side wall mounted 20 heavy guns on a face of 500 yards. At the opposite end was a 60 foot high mound battery with two heavy guns that could send plunging fire into any Union ship attempting to run into the harbor. Still, Hobart Pasha had run into Wilmington on one of his blockade running operations late in the war and had commented on the fortifications that,

> We were much struck with the weakness of Fort Fisher, which, with a garrison of twelve hundred men, and only half finished, could have been easily taken at any time since the war began by a resolute ... night attack. It is true that at the time of its capture it was somewhat stronger than at the time I visited it, but even then its garrison was comparatively small, and its defences unfinished.

The initial assault was made at 01:40 on 24 December 1864 and was opened with the exploding of a 295 ton steamer, the *Louisiana*, loaded with 215 tons of gunpowder, 500 yards from Fort Fisher. High hopes were placed in this device, hopes that it would level the fortifications and stun the garrison into submission, but when it went off it was little more than a large boiler explosion on a warship at sea wakening the Confederate garrison from their slumber. The notorious Federal Army General Ben Butler, commanding the army, and Admiral Porter both expected great results from the explosion.

Porter then moved over fifty warships that morning into position and opened a bombardment. The *New Ironsides* led the attack to within a mile of Fort Fisher, supported by the monitors *Canonicus, Monadnock,* and *Mahopac.* The first and the third were improved *Passaic* class monitors, being slightly longer and with a higher speed. Known as "Harbor and River Monitors," they were armed with two 15" guns, had 10 inch armor placed on their turrets, and were probably the first United States warships with bunks for the crew. Also present was the twin turreted *Monadnock.*

The accuracy of the attack was poor, with much overshooting of the fortifications (apparently the fort's flag was used as a mark instead of the emplacements resulting in overshooting). The Confederacy reserved its fire, largely due to ammunition shortages, so fired irregularly, giving the Union the impression that their fire was destroying the Confederate positions.

Fort Fisher fired only 672 shots that day, while the Union rained 115 to 180 shot and shell *a minute* on the fort. It caused Colonel William Lamb, the Confederate commander to remark that "Never, since the invention of gunpowder, was there so much harmlessly expended, as in the first day's attack on Fort Fisher." Butler arrived late with his troops so it would be the next day, Christmas, for the army to make its attempt.

The bombardment that day kept the Confederacy in their bombproofs, while 2,300 troops landed. Butler examined the fort's wall he was supposed to attack and announced that the naval bombardment had failed, which it had, and so withdrew his troops at the end of the day back on board the transports. During the fighting the fort had fired 1272 shot and shell and had suffered three dead and 61 wounded. Five guns had been disabled, two of those from bursting while firing. The fleet had fired 21,000 shot and shell and used one million pounds of powder and lost about 69 dead and wounded on board.

The final battle for Wilmington started on 12 January. Major General Braxton Bragg had arrived to relieve the Confederate area commander, Major General Whiting, who then joined Colonel Lamb at the fort. Bragg would end his military career here in a particularly unspectacular manner, sending no reinforcements to Fort Fisher and beginning the evacuation of Wilmington too early. In his defense, it should be noted that Sherman was advancing through South Carolina and preparing for a move north into North Carolina, which Bragg could not defend against. Still, with this being the last major port supplying the eastern Confederate armies, and blockade runners passing in right up to the fall of Fort Fisher, the fight should have been carried on more vigorously.

Butler also was gone.

The second attack began on 13 January 1864 with the army now under the command of the capable Major General Alfred E. Terry. The second attack had three major differences: it was in greater force, Porter had gunfire concentrated on the fort walls so as to be more effective, and finally, the gunboats maintained fire on the fort on the night of the 13th-14th so that repairs could not be made by the garrison.

The Confederates again replied with "slow and deliberate firing." Terry landed about 8,000 troops on 14 January. In a day and night of fighting, much of it hand to hand, and with the fleet supporting the advance of the army with a brigade of marines and seamen, as well as with support fire from the guns of the fleet, the Union force slowly moved forward. Whiting and Lamb were both wounded in the fighting, and Bragg sent no reinforcements to the fort and did not lead an attack, nor a creditable feint on the rear of the Union forces from the defense lines of Wilmington.

"This well-executed and well-coordinated amphibious assault was a great stroke for the Union." The price tag was not too high either, this final assault had cost 1,000 Union soldiers, and the Navy suffered 400 killed and wounded. The warships in the two assaults had fired over 50,000 shells into the fort and had suffered little in the way of damage.

Not only was the last main port captured, which effectively ended the supply of Lee's army from outside of the ever shrinking Confederate controlled territory, but Sherman's army now had another port to supply its advance. By the New Year, Sherman had captured Savannah and was moving north, forcing the evacuation of Charleston.

THE END OF THE FIRST MODERN WAR

The South might have solved some of its most crucial transportation problems had the blockade never been implemented. The South would have enjoyed the luxury of importing rails, locomotives, iron, manufacturing equipment, and marine engines. The South instead had to choose between the manufacture of naval ironclads or an expansion of its railroads.
—Robert M. Browning, Jr.

Gideon Welles must be given credit for creating a powerful steam navy in the course of the war, and the Union Navy was clearly a decisive factor in the victory of the North. Yet at least one scholar of the war states that steam navies were largely untried at this time, which we have clearly shown as not true. The use of steam, as of ironclads, in the Crimean War (as well as their general use) was widespread *before* the American Civil War.

The Union steam navy allowed for speedy vessels to chase and capture blockade runners. It also allowed for decisive movements on the extensive river systems of the South, supplying Union armies and giving them the ability to move and withdraw when needed. Another overlooked factor was that Union control of waterways forced the Confederacy to rely even more on their deteriorating and limited railroad facilities—and the Union could and did cut off those rail lines at key river crossings and towns.

Ivan Musicant, in his recent *Troubled Waters,* argues that "by the end of the Civil War, the U.S. Navy had become arguably the most powerful sea force in the world, with a total of 670 ships led by an impressive fleet of turreted, ironclad monitors ... ." When one considers that Great Britain in 1859 had *more* than 700 ships in her navy, virtually entirely built for war from keel up, compared to Union ships which were converted from civilian use, and that British ironclads were, for the most part, seagoing and designed for sea warfare—and not for coastal operations—one begins to see how ethnocentric many American histories are. Clearly, the British, and possibly the French, were more powerful in this time period.

Professor Luraghi has recently argued that the South's navy never was crushed in spirit and that up to the end it was still contending against the Union. Also, in the course of the war, the navy often covered the "back door" for the Confederate armies. With these two points we agree.

However, his contention that only one of the South's six main ports was taken from the sea, we think, is bending and twisting reality. For example, yes, the City of Mobile was captured in 1865 by the Union *army,* but with Farragut's victory and the passing of the fleet into Mobile Bay, the damage was done and as a blockade running port Mobile was no longer a factor. This is also true of Richmond, Wilmington, Savannah, and to a degree Charleston. The Union navy may not have captured particular major ports but they certainly cut them off from overseas trade.

But what if the Confederacy had gained her independence? What would have resulted?

The Southern states suffered for many decades after being forcibly reintegrated into the United States of America. For too many years the "bloody banner" was waved at election time, the Republican Party controlled politics, and the thought of a president from a southern state was anathema. Economically and culturally the South would suffer, especially after having spent so much of her treasure and so much of her blood in this futile war. She would take her place in the backseat of progress, as the rest of the United States forged ahead to take up a leading position in the modern industrialized world. Some have argued that the South was fighting to hold onto a way of life that history was already passing by, and this may be so, but in losing this war, she suffered the additional physical wrecking of her economic base.

But if the Confederacy had won her independence, it would have been likely that another war(s) between the Confederacy and the truncated United States would have followed. Both nations would have built up military and naval facilities as soon as peace occurred. Boundary disputes would have continued, and the slavery issue would not have vanished. North America would have become a militarized continent, with the potential for further international violence spilling over into Canada, Mexico, the Caribbean, and possibly including European powers. In retrospect, it would have been best if the war had never been fought and the issues then dividing our nation had been settled by other means, but it also was best that when finally fought, that the Union won.

After the long and bloody war was over, lessons of this war filtered throughout the world. Some of the ships used in this war were purchased by other nations on four continents. Yet the romance and some of the shadow of this war lives on, long after the carnage of it has disappeared.

Guerre De Course

The protection of commerce and food supplies was the piece de resistance of all arguments for building an unchallengeable fleet.
> —**Arthur Marder on the development of British seapower in the 19th century**

Guerre de Course would be one of the engines of warfare that would drive Great Britain towards the Naval Defence Act of 1889 and ultimately a navy that would dominate the world by the end of the 19th century. Part of the reasoning for building the British navy was to control the seas and allow free passage of food and goods, as she was dependent upon trade, and in the 1890s employed "two-thirds of the world's (seagoing) carrying power."

Even as early as 1850 one quarter of all bread corn was imported into Great Britain. By the 1880s the agricultural sector of Britain was subordinated to the Free Trade school and industrial might of Great Britain. Famine, or the "starving out" in Great Britain was a popular theme among naval writers and novelists of this period, and now possible, as the populace was dependent upon imported food, a condition that had not existed in the previous century.

So British interest in the exploits of the CSS *Alabama* and fellow Confederate raiders was strong—motivated by self-interest. It was these raiders, along with the use of iron built ships, and the requisitions for the Union navy, that had combined to cripple American merchant shipping. The Confederacy in the course of the war took 261 ships, virtually all sailing ships. Much of the Union's shipping was driven from the seas or sought other flags to fly under because of the threat and actual exploits of those Gray Raiders, and never recovered. As the 19th century British writer G.W. Steevens said, "The United States, before the Civil War, had a flourishing carrying trade. The depredations of the Confederate privateers drove it into our hands, and we have kept it ever since." An example of this new maritime order wrought by the raiders was shown by the change at the port of New York City. In 1860, two-thirds of the trade arriving and departing flew the Stars and Stripes flag. By 1863 this was down to one quarter.

The Confederate raiders had been built to perform two duties. One was to draw away Union warships from the blockaded coast to allow easier entry into her ports. Secondly, there was a goal of motivating the ship owners and bankers of the Union to push for peace to stop the depredations on the ships and their profits. Failure on both counts was the ultimate crop that the Confederacy harvested from those raiders.

The Union, fearing possible war with European powers, also built a class of extremely fast warships of the *Wampanoag* class, some of which could touch a high speed of 17 knots. Designed to chase ships such as the *Alabama,* they also were built with "an eye to causing equal damage to British shipping" if war had transpired.

Much of this fear of future raiders in the post American Civil War atmosphere evolved around French naval policies for building cruisers for long range raiding, bases around the world to support those raiders, as well as torpedo boats operating in European waters and possibly acting in a way that presaged the German submarine attacks of World War I—ruthless attacks against merchant ships and the enemy's coast. In France this was known as the *Jeune Ecole* or literally "Young School," which came to the fore in France in 1886. As with much of French politics under the Third Republic, her naval policies were constantly changing as governments were often revolving doors, more noted for replacing ministers than for stability. Still the *Jeune Ecole* was a school that developed throughout the end of the century in France, even if in fits and starts.

This school taught that one was not simply chasing and capturing Great Britain's commerce off the seas, a difficult goal at best. During 1794-1815 Great Britain lost approximately 11,000 merchant ships, but still kept commerce flowing and won the war against Napoleon largely through seapower. It did not emphasize large warships, as "it was based on doubts whether new technical developments left a future for big ship naval warfare."

It also presupposed that the day of the close blockade of France's ports was impossible. Ironclads were not wooden ships-of-the-line, that is they needed to coal (coaling at sea, except under ideal conditions, was not possible in the 19th century) and needed to visit ports more than the old style warship. Also, the torpedo boat made a close blockade difficult, and that in a future war, at best, a distant blockade would be all that could be attempted. From such blockaded ports it would be easier for French raiders to issue forth.

The French goal was to cripple the financial houses and commerce of Great Britain by driving up insurance policies for shipping above 25% of the value of the ships and cargo. This might occur almost as soon as war started as one of the ploys of France was to unleash raiders immediately at the outbreak of hostilities.

So what was the response to the French *Jeune Ecole* by her nearest neighbors?

In Germany according to Joest Dueffer, the head of Germany's navy, Count Georg Leo Caprivi, in the 1880s also adopted some of the points of the *Jeune Ecole*. Faced with a French navy superior to Germany's, he argued that "Against naval powers with considerable sea trade, after the advances made in the technology of ship and machine construction, cruiser warfare, even if slow in its effects, can none the less become decisive." This translated, until Grand Admiral Tirpitz and the German battleship program at the end of the century, into building coastal defense ironclads and torpedo boats for coast defense and cruisers for commerce warfare and showing the flag.

Italy adopted the gun carried on the battleship as the answer for her naval situation vis-a-vis France. While she saw a role for raiding, in maneuvers she also noted that it was time and time again difficult for the small torpedo boat to even *find* the large cruising warship on the high seas. Since in a war with a likely enemy such as France, Italy realized that such a nation could convoy a large invasion force, say from Africa, to her long coasts for an invasion and Italy's best answer was a battlefleet that could stop such an invasion.

The British response was more comprehensive. One obvious defense against this method of warfare, other than attacking and taking all of the enemy's ports and raiders, was the convoy system. The convoy system had worked for many of the wars in the previous two centuries. But there was always much resistance to convoys, especially with ships travelling at various speeds, in this new age of steam, and having to be gathered together in the first place. Some argued that the various speeds of steamships and sailing merchant ships were such that convoys were no longer possible. Later, in World War I, it took a severe shipping crisis for Great Britain to adopt the convoy system.

Another method proposed advocated National Insurance. This insurance would be offered by the British Government and would guarantee against shipping and cargo losses, especially in the first days of war when British seapower was still mobilizing and deploying and the enemy's naval strength was strongest. This system, would, most likely, have mitigated the worst dislocations brought on by the outbreak of war, primarily on the poorer peoples of Great Britain.

British writers were of the opinion that the Union Navy response to the Confederate raiders was poor. In their opinion, not enough warships were dispatched to various points around the globe to chase and capture the raiders. British policy always saw the building and heavy employment of cruisers to chase down raiders. Both world wars would see the success of this policy in handling surface raiders. Whether this would have been successful against a nation like France, ready to *heavily* employ this strategic ploy from the opening of the war is difficult to determine. Traditionally, though, raiding was a move that failed.

Cruisers in this period would constantly evolve, in much the same way as the ironclad, and like it, speed, endurance, gun power, armor, and new types like the armored cruiser would also be part and parcel with this period of *Pax Britannica*. Much of this evolution would be fueled by the *Guerre de Course*.

The Russian Visit

One of the greatest practical achievements of the Navy.
—Tsar Alexander II

One of the reforms of the new Tsar Alexander II involved the easing of his rule in Russian occupied Poland. This resulted in the return of exiled patriots, lessening of police restrictions, and other reform acts which allowed the Polish patriots to conduct internal agitation. A revolt simmered in 1861-62 and came to a full head in 1863-64. In the process of the brutal repression of this rebellion, the more liberal European powers of Great Britain and France threatened to intervene on the side of the Poles, in this so called "Polish Question" dispute.

With the crisis beginning to come to boil in 1862, the Russian Navy was given orders to send several of her cruising ships to foreign waters. It was explained to the Tsar that such a move would keep these warships from being trapped at Kronstadt and other Russian ports by the immensely superior British and/or French fleets and would also act as a deterrent to those powers, as the warships could threaten those powers' commerce. On leaving in 1862, the orders to the Russian Vice-Admiral Stepan S. Lesovskii, in charge of six warships read,

> ...In case of war, destroy the enemy's commerce and attack his weakly defended possessions. Although you are primarily expected to operate in the Atlantic, still you are at liberty to shift your activities to another part of the globe and divide your forces as you think best....

His destination was New York City. One of the important advantages of this port was that it was within striking distance of British and French shipping lines in the West Indies.

Rear-Admiral A.A. Popov also left the Baltic with a small squadron of six wooden warships. He left in January of 1862 and arrived at Hong Kong in April. From there he visited several ports in the Pacific, arriving at San Francisco on 28 September 1862. His squadron would winter at Nagasaki. With the threat of war still hanging over the Russian Empire, it returned to San Francisco, arriving for a second time on 12 October 1863.

The Russian fleet visits were hailed by the Northern newspapers as showing support for their cause by the Russian tsar, the same Russian tsar who had freed the serfs in Imperial Russia. Much of the Union press assumed that the Russian tsar supported the North over the Confederacy. But the purpose of the visit was primarily to protect the Russian cruising fleet, and the Russian government believed that "President Abraham Lincoln was maintaining a strict neutrality *vis-a-vis* European affairs, which pleased Russia immensely."

Still, much of the Union and Confederate press recognized the real reasons for the presence of the Russian squadrons and several articles were written at the time that were quite accurate in their appraisal. Only Popov, of the two Russian admirals, played up to the press, promising to defend San Francisco against Confederate raiders!

As an aside, it was Popov who later designed and built two circular battleships in the Black Sea, as well as the first armored cruiser, the *General-Admiral*. On board his ship was the future Russian naval hero Vice-Admiral Stepan Osipovich Makarov, who would fight the Turks in 1877-78 and go down in his flagship off Port Arthur in the Russo-Japanese War.

Did this move deter war? That is difficult to answer, but it certainly did not hurt Russia's cause. What else is interesting is how the Russian navy had improved in just a few short years from its disastrous showing in the Crimean War. As Kipp points out, "As a result of the incompetency of her naval planners Russia had entered the Crimean War with an obsolete fleet and a bankrupt naval strategy." She now had a screw propelled fleet, was building ironclads (initially broadside ironclads similar to the *Gloire* and later monitors for coast defense), and deployed two ocean squadrons based around steam frigates and speedy screw "clippers" designed to raid the enemy's shipping.

After the experience of the American Civil War, the Russians continued to build a cruiser fleet as raiders and a threat to the British maritime trade. She foresaw four squadrons of two ships each, one for the Baltic, one for the Black Sea, one for the Far East, and a final squadron in reserve. By the end of the 1870s this force would be augmented by a series of armored cruisers. The naval ministry encouraged ocean cruising throughout this period around the globe which improved skills and cultivated initiative in Russia's sailors. It would pay dividends in the Russo-Turkish War.

CHAPTER VI

German and Italian Wars of Unification

Nevertheless, at least during the 1860s, the manufacturers of armor managed to keep pace, and battleships retained a high degree of resistance to shot and shell.
—C.I. Hamilton

The spread of nationalism across the planet began in Europe. It was expressed in the wars that the "Iron Chancellor," Otto von Bismarck, fought in the 1860s and early 1870s that brought Prussia to the head of the German nation and made the King of Prussia the kaiser of Imperial Germany.

In tandem with these wars and starting earlier were the Italian wars of unification. Most were led by Count Camillo Benso Cavour, the Prime Minister for the north Italian Kingdom of Sardinia. Bismarck never envisioned a powerful role for the Prussian or the German navies, other than to defend the naval frontier. Cavour, on the other hand, had early on recognized the need for an Italian navy that was to be ironclad.

In 1859, Imperial France and the Kingdom of Sardinia fought a war with the Austrian Empire. This short war brought about the annexation of the northern Italian province of Lombardy, then owned by Austria, to Sardinia. This was followed in 1860-62 with the unification of all Italy under Sardinia except for Rome, then under French protection, and the Austrian owned province of Venetia, which had the port of Venice. To gain Venetia, the now Kingdom of Italy brokered a deal with Bismarck's Prussia in 1866.

Bismarck, to bring about the unification of Germany, realized that he had to eliminate the Austrian Empire's power in Germany. Several of the smaller states, primarily the Kingdoms of Bavaria and Saxony, were allied to Austria to help check Bismarck and Prussia's power. These political struggles would be played out in the weak German Diet which was a liberal framework for a united Germany born from the revolutions of 1848-49.

Bismarck first moved against Austria by involving Austria and Prussia in the Danish problem. This would ultimately lead to the establishment of the German Empire and the united Kingdom of Italy.

THE SCHLESWIG-HOLSTEIN WAR OF 1864: TEGETTHOFF BECOMES A HERO

If the Danish Navy had been able to assert an effective command of the Baltic, the Prusso-Austrian operations against Duppel and the island of Alsen would have been greatly embarrassed. But the Danes were too weak at sea to watch closely the narrow channel between Schleswig and the island of Alsen, where the main Danish force concentrated after the loss of the Danish territories on the mainland.
—H.W. Wilson

Our armies fought victoriously, let us do the same.
—Wilhelm von Tegetthoff at Helgoland

At 13:30 on 9 May 1864, the Danish naval forces met an Austrian dominated squadron near the isle of Helgoland. It was one of the few sea actions of this period, and lasted two and a half hours. The Danes were at war again because after what they called the first Schleswig war in 1848-1850, the question of the possession of the boundary duchies of Schleswig, Holstein, and tiny Lauenburg in the Jutland Peninsula was still on the table. But this time they had to deal with the joint effort of Prussia and Austria.

The crisis had been brewing for some months. On October 1, 1863, the German Diet had ordered a "federal execution" against Denmark over the question of these three duchies. In November Prussia recalled her overseas warships. Several were in the Aegean Sea, under Captain Klatt, protecting Prussian interests there during a Greek revolution against King Otto, and took some time to return home due to engine difficulties.

On 8 December the Prussian fleet was ordered to mobilize.

> This was hampered by a shortage of personnel, the need to pay off sailing ships used for training to man the steam-driven vessels, and by the removal without replacement of certain army officers employed on administrative duties in the navy ministry.

In addition several gunboats near Stralsund had to be reassembled from their laid up condition on shore. The Prussian gunboats were formed into the *Commando der Flotillen* under Captain Kuhn who would fly his flag on the steam paddlewheel yacht *Loreley.* Throughout February and March the Prussian navy

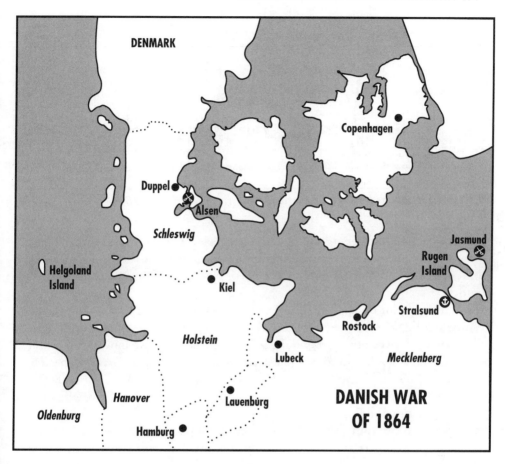

Helgoland Island

Duppel

Alsen

Schleswig

Kiel

Holstein

Lubeck

Hanover

Lauenburg

Oldenburg

Hamburg

DENMARK

Copenhagen

Jasmund

Rugen Island

Stralsund

Rostock

Mecklenberg

DANISH WAR OF 1864

would be busily readying both small and large ships for sea duty in the Baltic. On 27 March Prinz Adalbert von Preussen was appointed Commander in Chief.

Meanwhile, Holstein had been occupied by Hannoverians and Saxon troops at the behest of the German Confederation to free the German populace in Holstein from Danish rule, after Denmark had formally annexed Schleswig. This had been achieved by 24 December, with the Danish army withdrawing without fighting.

On 16 January 1864 Austria and Prussia delivered an ultimatum to Denmark, demanding the evacuation of Schleswig. They refused and the first fighting began on 1 February 1864.

The Austrian contribution to the war was aimed at not being excluded by Prussia in dealing with the question, as would be clear when the victorious armies occupied with mutual distrust the acquired provinces. So it was not on Bismarck's insistence alone that Austria agreed to join the ultimatum to the Danish Govern-

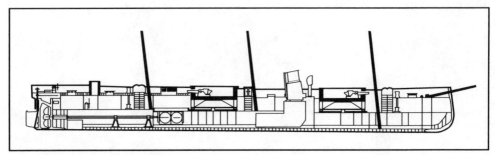

The **Rolf Krake** *engaged Prussian batteries on numerous occasions in 1864.*

ment to free *both* Schleswig and Holstein territories. This last diplomatic step saw Hannover, Saxony and Bavaria hindering the passage of Austro-Prussian troops through their territories, and in occupied Holstein refusing Austro-Prussian orders.

While inferior on land, the Danes were superior at sea, at least as long as the Austrians did not send their fleet from the Adriatic, 3,000 miles away, to the North Sea waters. Between the first and the second Schleswig-Holstein wars, the Royal Danish Navy had begun to develop steam power, acquiring at Glasgow the *Rolf Krake* in 1863, and importing technology and personnel from Great Britain. The chief engineer of the Danish navy was an Englishman, William Wain, who took part in the shipbuilding enterprise Burmeister & Wain Company. The Danish kingdom was not only forced to rely upon the workshop of the world for naval technology, but was also diplomatically supported to some extent by Great Britain.

When war broke out with Austro-Prussian troops crossing into Schleswig, the Danish fleet's main duty was the blockade of German ports. She had one ship-of-the-line, four frigates, three corvettes, seven gunboats, and some smaller vessels. Meanwhile, on 3 February the Danish government issued orders to take possession of all the Austrian and Prussian ships in Danish ports, and Prussia applied an embargo on Danish ships in Prussian ports. The blockade established by the superior Danish forces was not strict, and the Danes entered the Baltic Sea only on 10 February, due to the severe climatic conditions.

While the Prussian navy was still young, limited initially to three frigates, one corvette, and 22 gunboats, the combined forces of the two allies had numerical superiority over the Danish fleet, since Austria, ally of Prussia, had a fleet able to contest the blockade, but was distant from the theater of operations. In a strange case of destiny, the Austrian fleet began reorganizing in 1849, asking advice of the Danish Rear-Admiral Freiherr Birch von Dahlerup, who brought with him some other Danish naval officers. Dahlerup, a vice-admiral at the time of war, would postpone his retirement, but was not sent to fight his native country.

Denmark fought essentially two types of war at sea. She had coastal warships, including ironclads, which supported her army as much as possible. She also had a seagoing fleet that would receive an ironclad toward the end of the short war. The immediate activity of the Danish fleet was limited to a distant blockade of the mouths of the Weichsel and Oder rivers. We will first address the coastal war, which was interrupted by the armistice of 13 May—with the first armistice ending on 26 June 1864.

On 1 February 1864, as Prussian and Austrian land forces advanced on a Danish position, a Prussian unit that was marching there was taken under fire by the Danish steam corvette *Thor* and the ironclad *Esbern Snare*. Three field batteries opened fire and *Thor* was hit several times while the plates of *Esbern Snare* were pierced in several points. The ships withdrew from the bay without having done damage to the Prussians. *Esbern Snare* was one of two steam ironclad schooners ready for action at the outbreak of the war, the other being the *Absalon*. Each was armed with three guns and powered by a 100 horsepower engine. Their broadsides were armored with about 2 inches of iron (55 and 52 mm respectively).

On 18 February a couple of Allied battalions carried out a reconnaissance, employing a pontoon bridge. They were taken under fire on the bridge from the sea; it was the *Rolf Krake* that engaged in an exchange with some Prussian batteries. This ship was a twin turreted ship, the first of its kind in the European navies, and built by Napier & Sons in Glasgow, under influence of the American Civil War and on Captain Coles' concept.

A similar ship was also ordered by the Prussians in England; she was the S.M. *Panzerfahrzeug Arminius,* under construction during the Danish-Prussian War and did not take part in the campaign. She was commissioned at Samuda Brothers in Poplar (London). Due to the state of war and the fact that Britain sympathized with the Danish cause, the ship was delivered to the Prussian navy only in April of 1865, after the war.

The *Arminius* was also the oldest Prussian armored ship with twin turrets and was built according to Coles' design of *Kuppelprinzip* (cupola principle), an alternative design to the Ericsson monitor principle. She displaced about 1,600 tons. Later, on 3 October 1866, the *Arminius* had a race against the United States monitor *Miantonomoh* at Kiel, showing the higher speed. The ship was employed twice in war, and in the 1866 and 1870/71 campaigns, but did not see action.

As a side note, the *Miantonomoh* was a twin turreted monitor ordered in July of 1862. Named for a Narragansett Indian chief of the 1830s, she was wood hulled, and 250 feet long. She would have the distinction of being the only U. S. built monitor to cross the Atlantic, doing so in 1866 on a diplomatic mission to Imperial Russia. During her visit she also touched land at Great Britain and

American monitors could operate in rough seas.

Denmark, generally creating quite a stir in Europe (the London *Times* reported that the British Navy was "henceforth useless"). Credited with a speed of nine knots to the *Arminius'* 11 knots, her defeat in the race is not surprising.

On 8 February the *Rolf Krake* had entered service. It was envisioned that her role would be one of supporting the land forces. According to the study published by the Dutch Navy in its *Marineblad* in 1913/14, the *Rolf Krake* sailed on 11 February from Copenhagen with a gunboat, a fact that points to the authorities not being sure of her steaming qualities in the high seas.

So, on 18 February at 08:00 the ship steamed near a Prussian battery at Hollnis at 1,500 meters and opened fire, receiving fire in return from rifled 12 pounders at Alnoer, with the range falling to 750 meters. Like other early ironclads, she could lower herself in the water by filling watertight tanks, thus making her a smaller target. She pumped water inside the hull to become almost invisible as a target. The *Rolf Krake* fired 42 shells with the heavy guns, hitting the Alnur battery 12 times, but without inflicting much damage. One shell hit the pontoon and two men were hurt; many shells hit a nearby farm. The pontoon was not damaged and there was some wonder that the ship did not apply herself more to destroy it. As written in *Marineblad,*

> According to one Navy officer the Prussians had fired more than 2,500 pounds of iron. The iron plates were hit in 66 points but did not show much damage, some hit the turrets, 16 went through the smokestack, one through the steam pipe, five in the masts and 60-70 pierced the superstructure, the boats and bulwarks. The deck was opened in some point by flying splinters which passed through the deck's iron grate. According to eyewitnesses there was not a single safe place on the deck. The ship left pumping water out (though this was in part due to her ability to lower herself).

The *Rolf Krake* again bombarded the Prussian lines at Dybbol on 28 March, without much result, and again saw action on 18 April at Gammelsmark, and followed that up by a bombardment on the 19th at Alssund.

Also the *Rolf Krake* did not battle effectively against the Prussians' 26 battalions when they landed at Alsen on 29 June, using 160 flat-bottomed boats. This attack spelled doom to Danish resistance in this war. At the time of the attack the *Rolf Krake* was at anchor in nearby Andersen fjord. At 02:00 the Prussians put the boats, hidden in nearby woods, into the water in silence. The *Rolf Krake*, however, immediately sailed and appeared at 03:00, commencing firing at 1200 meters upon the boats. Prussian rifled batteries replied and hit the *Rolf Krake* 12 times, at the same time some of the boats were struck. Her action was much criticized, although the cautious performance of the ironclad could be explained on the basis that the Danes did not want to expose the ship to possible destruction by mines. (From this point forward we adopt the respective modern terms for torpedoes and mines.) Especially in the role against the Prussian landing boats filled with soldiers, the 60 pounder smoothbore guns seemed too large and unsuitable for the task at hand, particularly when combined with the large turning radius of the *Rolf Krake* and its need to turn each time in a long arc to renew the attack—it had only one screw.

Nevertheless, the *Rolf Krake* was held in some respect by the Prussians, who deployed a new battery with two rifled 12 pounders and two rifled 24 pounders, as shore batteries before the attack on the Duppler position, just to counter the ironclad. This landing was a decisive defeat for the Danish.

A second armistice would be declared on 20 July, and the peace conference would open in Vienna on 25 July. On 30 October 1864 Denmark ceded the Duchies of Schleswig, Holstein, and Lauenburg jointly to Prussia and Austria "to be disposed of as they might wish."

During this short war there were other actions on the high seas. First we will look at the actions in the Baltic Sea, and then turn to the North Sea.

At the end of December on the eve of the war, Denmark bought a Confederate ironclad under construction in Scotland and named it the *Danmark*. The *Danmark* was a broadside frigate outfitted with a ram, begun for the Confederacy in Britain early in 1862. With seizure likely by British authorities, it was sold to Denmark but could not be delivered until December 1864, too late for the war. Interestingly enough this ship displaced 4,770 tons and had a draft of 18.7 feet with a low speed of eight and a half knots. Her guns were 24: twelve 8" and twelve 6", all rifled, while her armor varied up to 4.5 inches on her belt and 3 inches in thickness carried four feet below her waterline. She reminds one of the Union navy's *New Ironsides*.

Almost available was the *Dannebrog*, a sailing ship-of-the-line modified before and during the war with an armor protection of 10cm thick plates from stem to stern and steam power. Armed originally with smoothbore guns, they would be exchanged for 16 rifles, six 8" and ten 6". She drew too much water (23.3 feet) for effective employment along the coasts of Jutland.

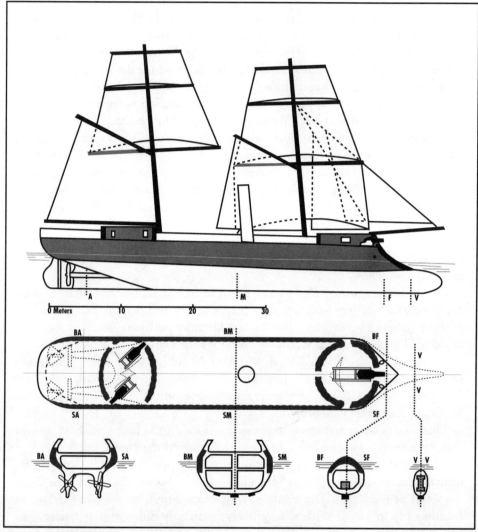

Danish Staerkodder *(ex* Stonewall*).*

Also in Scotland was the *Staerkodder,* the former Confederate ship *Stonewall,* which was not purchased by the Danish Government due to the end of the war. She was resold to the Confederacy and sailed for America arriving at Havana, Cuba, in time to learn of the end of the war and the defeat of the Confederate States of America. Ending up in the hands of the United States, she was sold to Japan—where she finally saw action in Japan's Civil War.

The Danes did not try to attack the inferior Prussian fleet, and very few actions occurred. The Prussian navy began operations in the Baltic on 21 February. Kuhn was exercising the steam gunboats near the island of Rugen on 15 March when he was ordered to join Captain Jachmann's squadron made up of the larger wooden warships.

On 17 March 1864, the little Prussian navy met the enemy. At the outbreak of the war she had two ships with trained crew, namely the *Arcona* and 19 gun corvette *Nymphe*, the former being partly manned by seamen taken from the *Niobe*, which was put out of service. Commander of this division was Kapitan zur See Eduard von Jachmann, who hoisted his flag on the 30 gun steam frigate *Arcona*, capable of 12 knots, and sailed from Swinemunde to join some gunboats, possibly five, and the yacht *Loreley* at Stralsund. Together they steamed along the east coast of Rugen Isle. His plan was to catch an isolated enemy ship, and to sink or capture her, but instead he encountered a Danish squadron. The Danes had the frigate *Sjaelland*, the flagship of Rear-Admiral van Dockum, the 64 gun, eight knot ship-of-the-line *Skjold*, and the corvettes *Hejmdal* and *Thor*, also the frigate *Tordenskjold*, though the latter may not have been engaged in the action. The Prussians had 68 guns to counter the 168 guns of the Danes. Both flagships turned eastwards, fighting broadside to broadside.

Nevertheless Jachmann bore down on the enemy and opened fire at 2,000 meters with his bow guns. Jachmann ordered his squadron into a line ahead at 1,500 meters.

On the Prussian side the signals were not seen, so the *Nymphe* and the *Loreley* did not turn until they were only 1,000 meters from the *Sjaelland* and 1,200 from the *Skjold*. The *Sjaelland*, with her higher speed tried to exploit the situation putting herself between *Arcona* and *Nymphe*, but failed in this rapid attempt, probably because of a mechanical breakdown, and suffered some from the Prussians' fire.

The Prussians turned back toward Swinemunde. The gunboats and *Loreley* retreated toward Rugensche Bodden. The Danish squadron pursued but only the *Sjaelland* proved to be able to keep pace with the Prussians' superior speed. While maneuvering the ship came under Prussian gunboat fire. The *Skjold* fired only with her small pieces to avoid losing ground. The last shot fired by the Danes came at 17:00, thus ending the fighting, although they had pursued the Prussians until they were only 11 miles from Swinemunde, before retiring.

The Prussian ships *Arcona* and *Nymphe* anchored at Swinemunde at 19:00. The Danes had fired more than 1,200 shots: the *Nymphe* received the most damage, with 23 hits on the hull and 50 through the masts and rigging. The *Arcona* was hit five times on the hull, once on the deck, and suffered damage to her guns and equipment. Nevertheless the ship was back in service after two days of repairs. The *Loreley* had one boat destroyed. From the Prussian side, the *Arcona* fired 156 shots, *Nymphe* 84, *Loreley* 22, and the gunboats 20 shots, altogether causing substantial damage to the *Sjaelland* and some to the *Skjold*.

Austro-Prussian fleet, showing Schwarzenberg *and* Radetzky.

There were some losses of personnel. The *Sjaelland* had 3 dead and 19 wounded, the *Arcona* three dead and three wounded, the *Nymphe* had two dead and five wounded, the *Loreley* one dead. Fighting at Jasmund was later remembered with great pride by the German navy for the spirited and daring attack staged by their seamen (Jachmann was promoted to *Konteradmiral,* or rear-admiral, for the action).

Jachmann sortied again with his squadron on 19 March, making no contact with the Danes, but the situation at sea was radically changing. The balance turned on 30 March, when the ironclad *Dannebrog,* converted from a two decked ship-of-the-line into a single gun deck armored frigate, joined the Danish Baltic squadron. While too deep drafted for coastal work, and slow at nine knots, the Prussians had nothing that could defeat her at sea. The conversion of ships-of-the-line to armored frigates was not unusual and was a relatively inexpensive way to get an ironclad. The British did this the most, but problems converting the ships were twofold. One, they remained wooden, so they did not have a long life, and two, they usually were not fast ships in their new role.

Still, Jachmann was not to be deterred and sortied again on 9 April, sighting four Danish warships that refused action. On the 14th, with Jachmann at sea nearby, Prinz Adalbert von Preussen with the armed yacht *Grille* and several gunboats engaged the Danish *Skjold* and *Sjaelland* west of Rugen off Hiddensee. Another skirmish occurred on 24 April between the Prussian gunboats, under Kuhn, and the *Tordenskjold,* but again with no result.

Now followed a series of minor skirmishes. Another desultory action occurred on 26 April. On 30 April the *Skjold* arrived off Danzig and tried to lure the newly commissioned steam frigate *Vineta,* sister ship to the *Arcona,* out. The 11 knot *Vineta* tried to draw the *Skjold* under the coast defense batteries, but both failed in their attempts.

On 6 May, when Jachmann and Kuhn offered battle, the Danes refused it. On 12 May the Prussians attempted to seize "the Danish armed steamer *Freya*" and skirmished with the *Sjaelland* and the ironclad *Dannebrog*.

With the armistice, Prussia ordered several ships that were being built for the Confederacy. This would eventually bring the *Prinz Adalbert* ironclad ram (sister to *Stonewall)* and two steam corvettes, the *Augusta* (ex-CSS *Mississippi*) and *Victoria* (ex-CSS *Louisiana),* into Prussian service after the close of war.

With the end of the armistice, there was one minor action off Hiddensee on either 2 or 3 July. The war in the Baltic was now over, and the Prussian fleet could be justly proud of their aggressive conduct.

The North Sea was different. The situation urged additional naval help that could only come from the Austrian ally. Klatt's squadron slowly returning from the Aegean finally arrived at Den Helder in the Netherlands on 15 April. A stronger Danish squadron under Captain Edouard Suenson had been maintaining a blockade of the German North Sea ports, so Klatt was very careful in his approach. On 21 April, Suenson entered Den Helder, but he respected the neutrality of the port, and shortly after left. Klatt waited for the arrival of the Austrian squadron under Tegetthoff.

The Adriatic based Austrian fleet, composed of one steam ship-of-the-line, five frigates, five armored frigates and two corvettes, sent one squadron to the North Sea with orders to break the Danish blockade and to defend the Prussian sea commerce routes. That Levant squadron consisted of the steam frigates *Schwarzenberg, Radetzky,* the corvette *Dandolo* and gunboat *Seehund* and had orders to break the Hamburg blockade at any price. Of these ships, only the *Radetzky* and *Schwarzenberg,* under the command of Commodore Wilhelm von Tegetthoff, arrived near Helgoland. The gunboat *Seehund* was picking up coal in Great Britain, and while under the control of an English pilot, ran aground. (Austrian histories consider this a deliberate "accident.") The *Dandolo* suffered a boiler breakdown.

On his arrival on 1 May, von Tegetthoff also took under his command three Prussian ships, namely the *Preussischer Adler, Basilisk* and *Blitz,* whose guns played a minor role in the ensuing battle. He then had 87 guns on the allied squadron against the 102 available to the Danes on board their three ships.

Schwarzenberg
    6 smoothbore 60 pounders
    40 smoothbore 30 pounders
    4 rifled 24 pounders
Radetzky
    4 smoothbore 60 pounders
    24 smoothbore 30 pounders

> 3 rifled 24 pounders
>
> *Preussischer Adler*
>
> 2 smoothbore 68 pounders
>
> *Blitz*
>
> 1 smoothbore 68 pounder
>
> 1 rifled 24 pounder
>
> *Basilisk*
>
> 1 smoothbore 68 pounder
>
> 1 rifled 24 pounder

The Danish North Sea squadron, under command of Suenson, was composed of the screw frigates *Niels Juel* with 42 guns and the *Jylland* (also called *Jutland* by some historians) with 44, and the steam corvette *Hejmdal* with 16 guns. In terms of rifled ordnance, the Austrians had seven 24 pounder rifled guns (plus the two Prussian rifles), against the twenty-two 18 pounder and four 12 pounder rifles of the Danes.

The Danes had the following guns:

> *Jylland*
>
> 32 smoothbore 30 pounders
>
> 8 rifled 18 pounders
>
> 4 rifled 12 pounders
>
> *Niels Juel*
>
> 30 smoothbore 30 pounders
>
> 12 rifled 18 pounders
>
> *Hejmdal*
>
> 14 smoothbore 30 pounders
>
> 2 rifled 18 pounders

The ratio was thus in favor of the Danes who enjoyed 76 smoothbore and 26 rifled guns, against the 78 and 9 of the Austro-Prussians.

It was just after 11:00, 9 May 1864, when each side spotted the other's smoke and by 13:00 could see each other. What followed was one of the last fights between wooden ships and one of the first between steam powered ones where sail proved a disadvantage. As the opposing warships came on, the Danes were in an arc formation, while Tegetthoff deployed his ships in line. The exchange of gunfire began when the *Schwarzenberg* opened fire at 3,500 meters and at about 1,800 meters all ships were firing, apart from the Prussians whose slow speed did not allow them to close the range. The *Schwarzenberg* had one gun hit early on and the Danish *Jylland* had received much of the enemy fire. Tegetthoff tried to cut off the Danes from Helgoland and to close with their ships, while Suenson maneuvered to bring both fleets on a broadside bearing at short range while steaming on parallel lines. Since the Danes concentrated their shots on the flagship *Schwarzenberg*, while the Prussians fired from afar, it was this ship that caught fire. The fire which started in a sail locker, near a powder magazine placed the ship in danger. By about 16:00 the foresail was burning, spreading fire to the mast. Losses among the crew had reduced the guns in action, and while fire spread on the ship she made for Helgoland—which was British at the time—in the direction west northwest, covered by the *Radetzky*. Suenson ordered the pursuit of the retreating enemy, but meanwhile the *Jylland's* rudder was hit, and the battle was over by 16:30, when Tegetthoff succeeded in reaching neutral waters.

Both sides claimed victory after the battle and much has been said by historians on the matter. For example the biographers of Tegetthoff, Handel-Mazzetti and Hans Hugo Sokol, wrote:

> The soldiers cannot say that Helgoland was a tactical success for the Austrian Sea arms, notwithstanding the courage and valor of Tegetthoff and his men.
>
> But if the success is evaluated, thus it is without any doubt on the Austrian side because the superior Danish forces abandoned the combat waters without pursuing the wounded enemy, and lifted the blockade.

At the same time, both in Denmark and in Britain, there were different opinions. The Ole Lisberg Jensen booklet on the Danish Naval Museum states:

> For the Danes, the Battle of Helgoland was both a tactical and moral victory, but in the meantime the army had been defeated in Schleswig, and a cease-fire was negotiated a few days later.

Surely, both sides fought gallantly and the Austrians suffered more than the opponents, 32 dead and 69 wounded on *Schwarzenberg* and five and 24 on the *Radetzky*. Nevertheless, Tegetthoff refused the help offered for the wounded by the commander of the British *Aurora*. The Danes had two dead and 23 wounded on the *Niels Juel*, 12 dead and 29 wounded on the *Jylland* and two wounded on the *Hejmdal*. The good performance of the Danish gunnery was not only because they enjoyed the superiority of 102 against 87 pieces, but also because, as pointed out by Klaus Mueller, who considers this battle as a draw:

> Confrontation between opponents was 26 to 9 for the Danes; that is about 25% of all guns taking part in the fight on the Danish side were rifled, while the Allied ships were armed only with 10% of this modern gun type. The advantage of the rifled gun over the smoothbore one was that the elongated projectiles here employed (are more accurate) after having been fired from the gun…. (so there was improved) gun precision, and the range of fire was highly increased over that of smoothbore guns.

The same day, while the ships were under repair and the fire on board *Schwarzenberg* had been checked with much difficulty, Tegetthoff was promoted to Rear-Admiral by the Emperor Francis Joseph I for his gallant behavior. During the night he sailed back to Cuxhaven, where he anchored at 04:00 on 10 May. During the following days a visitor on the flagship noted that the Danish shots had made holes of four to five inches in the ship's 12 inch thick wooden walls. He noted that the crew were Italians and Dalmatians (Slavic), while the Marines were German. The language of the Austrian sailors was predominantly Italian, while to be an officer, an Austrian had to be able to speak German.

The steam frigate *Jylland* was hit the most on the Danish side, but managed to survive (displayed today as the Danish Museum ship in Ebeletoft at Jutland).

Suenson remained in the waters of the battle, after having disembarked wounded, cruising between Helgoland and the mouth of the Elbe, ready to resume combat against the Allies. But on the day of the battle of Helgoland, an armistice was signed in London, to go into effect on 12 May. This foresaw the stopping of hostilities, the blockade ceasing, and any reinforcement of land and sea positions forbidden. For this reason Suenson received a last minute despatch suggesting he leave for neutral Norway. From there he would retain a greater degree of freedom of movement.

Surely the Danes could have won a major victory if they had kept more ships on the North Sea, or used the more inactive ones in the Baltic Sea in the North Sea. They had during the fighting a clear superiority in rifled guns that allowed them a superior effectiveness of fire against the Allies. It was noted that the *Jylland* was hit about 20 times against the 80 hits on the *Schwarzenberg*.

Comparison of Warships Taking Part in the Action Off Helgoland

Ship	Displacement		Guns	Speed in knots
Schwarzenberg	1853	2614	50	11
Radetzky	1854	2334	31	9
Niels Juel	1855	1935	42	9.3
Jylland	1860	2450	44	12
Hejmdal	1856	1170	16	9
Preuss. A.	1847	1171	2	10
Blitz	1862	353	2	9.3
Basilisk	1862	353	2	9.3

Helgoland was Tegetthoff's day, although he was courageous and lucky at the same time, because Suenson wanted to pursue him and use his gunnery superiority, and it was only the sudden inability to maneuver the *Jylland*, after it was hit on the rudder while ordering the pursuit that hindered a prosecution of the battle. When the Danes resumed movement it was too late because of the

*Austrian Squadron concentrated in the North Sea at the end of the 1864 war with Denmark.
Note the Austrian ironclad* Kaiser Max*'s bow on extreme left of picture. It was later modified,
as it was too low for safe operation on the high seas.*

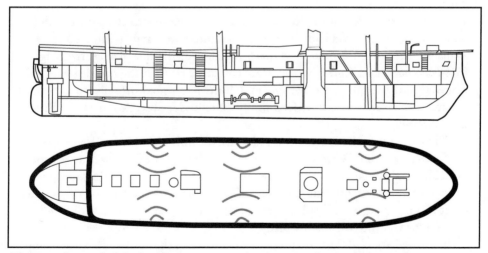

The Danish ironclad Peder Skram, *not completed in time for the Schleswig-Holstein War
of 1864.*

advantage Tegetthoff had enjoyed in the meantime, and moreover he was now near neutral waters. It can be argued that the situation was in some way similar to that faced by Tegetthoff at Lissa, where his guns were inferior and he responded to the situation by charging the enemy. Also at Helgoland the risk for Suenson was that Tegetthoff would be able to capture or destroy one of his ships and thus end Danish superiority.

At the start of the war, while the Austrians had some "old" ironclads like the *Drache* and *Salamander*, and the newer *Prinz Eugen* guarding the Adriatic, a squadron under command of Vice-Admiral Bernhard von Wullerstorf, more of a "mathematician and scientist" than admiral, was now approaching the North Sea. It had been shadowed by British warships and was anchored at Cherbourg when it heard about the battle of Helgoland. It comprised the new ironclad *Don Juan de Austria*, the steam ship-of-the-line *Kaiser* with ninety-two guns, the steam powered corvette *Friedrich*, and the paddle steamer *Elisabeth*. This force, which was soon followed by another new ironclad completed the previous year, the *Kaiser Max*, arrived in North Sea waters when the war was almost over. But with the *Kaiser Max* and *Don Juan de Austria* (each armed with sixteen 48 pounder smoothbores and fifteen 24 pounder rifles), although plagued by mechanical problems during a long voyage, the Austrians achieved a clear superiority at sea. They enjoyed five to two ironclads over the Italians in the Mediterranean, so they did not feel threatened by dispatching two ironclads to the North Sea, even when the British next threatened to deploy a squadron to the Adriatic—which turned out to be but a bluff.

The armistice lasted until 26 June. On 27 June the Austro-Prussian North Sea Squadron based at Den Helder in the Netherlands was heavily reinforced and had available: the ironclad *Juan de Austria*, the ship-of-the-line *Kaiser*, two frigates (*Schwarzenberg* and *Radetzky*,) the steam corvette *Friedrich*, the paddle steam ship *Elisabeth* and the gunboats *Seehund* and *Wall.* The squadron sailed on 29 June toward Cuxhaven where it arrived on 30 June under observation of the British aviso *Salamis.*

While the Danes had some armored ships, the only effective ironclads were the *Rolf Krake* and the *Dannebrog*, making a continuation of the war at sea more difficult for Denmark. Also, the *Peder Skram*, was being converted to an ironclad from a wooden warship but she was not ready for war. She had 16 rifled guns, eight 8" and eight 6", a displacement of 3379 tons and could develop some 11 knots. Nor was the *Staerkodder* ready.

If all these ironclads had fought on the Danish side the results of a battle against Wullerstorf's squadron would have been unpredictable. No major power's support could be obtained, although an unauthorized Prussian move at the little border town of Kolding on 18 April caused Great Britain to consider for a while sending a naval force to Copenhagen.

Resuming war on 26 June, the combined Allied naval force supported the seizure of the North Isles (northeast of Helgoland, along the west Danish coast), whose defense was gallantly conducted by Lieutenant Otto Christian Hammer, with his forces organized mainly on the isles of Sylt, Amrum and Foehr. This, combined with the Prussians crossing the Sound on boats and taking Als on the night of 29 June while facing the *Rolf Krake,* compelled the Danes to ask for a second armistice.

With the war lost on land, the Danes had to accept the peace. The war was over, and the *Rolf Krake* had not prevented the defeat on land. With peace, the disputed provinces were jointly occupied and governed by the Austrian and Prussian governments. Friction over the occupation, in part instigated by that master of intrigue, Bismarck, began almost immediately.

THE SEVEN WEEKS WAR
The Austrian and Italian Fleets Encounter in the Adriatic

Nevertheless, at least during the 1860s, the manufacturers of armor managed to keep pace, and battleships retained a high degree of resistance to shot and shell.
—C.I. Hamilton

Fought with valour at Helgoland gloriously won at Lissa ...
—on Tegetthoff's monument at Vienna

In 1864 Wilhelm von Tegetthoff fought shoulder to shoulder with the Prussians, but two years later he found himself an enemy of the former ally and in command on 9 May 1866 of the Austrian fleet based at Pola on the Adriatic sea. Tegetthoff was 39 years old, having been born in Marburg on 23 December 1827. In 1866 the Austrian and Prussian rivalry over the question of hegemony over the many German states reached its climax and Bismarck forced the war, allying with Italy, which still had Venice to gain in the northeast in order to complete the *Risorgimento.*

The new Austrian navy was born in 1848-49, as detailed by Lawrence Sondhaus, when at the end of the war against Piedmont, during which most of the Austro-Venetian (i.e., Italian) navy officers revolted along with the city against Austria, and a Dane, Count Hans Birch von Dahlerup was appointed to the duty of reorganizing the old navy on a new basis. This new basis was one that reflected Imperial *Austrian* interests. The Venetian legacy especially bothered the Austrians, who feared possible sympathy for the dangerous revolutionary new Piedmont

Kingdom of Sardinia, a state that was leading the way to the united Italy of the future.

Dahlerup had to deal with the unique Austrian mentality and failed to give more independence to the navy and the navy ministry in Vienna, because of the firm Austrian principle of dependence of armed forces on the Emperor (and his military chancellery) and on the state administration. In spite of these difficulties, he introduced German as the service language, as well as strict discipline, replacing many Venetian officers with Austrian, or even German or Scandinavian ones. Another important measure was the movement of the main naval base from Venice to Pola.

However, the founder of Austrian seapower is often considered to be the Archduke Ferdinand Maximilian, who was appointed in 1854 Commander in Chief of the Austrian navy. Originally he wanted to create a fleet built around a "half dozen wooden ships-of-the-line" but later abandoned this when Italy ordered ironclads. He fought and won a battle of principles against the theory of the defensive Austrian navy armed with minor vessels, endorsing instead the view that the navy should be as strong as the Italian one. The ironclad was finally adopted by Austria in 1862 after the Battle of Hampton Roads. Until 1862 when he left the command, he studied the British Royal Navy organization and urged the strengthening of the Austrian one. As a result, backed up by a strong shipyard industry based at Venice, Pola and Trieste, the navy could put to sea in 1866 a fleet of seven ironclads, all built in Austria.

In the 1849 war with Piedmont the Austrian navy placed Venice under blockade, but during the following 1859 war against France and Piedmont she had less to do, as the French navy was overwhelmingly strong. Five years later Wilhelm von Tegetthoff, in the meanwhile rapidly promoted after the dismissal of many Venetian officers, commanded the expedition to the North Sea against the Danes in 1864.

In Central Europe a new limited war was about to break out. After the question of rule over the Schleswig and Holstein provinces was settled with the defeat of the Danish kingdom and the occupation by Austrian and Prussian forces, Bismarck wanted to achieve the unification of German states under Prussian hegemony, rather than under the rule of the Austrian Habsburg house. The contest was settled with the war of 1866 in which the states of South Germany and the Kingdom of Saxony took the side of the Habsburgs, and Prussia allied from the beginning of the year with the new Kingdom of Italy. At the same time both the French and British pursued a policy of little or no intervention. The French had their hands tied because the French army was heavily involved in the Mexican adventure. Nevertheless, Emperor Napoleon III committed himself to an active diplomacy between the belligerents.

Bismarck provoked the war when the Holstein province was occupied by Prussian troops and Austria asked retaliation against Prussia from the German Federation on 14 June; on the 17th Austria declared war, Prussia did so the following day, and on the 20th Italy declared war on Austria.

Preparation for Battle

The Italians are a seafaring people with a past of great naval achievement. But nearly all the Italian ships were new; the guns which they mounted had for the most part been recently acquired; and their officers and crews had not been sufficiently practiced in their use. Though considerable squadrons had been maintained in commission in time of peace, they had received a totally inadequate tactical training. Moreover, the navy suffered from personal jealousies and antagonisms; it had been formed by the fusion of two distinct services, the Sardinian and Neapolitan, and there had not been time to make the fusion complete ... . Of bravery there was no lack. What was wanted was staff work, leadership and skill.
—H.W. Wilson

At the end of April 1866 Austria began to prepare for possible war against Italy and Prussia, which involved the navy. Since the main enemy fleet was the Italian, little attention was paid to the small and distant Prussian one. The appointment of Tegetthoff in May 1866 as commander of the fleet was a decisive factor, since the man was widely known in the navy, especially after his charge at Helgoland, and his mere presence succeeded in raising the morale of the sailors while improving the effectiveness of the battle squadrons. All the naval yards were pressed to have ships ready for action in a short time, and the new ironclads *Erzherzog Ferdinand Max* (Erzherzog is "Archduke") and the *Habsburg* entered service from the Trieste shipyard before their planned completion date. Hectic activity allowed these two man-of-wars to be fitted with side armor plates and to be ready for battle, the former by 21 June and the latter by 27 June. The older steam ship-of-the-line *Kaiser* under repair was also ready for action on 25 June, while another old ship, the *Novara*, which suffered on 3 May from a fire incident probably provoked by sabotage, also joined the fleet on 4 July, anchored in the Fasana Channel, just north of Pola.

Tegetthoff was under Archduke Albert, commander of the South Army, and was instructed to support the land operations from the sea. At the outset of the war the Austrian battle fleet was composed of five broadside ironclads, that is *Drache, Salamander, Prinz Eugen, Kaiser Max,* and *Don Juan de Austria,* plus the two above mentioned, for a total of seven. Moreover there were seven unarmored ships and seven smaller gunboats. The weakest contingent of the fleet, the wooden ships, were strengthened about the waterline, and protection of the boilers and guns was provided by iron chains, such as utilized in the American Civil War. The

Ship	Armament							
	48 Pdr R	24 Pdr R	12 Pdr R	6 Pdr R	48 Pdr	30 Pdr	12 Pdr	Total
Ferdinand Max					16			16
Habsburg	1				15			16
Kaiser Max		14			16			30
Prinz Eugen		14			16			30
Don Juan de Austria		14			14			28
Drache		16			10			26
Salamander		16			10			26
Total Ironclads	1	74			97			172
Kaiser		2				74	16	92
Novara		3				44	4	51
Schwarzenberg		4				36	6	46
Radetzky		3				24	4	31
Adria		3				24	4	31
Donau		3				24	4	31
Fredrich		2				16	4	22
Hum		2			2			4
Dalmat		2			2			4
Vellebich		2			2			4
Wall		2			2			4
Reka		2			2			4
Seehund		2			2			4
Streiter		2			2			4
Kerka		2				4		6
Narrenta		2				4		6
Kaiserin Elisabeth		2	4					6
Greif			2					2
Andreas Hofer		1				3		6
Stadium								0
Santa Lucia			2			4		12
Vulkan			2					4
Triest				4				4
								432

Novara received rail pieces. Coal shortages did not impede the Austrians from exercising at sea almost every day, although by night they moved under sail, and by day they steamed at only five and a half knots. Training consisted of gunnery shooting at targets with a concentrated broadside and maneuver, especially bold ones, and ramming. The focused fire allowed the inferior Austrian naval artillery of a particular ship to be directed to a specific target, raising the effectiveness of the broadside.

With war unavoidable, the Italian navy ministry on 3 May 1866 ordered the formation of an operational fleet of 31 warships out of a variety of 69 steam and 75 sail vessels available at the beginning of 1866, many of which were unfit for war actions.

Such a fleet had to be completed in number, armament, and equipment by 20 June, the day that war was declared. By that date 29 ships were ready, although not all scheduled changes were complete, especially in regard to guns. In terms of gun armament, the navy ministry ordered the exchange of the 16cm rifled guns not banded (often referred to as "hooped") for the banded and rifled ones, giving an armament increase to the ironclads. The alterations were made in Taranto from which the fleet departed on 21 June, the day after the declaration of war, to Ancona in the Adriatic Sea. There the fleet arrived on 25 June, held back by limited speed of 4-5 knots of some very slow ships. There they waited for supply and new orders, while the exchange of old guns with new ones was resumed.

The fleet was almost completed at Ancona before the battle—"all, with very few exceptions, and this limited to the inferior ships, had them [the artillery] according to the Ministry directives." This report also states that "the ships were reorganized in Ancona on 20 June and that the artillery were changed on all ships, except one, when on 27th the Austrian commander appeared before Ancona." On that occasion *Principe di Carignano*, which was changing eight guns from the ironclad gunboat *Terribile*, although delayed, steamed against the Austrians.

Heading the fleet was Admiral Carlo Pellion di Persano, born on 11 March 1806 at Vercelli. He had distinguished himself in the Tripoli action of 1825 when he commanded an assault boat, but on another occasion was tried by a court martial as being imprudent. He was navy minister from 3 March 1862. When he became on 3 May 1866 the Commander in Chief of the *Armata di Operazione* (Operation Fleet) he was in his sixties and perhaps too old for such duty, no longer the imprudent and impetuous commander of the past. In 1862 he chose the ironclad construction policy against the former wooden ship policy sponsored by minister Urbano Rattazzi, an important change in the new Italian navy. Moreover he planned a Royal Academy for the united navy, to overcome the strong rivalry between Sardinian and Neapolitan officers who formed the new Italian one. This was the time when Italy adopted armor plate. Persano stated on June 1862 before the Italian Parliament that "… the recent events in the American war have shown

Ship	25cm Arm	20cm Arm	16cm R	16cm H R	20cm	16cm	20cm How	12cm R	TOTAL
Re d'Italia		2	16	14	4				36
Re di Portogallo	2		12	14					28
Ancona			22	1	4				27
Maria Pia			18	4	4				26
Castelfidardo			22	1	4				27
San Martino			16	6	4				26
P. Di Carignano			12	6	4				22
Affondatore	2								2
Terribile			10	6	4				20*
Formidabile			10	6	4				20**
Palestro		2			2			1	3
Varese		2	2					1	6
total ironclads	**4**	**6**	**140**	**58**	**34**			**2**	**244**
Maria Adelaide				10	22				32
Re Galantuomo				8		32	10		40
Duca di Genova				8		32	10		40
Carlo Alberto				8		32	10		50
Vittorio Emanuele				8		32	10		51***
Garibaldi				8		34	12		54
Italia				8		32	10		50
Principe Umberto				8		32	10		50
Gaeta				8		34	12		54
San Giovanni				6		14			20
Principessa Clotilde			6			14			20
Etna				2		8			10
Governolo							10		10
Fulminante				2			8		10
Costituzione							10		10
Guisardo				2		4			6
Ettore Fieramosca				2		4			6
Archimede				2		4			6
Tancredi				2		4			6
Montebello								4	4
Vinzaglio								4	4
Etna				2		8			10

NOTES:

*Arrived too late for battle **Not present at Lissa on 20th ***Had also 1 Dahlgren

Arm = Armstrong   R = Rifled

How = howitzer   H = Hooped or banded

that wooden warships can be taken into little account, given the incontestable superiority of the ironclad ships, only one of which could with her ram sink an entire wooden fleet."

While Persano proved a good politician and organizer, displaying positive ideas for the navy administration, he would be a failure as a fleet commander. On 20 July the entire fleet had 56 ships available. Among them Persano could rely upon 11 ironclads and a twelfth would arrive a few hours before the battle. This was the *Affondatore*, which arrived nearly completed from Millwall on the Thames where she was built. The *Affondatore* was a unique sea-going turreted ironclad, with a ram which extended 26 feet.

Two other ironclad 1st class frigates had been built in New York by Webb during the American Civil War (*Re di Portogallo* and *Re d'Italia*, which were also armed with spar torpedoes) but the rest, except the 2nd class frigate *Principe di Carignano* built in Italy, were coming from French shipyards. They were the 2nd class frigates *Maria Pia, Ancona, Castelfidardo, San Martino*, the ironclad corvettes *Terribile* and *Formidabile*, and the armored gunboats *Varese* and *Palestro*. The *Re d'Italia* was the first unescorted ironclad to cross the Atlantic in March of 1864.

Vice-Admiral Giovanni Battista Albini Count of Sarda was in command of the wooden squadron, hoisting his flag on *Maria Adelaide*. The other ships were the 1st class steam frigates *Duca di Genova, Vittorio Emanuele, Gaeta, Principe Umberto, Carlo Alberto*, and *Garibaldi* and the corvettes *Principessa Clotilde, Etna, San Giovanni* and *Guiscardo*. A third group of ships was formed with four gunboats under command of Captain Antonio Sandri, each armed with four rifled 12cm guns.

According to Persano's critics, he did not order any target exercises, while they were the rule for the Austrians, who trained crews continuously at gunnery. The navy section of the Italian war ministry had made available an increased amount of ammunition precisely for gunnery practice.

Persano first displayed weakness when he did not react more quickly when Tegetthoff appeared before the Italian base of Ancona on 27 July. Later it was said that the moral effect of the insult inflicted on a superior force by the Austrians was great on both sides. Tegetthoff had sent the yacht *Stadium* on a reconnaissance of the enemy coast to see if the Italian fleet had moved into the Adriatic. Receiving a negative report, he asked Archduke Albert permission for a personal reconnaissance to look for the enemy fleet. Permission was delayed, or else he could have shelled the enemy base at Ancona before the Italian fleet arrived. When permission was granted, he arrived off the enemy base with six ironclads and several wooden warships to find the entire Italian fleet. He waited off the port, offering battle, while the Italian fleet slowly assembled under the port's guns. Finally, he steamed off, having achieved no material success, but having a moral victory. He was well aware that to "reach a success ... not material, but moral, that is not to be undervalued" as he wrote to his friend Emma Lutteroth.

So, why did Persano react slowly to the Austrian attack on Ancona? In part it was because the ships were unprepared: the *Principe di Carignano* was getting guns from the *Terribile*, the *Re d'Italia* and *Re di Portogallo* were changing their coal, which was smoldering in their bunkers, and finally the *Ancona* was under repair. Additionally the warships were working among a lot of small vessels, launches, etc., which slowed movements considerably. According to Tegetthoff's report, half of the warships in the harbor were under steam and could sail to check the Austrians. Persano urged the ships to move as soon as possible out of the port, using a scout boat to personally visit the ships, but under the present conditions it was only after a couple of hours that the fleet was assembled in two lines ready for combat. Being scattered, they were put in formation as soon as they were ready under protection of the guns of Mount Conero, a fort at the entrance to the harbor, a logical move. When they were ready Persano advanced on the Austrian ships that meanwhile had begun to retire and disappear.

The reason why is easily explainable: Tegetthoff was also surprised to find the enemy fleet at Ancona and did not want to accept battle at that moment. He was satisfied by the fact that he had surprised the enemy fleet in their harbor, and thought he had inflicted some damage on the little *Esploratore* that had first spotted him, and raced away as his fleet fired on it (the boat was only hit by some splinters).

Meanwhile the campaign on land in north Italy was developing favorably for the Austrians. The Italians divided their army into two parts, one of 12 divisions under General Alfonso La Marmora (who was also Prime Minister), the other with eight divisions under General Enrico Cialdini deployed on the lower Po River, both ready for concerted action. But they managed to fight independently their private wars, since neither one of them wanted to play the secondary role of conducting a diversionary attack, with the result that La Marmora was defeated at Custoza on 24 June. Cialdini, who had before his corps only one Austrian battalion, was not ready for action and remained passive, partly because the dispatches sent him were too pessimistic on the outcome of the battle. Only Garibaldi managed to penetrate into the Trentino mountain valleys of the Alps, but was stopped by La Marmora who instructed him to protect the northern flank of his retreating army after the battle of Custoza. Garibaldi resumed movement only in July, after the battle of Sadowa on 3 July, gaining some success at Bezzecca against General Kuhn, while Cialdini, now in command of all Italian forces, began to move beyond the Po River.

On the North Sea and in the Baltic the Prussian navy had little trouble, with the Austrians fully engaged in the Adriatic. Her presence was symbolic and limited to the occupation of the Hannoverians' coastal forts, since Hannover was on the

Austrian side, which gave Prussia and her small Allied states control over the Baltic and North Sea from Memel to the Ems mouth. During these operations the little ironclad *Arminius* with the gunboats *Cyclop* and *Tiger,* helped General von Manteuffel and 13,500 troops with guns and horses, to cross the Elbe in the presence of the enemy.

If the navy minister, Agostino Depretis, had until that moment quietly been waiting for Persano's moves, he was now in a new political situation. The Austrians offered an armistice and in it promised to give the Venetian province to Napoleon III (Austria signed a secret agreement with France on 12 June). Napoleon in turn would give the province to Italy, to save some face.

Depretis urged Persano to move as soon as possible to show the world that Italy had *won* Venice. Forced to show some activity, the Admiral decided to search for the enemy in the Adriatic. The last of the many dispatches exchanged between the Minister and fleet commander could not still be ignored by Persano, who was instructed to look for the enemy even if he was not completely ready for action. Orders, already issued on 8 June, to master the Adriatic were compelling him to bar the sea to the Austrian fleet by either attacking it or blockading it at Pola, and now these orders were strongly emphasized and underlined by the Minister.

Persano sailed on the afternoon of 8 July, with the complete fleet, although some minor vessels remained in port and the *Affondatore* was still on the way, having passed Gibraltar on 28 June. Still, Persano was superior in numbers and could have attacked the Austrian fleet. His intention not to deal with the enemy was still obvious from the fact that he steamed in the Adriatic taking a north-south route just beyond the sight of the Dalmatian and Italian coasts until the 13th. Later he was much criticized that this allowed him not to be seen by friend and foe alike.

Interestingly enough, during what was later called "cruising in the right middle" Persano was also not attacked by the Austrians, who had learned of his presence. Tegetthoff was aware of the Italian fleet cruising the Adriatic because on 10 July two messages signaled word of the Italian ships, one time some 25 miles from Lissa, and another near Isola Grossa on the Dalmatian coast. It is possible that he did not react because the situation was not as favorable as he desired. On the 9th Tegetthoff received the news that the Italian General Cialdini had passed the Po River; like the later actions of Vice-Admiral Albini, Cialdini had taken the role of spectator during La Marmora's operation at Custoza.

Earlier, Tegetthoff had briefed his commanders on board his flagship, (transferred from *Schwarzenberg* to *Ferdinand Max* on 24 June,) about his plans and tactics to be used in the event of a battle with the Italians. Tegetthoff's decision to charge and ram the enemy was the only naval tactic practicable in a battle in which the enemy had a gun superiority, both in number and in quality; it was not a new idea, and there is evidence that the Austrian navy followed the experiences

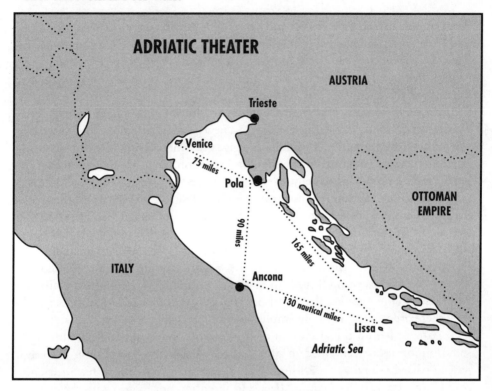

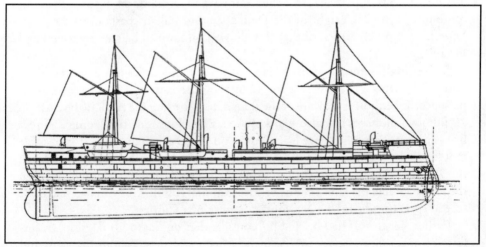

Erzherzog Ferdinand Max

gleaned from the American Civil War. Ritter von Attlmayr brings this point out in his book which appeared in 1896: *Der Krieg Osterreichs in der Adria im Jahre 1866:* "He chose the same solution as Farragut" when he referred to the briefing held by the Austrian admiral in several meetings to explain how the ramming tactics worked and how to carry them out for the best effect. Farragut was also quoted by Tegetthoff in the final report of the battle. This comparison is often repeated and we can assume that the American Civil War had really influenced naval tactics in the first ironclad steam powered battle fought in the open sea. In fact Tegetthoff wrote after the battle:

> In the American Civil War, wooden ships were already successfully employed among ironclads, for they were employed against ironclads at Mobile, and in the battle of Lissa the Austrian fleet offered again the proof that this can always be done without danger.

Also Tegetthoff had received the news of the French mediation between the belligerent, and that Venice would be lost to Italy, which greatly bothered him. Of the 10,000 Austrian naval personnel, about 2,000 were Venetian (i.e., Italian), and of these some 800 were in key positions such as helmsmen and seamen. This was difficult news and he asked about the possibility of disembarking these sailors. He was reassured by the War Ministry, who sent a reply which Tegetthoff published as the order of the day to assure his crews: "Venice not lost, duty unchanged."

Meanwhile Persano had returned to Ancona on the 13th to take on coal and to report to the minister that he had tried to draw Tegetthoff out with his fleet, but really Persano had never come in sight of Pola and his brief night probe toward Venice remained unobserved. Nor had he spotted unescorted Austrian ships transporting troops along the Dalmatian coast but he had approached within 12 miles of Lissa and been sighted. The Adriatic cruising was surely of good value as a tactical exercise (although no target practice was undertaken) but it delivered a severe blow to the spirit of the sailors and officers who were astonished by Persano's lackluster activity.

Persano had a continuous exchange of telegrams with the minister of the navy, Agostino Depretis. From his letters, it appears that Persano was unsure of the state of his fleet, and this was in regard to many aspects. He asked the minister numerous questions, probably in order to wait for a diplomatic conclusion to the war, and to try to have the Minister take responsibility for issuing orders.

Depretis arrived at Ancona on the same 13th to urge Persano to take action against the enemy, otherwise he would relieve him of command. Depretis had with him a letter, ready to fire Persano on the spot, but he spoke with the fleet commander before taking action against him. Prior to that fateful meeting, he summoned some high ranking officers and asked them about the inactivity of the fleet. Admirals Giovanni Vacca and Albini, and moreover the Chief of Staff, the

36 year old Neapolitan D'Amico declared themselves to be against Persano's strategy. The clever D'Amico, although not having served at sea in the previous five years, had placed this question openly before Persano on the 11th.

It is interesting to note that at this point Persano had lost the confidence of his men and officers, and was openly rumored to be a coward, but the Minister would have problems if he relieved him. The problem was connected to the mixed nature of the "Italian" fleet that was still broken down into Neapolitan and Sardinian factions. It was difficult to choose between Albini and Vacca, since neither one of the two would probably have fought under the other's orders. To put this in perspective, it must be recalled that at this point in history the Italian language was not accepted throughout that nation—it was a nation still riven by dialects, which reflected its very recent unification.

Moreover, Persano declared he was still not thinking of moving against the Austrians ... yet, but he wanted to go to Pola as soon as he received the powerful *Affondatore*. This view was accepted and the following day a war council held in Ferrara confirmed to Persano that he could wait for the *Affondatore*, but "as soon as it reaches the fleet you must take to the sea and begin against the fortresses and against the enemy fleet those operations you think most convenient in order to obtain an important success." Such an order was to be strictly observed, otherwise Depretis "will be forced to relieve you of command."

On 15 July, Depretis was still in Ancona to discuss the situation with Persano and to urge him to attack Lissa. The idea was probably given by Vacca to the minister who in turn proposed it to Persano. He was asked about the possibility of attacking the island of Lissa, and Chief of Staff D'Amico, along with Rear-Admiral Vacca agreed that it was a good idea. Persano himself was of the same opinion, for he had already mentioned such an attack in at least two of his letters of 7 June to Minister Angioletti (General Angioletti had been navy minister at the time, before Depretis) and to Depretis on 13 July. On the other hand his intention was to deal with Lissa only after the destruction of the enemy fleet, an affair in which Persano did not want to be involved, since, as he explained to journalist and friend Pier Carlo Boggio (who was also a member of the Parliament), "you do not think of the responsibility I have toward the country which entrusted me with this fleet, and the irreparable loss if we suffer a defeat." Often, when you are more afraid of defeat than you are of gaining a victory, you have already lost the battle. This may have been Persano's crisis of confidence which would cost him the defeat at Lissa.

After the news of French intervention to settle the question of the Venetia, which would be passed to Italy from Austria via France, the Italian government wanted a naval victory to avoid such a humiliating situation; on the contrary Persano did not want any risk before the impending armistice. However, he tried to throw obstacles in the way by saying he wanted six thousand men with engineer officers and an army general to be responsible for the operation. Since this was not possible in the short period of time left, the attack on Lissa was seen as being a *coup de main* and offered him the possibility of avoiding the direct confrontation with the enemy fleet and the possible risk of losing some ships in a naval battle. It is interesting to note that Admiral Albini was against the attack on Lissa, for his Chief of Staff Paolucci was a Venetian officer who had been stationed at Lissa under the Austrian flag, and thought this was not a good move—the island defenses were too strong. The fleet would thus begin an operation without being prepared, having too few marines on board, and lacking a single map of the isle.

No questions were posed by the higher commanders about the attitude Tegetthoff would take if Lissa was attacked, but a letter was written by the *Varese* commander Fincati, who argued that the Austrians could attack Ancona while the Italians were engaged at Lissa.

At 15:00 on 16 July the fleet sailed from Ancona with 11 ironclads, seven large wooden warships, three gunboats and seven steamers, a total of 28 ships. Their destination was Lissa.

The Bombardment of Lissa

While the ironclads, kept in continual motion, rained heavy projectiles on the forts, the latter returned the fire with steadiness. Aware of the small size of the guns on shore, the enemy often ventured within 1,500 yards of the defences.
   —W. Laird Clowes

The isle of Lissa is 11 miles in length and 4 miles broad, dominated by the almost 2,000 foot Mount Hum. Porto San Giorgio (the port of San Giorgio) with the town of Lissa, was a very safe harbor for this period, being one mile long and a half mile wide on the north-east corner, while Porto Manego was on the south-east. The coasts are generally rough and only on the east side is the water shallow. On the west side of the island there is Comisa Bay, a third point of approach. The Austrian defenses were connected with Zara on the coast with an underwater cable and an older semaphore system. The cable was cut too late, and the defenders sent messages asking for help.

The defenses of Lissa had been placed there by the British who fortified the island during the Napoleonic wars, after which they passed them on to the Austrians. In 1860 Lissa was declared a military port and with the war approaching, the existing batteries were reinforced and old fortifications placed in good order. Persano did not have a decent map of Lissa and sent the ship *Messaggero* with his Chief of Staff D'Amico on reconnaissance. He compiled a rather good map, although, understandably, he inaccurately drafted the Madonna battery and failed to appreciate the height advantage of many other batteries. To accomplish his mission, D'Amico sailed under British colors, but his activity was observed by defenders and a corresponding dispatch was sent to Tegetthoff.

The garrison under the command of Colonel Urs de Mangina was about 1,200 men of the 4th, 9th, 10th, 11th, and 12th marine infantry companies and 1,047 men of the newly arrived 69th Jellacic battalion, besides about 562 artillerists of the 3rd and 5th coastal artillery companies, 27 engineers and 44 sailors. On 12 July the Jellacic battalion was shipped to Trieste, and the garrison was reduced to 1,833 men. The batteries at Lissa were mainly concentrated near Port San Giorgio, where there were eight. On the west side of the Comisa Bay there were two, while the little port Manego on the south-east corner was defended by the battery Nadpostranje.

Inside the island there were other batteries, like Fort Erzherzog Max-Feste armed with two 24 pounder short guns and two 7 pounder shell guns, a total of some ninety guns, but these did not engage the Italian fleet because of their position.

On leaving Ancona, Persano steamed at six knots toward Lussino, a different area on the Dalmatian coast, to deceive possible enemy intelligence in Ancona, and at night turned toward Lissa. Near evening on the 17th, the *Messaggero* met the fleet and Persano now had information upon which to issue orders to the fleet. He divided the ironclads into three groups, two of which would attack Port San Giorgio and one Port Comiso, while the wooden ships were to bombard Port Manego. Use of steel projectiles was strictly forbidden—they were to be saved for fighting enemy ironclads.

On the following day the Italian ships appeared at about 10:00 to open fire on the coastal batteries, while the gunboat *Montebello*, leading a flotilla, arrived nearby at the island of Spalmadore to cut the telegraph cable, too late to avoid the dispatch sent to Vienna warning of the start of the Italian attack.

At Port Comiso the *Carignano* and *Castelfidardo* responded to fire started by Austrian guns at 11:30, shelling battery Magnaremi, while the *Ancona* was firing onto Battery Perlic. It was soon clear that the Austrian batteries were too high to be hit by naval fire, although such an appreciation was also inaccurate. They could have been bombarded if the ships had been further away from the coast, and Rear-Admiral Vacca thought they were too high, but in reality the batteries were not placed at as high an elevation as he thought. After the *Carignano* fired 116 times against battery Magnaremi, and in return was hit three times, Vacca ordered his ships to abandon Comisa Bay and to head for Porto Manego to help the wooden squadron of Albini.

Albini in turn had the same problem with the battery San Vito (as the Italians called the Nadpostranje battery), which was attacked by the *Maria Adelaide* and *Vittorio Emanuele*, but had retreated, asking for further orders from Persano. It is interesting that Vice-Admiral Albini refused Vacca's offer to try to fire on the forts of Porto Manego; of his five ships only two fired, the *Maria Adelaide* 14 rounds and the *Vittorio Emanuele* only one, but they were too near the coast to hit the Austrian battery which was placed very high. The half-hearted conduct of the operation by Albini was probably due to the fact he was convinced from the outset that this operation was an error. Vacca now took his three ironclads and steamed to join Persano.

At Porto San Giorgio meanwhile the two ironclad groups began operations at 11:30, shelling with *Re d'Italia, Formidabile, San Martino* and *Palestro* the west side of the port. The east defenses were attacked by *capitano di vascello* Riboty with the ironclads *Re di Portogallo, Maria Pia, Terribile* and *Varese*. At first the gun action was ineffective, and Persano ordered *Formidabile* (commanded by Simon Pacoret de Saint Bon) to bombard at close range Fort San Giorgio which was silenced at 16:00 after a lucky shot by the *Maria Pia* which exploded a powder magazine. Battery Schmidt suffered the same fate at 13:30 with the loss of 35 men. At that point Persano ordered the port to be entered by the *Maria Pia* and *San Martino*. The former was caught by enfilade fire by batteries Madonna and Wellington without being able to maneuver in narrow waters, and the approaching *San Martino* was hit several times, but pierced by only one shot that started a fire on board, compelling the ship to retreat out of the port. The *San Martino* also exchanged shots with battery Madonna without any results. Toward 17:00 the Vacca group arrived and helped Riboty to bombard Bentinck and Wellington towers. These were damaged at 17:30 but continued to reply fiercely to the fire of the Italian ironclads. While battery Manula had ceased fire, the Zupparina and Madonna were still fully engaged with the Italians and intact.

By evening the Italians had suffered seven dead and 41 wounded. The *Re d'Italia* alone had fired 1,300 projectiles. Persano suspended operations. He had reached the commander of the gunboat flotilla, who reported that according to intelligence gained from the enemy, Tegetthoff had assured the garrison of his coming aid. This seems doubtful, since Tegetthoff sent only one dispatch to Lissa on 18 July, at 14:20, asking what type of ships were attacking, trying to gain an understanding of what was really happening. He was reacting cautiously, asking instructions of the war ministry and waiting on events, probably fearing a trap. It is interesting that Persano and D'Amico did not give much credit to such moves, but that night the crews were kept at a state of alert, and the ironclads were cruising 40 miles away in the Lissa channel between the Dalmatian coast and the island.

Persano took this occasion to rebuke Vacca for his weak action at the port of Comisa, and for his leaving the operation without permission. His dispatch to the Vice-Admiral Albini for his operations at Port Manego was also sharp. It was sent to Albini at dawn of the 19th, before Persano had all the reports on the action, and this raised the rivalry that already existing between the two men. They were sent on the morning of the 19th to bombard again the ruins of the Porto San

Giorgio fort which Persano suspected could be brought back to a state of readiness during the night.

Tegetthoff was still receiving despatches from Lissa reporting the development of the Italian attack. He feared that the attack was a diversion and that the main objective was Venice or Trieste, and asked for instruction from Archduke Albert, who had his Headquarters at Codroipo, in north-east Italy, receiving the reply that Istria and Trieste should be defended by an undivided fleet. More light on the matter came the following morning with further messages from Lissa, announcing that 22 Italian ships were taking part in the operations. He now understood that this was not a secondary operation, and ordered his ships to prepare for movement, sending at the same time dispatches to the war minister and Archduke Albert, explaining the situation and asking for orders.

In the waters off Lissa, the *Affondatore* arrived before noon and shortly thereafter the screw frigates *Principe Umberto* and *Carlo Alberto* with the paddle frigate *Governolo*. Thinking of a possible appearance by the Austrian fleet, Persano waited all morning without continuing the bombardment of the forts. Only then did he issue orders for the prosecution of the attack on Lissa, especially to the *Formidabile* that was to enter the port and silence the batteries there.

The ship begun to move slowly because it did not have a chart of the waters, but fired successfully along with the *Affondatore* against the Mamula, Zupparina and Robertson batteries. The battery Madonna proved an especially hard nut to crack. Madonna's eight guns equalled one broadside of the *Formidabile*—which was also one of Italy's less protected ironclads. The commander was the same Saint Bon later to be navy minister, who now performed a daring maneuver, anchoring his ship before the battery. A tremendous fusillade was now opened up at 400 yards causing heavy damage to the ironclad, whose crew was also targeted by infantry fire, with the loss of three killed and 55 wounded (41 according to other sources). At the same time the shots of the *Formidabile* proved ineffective against the approximately 20 feet thick stone wall of the battery; moreover many of the projectiles passed *over* the battery. Vacca briefly entered the port with *Principe di Carignano, Castelfidardo* and *Ancona,* coming under heavy fire. This caused one armor plate to almost break off, casualties of 6 killed and 19 wounded on the *Ancona,* in addition to a fire breaking out on board, and the retreat of these three ironclads, leaving the *Formidabile* alone in the contest. Saint Bon was thus compelled to retreat after having fired 688 projectiles and was later awarded with the Gold Valor medal *(Medaglie d'Oro)* for his performance (this is Italy's highest award and is given for bravery). The ironclad had also suffered the loss of one of her guns and other damage, the worst being the fact that gunport covers were broken, and that for this reason on the following day the ship did not take part in the battle since there was the possibility of her shipping water in heavy seas, which would cause the sinking of the *Affondatore* during a storm on 6 August.

On the other hand it should be noted that the *Formidabile*'s armor plates were not pierced by the Austrian shots.

Thanks to the inactivity of Vice-Admiral Albini the landing at Karober ordered by Persano, with 2,600 men now available after the arrival of further troops, was not attempted since Albini reported difficult conditions at the landing place. A later confirmation by Persano to carry out his orders in some other landing place, led to a half-hearted attempt at 20:00 that failed in the face of Austrian infantry fire. This episode confirms the general attitude of this high officer during the whole operation. At the same time, a probe by Vice-Admiral Vacca was repulsed by gun fire at Comisa Bay.

During the same day Tegetthoff had ordered the fleet out of Fasana after a briefing with his commanders at 10:30 and was waiting for a reply with only the flagship at anchor. About noon the war ministry replied, giving him a free hand, with the restriction of not attacking the enemy if Lissa was a diversionary attack. Thus the fleet commander sailed with the *Ferdinand Max* and the whole fleet steamed south-east at six knots.

At 20:00 Persano rounded up his ships and stationed them about eight miles from the island. The day's losses were 9 more Italians killed and 73 wounded, giving a total in the two days of 16 killed and 114 wounded, compared with the 26 killed and 68 wounded suffered by the defense in two days of bombardment, during which it had fired 2,733 projectiles against the Italian ships. Of the Austrian batteries at Port San Giorgio, only Madonna was untouched, while the others had only 8 guns available. Total Italian ammunition expenditure is difficult to determine but it varied greatly from ship to ship. For example, the *San Martino* fired 776 times at the fortifications, while the *Principe Umberto* fired but 80, the *Terribile* 50 times, the *Castelfidardo* about 1,000 times, and the *Re di Portogallo* a total during the bombardment and subsequent battle of about 500 times.

During the night the fleet remained in place and Persano consulted D'Amico and other officers. Since he was running low on coal and required more troops for a successful landing, D'Amico proposed to anchor at Lesina, where the fleet could wait for replenishment and also for the possible arrival of the Austrian fleet. Rear-Admiral Vacca instead proposed to resupply at Ancona, but such a move without having completed the operational orders would be seen as a defeat and was rejected by Persano. His intention was altered by the arrival on the scene of the paddle transport *Piemonte* with 500 marines that allowed Persano to go on with the landing attempt under the protection of the heavy Armstrong guns whose fire could silence the last of the Austrian coastal guns.

It was just then, with the landing operations in progress that suddenly at 07:50 the *Esploratore* appeared from the heavy rains just to the north with the signal "Suspicious ships in sight."

The Battle

...the war value of a navy is measured by the capacity of the admirals who control it, and by the spirit that animates the captains, officers, and men rather than by size or special characteristics of the ships.
—Admiral Sir Reginald Custance in "The Ship of the Line in Battle"

The Italian fleet around 08:00 was caught scattered to the north and partly on the opposite side of the island of Lissa. The ironclads *Terribile* and *Varese* were preparing for attack at Comisa, the *Re di Portogallo* and *Castelfidardo* had problems with their machinery while the *Formidabile* was busy with transshipping of wounded, and did not take part in the battle due to her damaged condition. Also Albini's wooden warship division, with the gunboat flotilla, was preparing for landing at Karober. So it came about that when Persano had been urged to attack Lissa, he steamed for Lissa without apparently having given much thought to the fact that such an operation would provoke Tegetthoff out of his base to check the Italian move. However he was aware of this possibility, having dispatched the *Esploratore* for scouting duty between Punta Bianca and San Andrea island and the *Stella d'Italia* between San Andrea and Pelagosa island. On the other hand he did not summon his commanders to discuss any tactic or measure to be taken should the enemy fleet appear.

Tegetthoff had approached while reducing speed to five and a half knots because the sea conditions were worsening. He intended to adopt the same formation used during his reconnaissance at Ancona, three divisions formed in salient angle, almost like a flying wedge, each following the other, with the ironclads in the first line, the wooden warships in the second, and the gunboats in the third. Each angle had one leading boat with three each side and one minor vessel going ahead of it. This was a cruising and tactical formation alike. The duty of the ironclads was to pierce the enemy line and therefore attack it aggressively at close range. The wooden ships had to act according to the intentions of their commander, Commodore von Petz, and the gunboats should divide in three parties to help the wooden ships—possibly by enfilading the enemy ships. Should Tegetthoff fall in combat, commanders were instructed to withhold the fact from the crews until the end of the battle.

Steaming south, after sighting an enemy ship at about 07:00, the rain impeded any further observation until about 09:00, when the weather begun to clear and the wind quieted. When at 10:00 the Austrian ships emerged from the mist they saw the Italian fleet assembling north of Lissa. Orders were quickly issued in rapid succession to "Clear for action," "Close up," "Advanced ships take station," "Full speed," and at 10:35 a.m., "Armored ships charge the enemy and sink him."

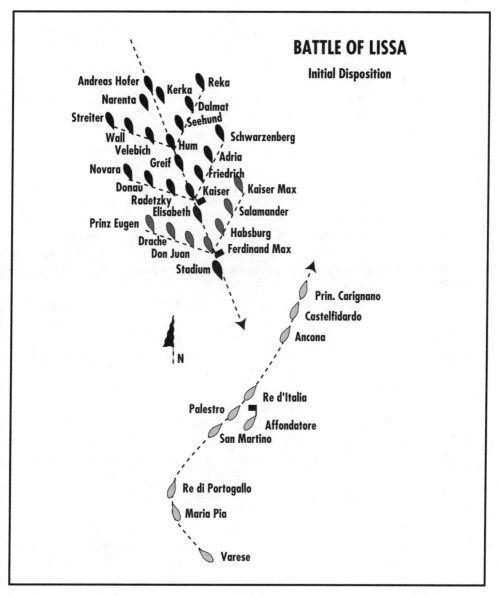

BATTLE OF LISSA

Initial Disposition

Andreas Hofer
Kerka   Reka
Narenta   Dalmat
Streiter   Seehund
Wall   Hum   Schwarzenberg
Velebich
Greif   Adria
Novara   Friedrich
Donau   Kaiser   Kaiser Max
Radetzky
Elisabeth   Salamander
Prinz Eugen
Drache   Habsburg
Don Juan   Ferdinand Max
Stadium

N

Prin. Carignano
Castelfidardo
Ancona

Re d'Italia
Palestro
Affondatore
San Martino

Re di Portogallo
Maria Pia

Varese

In the meantime Persano, after the report of the *Esploratore,* took measures to assemble his forces. Albini was ordered to suspend landing operations and to join the ironclads, 3,000 meters behind them. The two ironclads *Terribile* and *Varese* were recalled from Comisa Bay while the two others with machinery problems, the *Castelfidardo* and *Re di Portogallo,* were towed away and repairs accelerated. The available ironclads were assembled in line. When Austrian smoke appeared at 09:30 the situation of the Italian ships was reordered and the line ahead of the ironclads formed with the direction west southwest. Problems were solved and new ones appeared: the *Varese* joined Persano, but the *Terribile* arrived slowly for reasons never completely clarified and finally joined the wooden ships without taking part to the battle, apart from some long range shot fired against the wooden *Kaiser* when that ship left the battle to take cover at Port San Giorgio. *Castelfidardo* and *Re di Portogallo* had repaired their breakdowns.

Persano was about to confront the Austrians with the Italian ironclads alone and only nine were available, since the *Formidabile, Varese* and *Terribile* had not reached the main group. Of these three the *Formidabile* signalled her intention to go back to Ancona due to her damaged condition. Persano signalled only that he had received the message, but did not agree. However the *Formidabile* abandoned the Lissa waters. The *Terribile* arrived too late and Albini's squadron remained passive in the battle, only participating in the end. The *Varese* joined the line of the ironclads although somewhat distant from other ships. The ship formation Persano had assumed was the line ahead according to *Tactique supplementaire rules* published by French Rear-Admiral Louis Eduard Bouet-Willaumez, who was also commander of the squadron sent to the Adriatic during the 1859 campaign and later in 1865-1866 commanded a six ironclad squadron in the Mediterranean. His handbook was quoted by Persano in his instructions: "The armored squadron will use, besides the regular tactics, also the supplementary one of the Vice-Admiral Bouet-Willaumez. The wooden squadron will use only the regular tactic." Steamship tactics had been developed by naval officers in several countries, such as the already quoted French, the British General Sir Howard Douglas, and the Russian Admiral G. I. Butakov. Also Tegetthoff referred to such regulation and adopted one of the formations suggested by Bouet-Willaumez (*pelotons d'escadres* number 3). It should be noted this had also been proposed by Sir Howard Douglas, but it was also observed that this was a difficult formation for warships to hold for any length of time.

Persano first ordered a turning to the west when the Austrians appeared at 10:00. Having seen the Austrian fleet heading towards Port San Giorgio, he ordered another turn in a north northeast direction to cut off the Austrian advance. This maneuver greatly reduced the range, losing part of the advantage of Italian gunnery superiority, and at 10.43 the *Principe di Carignano* opened fire at about 1,000 yards. At this point the nine Italian ironclads were in a line ahead, heading towards the north northeast, with a tenth ironclad, the *Varese,* approaching. The Italian line had three gaps, one after the three first ships, that is the group of Rear-Admiral Vacca, and the second gap left the last two ships behind.

It had transpired that Persano had changed his flagship from the *Re d'Italia* to the *Affondatore* amidst the ensuing combat without Vacca and other ship commanders being informed of such a move, although Vacca was probably aware of it. This operation took about ten minutes and consequently Persano had accelerated the contact with the enemy with a broken formation. Such a quick turn ordered by Persano was probably due to his being criticized for his conduct on 27 June when the Austrians appeared off Ancona, when he waited too long to have all the ships well disposed for combat, leaving time to the enemy to disengage. By advancing on the enemy he lost gunnery superiority because this advantage could be maintained by falling back from the Austrian fleet, and giving time for the wooden squadron to join the battle, provided that Albini had any intention to do so.

Incidentally, such a quick approach left almost no time for Tegetthoff to deliver his last signal, "Lissa must be a victory." He was steaming at 10 knots in a south southeast direction towards the Italians and when making contact with the enemy line, just where Vacca's ships were leaving a hole, the starboard part of the first wave was directed to the main group of the enemy, and the port one to the Vacca's ships. The main group of the Italian ironclads turned slightly to port to attack the wooden ships of the Austrian second line which in turn charged the rear ships of the Italian line. The resulting *melee* was a continuous passing of ships, one near another, of unlimited attempts to ram, and maneuver to avoid such threats, and of discharging broadsides in the middle of an increasing cloud of smoke generated from the steaming and gunfire. At a certain point the *Affondatore,* which tried many times to ram black ships, the Austrian color (the Italians were gray), broke out of the smoke and tried twice to ram the old *Kaiser* steam ship-of-the-line, also firing its heavy Armstrong guns, one shot dismounting an upper deck gun. After the second charge, the *Kaiser* fired a broadside that caused great damage to the upper deck structures of the Italian ship, and thereafter the two vessels passed alongside exchanging rifle fire. It was 11:00 when the *Kaiser* and the *Re di Portogallo* tried to sink each other and scraped alongside with the Italian ship firing her broadside. The *Kaiser* suffered considerably in this encounter and left her bow sculpture on the deck of *Re di Portogallo,* and after receiving another broadside from the *Maria Pia,* left the melee in a cloud of smoke and on fire, steaming toward Port San Giorgio. In the process the *Terribile,* which arriving on the battlefield had joined the wooden squadron under Albini, was satisfied in firing some long range shots without any result. The *Kaiser* was helped in her retreat by the *Erzherzog Friedrich, Seehund* and *Reka,* and was attacked by the *Affondatore,* which tried twice to ram her but was hindered by the wooden ships and later by the intervention of the ironclads *Don Juan de Austria* and *Prinz Eugen.* A third time the *Affondatore* tried ramming but failed when Persano ordered her to turn away. The *Affondatore* did have the chance to fire 300 pounder shots at the *Don Juan de Austria,* hitting her three times and breaking off some armor plates from the Austrian ship.

Other significant features of this confusing battle were the ramming and sinking of *Re d'Italia*, and the striking and eventual sinking of the *Palestro*. It happened that the ironclad group under Rear-Admiral Vacca remained isolated, with the *Principe di Carignano* and *Castelfidardo* turning to port while the middle of Persano's ironclad line was assailed by most of the Austrian fleet. Two of Vacca's ships turned towards the wooden Austrian vessels but were checked by concentrated Austrian fire of the steam frigates *Donau, Radetzky* and *Schwarzenberg*. Vacca's left instead of right turn was later strongly criticized. He has been considered by Austrian and Italian writers alike as just a little less responsible than Persano and Albini for the Italian defeat at Lissa. The Austrian ships could concentrate against the middle of the Italian line, where the supposed Italian flagship was located. It should be noted that a general navy rule of the time prescribed that during battle the ships had to support the flagship. Two attempts by the Austrian flagship *Ferdinand Max* failed because the Italian ironclads managed to avoid the assault, during one of which an Italian national flag, part of the combat insignia of the *Palestro*, fell on the deck of the Austrian ship and remained there as war booty. Also the *Re d'Italia*, still thought to be the Italian flagship, was soon beset by four Austrian ironclads and the attempt of the *Palestro* to come to her aid failed because of the barrage of fire from two Austrian vessels; the *Ferdinand Max* tried to ram her but the *Palestro* managed to avoid the attack. One shell fired by *Drache* started a fire on board because the *Palestro* went into battle with extra coal on deck to increase her steaming range. This circumstance would prove fatal to the *Palestro*, which now had to abandon the struggle.

The *Re d'Italia* was meanwhile hit in her steering gear which, being above water and well exposed, was disabled. She was maneuvering solely on her engines. Lieutenant Enrico Gualterio, one of the survivors and an eyewitness, wrote:

> About the sinking I think the main and lone cause was the fact the rudder was exposed, therefore was blown off by enemy shots. Since we were steaming without steering we were cut off from the Fleet ... We tried at full speed to avoid the shock of the ironclad that headed toward our midships, but since we would have received those of another ship coming from bow, we reversed engines hoping to have as always some movement ... but the reverse movement stopped the ship ...
>
> The ship sank with all the flags high, officer Razzetti used his saber to keep any sailor from taking down the flag. After being hit we fired a broadside and the men with boarding duty, along with those on the mast fired their small arms a last time. Then the crew threw themselves overboard into the sea without cries and confusion. When we were in the water we were targeted by some rifle shots from an Austrian gunboat which wounded two sailors and killed two others.

The ship was almost dead in the water and unable to maneuver, thus enabling the *Ferdinand Max* to deliver a fatal blow at full speed. As the war diary of the *Ferdinand Max* says:

The Battle of Lissa, 9 May 1866. The Re d'Italia *sinks after being rammed by the* Ferdinand Max.

The engagement with the enemy ironclads was going on when at 11.30 am we succeeded, while steaming at full speed, to ram a large enemy ship that moved across, about on the quarter near the foremast. The enemy ship rolled back one time and sunk a minute and a half after the shock.

The Italian ex-flagship was caught when she was trying to reverse her movement because her advance was impeded by an Austrian ironclad, thus she was nearly stopped when rammed. Hit in her midships at eleven and a half knots by 4,500 tons of solid iron, the *Re d'Italia* had an enormous hole opened in her flank, about half of which was under the water line, about six and half feet deep. The Austrian ship quickly reversed its direction to free itself from the enemy ship that sank almost instantly after such a shock, while sailors were still firing with muskets, Boggio, a friend of Persano, used his revolver. An outburst of "hurrah!" was spreading on all the Austrian ships in sight. At that moment the *Ancona* was trying to ram the Austrian flagship, but failing, fired a broadside which had no effect. Commander Piola-Caselli stated later, at the Inquiry Commission for the state of materials of *Regia Marina (Royal Navy):*

> ...since a commander had to wait until the moment to fire in order to choose to load the gun with wrought iron or steel shot (and to this last more powder must be added), it is possible that the Chief gunner fired with powder *alone,* forgetting how the gun was loaded.

Commander Piola-Caselli had suggested on the same occasion that steel projectiles would be excluded from employment since they wore down the gun barrel after being fired only 25 times. After the fight with the *Ferdinand Max* the *Ancona* had a collision with the *Varese* while trying to reach and help the *Re di Portogallo*. The shock left some damage to both ships, and the *Varese* had a plate displaced. Another collision took place between *Maria Pia* and *San Martino* when the former, after a wide maneuver, tried to intercept two Austrian ironclads and failing in a ramming attempt, exchanged ordinary infantry fire, and then headed to join with Rear-Admiral Vacca.

At 12:10 Tegetthoff signalled to his ships to join the commander, and arranged them in three columns on a northeasterly course, with the ironclads closest to the enemy. Persano signalled also to his ships to attack the enemy, but Albini's wooden division, which was still a spectator, did not move at all. At 13:00 Tegetthoff ordered the *Kaiser Max* to cut off the *Palestro,* but the burning ship slipped away in the chase, while protected by the *Indipendenza* and the supporting *Affondatore* and towed by *Governolo.*

Persano wanted to resume action after having reunited the fleet, but there were several obstacles to this course of action; the *Re d'Italia* had been sunk, the *Palestro* was on fire and the *San Martino* was unable to resume combat immediately due to damage. Moreover the wooden ships displayed the greatest inactivity, although Persano signalled that whoever "is not in action is not in her station," clearly saying that Albini was disobeying orders. The Italian fleet therefore headed away from the battle scene, and Tegetthoff sent his gunboats to try for Port San Giorgio, where all the fleet assembled by the evening, the last to arrive being the *Ferdinand Max.* Before this, the *Palestro* was still fighting the fire on board and the commander Alfredo Cappellini wanted to remain at his post with all the crew, but fire reached some shells that exploded. At 14:30 she blew up and sank.

After some hours of cruising near the waters of Lissa, Persano made the decision to go to Ancona, but he sailed only at 22:30 for his base, when Tegetthoff was anchoring at Fasana. By 14:00 Tegetthoff has been promoted to Vice-Admiral.

Aftermath

The effect of the battle on naval development was marked. For nearly a generation it fastened attention on the ram, and led all navies to build ships designed for end-on attack. Only with the progress of the torpedo which rendered close action too hazardous and uncertain for any but the most resolute, did this inclination towards a line-abreast formation pass.
—H.W. Wilson

The Austrians lost 3 officers and 35 sailors, 15 officers and 123 men were wounded. The Italians lost the crews of *Palestro* (11 officers and 193 sailors) and

Re d'Italia (408 dead, 159 were rescued and 18 reached Lissa by swimming). There were 7 other officers wounded, 7 sailors killed and 32 wounded on the other ships.

The sea encounter between the Austrian and Italian fleets near Lissa was over in some two hours and the true fight did not last more than three quarters of an hour, but it had many consequences. The fact that an inferior fleet had won the battle raised some questions, first about personal responsibility and secondly about technical matters. The questions about personal responsibility were focused almost exclusively on the Italian fleet commander Admiral Persano who was indicted for either not having carried out or having fulfilled his orders so badly that he was dismissed, with the loss of his rank and pension. He survived only thanks to secret help from the King (presumably to keep him quiet and silence the scandal) and died in poverty in 1883. His defense was summed up in a pamphlet he put in circulation in September of 1866 to counter the scandalmongering campaign mounted against him to satisfy Italian public opinion demanding to know who was responsible. "All were lions before the fight, but when coming to the proof they become rabbits, except for some few exceptions." His two reluctant subordinates Vice-Admiral Albini and Rear-Admiral Vacca were forced to retire as a consequence of an inquiry in 1867, but this did not gain the same publicity. For comparison, during the 1849 campaign that ended with the Italian military defeat at Novara, the Piedmontese General Ramorino was brought before a firing squad for not having moved his troops in good time. This story was often quoted when Albini's behavior was discussed.

Even if the penalty was too harsh, since he paid for the mistakes of others, Persano had to take ultimate responsibility. It is true however that the navy minister should have relieved him of command when the fleet commander—a rank and honor never reached by Nelson—proved to be so weak, moreover the influence of the minister upon the expedition to Lissa was great.

Persano appeared to lack a definite strategic plan, other than to try to wait for the coming armistice, nor did he have a tactical plan to be given to his officers and sailors. When compelled to take action by threats to relieve him of his command, he attacked Lissa to satisfy the navy minister without any sort of preparation. His main weakness was his inactivity inspired by prudence, which gave a painful impression to the navy crews and officers, effectively demoralizing them on the eve of battle. The trial, but especially the public discussion before and after, made clear that he was far from loved in the fleet, just the opposite of his adversary. He was warmly hated by Saint Bon, Vacca, and Albini to give some examples, and as a consequence there was never a common discussion of tactics and operations planning. The aversion was not just between Sardinian and Neapolitan officers and therefore between Persano and the officers mentioned because he was even more hated by the Venetian officers.

In many cases Persano summoned friends and cronies, as well as his Chief of Staff Captain D'Amico, his deputy and friend Boggio, and other ship commanders, instead of Vacca and Albini. They in return undertook their tasks with little or no interest, leaving the commander in the lurch. Some authors have argued from the attitude displayed in the campaign that these high officers were incompetent or, worse, cowards. But it should be remembered that Vacca was chosen by Cavour for his energy and courage, although he appeared unscrupulous, and Albini displayed much valor in the fight against Ancona in 1860 when he was commander of the ship *Vittorio Emanuele*. But he was no "brain" and, moreover, hated the ironclads and new naval technologies.

After the battle, historians' discussions in Italy was largely dominated by the Persano question, with some obvious political input, without many considerations of the technical aspects of the battle, i.e., who fired at whom and so on. But worldwide Lissa become the victory of the ram over the gun. As one Austrian officer wrote later of the guns, "we could have left them at home" that day. This was because both the Austrian and the Italian gunfire "proved so uneven and without effectiveness against ironclads."

On the other hand, of the many ramming attempts of the day, only one was successful and won the battle on the Austrian side. This was only because the *Re d'Italia* had her rudder broken, and yet this deeply influenced naval circles until the 1890's, since no other major naval engagement occurred in the quiet seas of the second half of the 19th century. At the same time there had been no particular examples of battles between ironclads in the open sea before Lissa, while those of the American Civil War generally took place in coastal waters.

As already mentioned, an Inquiry Commission was established by the navy ministry on 8 August 1866 in order to clarify "the state of the materials and administration of the *Regia Marina.*" We can also add that the commission had to charge Persano with all the blame. Of course this was not its main duty, since it was one of the two the Royal Italian Government had decided to establish. The other was a judicial inquiry to clarify the question of personal responsibility.

The commission held its duty as most important not only to identify the responsibilities for the defeat, but also in order to understand the steps that needed to be taken for the future effectiveness of the navy, as pointed out in the commission's final words, "Italy will have in a short time a better navy, with one third expense cut." The commission said this had also been done in other countries, like the Netherlands in 1852, in Great Britain between 1802 and 1861 and in France in the years 1849-1851, with an improvement of the navies of those countries. Essentially, the retirement of older wooden ships, even with the reduction in the budget, allowed for the modern ironclads to be kept in commission and with trained crews.

Much information came to light during the commission's work. For example, in the field of orders to the shipbuilding industry, often made without following the contract rules. There was often a lack of test minutes, or a discrepancy found in operations from the final trial data, as in the case of ·the *Ancona,* a ship built for 13 and a half knots and developing, instead, 12 and a half knots. The *Re d'Italia,* sunk in the battle, was 15 months under repair after her acceptance by the navy for boiler problems and the poor quality of timber with which she was built, although this did not justify the lack of resistance of the ship to the ramming; the *Varese* was accepted because of the approaching war but did not run her trials and was slower than foreseen, also needing repairs, which the French dockyard had to undertake.

Generally speaking, the commission said that many documents were lacking, and especially the most important ones. The *Terribile* and *Formidabile* were built with a one year delay by the French owned *Societe de Forges et Chantiers de la Mediterranee* and were in reality such bad steamers that one can understand why the trial minutes, building contracts, bids by constructors and ship design etc., were not available. According to these ships' officers, neither ironclads could hold the line, unless the sea was calm and the weather good.

Also the *Varese* and *Palestro* were built by the same company without any design and the commission established that the speed of the *Varese* developed only six out of the ten designed knots, that only one fourth of the ship's length was armored, and that powder and shells were delivered through an unarmored section of the ship. This could explain in part why the sister ship *Palestro* was so decisively hit during the battle. The loss was caused by the fire on board which in turn was due to the lack of armor over all the ship's length, since she was armored only in the central part of the hull.

The ram *Affondatore* appeared to the commission to be both a shipbuilding failure and an administrative scandal at the same time. At first commissioned without expense approval by the Government to the Mare Company in London, which did not survive long enough to build the ship, the second order was given to the Harrison shipyard without the need of approval. The coming of the war required the acceptance of the ship without making difficulties for the building company, although during unofficial trials, the ship failed to make her speed or projected draft. She was not lost because of damages received during the battle, as has been argued, but due to a storm in August, when she shipped storm water and sank at the port entrance, from where she was later raised and recovered.

Such severe statements were partly refuted by the "Observations and Justifications," a booklet printed by the navy, a remarkable case of reaction in this sort of affair. The navy argued that the commission made some errors in the request and evaluation of the documents, probably due to the incompetence of some of its members. Some papers came to light and in some cases justifications were offered concerning the low speed of the *Varese,* due to the fact that French machinery personnel were disembarked and the replacements were untrained. Ships were in danger of impoundment by the French or British governments, causing many to be accepted without sea trials. Some ships like the *Ancona* had a lower speed than expected because her trials were made with perfect conditions and clean hull—when later having a fouled hull she was substantially slower. The fact that there were fouling problems is a difference between the Austrian and Italian fleets—upkeep on the Austrian fleet was better.

The general opinion of the Italian officers was that their navy was far superior to the Austrian one. This is reflected in all the testimony the commission took from various Italian officers appointed to different duties, and the commission's conclusions adhered to this statement.

The exact distribution of the guns between the ships was not determined by the commission. There had been so many changes, with old guns landed, new ones embarked, and others shifted from one ship to another on the eve of battle, that it simply could not be exactly determined.

After the battle, the Armament Director at Ancona visited all the ships of the fleet, checked all the guns, and not one was changed, for they were all still fit for further action. There was little serious damage, all which was repaired in one week, except for the *Re di Portogallo,* which was repaired by 2 August. The armor plates were rarely displaced, in most cases they had been deeply crushed, and only two were pierced. It could not even be determined if the plates were pierced by Austrian or Italian projectiles. The director wrote on 23 July that "having visited on your order the Royal ships of the Lissa operation, I have found all materials in a very good state, and more than capable enough to bear with safety any war action."

In 1871, in Streffleur's Austrian military magazine, the Austrian naval Captain Engelmann commented on ironclad tactics based on the experiences learned in the battle of Lissa. One fact noted was that steam allowed little time to prepare for action after the enemy was spotted—one example was the surprise of the scattered Italian fleet. It was also noted that the formation used by Tegetthoff in his assault had actually a considerable disadvantage when used against an enemy in line formation, because the side ships would enter the battle later. A line abreast would be more effective.

In his analysis of the battle, Engelmann outlined four main points that caused the Italian defeat. First the fact that the Italians expected a gunnery duel with the Austrians. Secondly, they were deceived by the formation Tegetthoff adopted. Thirdly, the Italian ship commanders waited for Persano to signal instructions for the battle, instead of acting independently. And finally there was little confidence in the ram as a weapon. As Engelmann comments, these points were not mentioned during the Persano trial. In effect, the trial was to hold Persano responsible for every blunder of the campaign.

Persano himself was highly impressed by the Lissa fighting results and stated that it "being possible that the ironclads can be sunk by the shock of the ram, just as the wooden ships are," he recommended that hulls be built with numerous watertight compartments. He also suggested building rams with two screws because the battle was decided more by rams than by guns and because the ram tactics were "simpler," and preferable to Bouet-Willaumez or Butakov's tactical books. Such was the impact on world navies, that the Austrians held ram tactics for many years in great esteem. Even in the 1890's old officers who were at Lissa, like von Sterneck, proposed to build rams, when gun development and torpedoes had rendered hopeless any ram charge. In his paper on the battle, Captain Colomb underlined that in a time of quick technological change, the ram should be considered as a naval weapon, although the gun would continue to be important and the main armament of a fleet.

Important effects of the battle were visible also in the following years in Austrian and Italian shipbuilding. In fact, Tegetthoff's conclusions after deep technical investigation into future shipbuilding, were that future ships should have complete armor protection, be powered by twin screws, and armed with many powerful guns on board. This was reflected in the construction of the wooden central battery armored ship *Lissa,* which was begun the following year, with an increased thickness of her armor plates (to 158mm), and the powerful armament of ten 24cm Krupp guns. Also the *Kaiser* was reconstructed and armored and strengthened by ten 23cm Armstrong guns and both ships were also armed with four 9cm and two 7cm guns as a secondary battery. Also the two following ironclads, named the *Custoza* and *Erzherzog Albrecht,* were laid down in 1869 under Tegetthoff's influence, with the important change that their hulls were iron built. The central battery *Erzherzog Albrecht* was 5,940 tons and could steam at 13.38 knots. She was armed with eight 24cm breechloading rifles built by Krupp, and protected by 177mm armor plates over 254mm of wood. Maximum thickness of the plates was 203mm on waterline belt, supported on 203mm of wood. The central battery *Custoza* displaced 7,060 tons and developed almost 14 knots while protected by 227mm of iron over her machinery and 177mm on her batteries. Her main guns were eight 26cm Krupp guns. However with the death of Tegetthoff in 1871, this trend ended.

A new form of warfare was born for the young Austrian navy, to be conducted by torpedo boats with the weapon that was also called "the devil's device." Geographically the Austrian side of the Adriatic had a thousand islands which were conducive to a guerrilla war to be carried on with small ships rather than with cruisers. Moreover there was the fact that the Austro-Hungarian Empire (no longer known as the Austrian Empire after 1866) always remained behind in the naval race with Italy, a fact that led to some interest under the Admiral Sterneck naval administration in the French *Jeune Ecole*, although the Austrian light craft were larger than those conceived by the leader of that school, French Admiral Aube.

Some 30 large torpedo boats existed in this later period, while in 1887 a larger type, the torpedo-gunboat of about 1,500 tons was also placed in service. Still, naval maneuvers in the 1880's proved that a daylight attack with torpedoes against enemy ships usually failed, as torpedo craft were disabled before they could reach the one kilometer range needed to launch the torpedoes.

Sterneck, a hero at Lissa, advocated the ram until the 1890's, reflecting the strong influence over the Austrian navy of the events of 20 July 1866. He wanted unarmored ships of 3,000-4,000 tons, with high speed, to directly attack the enemy. He considered the ram as "the ship of the future." Of course, the rapid development of gun technology, especially in the small and medium calibers, turned ramming into a hopeless enterprise for ships in close combat.

In the 1880's the Austrian navy technical department evaluated the important building points of a warship, such as speed and compartmentalization, as well as armor and guns. Interestingly enough, it held torpedo armament in low consideration.

Until the signature of the Triple Alliance with Germany and Italy, the main Austrian enemy was the Italian kingdom, and the Adriatic was the field of contest. Russia was the second most likely enemy that she faced. War scenarios involving Russia foresaw the coming of a Russian squadron into the Adriatic to support the Turkish position in Bosnia-Herzegovina against Austria, while Prussia had to deal with the Russian giant in the Baltic Sea. A more favorable situation would be one in which Italy and England would be supporting the Austrian action, which is what really happened during the Greek blockade in 1886, and more so in the 1887 cooperation of the Western Powers against Russia.

The year 1891 was a turning point for Austrian shipbuilding, the starting point of the *"Flottenpolitik,"* since the summer construction plan of Sterneck was changed by an admiral's commission. This foresaw three fleets, only one of which was at hand, with the others built in a five year program. The Russians had helped the Austrian navy in obtaining an increase of budget by establishing a larger Russian force in the Black Sea.

After the conclusions of the already cited Inquiry Commission, Italy developed rather quickly a policy to deal with the main concerns in the Italian navy; one was the professional education of the personnel and the other big ship construction that would be represented by the former commander of the *Formidabile*, Saint Bon. He became navy minister and developed the new *Duilio* capital ships class in strict collaboration with the naval designer Benedetto Brin.

Just after the war two new ironclads entered service, but they were laid down in 1863 at Genoa, the *Roma* and *Venezia*. Both arrived too late for the war; the former was completed in 1868 and the latter in 1873. Both were wooden hull, central battery ironclads and were armored with plates 150mm thick on the waterline and 120mm on batteries, with a speed of 13 knots. Armament at first was of several calibers, but was soon standardized between the years 1874 and 1875 with the 250mm gun. The *Roma* received eleven pieces and eight were given to *Venezia,* which also had one of 220mm. Before laying down the big ships promoted by Saint Bon and Brin, Italy received two more wooden armorclads from the yards at Castellamare di Stabia and at La Spezia named *Principe Amedeo* and *Palestro.* The long time required for construction rendered both obsolete; laid down in 1871 *(Palestro)* and 1872 *(Principe Amedeo),* they entered service only in 1875-1876. Armor thickness was meanwhile increased to 220mm at waterline and limited to 140mm on the gun batteries, but the remaining parts of the ships were unprotected. Their guns were changed from the old 16cm guns to one 280mm and six 250mm each.

The time of the big ships was about to begin.

THE FRANCO-PRUSSIAN WAR

...our war service on the Outer-Jahde, inactive from a military point of view, was burdensome and heavy...
—Grossadmiral von Tirpitz

France had not only an army but a navy which ... even the British for twelve years past had regarded ... as a deadly threat ...
—Michael Howard, *The Franco-Prussian War*

Bouet-Willaumez never passed beyond the blockading stage in the Baltic, imitating therein the conduct of the larger proportion of British admirals in command for years in the North Sea, the Channel, and the Mediterranean. There was a furious outcry against him in France by a people profoundly ignorant of the conditions, yet his answer was complete. He had not troops, no small vessels; none of the appliances for territorial attack; and the masking of the very inferior German fleet was not complete.
—Vice-Admiral P.H. Colomb

The roar of the Krupp guns at Sedan smothered the naval dimension of the war between France and the new Germany. In effect, some historians have defined the naval events of this war as actions without significance.

The outbreak of war between France and Prussia and the smaller German states on 19 October 1870 is widely known for its land warfare aspect and the exploits of Helmuth von Moltke the elder's army at Sedan. The young Prussian navy was in a much worst situation, having to deal with an Imperial French navy four times its strength. Apart from the much talked about episode of the minor fighting in the West Indies between the *Meteor* and the French *Bouvet,* the campaign deserves little attention, but the moves behind the scenes and the political and strategic considerations are worth some attention.

The total French sea control compelled the little Prussian navy to limit her activity to defending the coasts, where she was under the protection of her coastal guns. It is interesting that just after the declaration of war, the navy obtained a supply of Krupp guns that enhanced the defense of the two main war harbors, Kiel and Wilhelmshaven. Kiel had just been acquired in the recent war with Denmark in 1864.

Some days before the outbreak of the war the most important part of the Prussian fleet, composed of the ironclads *Koenig Wilhelm, Friedrich Karl, Kronprinz* and the little *Prinz Adalbert,* were in training, steaming through the Channel to the Atlantic, under the command of Prince Adalbert von Preussen. The first three German warships were broadside armored frigates—all were foreign built.

The French planned to cut off this important squadron but on 10 July the Prussian intelligence service working in London gained important information—a considerable success of the Prussian/German intelligence service, and delivered a timely warning directly from the Ambassador to Prince Adalbert. He was able to head for home arriving on 16 July at Wilhelmshaven, despite the fact that the squadron was slowed due to engine difficulties with some of the ships. The Germans were not in great danger as the French Atlantic squadron was slow to react, as it was not ready for this sudden war. A squadron of seven ironclads did not leave Cherbourg until 24 July.

The French also kept their Mediterranean squadron there, in case the Prussian fleet steamed for the Mediterranean, where it could disrupt troop movement from North Africa and French shipping in general. Ironically, it was foreseeing what the German battlecruiser *Goeben* would try to do in 1914.

Criticism was then raised against the Prussian fleet—that they were unfit for confronting the enemy. Mechanical problems with the *Koenig Wilhelm* and the *Friedrich Carl* were not repairable in Germany; it should be taken into account that only in December were these ships able to enter the first basin at Wilhelmshaven. The former had never had her hull cleaned and some 60 tons of growth was removed. Because of this, the Prussian ironclads had their speed reduced to 10 knots instead of 14, which hindered their employment against superior forces and robbed them of the chance to disengage the enemy if needed. Moreover, with the lack of adequate naval facilities, any damage was very difficult to repair.

Confronting the German/Prussian fleet was the French navy, the second most powerful force in the world, which could rely upon a fine ironclad fleet in which she had led the world in construction for about a decade. In the Channel France deployed under the command of Rear-Admiral Dieudonne, the ironclads *Thetis*, *Gauloise* and *Flandre*. Another squadron was in the Mediterranean with the *Atalante*, *Couronne*, *Heroine*, *Magnanime*, *Montcalm*, and *Provence*. The squadron commander was Vice-Admiral Fourichon, who also had the *Renard*, a dispatch boat. Around the world the French had some other armored vessels, like the small ironclad *Alma* that was sailing from the Mediterranean to China, and the *Belliqueuse*, detached from the Channel squadron to the Levant. Moreover, they had a number of ironclads under construction or in reserve. All these ships were primarily deep draft broadside ironclads.

On 24 July, Vice-Admiral Bouet-Willaumez (who had inspired ironclads tactics at Lissa), appointed by the Emperor commander in chief of the navy, caused a small fleet of seven ironclads and one dispatch ship put to sea. By November two French squadrons would be cruising the North Sea waiting and hoping for a Prussian attempt to exit into the open sea. Later squadrons would operate in the North Sea and the Baltic. The French did maintain a blockade of the German ports for much of the war which "prevented regular trade." In fact this was the real benefit of the French Navy to France—"French commerce was safe and secure on the high seas while German shipping activities ceased." As winter came on the ironclads were withdrawn and the numerous French wooden warships maintained the blockade.

The French fleet was composed of many ironclads but all were unfit for shallow waters operations; her reference point over the years had been the Royal Navy. But this was not to be a war of squadrons on the open sea but a coastal war. Although eleven good copies of the Crimean *batterie flottante* had been built between 1859 and 1867, there were no well designed warships for coastal operation, since the ironclads drew twenty-three feet and the armored steam batteries about twenty. This state of affairs, coupled with the French aim to strive for a sea battle with the greatest possible advantage, hindered any operation of significance during the war.

The French had an interesting strategic point of view for the war, namely the opening of a new north front, near Kiel, since the only possible landing operations could take place in the Baltic. This would have required an alliance with the Danes. This *could* occur, thanks to the large sea power enjoyed by the French, who might have sent an expeditionary corps to the Danish peninsula. It was originally envisioned that 30,000 Frenchmen would join with 40,000 Danes. The French wanted the Danish cooperation, also the Prussian Chief of Staff von

Moltke had theorized in the past years about such a situation, but during the campaign the main attention was paid to land operations. The Danes did not join the French in an alliance, although the arrival at Copenhagen on 28 July of the French squadron was warmly cheered by the populace. But Denmark stayed neutral. Bouet-Willaumez studied possible landing operations and numerous German troops were retained in the north until the situation was fully clarified. However, with the defeat on land of the French armies, there were no troops to land in the Baltic.

This stalemate on the sea had few exceptions that allowed for fighting around the world. In East Asia the Prussians had the corvettes *Hertha* and *Medusa*. The *Arcona*, which had earlier served in the Schleswig-Holstein War, was in the Atlantic on her way home, when she received orders to reach a neutral port. Her commander, von Schleinitz, sent some sailors home with a transport ship, while making for Lisbon, where she was again repaired. This old ship would reach Wilhelmshaven at the end of the war only to be again put under repair. The more modern frigate *Elisabeth* (same class as *Arcona)* remained at home since Bismarck did not want to unleash a *guerre de course* against the French commercial shipping, because this would be a disaster for Prussian commerce. Consequently, the intention of employing the ironclad *Friedrich Karl* and the *Elisabeth* in raiding missions was canceled.

Another reason this was not done was that though France received war materials from Great Britain and the United States, attacking such traffic could have resulted in friction with Great Britain, which was an undesired complication.

The only ship sent to raid commerce was the *Augusta,* which sailed on 12 December 1870 toward the north French coasts. The *Augusta* cruised from 26 December waiting for an arms shipment from the United States. It was not found, but three transports were captured. Steaming toward Cape Finisterre, to avoid French warships, the *Augusta* arrived at Vigo, Spain, where she anchored near the French ironclad frigate *Heroine*. Three more warships arrived to blockade her but with the armistice, the *Augusta* sailed for home.

The Prussian *Arminius* reported, for example, some forty skirmishes at sea, but the only worthy fight was between two vessels that met and fought in the waters of the West Indies. From the Prussian side it was the gunboat *Meteor,* whose poor seagoing qualities compelled the commander, von Knorr, to take refuge at Key West in Florida at the outbreak of war. The gunboat arrived on 7 November at Havana where there was also the French dispatch boat *Bouvet*. The next day at evening, after making a "duel" agreement, the French commander Franquet sailed and waited in international waters for the enemy vessel.

The artillery strength ratio was the same; both ships had one 16cm rifled and two 12cm rifled guns on the German ship and four 12cm guns on the French ship, but the French was more powerfully engined, while the *Meteor* had a stouter hull. The *Bouvet* had 85 men and the opposite ship 64. In accord with the international neutrality laws the *Meteor* sailed twenty-four hour later.

On 9 November 1870, only two miles off Havana the two ships spotted each other and outside neutral waters the ships began the fight. At 2,000 meters the *Meteor* opened fire against the *Bouvet* firing eight salvos without effect. In return, the *Bouvet* only opened fire at 14:30 when the range was about 800 meters, steaming northwards at a speed of 10 knots under a light breeze. Accuracy was poor and the ships tended to circle around each other, a common tactic between two ships in a duel. When range dropped to 300 meters, the French ordered full speed and tried to ram the enemy ship. The *Meteor* succeeded in avoiding direct impact, but she was hit at a forty-five degree angle, suffering some damage to her small boats and losing two masts which fell. The main mast fell over on to the starboard side, fouled the screw and hinded the proper employment of the guns. The *Bouvet* suffered bow damage. While the two ships were very close the crews opened fire with rifles and pistols.

While tacking, the *Bouvet* came in sight of the aft gun, where the gun commander made the personal decision, without waiting for an order, to fire. This shot hit the *Bouvet* under the funnel, putting her boiler out of action, which was detected by the steam cloud coming from the French ship. She was out of combat because she could only maneuver with sails. The *Meteor* tried to free herself from her mast and to reach the enemy to board it, but at 15:30 the screw was slowing due to the entangling shrouds, preventing her pursuit of the *Bouvet* that was retiring on Havana. When the *Meteor* was ready to continue the fight at 16:30, the French were already four miles into neutral waters and the Spanish steam corvette *Hernan Cortez*, which had stood by during the combat, fired a warning gun and advised her to cease combat.

The French had three wounded and the Prussians two dead and one wounded according to a contemporary Prussian account, while other sources give two killed for the *Meteor* and ten killed and wounded for the *Bouvet*.

Another skirmish was on the night of 22/23 July 1870 at Putzig Bay, near Danzig, where the German wooden corvette *Nymphe* was stationed. Four French warships anchored before the bay at about 18:00. That night the *Nymphe* slipped out, fired two broadsides at the French ironclad *Thetis,* and raced back, arriving safely at 03:00 on the 23rd.

Besides difficulties in keeping ironclads at sea for the blockade, and the fact that German traffic under neutral flags, i.e., British, was hardly disturbed, after the land defeat France was forced to withdraw from the Baltic and end the blockade, having done very little. If criticism was very bitter among public opinion—the cry was "what has the navy done," the proud spirit displayed by the many sailors employed as land troops in the last defense of the second empire gained wide admiration for the navy.

On 18 January 1871, with the proclamation of the German Empire under the Kaiser, there was also born the *Kaiserliche Marine* from the ashes of the *Norddeut-schen Bundesmarine*. With the end of the war later that year a reinforcement of the new navy with vessels taken from the French navy was not undertaken, as the problem of the Imperial German Navy was a question of trained officers and sailors rather than ships to be manned.

Turkish Support of Austria, 1866

by Dr. Mike Bennighof

When the telegram arrived at the headquarters of Austria's Southern Army in the early summer of 1866, none of the staff officers could believe it. Turkish soldiers and sailors—the Habsburg monarchy's sworn enemies for five centuries—were deploying to *defend* the empire's southern regions from possible Italian, Serb and Romanian invaders.

"Das hätte Mamula nie erlaubt," snorted Archduke Albrecht, the army commander. "Mamula would never have allowed this." Mamula, a highly conservative Croat until recently governor of Dalmatia, would never have stained Austrian honor by accepting the aid of the infidel Turk, and few at headquarters could truly believe that such help was being offered.

Yet the news was accurate; the Sublime Porte had dispatched naval and army units to key points near the Austrian border as a clear warning to the radical nationalists in Florence and Turin. Plans to make the Adriatic an Italian lake and spark similar nationalist movements across the Balkans, frightened the Ottoman government no less than Austria's leaders. Like the Austrian Habsburgs, the Porte would fight if necessary to protect its similarly conservative principles of legitimacy and tradition.

The rebellion which began on the island of Crete in April had focused Turkish concerns on foreign intrigues in the area. The Greek government had pledged not to aid the Cretan rebels, but individual Greeks were smuggling weapons to the island and the Turks suspected an Italian connection as well. An Egyptian division would eventually have to be called in to help the Turks take firm control of the island. The Porte sought not only to seal off outside help to the Cretan rebels, but also to prevent other movements from gaining a foothold on the mainland. And during an international crisis such as that brewing in Germany, few European eyes would be watching while the Cretan rebellion was suppressed.

War scares grew steadily stronger in Europe during the spring of 1866, as a showdown between Austria and Prussia for the future of Germany loomed. While most of the smaller German states lined up behind Austria, Italy sided with Prussia in hopes of obtaining Austrian-ruled Venetia. Both sides sought further allies, with Prussian chancellor Otto von Bismarck hoping to divert Austrian troops away from the main theater with attacks from Austria's small Balkan neighbors, semi-independent Serbia and Romania.

Southeastern Europe saw a few troop movements before war broke out in June, though none as dramatic as the mustering of armies across the German Confederation. Turkish troops gathered in Bosnia and in the Turkish coastal enclaves along the Adriatic, discouraging Italian amphibious landings and Serb attempts to invade the Banat region of southern Hungary. A large Turkish army assembled at Rushchuk in Turkish-ruled Bulgaria, across the Danube from Romania. And a Turkish naval squadron entered the Adriatic as well.

The implication was clear to all interested observers; the Ottoman Empire would stand alongside Austria to defend the *status quo*. In particular, as these movements show, the Porte sought to prevent independent action by, and the possible aggrandizement of, its vassal states of Serbia and Romania. Even more importantly, the Turks were determined to prevent Italian control of the Adriatic coast, especially the important port of Dubrovnik, historically an Ottoman protectorate.

The understanding between Turkey and Austria stopped short of a formal alliance, but Turkish interests clashed directly with those of both Italy and Prussia. Italian leaders had talked openly for several years of assisting Greek and Slavic rebels in their struggles with the Turks. And Italian designs on Dubrovnik, the main outlet for Bosnian trade, concerned Turkish leaders. Thus Turkish deployment around Dubrovnik in 1866 represented a level of protection never offered the independent republic.

In mid-May, 1866, the Austrian embassy in Constantinople reported Turkish troop strengths of 12,000 in Bosnia with about the same number in Herzegovina. Albania held 5,000 troops, Thessaly and Macedonia about 10,000 together and 40,000 concentrated at Rushchuk on the Danube to threaten Romania. Austrian Foreign Minister Alexander von Mensdorff-Pouilly told his diplomats to prod the Turks toward an outright invasion of Romania.

In late May another 6,000 Turkish regulars and 2,000 irregulars known as *bashi-bazouks* (literally "crazy heads") moved into Bosnia, while other Turkish units entered northern Albania. On June 25, two days after the Italian declaration of war against Austria, the Turkish commander in Bosnia, Farouk Pasha, ordered full-scale mobilization. Sixty thousand men were called to the colors, representing all three classes of Turkish reservists. The third group, the *Moustafiz*, was only called out for dire emergencies. During the Russo-Turkish War a decade later the *Moustafiz* did not receive mobilization orders until several weeks after the war began. Thus the mobilization to support Austria in 1866 represented a greater effort and expense than the one to fight Russia in 1877.

The Austrians, meanwhile, took advantage of the Turkish moves to strip Dalmatia of almost all its garrisons, shipping all the regular army battalions from the coast to Trieste. From there they took the rail line to Vienna to join the forces gathering to defend the capital from the advancing Prussians.

On May 28 the Austrian consul in Mostar informed the military governor of Dalmatia that a Turkish naval squadron would soon enter the Adriatic to protect the coastal enclaves of Klek and Sutorina, on the Adriatic coast north and south of Dubrovnik respectively. Though Klek was a Turkish port, provisions dating from 1718 required Austrian permission for the entry of Ottoman warships there.

The small port, though economically insignificant, would be of enormous strategic importance if seized by Italy. Both Dubrovnik and the Austrian enclave around Cattaro, further south, would be cut off from Austrian reinforcements and easily taken. Turkish warships at Klek would not only prevent an Italian landing there, but also provide indirect protection to Austrian coastal shipping.

The first Turkish warship, the screw corvette *Mansure,* arrived on 29 May, followed by the *kalyon* (steam-powered ship-of-the-line) *Kossovo.* Over the next three weeks they were joined by Vice-Admiral Ethem Pasha and his flagship, the screw frigate *Hüdavandigar* ("Sovereign") as well as the ship-of-the-line *Peyk-I-Zafer* ("Satellite of Victory"), the screw corvette *Sinop,* the gunboat *Beyrut* and an unarmed transport. The Austrians expected the *Peyk-I-Zafer* to replace the *Kossovo,* but both ships seem to have remained on station. Soon after her arrival Austrian agents reported that the *Peyk-I-Zafer* left the squadron for a patrol along the Albanian coast. Turkish supply ships continued to arrive as well, the brig *Genuz-Dundja* delivering hundreds of crates of ammunition each to Salonika, Antivari and Klek on the 15th and 16th of June.

Officially titled the *Rumeli Filo,* or European Fleet, the stated mission of Ethem Pasha's squadron was to suppress gun-running. He was also ordered to resist with force any Italian landings on Turkish territory.

The size of the Turkish squadron seems to have surprised some Austrian officials, but Austrian officers were under strict orders not to interfere with Turkish movements and to accommodate any requests for assistance.

The Turkish squadron represented a fair portion of the Ottoman fleet, much of which was built in Great Britain, but omitted its most powerful warships. The four large armored frigates of the *Osmanieh* class, at least two of which should have been available for operations, remained outside the Adriatic. In fact, none of them are listed for any active Turkish squadron at the time, making their battle-worthiness questionable a year after commissioning. On paper at least, these large, modern warships were far larger and more powerful than anything in either the Italian or Austrian squadrons. They displaced over 10,000 tons each, could steam at 13 knots, and were armed with one 9" Armstrong rifled muzzle-loader as a pivot gun, and thirteen 8" Armstrong rifled muzzle-loaders on the broadside, as well as ten 36 pounders. They could, if competently handled, have made a significant difference in battle, giving the smaller Austrian fleet parity with if not superiority over the Italians.

Steam-powered ships-of-the-line like the *Kossovo* and *Peyk-I-Zafer* still carried great weight in the minds of diplomats, despite the obvious fighting power of armored frigates. And even after the successes of ironclads in the American Civil War, wooden ships remained in service in most navies, as the great cost of ironclad warships worked against the quick replacement of wooden warships. The Austrian wooden ships fought well at Lissa in July 1866, especially the ship-of-the-line *Kaiser*. The *Kaiser* and her consorts had the added protection of railroad iron and heavy chains around their engine rooms and magazines, an additional step neglected by the Italians for their wooden ships and probably by the Turks as well.

The *Kossovo* and *Peyk-I-Zafer*, converted sailing ships two-thirds the size of the built-for-steam *Kaiser* and probably much less maneuverable, would have proved easier marks for the Italian armored ships. The very similar Italian *Re Galantuomo* was considered fit only for patrols in the lower Adriatic (and may have been the ship spotted off the Albanian coast by the Austrians). Thus, with the Turkish ironclads kept out of the war zone and the Adriatic squadron too weak to independently influence events, the Porte probably did not intend its squadron to actually engage the Italians in battle.

Guns at Lissa

The name of the little island of Lissa was recorded for years in naval circles for showing the supremacy of the ram over the gun. After the battle many ship commanders said that future ships should be armored with a strong ram. The reason why the guns were apparently less effective than the ram led to an inquiry into Persano's underemployment of his guns at Lissa. This requires a different look at the battle from the view of a time of technological change. The inquiry commission established after the defeat by the Italian government, was unable to arrive at complete conclusions about what would be the future of warship construction, quoting only the opinions of officers in charge of armament duties or commanders of some of the various warships during the campaign.

It is interesting to note what changes occurred during the preparation for the battle. This is in part due to conflicting information that has appeared over the years. Besides the changes ordered by the navy minister, Persano asked permission to change other pieces, writing on 29 May and begging that the "ironclad gunboats be supplied with a 12" rifled gun of wrought iron." This was because those ships were provided with a bow gunport, which allowed them to pivot to either broadside or forward. Persano concluded that "it is only a pity that it cannot be used with a gun of more powerful caliber, but the requested gun will be always effective against wooden ships." Other changes were made, when on 12 June Depretis agreed with Persano's proposal on 7 June which had said that since the steam corvettes *Formidabile* and *Terribile* were called upon to operate against fortifications rather than against ironclads, their guns should be transferred to other ships. The wooden frigate *Duca degli Abruzzi* transferred her 16cm rifled guns to the *San Martino,* which had only eight rifled and banded guns, while the *Carignano* received eight guns of the same type from the *Terribile* and another eight from the *Formidabile.* On the other hand it should be noted that only in the first days of July did the steel projectiles arrive for Persano to substitute for the iron ones in the ammunition supply.

By 20 July, Persano had changed guns on his ironclads to have the highest possible number of rifled and banded 16 cm guns on his armored ships, although he was unable to get all the ordered Armstrong guns in time.

On the other side the Austrian armor plates, supplied by the Styrian industries of Zeltweg and Store for the protection of the Austrian armorclads, were of high production quality, and particularly glorified by newspapers. The Austrian newspaper *Grazer Tagespost* wrote that Styrian iron was much better than any other and that it resisted the 300 pound iron balls fired by the heaviest Armstrong guns of the Italians. The same newspaper was sure that the Styrian iron projectiles smashed the Italian iron turrets, although they were built in the best French,

American and British arsenals. Despite such war propaganda, no Italian turrets were pierced in the battle, and only two shots pierced Italian armor plates.

Most of the armor plate used in the construction of Austrian ironclads was from foreign sources; moreover all the guns were ordered from foreign suppliers. Austria was driven at one point to secretly import plate from France from an office in Austria posing as an American contact point set up because of the American Civil War! Another example are the guns of the armored frigates *Erzherzog Ferdinand Max* and *Habsburg* that were ordered from Krupp but which did not arrive before the outbreak of the war. The Italian armor plates were generally purchased in France and in Britain.

All in all Persano succeeded in exchanging between ships of the fleet some eighty 16cm guns to improve his ironclad gunnery strength, taking them from the wooden ships where they were originally mounted. These exchanges were carried out in such manner that a precise record does not exist but we believe the planned eighty guns to have been distributed as follows:

12 to *Re di Portogallo*
8 to *San Martino*
16 to *Maria Pia*
8 to *Principe di Carignano*
12 to *Re d'Italia*
20 to *Castelfidardo*
4 to *Varese*

Of these, only four were supplied by the Naples artillery depot, and were delivered to *Castelfidardo* and *Varese*. The others were given up by the wooden warships.

The comparisons between the opposing forces at Lissa contain some difficulties to clear up. In fact, tables showing the strength of the Italian fleet as for the Royal Decree of 3 May 1866 are quite different from the true strength present at Lissa, because the ships were changing their armament already before the declaration of war (20 June) and these changes were still in progress just before the battle. As we have seen, these changes were ordered by Depretis and in some cases proposed by the fleet commander, Persano. An account of these changes was very difficult because not all of them were carried out before the battle. As a result, the many sources dealing with the battle disagree and considerable differences appeared in gun totals and type. This seems to be the reason why almost every account of the Italian ships' armament is wrong, Iachino included. Iachino was the Admiral in command of the Italian battle fleet for much of World War II and later wrote the scholarly *La Campagna Navale di Lissa 1866.* He listed under the heading of *smoothbore* the 16 cm *rifled* guns, although he did get some correct data in the text of his overall detailed account of the campaign.

For much of our information, we relied upon the report of the Inquiry Commission established by the navy ministry on 8 August 1866 after the battle in order to clarify what was the true condition of the "the state of the materials and administration of the *Regia Marina.*"

It should be noted that during the battle the Italian ironclads fought (according to some recent calculations) with nearly 205 guns against the 130 rifled and 410 smoothbore Austrian guns, and this because the 400 guns of the Albini wooden warships remained silent. The ineffectiveness of Italian guns and gunners was also one of the points of the after-the-battle inquiry, which stated that the main gun on Italian ships (the wrought iron 16cm banded rifle) could pierce an armor plate about 2 inches thick at 200 yards; such results could only be obtained with the highest powder charge, which allowed for a gun life of 50 to 60 rounds. Steel built Armstrong 150 pounder rifles could pierce such plates at nearly 1,000 yards. Of course the 300 pounder Armstrong guns could perform better but there were very few of these pieces and the two on *Re di Portogallo* had only 12 wrought iron shots.

The 16cm guns were banded partly before Lissa in Italy by the Ansaldo company. The bands were often purchased abroad, in this case from Petin Gaudet & Company and from Routin Cyprien, both in Paris, while the guns were purchased mainly from Sweden. Although Ansaldo did not work badly, it was proposed after the battle to change the banding system because the French system allowed fire with 15 and a half pounds powder and steel shot without danger. Although built of wrought iron, not one exploded during the battle; only one was about to, but was put out of action.

Apparently many shots were fired over the Austrian ships, as when the Vacca ironclads fired on the wooden Austrian ones. The Austrians fired 4,456 shots and received in return 414 hits. There are different figures for the projectiles fired by Italian ships, since several ships had fired more on the 18th and 19th than on 20 July. For example the *San Martino* fired 776 against Lissa and 133 during the battle. The *Maria Pia* fired a total of 780, and the *Principe di Carignano* fired all her 20 cm smoothbore shells. The *Re di Portogallo* had fired 500 over all the three days. In the battle of Lissa, according to Vacca, they fired about 2,000 projectiles, but documents give a total of 1,452 against some 500 received. The *Kaiser Max* was hit 28 times, *Salamander* hit 35 times, and the *Kaiser* 80 times. The *Don Juan de Austria* suffered from some heavy hits among the 41 shells she received. The *Affondatore*, by comparison, was hit 22 times.

The ratio of shots fired by the two sides varies from eight to nine per gun for the Austrians to less than seven for the Italians. This seems to prove that the gun crews were not well trained. But since out of 1,452 shots fired by the Italians, 412 reached the target, this was not a bad result. However, the Italians scored scattered hits while the Austrians had more concentrated broadsides, and this was confirmed at Persano's trial. Only two shots made any real difference: on the *Re d'Italia's* rudder and on the coal bunker of the *Palestro*.

In one paper read at the Royal United Service Institution, Captain P. H. Colomb, later Admiral Colomb, stressed how difficult it was for a fleet in line formation to fire with accuracy against a force under steam advancing at full speed, thus compelling a rapid change of gun elevation. This would be a problem for the Austrians, for one after battle report, signed by the commander of the *Erzherzog Friedrich,* Markus Florio, urged improved devices for gun aiming, because the 24 pounder guns experienced difficulties in changing range quickly. At the same time Austrian appraisal of the Italian guns' performance noted that fire control was carried out by individual gunnery commanders and salvo fire was seldom undertaken. Gunners seemed too excited to aim correctly during close fighting. Commander Adolf Noelting of the gunboat *Reka* noted that enormous numbers of the shells fired at the Austrian ships were intact—i.e., did not explode, which suggested at first that they were training projectiles, but later it was realized that they had faulty fuses. Noelting's opinion was that Austrian guns had fired more quickly and with more effectiveness than the Italians since they had a habit of firing concentrated salvos. However Austrian fleet artillery was inferior to the Italians and in the future "we should become not only even with our enemy, but also superior to him." That the Italian rate of fire was slower than the Austrians' was appreciated also by Carl Kern of the *Salamander* who praised his armor plates, hit but never pierced. The final word was written by Tegetthoff:

> As far as the artillery aspects are concerned, the lack of results on the part of the enemy have shown that smoothbore guns on the sea have much more value than a rifled one, since a rifle requires for best results at long range a still position, difficult to find on the sea. Against wooden ships, or for fire against objectives of lesser value, only rifled guns of a small caliber like 24 or 12 Pounders, which should be present on the ships in greater numbers, and be able to fire canister during close combat. From what I am aware of, this last kind of projectile had little or no use made at all by both sides during the battle, although the ships fought often very close. And the effect of this kind of fire should be very high, even against ironclads since the fragmented ammunition from canister could find a way into the batteries through the gunports.

HMS Devastation: The First Capital Ship

As it was, they had simply to improve now upon the Devastation, the prototype of the modern battleship.
—Stanley Sandler

With the introduction of the ironclad, and all the technological changes that went hand in hand with it, the ideal design for a battleship of this modern age went through an evolutionary process in which certain branches would wither and die out. From this developmental struggle, the ideal design evolved to its final expression and form. Stanley Sandler has written an excellent book, *The Emergence of the Modern Capital Ship,* on this development.

Sandler argues that the classic late 19th Century battleship was born from the design of HMS *Devastation* and her sistership *Thunderer.* They would be designed by Edward James Reed, Chief Constructor of the Royal Navy from 1863 to 1870, who also introduced the central battery design. The mix of tactics, various ship designs, ordnance, the need to keep the sea—possibly as a part of a blockading squadron—more efficient engines, all combined with the turret to suggest this new ship design.

The *Devastation* had a displacement of 9,330 tons, 12 inch armored belt, 3 inch deck, carried 358 men and could steam at 13 knots. She was laid down in 1869 and completed in 1873. The *Devastation* owes her basic design concept to several seagoing coastal ironclads, somewhat like the *Rolf Krake* or *Huascar.* Reed took this a step further and designed a ship with twin screws, the complete absence of masts for propulsion, placed turrets at each end of the ship with powerful guns, gave her a high freeboard so she could steam easily in the oceans of the world, and good bunkerage to allow her to remain at sea for extended periods of time. She also was well sub-divided internally to control flooding—104 total compartments. She only lacked a secondary battery; her four 12" muzzle-loader rifles being her sole armament. Later reconstructions would give her both torpedoes and a small secondary battery.

Reed saw this ship as "carrying war to any European port, or in an emergency, across the Atlantic, in addition defending our own shores when threatened." John Ericsson, when he learned details of the *Devastation,* commented that she "may steam up the Hudson in spite of our batteries and our monitors, and dictate terms off Castle Garden."

The Russian reply was the *Imperator Petr Veliki,* almost identical though somewhat slower. Commissioned in 1875, she was slightly larger than the *Devastation.* She had several problems in her career, some brought on by the cold weather of the Baltic, but during construction it was said of her by an English publication that "the relative power of the 'Peter the Great' is much over-estimated… ; and if half the stories which are told of the Russian dockyards are true, her construction is defective in many important particulars."

The design of the *Devastation* did not automatically sweep away the other warship evolutionary branches. The age of experiments was by no means over. New technology was still to foster evolutionary developments.

One event that had a large influence on future design, especially design dominated by larger and fewer guns, was the experimental firing by the *Hotspur* at the turret of the *Glatton*. These two British ships were turreted coastal ironclads/rams. Inside the *Glatton's* turret were placed some animals so that they could be later studied to see what was the effect of " …heavy blows on the brain." On 5 July 1872, the *Hotspur*, at 200 yards on a calm day firing in Portsmouth Harbor, missed with her first shot. This combined with some other gunnery errors led the British and other powers to question the power of large guns that fired slowly (the large 16" and 17.7" guns of the day took up to seven minutes to load and fire—a lot can happen in seven minutes in the heat of battle).

She did hit with her second and third shot, and did little in the way of damage to the *Glatton*. Both hits penetrated into the turret 20.5 inches and 15.5 inches, but the turret was still functional and the animals inside were not hurt.

With the building of the *Devastation*, the future battleship was now part of the age of the ironclad. While this design would not fully and immediately catch on with all maritime nations, the impact of the *Devastation* would influence future warship design. From her lineage one can directly trace the battleship design all the way to the *Bismarck, Yamato,* or *Iowa.*

The Prussian and Imperial Navies

The eagle has abandoned the nest and hovers again on the blue profoundness, to announce to foreign peoples that a new Germany is rising.
—**Admiral Reinhold Werner, Norddeutschen Flotte, 1867**

In the middle of the 19th century the Prussian navy, that is, what could be defined as the bulk of the future Imperial navy, was thought to be potentially the "second most powerful fleet of the world," or the "luxury fleet" in the words of Winston Churchill. Although deemed to pose the most serious threat to Britain's mastery of the seas, it was still very small. Besides the legacy of the little Prussian navy, the Imperial navy's other parent was the German navy, born as a result of the National German Congress that during the German revolution, on 13 June 1848, had assembled in Frankfurt's St. Paul church, and voted six million Thalers for the foundation of a German Navy. The expanding economy of the German states favored by the *Zollverein,* the customs union, raised enthusiasm for the idea of the formation of a German fleet with the roles of defending trade, the coasts, and appearing as a *national* symbol. The first war against Denmark and the blockade on German shipping showed how necessary this was.

The legacy of revolutionary liberalism remained in the future Imperial navy, and the conservative part of the Parliament would often vote against naval laws and increased budgets because of this origin. The navy would be opposed by the army which was linked with the *Junkers* landowners, against the *bourgeois,* best represented by the new emerging steel industries. Nevertheless the main body of the Prussian and later German navy would be, of course, officered by many representatives of the *Junkers* noble class.

Toward the end of 1849 Rear-Admiral Karl-Rudolf Brommy, commander of the Navy of the German Union, had nine frigates and corvettes, plus twenty-seven gunboats and two sailing ships. Political events led to the end of the German fleet in 1853, but the little Prussian navy remained active, taking part in the war against Denmark in 1864 and later becoming, after 1866, the navy of the North Germany Union. In 1864 the Prussians had a total of only 2,500 sailors and officers. Besides the little action at Jasmund and the presence of three gunboats at the battle of Helgoland, she had gained little battlefield glory.

It is noteworthy that the Prussian navy began to order ironclads in British yards, like the *Panzerfahrzeug* S. M. *Arminius,* of 1,600 tons, commissioned from Samuda Brothers in Poplar (London) and delivered on April 1865. The *Arminius* was a Captain Coles cupola design. Another foreign built ship was one being built in France for the Confederate States, an armored ram called *Cheops,* sister ship to the Danish *Staerkodder,* that was bought by the Prussian navy in January 1865 and renamed on 25 October the *Prinz Adalbert.* In 1869 her Armstrong muzzle-loader guns were replaced with breech-loaders by Krupp, one 21cm on the bow and two broadside 15cm.

In 1867 the Prussian navy became the *Norddeutschen Bundesmarine,* and the main base was moved from Danzig to Kiel. She also built some new ships, although the building plans were almost unchanged from those of the Prussian navy of 1865. Her strategy could only be the defense of the more than 800 miles of coast and especially the critical points of the mouths of the Elbe and Weser, and the ports of Kiel, Danzig, and Stettin.

By 1870 the German fleet had five ironclads, namely the *Koenig Wilhelm, Prinz Friedrich Karl, Kronprinz, Arminius* and *Prinz Adalbert.* Of these, the first one was a powerful broadside ship originally built to an Egyptian order, and later sold to Germany. She was like an enlarged *Warrior,* armed with eighteen 24cm and five 21cm Krupp breechloader guns and was for some time the flagship of Prince Adalbert von Preussen. The experiences of the Lissa campaign, the American Civil War, and the Prussian-Danish war all influenced the early orders of two armored central battery type warships, ordered in France (*Friedrich Karl,* 1865) and in Britain *(Kronprinz,* 1866), and entering service in 1868. Krupp guns for them were refused, being viewed as unfit for the duty required. They were smaller and more maneuverable than the large broadside flagship.

Adalbert von Preussen is credited as one of the creators of the German fleet, thanks to his memorandum that foresaw in May 1848 the creation of an independent sea power, and the fact that he created the Admiralty in 1853. Such an impressive force had many problems, for example, the lack of docking facilities in which to clean the ships' hulls. The future Grand Admiral Alfred von Tirpitz, while stationed on the flagship, remembered that some 60 tons of fouling were removed when the ship was cleaned and that such an amount of fouling had reduced the speed by a good four knots. This partly explains—along with their hopeless inferiority in strength—the attitude of the German fleet during the 1870-71 war, to the point that sailors were accused of cowardice, and that period of service was not counted at all for career benefits—it was as if they had seen no combat. Moreover their participation in the victory parade in Berlin was argued against by some, and barely allowed in the end.

The declaration of the foundation of the German Empire after the victorious Franco-Prussian war set a path to a unified German fleet, which received the legacy of the Prussian and German navies. The *Kaiserliche Marine* was born and the new political situation required a change in attitude towards the German role in Europe. Bismarck did not want any French ironclads incorporated in the German navy since the Germans did not have enough sailors and officers to man them, so they were not seized as war booty. Until that year the commander of the navy was Prince Adalbert, who was replaced by an army general, Albrecht von Stosch, from 1 January 1872, since there were no senior officers available and the famous

Jachmann, hero at Jasmund, had accepted another appointment. This confirmed the secondary role of the navy toward the army, a situation that only began to change in 1888. It is noteworthy that until 1890, the year the *Marine Rundschau* professional magazine was founded, no journal supported the navy's activity, and little was said by official historians, who suspected the "revolutionary" origins of the navy. After the decision to build a fleet, things begun to move and grow in the arena of public opinion.

Interestingly enough, by 1871 the navy was put under the Emperor's control, while her administration office was the Chief of Admiralty, which had to report to the Imperial chancellor. In 1873 there was launched a building plan that foresaw the building of eight ironclads, six armored corvettes, seven armored gunboats, twenty cruisers, six dispatch vessels, plus eighteen gunboats and twenty torpedo boats, but since the parliament approved only part of the expense, only the minor vessels were built. In the middle of the century the German navy had to rely upon British yards and machinery supplies, while domestic plants begun to emerge. In 1867-68 Krupp began to supply guns acceptable to the navy; for the navy officers it was difficult to understand that Krupp could produce guns in Germany, since the general opinion was that only Armstrong could produce effective naval guns. In 1841, Prussia had already introduced the first shell guns of 23cm and 28cm for coastal defense, which proved successful during the 1849 war against Denmark, when on 5 April they helped to a degree in the destruction of the ship-of-the-line *Christian VIII*. Later she adopted the Swedish Wahrendorff system of rifled breech-loader guns carrying out tests from 1851, and adopting them for the coastal artillery from 1859. The Prussian War Ministry made the decision to adopt a rifled gun for the navy of 15cm, but soon the caliber increased. The building of ships before 1870 had been ordered in British and sometimes in French yards, at least where the ironclads were concerned. Later the Germania yards at Kiel and Vulcan at Stettin become popular construction sites in Germany.

The "Stosch era" was one of organization. The poor situation of the naval officers (in 1861 the school ship *Amazone* sank with all the midshipmen lost) was improved with the creation of a naval academy at Kiel, staff officer training was planned, and many stations abroad were established. About two or three warships per year entered service, although they were mostly minor vessels. Eventually Stosch's many rivals took the opportunity to compel him to resign when a new warship, the *Grosser Kurfurst,* was sunk in 1878 due to a collision, creating a very poor impression of the navy to the public. However, it should be noted that in this era several navies suffered losses due to errors of seamanship. When he left, the navy had seven armored capital ships, of which four were of the new 14 knot *Sachsen* class, each armed with six 26cm guns, two in one bow barbette and four in an open central battery. Nevertheless the navy was mainly a coastal defense force, doomed to cover the sea flank of the army.

At the beginning of the 1880's the defensive strategy of the *Kaiserliche Marine* was reflected by the fact that during winter crews were often housed on land, and sailed only in the spring and summer for gun exercises, while tactics was generally given little consideration or practice.

Stosch's post was taken by another army officer, General Leo von Caprivi, whose work has received little or no consideration, because the streams of ink spent writing on the following period primarily concern the Imperial threat to Britain's sea power and the start of the Anglo-German naval race. Under the shadow of Tirpitz and his times, Caprivi's era disappears into obscurity. It was one of change and uncertainty in which he tried to go back to old concepts backed up by Adalbert von Preussen of a battleship fleet, but in reality such a policy was soon abandoned and new experiments were made with torpedoes, while overseas cruisers were built in accord with the political concept of colonial and trade interests abroad. Among the new theories favored was the so called French *Jeune Ecole,* or a war against enemy shipping trade. This view was particularly strong during the 1880's. The period was also called that of *"lebendige Küstenverteidigung"* or lively coastal defense.

During Caprivi's command little changed in the taking of gunnery exercises, though the introduction of the artillery school ship *Mars* was accomplished, and the practice firing ranges grew to 2,500 yards. But between 11 and 15 October 1885 some new improvements were put into action, with the battleship *Bayern* firing at a target near Courland at variable, and relatively long, ranges. It was decided to prepare firing tables to exploit the possibility of firing every gun up to maximum range and mounting the guns on ships so they could fire at maximum range. In this period and up through World War I, some guns would be mounted so that they could not be elevated very high. This self-imposed limitation would take some time to eliminate and would vary from navy to navy.

It was the beginning of long distance combat. Admirals Thomsen and Jacobsen both were committed to reforming gunnery practices, observing artillery exercises, and looking for new approaches. In 1890 Admiral Thomsen made it clear that firing at sea should take into account the variable of distances due to the target's movement, and that such movement could be observed and measured with modern equipment. According to Paul Schmalenbach, the Imperial German navy adopted the first firing training regulations of any navy in 1893, on the basis of the *Gabel-Strich* (fork-stretch) procedure which involved the observation of change in distance and position of the target under direct fire, giving the gunnery observation officers an outstanding role to play in training and fighting. Range finders become necessary and would improve over the years. In the same year the American naval officer Bradley Fiske patented (March 1891) a range telescope and Percy Scott in the Royal Navy, a gunnery specialist, increased from approximately 30% to over 70% the average hits on a target, introducing aiming devices like the dotter and deflection teacher. Still, the German navy asserts the claim, especially in the writings of Schmalenbach, to be the first navy to seriously pursue accuracy in long range gunnery, beginning in the late 1880's. In our opinion, the entire question of long range gunnery and range finding equipment and its introduction in the world navies, is one that needs to be further addressed by some future historian.

Interestingly enough, this regulation ran into bitter resistance because of the widely held opinion that ramming and torpedoing were the only means to attack the enemy at close range. Some articles appeared in the newly founded *Marine Rundschau* in 1892 on gunnery training in the German and British navies. Regular twice a week loading training sessions were calculated to offer 1,920 exercises in two years' service for the average crew member.

When Tirpitz in May 1878 became responsible for the "Commission for Tests and Examination of the Torpedo" he made strong efforts to improve this weapon. The navy had ordered in 1877 when its safety and effectiveness was still quite poor. Thus, before his conversion to the battleship doctrine, he was one of the strongest supporters of the "devil's device" whose adoption he favored, and of the building of torpedo boats displacing 100 tons at Schichau yards in Elbing. He was detached to Fiume to the Whitehead torpedo plants and later performed successful torpedo tests in 1879. Later he urged the production in Germany of such weapons.

By the end of the 1880's the German battle fleet was growing old, but toward the end of the decade there were to be some decisive events. Historians are still debating whether 1888 was the turning point in German naval policy, when the new Emperor Wilhelm II came to power. He was an enthusiastic navalist and held firmly the view that a world power, as Imperial Germany was about to become, needed a fleet of corresponding might. However, the first years of his rule did not see the start of new large building programs, and it would be later that Tirpitz would define this new program. On the other hand, 1888 was the year in which Count Monts, the first naval officer at the top of the Admiralty, pushed for a "High Seas Fleet," a move marked by the building of four units of the *Brandenburg* class (all laid down in 1890 and displacing 10,500 tons, armed with six 280mm guns).

As with other navies, the second half of the 19th Century was marked by endless discussions about the fleet of the future, and lacking proper war experience, navy officers and staff planners had to rely upon misleading ramming incidents in battles like Lissa, in which results were overestimated. Consequently the ram was held in great esteem until the eve of World War I.

An important change, especially in the relations with the army, happened in 1889, when the State secretary of the *Reichsmarineamt* (Imperial naval office) was created and placed under the direct responsibility of the Chancellor.

But the final important date was 1897, when Alfred von Tirpitz become State secretary of the *Reichsmarineamt*. In that office he would promote the so called "Tirpitz Plan" according to his *Denkschrift IX* and the second most powerful fleet in the world would be born, along with World War I.

CHAPTER VII

South America's Pacific Coast Wars and the Spanish Cartagena Revolt

The Spain of Isabella II was a nation of political turmoil, economic depression, financial crises and social unrest. Everywhere there were marks of sloth and improvidence and of starvation in the midst of plenty.... At its head was a queen hardly more notorious for her laxity of morals than for her lack of ability as a ruler.
—William Columbus Davis

During the period of the 1860's numerous overseas interventions and conflicts was conducted by successive governments of Spain's Queen Isabella II (reigned 1843-1868). This was especially the case with those governments led by General Leopoldo O'Donnell, the Duke of Tetuan (named Duke for a victory in Morocco), or his clients. Spain fought a war against Morocco in 1859-60. She was involved in a dispute in Indochina/Annam (now Vietnam) in 1859. She ordered a Spanish squadron to join with the French and the British off Mexico in 1861. Spain and Great Britain would quickly pull out of this effort, but it would eventually lead France into the morass of Mexico and the Emperor Maximilian. Also in 1861, at the invitation of a faction, Spain annexed the Dominican Republic. This annexation would last until May of 1865 when a successful revolution forced Spain out. Finally, as described below, in 1864-1867 Spain went to war with Peru, Chile, Ecuador, and Bolivia. Queen Isabella's ministers were probably primarily concerned with distracting the Spanish people from domestic problems, and less with the re-establishment of the Spanish Empire. Understandably however, several Latin American republics felt that Spain was trying to recapture portions of her lost territory, taking advantage of the American Civil War and the United States' temporary inability to enforce the Monroe Doctrine.

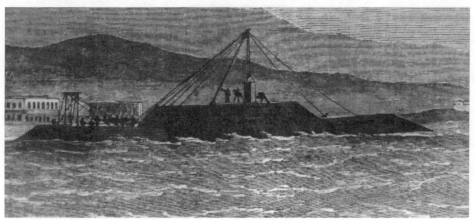

The Peruvian ironclad Loa.

In Spain, this war would be known as the Pacific War. In South America it is known as the War of the American Union.

It transpired in 1863 that some Spanish immigrants in northern Peru were assaulted by the local populace. To redress this, Spain ordered a squadron on the scene to seize the Chincha Islands, a small three island group 120 miles south of Callao, Peru's chief port. They were part of a so-called "scientific expedition" sent out to the area earlier. The seizure was easily accomplished on 14 April 1864. The Chinchas were just off the coast and were rich in guano, or bird droppings, used for fertilizer. This was so valuable a resource that custom duties from guano, between 1859 and 1864 paid between 50-75% of Peruvian government expenditure. Captain Parker, commander of the *Beaufort* at the Battle of Hampton Roads, recalled in 1858 visiting the islands on board the old *Merrimack* and seeing "forty or fifty vessels here" loading guano.

One of Spain's adventurous ministers actually thought that by seizing these islands, it might be possible to swap them for Gibraltar. In any event they did offer a large amount of income to a government strapped for funds. They also represented a territorial pledge that Spain thought would force Peru to comply with Spain's wishes.

However, after their seizure, the incensed Peruvian government and her people contributed thousands of dollars towards the armed forces. They would fight the Spanish. A commission was dispatched to Europe to raise a loan to buy armaments in the United States and Europe.

At home the war effort included the start of the conversion of the wooden warship *Loa* into an ironclad, mounting one 110 pounder forward, an old 32 pounder smoothbore aft, and protected with armor made with railroad iron. The *Loa* was originally named the *Collete* and built in 1855 in London. As the *Loa*,

The Spanish ironclad frigate Numancia *in the harbor of Callao.*

she displaced 648 tons, was 165 feet long, had a beam of 26 feet, and a draft varying between 20 and 21 feet. The *Loa* was designed in appearance to resemble one of the small Confederate casemated rams of the *Richmond* class and was completed in 1865. The *Loa* would run aground in Callao harbor on 5 February 1866 while "attempting to steam around the bay."

Another ironclad vessel was the *Victoria*. This monitor style warship was built at Maestranza Naval de Bellavista Callao by the "Ramos Brothers." About 300 tons and powered by a train engine, she was 150 feet long, 30 feet in beam, and 12 to 13 feet in draft. She was completed with a smoothbore 64 pounder and armored with 3 inches of armor. The Peruvians felt, incorrectly, that the only Spanish guns carried that could penetrate her armor were on board the Spanish ironclad *Numancia*.

The manufacture of gunpowder and building of coast defenses at Callao and elsewhere forged ahead. The depth of the Peruvian reaction can not be underestimated against their former colonial oppressors and the Peruvian president, Juan A. Pezet, was soon to be left behind by the wave of popular anger, which bypassed both him and his government.

As winter (June, July, and August in the Southern Hemisphere) turned into spring, and then summer, the stalemate did not seem to change, but subtle winds were blowing. The Peruvians faced only two modern Spanish wooden steam frigates and the gunboat *Covadonga* and when one of the frigates accidentally burned there was talk of sending the now completed *Loa* to attack. But Pezet felt that his assembled navy, which consisted of the *Loa* and two old steam frigates, supplemented by a ragtag wooden auxiliary naval force converted from commercial vessels, was not well enough trained to hazard an attack, though with approaching Spanish reinforcements, now would be their best chance.

At home in Spain the government changed yet again and a new rear-admiral was dispatched to help break the deadlock, Jose Manuel Pareja, the late Minister of Marine. He had been born in Peru and his Royalist father killed during the South American Wars of Independence. Pareja hated the usurpers of Spain's rich colony. He secretly travelled through Peru incognito and then arrived on board the Spanish flagship to take over command.

Though Pezet in April of 1864 had publicly stated that "I authorize any man to cut off my head if I compromise with the Spaniards," he had not acted decisively over the last few months of this standoff. Now Spain had sent out this new Admiral Pareja and additional Spanish reinforcements were also on their way, including the ironclad frigate *Numancia*. This French-built iron-hulled ship displaced 7,305 tons and could make 10 knots. Her iron armor comprised a 5½ inch belt with a 4½ inch battery above. She carried forty smoothbore 68 pounder guns and was similar in appearance to the *Warrior* or the *Gloire*. She was named for a Spanish Masada type incident that occurred in Spain during Imperial Rome's invasion of that land. Pezet's government now decided to enter into negotiations.

While negotiations were progressing between Pezet and the Spanish government, Admiral Pareja moved his fleet, now consisting of four wooden frigates and the gunboat *Covadonga* to Callao, which they entered. The Peruvian Government allowed the unopposed entry because the treaty of peace was under negotiations. Pareja, with the guns of the fleet now trained on the town and all its commercial facilities, demanded that Pezet accept the treaty. Most of the Peruvian fleet was present at Callao, that being one frigate and the *Loa*, as well as eight smaller ships, supported by coastal guns, but Pezet bowed to the threat. So a treaty was prepared on 27 January 1865. Part of the terms involved paying to Spain an indemnity of 3,000,000 pesos or (about $2,400,000 at that time), causing the Spanish squadron to withdraw from the islands. Additionally, there *may* have been some bribery involved of the high Peruvian leadership. Moreover the Spanish squadron did not withdraw from South American waters at the conclusion of this peace—which also meant they could return and take back the islands.

Within days, Spanish sailors on shore leave in Callao had been involved in an incident involving drunkenness and the townsfolk. One sailor and one citizen were killed. Anger over this incident and the treaty led to an attempted coup against Pezet's government. While this first attempt failed, as did a second, the discontent continued to spread.

The indemnity was decidedly unpopular and the humiliation that the people had suffered so deep, that a rebellion broke out in the provinces and the Peruvian government was finally overthrown. A new government was installed, led by

Colonel Mariano Ignacio Prado by November of 1865, driving Pezet into exile. Prado denounced the treaty, and began negotiations for an alliance with Chile, which would later be joined by Bolivia (which then had a desert seacoast province), and Ecuador. This alliance would be called the American Union.

We must now turn to events in Chile. When Spain first seized the Chincha Islands, the Chilean populace had also demonstrated against Spain. Spain was aware of this opposition and other anti-Spanish acts (including some uncomplimentary newspaper articles about Queen Isabella's lifestyle), but had also requested that Chile grant coaling rights, as Spain had no ports in the area. This was refused (along with coal to Peru, but that was meaningless with Spanish control of the sea) and at one point the Spanish flag was not saluted. It was this last insult to Spanish pride that may have brought about the war. Back in Spain, O'Donnell was once again in power and he granted Rear-Admiral Pareja full authority to negotiate with Chile.

Pareja now had the full credentials to pursue his goals. However, the process of sending an emissary to Spain, and returning, used up the best part of three months. But as soon as Pareja was armed with his new powers, he immediately headed south with his wooden squadron to attack Chile, leaving the newly arrived *Numancia* with the little *Covadonga* to watch Callao. In September of 1865, Pareja proclaimed a blockade of Chile; Chile declared war on 25 September. Valparaiso was the main Chilean port, the busiest on the Pacific in South America, and the one that the Spanish squadron most enforced the blockade against, bringing shipping there to a halt.

Chile at this time had the largest merchant fleet on the Pacific side of South America, and would lose it in this war as her ships sought new flags to fly under with the presence of a strong Spanish squadron. Chile's navy consisted of only two small wooden ships, and two being built in Great Britain, the 12 and a half knot unarmored cruisers *Chacabuco* and *O'Higgins* that were seized by Great Britain and held until the conclusion of the war. Both were *Alabama* type cruisers, quite a common design built for smaller powers after the American Civil War. Chile had only 38 naval officers, but they were well trained and the country enjoyed a naval tradition dating back to the Wars of Independence.

But while Chile suffered from an initial shock due to Spain's action, she made 38 other ports free of duty on cargo, which was an act that quickly redistributed trade routes. It was impossible for Spain to blockade all these open ports and she lacked an army to occupy any shore position. Again we have an example of the problems inherent in a war between the whale and the elephant. As with Peru, the public rallied around the Chilean government, and huge sums were subscribed for the war effort.

Pareja now began to suffer a series of setbacks, some small and some not so small. He could make no headway in his war with Chile, as his blockade

Warships of Chile in 1866		
Country	Name	Armament
Chile	Esmeralda	20-30 pounder smoothbores
Chile	Maipu (dispatch vessel)	4-30 pounder rifles, 1-68 pounder smoothbore
Chile	Covadonga	2-20 pounder rifles, 2-68 pounder smoothbores
Chile	Ancud (iron screw steamer)	6-32 pounder smoothbores
Chile	Abtao (Chilean flagship)	4-8" smoothbore guns, 5-40 pounder ""shunt"" guns
Chile	Arauco (wooden screw steamer)	10-70 pounder rifles, 1-100 pounder rifle (pivot gun)
Chile	Valdivia (iron screw steamer)	2-30 pounder rifles, 1-100 pounder rifle (pivot gun)
Chile	Nublia (screw steamer)	4-8" smoothbores, 1-100 pounder rifle (pivot gun)
Chile	Concepcion (iron paddle steamer)	2-30 pounder rifles, 1-70 pounder rifle (pivot gun)

deteriorated in effectiveness. Supplies were running low and his financial books had a difficult-to-explain shortfall of $175,000. Crews on his ships were dissatisfied, some having been on board for four years.

It all culminated for Pareja on 26 November 1865 when the little *Covadonga* was captured by Juan Williams Rebolledo, later Rear-Admiral Williams, who commanded the Chilean 900 ton steam corvette the *Esmeralda*. This smart little action, known as the Battle of Papudo, started with the *Esmeralda* approaching the *Covadonga*, flying the British flag and a distress signal. The *Covadonga* stopped, and when the *Esmeralda* closed, Williams at the last possible moment raised the Chilean flag and opened fire on the unprepared and stationary *Covadonga*. The battle was quickly over and the *Esmeralda* suffered no losses, while the Spanish gunboat lost four dead, 21 wounded, and a copy of the current Spanish signal book.

For Pareja this was the end. A day after hearing the news he took one of his pistols and killed himself in his cabin on the flagship. Commodore Casto Mendez Nunez of the *Numancia* now took command of the Spanish squadron. There is an interesting account of Nunez by Charles E. Clark. He and his fellow American officers knew him as "Mondays Tuesdays" and found him a "most attractive personality."

One of the ironic upshots of this entire affair was the reaction in Spain to the loss of the *Covadonga*. The Spanish were enraged and demanded revenge. One newspaper back in Spain would write that "Let our squadron perish in the Pacific if necessary, only let our honor be saved."

Unfortunately for Spain, Mendez Nunez's problems would not disappear. Peru had been withholding supplies to Spain and now re-entered the war by concluding an alliance with Chile on 5 December 1865. This would quickly grow into the

"American Union" with the addition of little Ecuador and Bolivia to the alliance, though they could offer little except the denial of their ports to the Spanish. Ecuador declared war against Spain on 27 February and by 4 April 1866, Bolivia had also thrown in her lot with the American Union.

With her re-entry into the war, Peru also brought her newly strengthened navy. Two former Confederate raiders building in France and now for sale had been purchased. Peru had purchased these from Voruz & Company of Nantes in 1864. Originally they had started life as the CSS *Georgia* and the CSS *Texas,* but they would become known in the Peruvian navy as the *Union* and *America,* respectively. The *America* would be lost in a tidal wave in 1868 while the *Union* would go on to serve in the next war. The *Union* was named for the American Union. They displaced 1,827 tons, had a speed of 12 knots, and mounted a dozen muzzle-loading Armstrong 70 pounder rifles.

Peru's ironclad strength was being increased by seagoing vessels. The Peruvian navy, after an abortive attempt to buy monitors from Ericsson as early as 1862 (forbidden by Lincoln so as to conserve the Federal Union's naval might), had turned to Great Britain for ironclad warships. There, two were built. One, the *Independencia,* resembled the *New Ironsides,* while the other was an ironclad ram, the *Huascar.* The *Independencia* was armed with two 150 rifled Armstrongs fore and aft on pivots and a dozen Armstrong 70 pounder rifles, and possibly four 30 pounders.

At 2,030 ton and maneuverable at 13 knots, the *Huascar* mounted two rifled 10" 300 pounder Armstrongs in a forward turret behind 5.5 inches of armor and rode high enough out of the water to be seagoing. She also carried two 40 pounders and one 12 pounder and all guns were muzzle-loaders. Her manually trained turret had two additional inches of armor near the gun ports, and her backing was 13 inches of teak wood (except where the two additional inches of armor were on her turret face), with an additional half inch of skin plate. Her conning tower was only armored with three inches of armor on eight inches of teak backing. She was subdivided into five watertight compartments, and had a crew of about 200. By 1877 her ammunition consisted of steel battering shot, chilled shot, common shell, and shrapnel for her 10" guns. The *Huascar* was named for one of the two Inca kings involved in a civil war on the eve of being conquered by the Spanish Conquistador Pizarro.

These two vessels put to sea before Great Britain had learned that Peru had rejoined the war and readied themselves off Spain's coast. While preparing for war, the *Huascar,* first to leave Great Britain, had announced her positions in such a way as to alarm the merchants of Spain without being in any danger of combat. This contributed to rumors of privateers or "sea robbers" being present off Spain's coast and hurt her trade.

Eventually these two ironclads would arrive in Chile in June of 1866, having captured three Spanish prizes while crossing the Atlantic and being damaged in a collision with each other. The plan called for them to rendezvous with the wooden Allied fleet in southern Chile and then to defeat the Spanish squadron.

Peru also secured the services of several former Confederate naval officers (after failing to obtain Union officers), including Commodore John Randolph Tucker, former commander of the Confederate Navy at Charleston during the latter part of the war. This would be the first naval mission, though unofficial, to be dispatched to Peru from the United States, and would reach Callao in June 1866. Also, powerful naval guns were purchased from Great Britain and the United States for her forts, primarily at Callao. The Blakely and Armstrong guns would arrive in time but the purchased Dahlgrens and apparently at least one Rodman would have to wait until the next war.

The only fleet action of the war was fought on 7 February 1866 between the Allied wooden fleet consisting of the 28 gun Peruvian frigate *Apurimac,* corvettes *America, Union,* and the Chilean *Covadonga* and the iron hulled ex-merchant ship five gun *Maipu,* against two Spanish frigates, the 50 gun *Villa de Madrid* and 36 gun *Blanca,* near the small island of Abtao (sometimes spelled Abato) off Chiloe in southern Chile. The vain Juan Williams Rebolledo, who was usually in command of the fleet, was absent, and so the Peruvian commander Acting Captain Manuel Villar was in command. The 2,300 ton Peruvian frigate *Amazonas* should also have been present, but it had struck a rock and been shipwrecked on 15 January near Abtao. The smaller ex-Peruvian, now Chilean six gun 850 ton paddle corvette *Lautaro* went aground during the action and took no part in it. She would later be destroyed to prevent possible capture. The Allied fleet was in a shallow bay effecting repairs with the little *Covadonga* on patrol when the two large Spanish frigates hove into sight.

In the ensuing action the attacking Spanish came off worse though they carried more guns. Part of the reason for this was that the Spanish ships drew more water (the *Blanca* grounded during the action) and could not get close to the Allied ships. They also only had old and unreliable Spanish charts of the area. But what is more important, the Spanish gunnery was dismal, while the Allied ships were anchored and fought better with their guns. The Spanish ships made two passes off the headland, where they were engaged by coastal batteries and men from the *Amazonas,* as well as some landed troops.

So after a little over one hour of combat at an approximate range of 1,850 meters, and the firing of about 1,500 shot and shell, the Spanish withdrew behind the headland. The *Covadonga* then moved to a position where she could fire over the headland at the Spanish warships. Their heavy returning fire quickly chased her off for her brave if impetuous attempt.

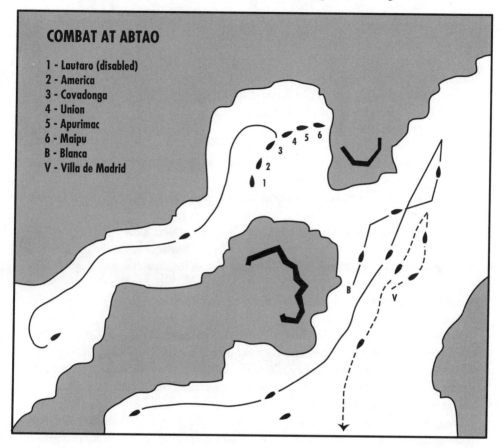

COMBAT AT ABTAO

1 - Lautaro (disabled)
2 - America
3 - Covadonga
4 - Union
5 - Apurimac
6 - Maipu
B - Blanca
V - Villa de Madrid

The *Reina Blanca* suffered some damage below her waterline near her screw that required plugging and had been hit a total of 16 times, while the *Madrid* was hit 11 times. The Spanish suffered only nine wounded while the *Apurimac* suffered three hits near the waterline and the *Union* lost 12 dead. One of the young midshipmen who distinguished themselves that day was the 16 year old Chilean Arturo Prat.

Upon learning of this setback, Mendez Nunez proceeded south with the *Numancia* and *Reina Blanca* to find the Allied squadron. Instead he anchored too close to land where, unknown to him, a half-battalion of Chilean troops were stationed. In the morning as the crew of the closest ship, the *Blanca,* mustered for review, the troops opened up at about 100 yards. Unable to elevate their guns to reply against troops up in the hills, the Spanish withdrew. Next Mendez Nunez found the Allied squadron in a small southern port, but it was too shallow for his ships, the fog was thick, and the anchorage was well fortified. So yet again the

Spanish headed north, though on the way north they captured a Chilean transport and some minor craft.

Now Mendez Nunez resorted to a move not popular with the world powers, but an action they chose not to stop. He decided on a course of bombarding the "open" town of Valparaiso. The Chileans had some time before decided that they did not have enough guns to defend the port, so had purposely removed existing guns, so they had no means of defending the town. They also hoped that the British and American economic interests, as well as other powers, backed by the military might of those nations would dissuade Spain from her course. Part of Mendez Nunez's reasons for the bombardment was his lack of supplies. By now his crews were eating only salt meat and dried vegetables and scurvy had broken out. He had to force a decision.

The Spanish squadron assembled at Valparaiso was now made up of the ironclad *Numancia,* four wooden frigates (the *Berenguela, Villa de Madrid, Resolucion,* and *Reina Blanca,)* the corvette *Vencedora,* two transports and some small coasting craft prize ships. Also present were warships of several nations with the British represented by two frigates and a small gunboat, and the United States by the monitor *Monadnock* and five wooden warships, including the speedy *Vanderbilt,* which was the flagship. The British commander, Rear-Admiral Denman, proposed, and the American commander, Captain John Rodgers, who had commanded the *Galena* at Drewy's Bluff in 1862 and later fought the CSS *Atlanta,* agreed, that if the Spanish would not give fair warning of the bombardment, that the two squadrons would stop the Spanish.

Rodgers informed Denman that he could destroy the Spanish squadron, including the *Numancia,* in no more than 30 minutes' time. The Chief Engineer of the *Vanderbilt* remarked that "if there's a battle, just you get this ship pointed right, and I'll drive her through the *Numantia* (sic) herself." This makes it clear that the British *needed* the help of the United States on this distant station, in part due to the presence of a powerful Spanish ironclad, no matter how poorly crewed. The *Monadnock* was viewed as the equalizer.

Denman requested an ironclad for this station and, in 1867, the 11 knot 6,100 ton *Zealous* arrived to join his command. She was a steam ship-of-the-line converted while under construction and armored with 4.5 inches of iron on her belt and battery. She was armed with twenty 7" muzzle-loader guns and was quite comparable to the *Numancia.*

Now for the Spanish part, Nunez offered the opinion to Commodore Rodgers, "If you feel you must interfere … your *Monadnock* may be too strong for my *Numancia,* but I think I can dispose of everything else, and then if I find I can't (defeat) the *Monadnock,* I will leave." It is interesting to note that at the time the American wooden squadron did take protective measures by placing bags of coal to protect vital points on their ships, and disposing of chain cables on their ship sides, etc., in case the Spanish and the Americans came to blows.

As the time neared for the bombardment, a unique proposal was put forward by the Chileans that Rodgers should act as an umpire. It entailed him establishing two squadrons of equal strength with wooden warships chosen from the Allied and the Spanish squadrons and to have them fight a battle to decide the war. Rodgers' decision would be enforced by the strength of his squadron. The Spanish declined this proposal. Ultimately, the view held by the American squadron was one of "that the affair was really none of our business. Chili [sic—the old style spelling] was at war with a nation possessing a navy, and could scarcely look to others to save her sea-ports from contribution or destruction."

Finally on 31 March 1866, after proper notification, the bombardment began against a city of 80,000. The bombardment lasted for three hours and was directed at government buildings, including the fort and the railway station. Not a Chilean gun replied and the *Numancia* acting as the flagship, along with the *Berenguela,* did not fire. Clark would later write of the bombardment that

> at first, except when a slanting roof was struck, we could not see that much damage was being done, for nearly all the buildings were of stone, but soon smoke began to rise above the bonded warehouses, and it was evident fires had started. Very shortly these began to spread, especially in the southern portion of the city. The firing from the ships was erratic. Sometimes a frigate would let go a whole broadside, and again the shots would be intermittent.

As William C. Davis has written, "the damage caused by the guns of the Spanish vessels was not confined to public buildings. This was probably due in a large measure to Spanish marksmanship that, as had been exhibited in recent encounters in Chilean waters, was notoriously poor." While only a handful of people were killed or wounded, the damage was given as $14,733,700, an extraordinary sum. Spain's honor had been avenged.

Mendez Nunez's next move was against Peru and the port of Callao. As he headed north, two weeks after the bombardment of Valparaiso and after announcing that the blockade of that port had now been lifted, he was accompanied by part of the United States squadron. The Spanish squadron now numbered 11 with the addition of the new steam frigate *Almansa* and two schooners, one of which was a prize ship. The *Almansa* had brought new supplies and 300 extra men to fill out the depleted crews.

Callao at the end of April and the first days of May was filled with feverish defensive preparation. President Prado himself would direct the defense of the port. Batteries were erected and earthworks dug (see details at end of the chapter in the sidebar on Callao's fortifications). On 2 May 1866 the Spanish squadron steamed in for the assault.

The Spanish squadron approached in the form of a "V." Sources vary as to the guns carried, but below we list them as they appear in Christian de Saint Hubert's listing from *Warship International.* On the right was the *Numancia* with 40 guns followed by the *Almansa* of 48 guns and the *Resolucion* of 41 guns, engaging the Peruvian left. The Spanish left line was headed by the *Villa de Madrid* of 48 guns, followed by the *Berenguela* of 37 guns and the *Reina Blanca* of 37 guns. The apex was covered by the corvette *Vencedora* with three guns, acting as a signal vessel. She was fired on the two weak Peruvian ironclads, and was available to tow disabled ships out of action. All the Spanish guns were smoothbore except for the *Madrid* and the *Almansa* which each had eight 160mm rifled muzzle-loaders.

The Peruvians fielded the *Loa* (acting as a floating battery after her accidental grounding in February), the small and underpowered monitor *Victoria,* the gunboat *Tumbes* carrying two rifled 70 pounder guns, and two armed transports, the *Sachaca* and *Colon,* carrying six and two smoothbore 12 pounder guns respectively, and shore batteries mounting 57 guns. These batteries included five (some sources incorrectly give four or six) 11" rifled Blakely guns firing a 450 pound shot and four 10" rifled Armstrong guns firing a 300 pound shot. Apparently there were rumors of 12" rifled Armstrong guns, but they were not present, and the weight of the round has been switched in some sources. The remaining Peruvian guns were smoothbore 32 pounders.

The Spanish fought at long range because of the fear of mines and harbor obstructions. The "torpedo" defenses were established and operated by former United States and Confederate personnel. So even though they had smaller guns, none larger than a 100 pounder, and they could fire more rapidly, their accuracy was still bad due to their poor training, the long range, and possible bad fuses on their shells.

In the early afternoon the *Numancia* opened the action with a single shot towards one of the Peruvian forts at about 1,500 yards. Shortly after, the *Villa de Madrid* was hit amidships by a Blakely 450 pound shell, disabling her engines, and killing 16 men and wounded 20. She was towed out by the *Vencedora.* Next the *Berenguela* was hit on the waterline by a Blakely that made a hole 20 feet square and she was quickly listing with the inrush of sea water. She too withdrew from action, and though there was fear of her sinking, she did not. The *Blanca* was also hit and now shifted to the other side of the "V," thus leaving the right side of the Peruvian position unengaged.

Accounts are confused here, but apparently about 14:30 the *Blanca* and the *Resolucion* retired from the action due to lack of ammunition. All four warships may have withdrawn for a few minutes here, but all accounts agree that the *Numancia* and the *Almansa* continued the action against the Peruvian fort Santa Rosa until 16:45. The *Numancia,* the main Peruvian target, suffered little damage from the small caliber guns, though the Spanish admiral was wounded by some splinters, and one Armstrong shot punched through her armor plate, but did not pierce the wood backing. She was hit 51 times.

One Spanish hero of the day was Captain Don Victoriano Sanchez-Barcaiztegui of the *Almansa*. In the action the *Almansa* was hit and at one point was on fire, when Sanchez-Barcaiztegui was urged due to the threat of explosion to throw exposed powder charges overboard and pull out of the fight. Sanchez-Barcaiztegui "declared that he would rather blow up his ship than wet his powder, returning with more eagerness to the tiresome punishment that he received" from Callao's defenses. He would later die during a bombardment of a Carlist controlled port in 1875 in one of the Spanish civil wars called the Carlist Wars.

There were several gunnery accidents on shore and the Peruvians tended to concentrate their fire on the essentially invulnerable *Numancia,* instead of the wooden ships. One bizarre incident occurred at one Peruvian turret battery, *Torre* (turret) *del Merced,* mounting two 10" Armstrong guns. A shell being lifted on a sling fell, exploded in the crowded turret, and killed 28 and wounded 66. Among those killed was the Minister of War, Jose Galvez, who had been observing the action from the turret. These gunnery deficiencies would cause President Prado to later ask for a United States "professor of artillery" to be hired to improve his men.

The action ended with the coming of darkness, the Spanish were running low on ammunition, and fire from the shore had slackened. The Spanish lost 43 dead and 83 wounded and 68 others with contusions while the Peruvians lost about 200 dead. The Spanish ships were hit a total of 185 times. Damage to the town was slight.

This was a Peruvian victory, and has been celebrated there since that day as the holiday of *Dos de Mayo.* Mendez Nunez declared victory and withdrew the Spanish squadron, after announcing that the Peruvians had been sufficiently chastised. Part of the squadron returned to Spain, while the *Numancia,* now under Captain Manuel de la Pezuela, returned via Manila in the Spanish Philippines, along with the *Berenguela,* the *Vencedora,* and three small ships. Surprisingly, Mendez Nunez and the remainder of the Spanish squadron returned via Rio de Janeiro and were hailed as victors upon their return to Spain.

Spain would convert the *Resolucion* to an ironclad and rename it the *Mendez Nunez* and later would have a light cruiser, laid down in 1917, named after the Admiral. The latter ship would serve in and survive the Spanish Civil War. Sanchez-Barcaiztegui would have a wooden cruiser named after him in 1875 and later a 1927 destroyer would carry his name in Spanish service.

There are however two final acts of this global war between two such unusual antagonists. One was a small footnote to history. A Confederate raider CSS *Texas,* codenamed the *Canton* and sometimes called a "super-*Alabama*" was being built in Scotland when the British government ordered that she not be sold to the

Confederacy. This 13 knot, 2,090 ton vessel was eventually sold to the Chileans and departed south in the summer of 1866 without her armament. She had a partial armored 4 inch belt protecting her boilers and engines. She was captured by the slower Spanish frigate *Gerona* while on passage and flying a British flag on 22 August 1866, near Madeira. The flag proved to be used illegally and she came into Spanish service as the *Tornado*. It would be the *Tornado* that in 1873 while serving in Cuban waters captured the *Virginius*, nearly bringing about war between the United States and Spain over the execution of American citizens.

The other act was more dramatic and portentious. Though the Peruvians and Chileans did not get along (and this antagonism would lead to war in a few years), they had stung the Spanish. Now they wanted to carry the war to Spanish territory. There had been rumors of Chilean and Peruvian privateers off Spain through most of the war. These rumors had adversely affected her trade, with many of her ships seeking other flags or remaining in port. Now the American Union was going to try to make a naval threat a reality for Spain.

The contrast between the two Allied navies was marked. The Chilean ship captains averaged about 20 years' service under a stable government. The Peruvians' four most modern ships were commanded by men who on the average had but 13 years' experience, and had served under an unstable government. Often as one faction won control of the government, the naval officers who were on the winning side were promoted, while the officers on the losing side would be stricken, only to be reinstated a few years later. Peruvian naval schooling was next to nonexistent.

When acting as a joint fleet leading up to the battle of Abtao, there had been much dissention between the Allies. This extended from rations (the Chileans ate lard and beef jerky, while the Peruvians preferred sausages and butter), to the amount of alcohol consumed and alleged discourtesies extended to the commanding officers. The earlier loss of the Peruvian frigate *Amazonas* that ran aground while in southern Chile was felt to be due to the poor Chilean pilot supplied by the Chilean Navy, and this rankled too.

Now they were to embark, as Allies, on a distant war against the Spanish Philippines and possibly Spain herself, and with officers lacking experience beyond their home waters. The decision to hire former Confederate naval officers was difficult, but was finally chosen as a way to placate the leaders of both navies, and also to introduce more professionalism into the two, especially the Peruvian navy.

With professional jealousies and rivalries rife, it seemed that the best course of action was to appoint the former Confederate Tucker as commander of the Peruvian fleet. He was appointed rear-admiral in command on 17 June 1866. Prado thought that the Spanish would be "terrorized" by knowing that they faced "two (seagoing) ironclads and a North American admiral."

This appointment would receive mixed reviews from the Chilean and Peruvian officers. One Peruvian condemned him as a "pro-slaverist and unknown rebel," whose lack of command of the Spanish language was an important deficiency. Others looked on him as a mercenary, while the Chileans wanted their own officers to command the fleet.

Eventually Tucker was installed on board his flagship the *Independencia*, and ambitious plans for continuing the war moved forward. While Chile wanted to pursue a conservative strategy of sending the entire fleet into the South Atlantic, hoping to find the retreating Spanish fleet, Peru wanted to launch an expedition against the Philippines in the hopes of sinking or capturing the powerful *Numancia*. Peru would dispatch the two new ironclads, with the *Union* and *America*, or substitute one of the Peruvian corvettes with the Chilean *Esmeralda*. The operation would last five months. If Tucker could not find the Spanish ironclad, he was to attack and bombard Manila.

While this operation was taking place, the remaining Allied ships would cruise in the South Atlantic with Chile fielding several converted merchant ships to act as raiders against Spanish supply vessels. Both Valparaiso and Callao were continuing to strengthen their defenses if the Allied squadron was absent. This would not present a large problem if the Spanish reappeared.

The even more ambitious final *coup de grace* would be the reunion of the Allied squadrons after their forays to launch an attack against Spanish Puerto Rico and Cuba. An army would be dispatched via Panama to help raise the flag of independence for the last colonies of Spain in the New World and even a possible reinforcement from the United States was hoped for—by purchasing warships there. This last hope was doubtful as the United States was trying to maintain neutrality and was exhausted after the American Civil War. To add insult to injury, it was envisioned that the fleet would then bombard some Spanish ports in Europe.

Tucker did an admirable job of preparing the fleet. Their bottoms were cleaned of marine growth, they drilled, and spar torpedoes were placed on board warships and carried in launches. Shell fuses were improved—using local manufacturers. New shells based on Brooke's designs were developed, and a new naval signal code developed. Ship complements were filled out as much as possible. Torpedo warfare was strengthened and three torpedo launches were carried on board the *Independencia*.

On 27 November 1866, the British steam frigate *Topaze* reported that the squadron assembling at Valparaiso was quite impressive. It was known that a Spanish colony was to be attacked, and while the Philippines was thought to be the target, it was not certain as to *which* colony it would be. The core ships were the two Peruvian ironclads and the *Union* and *America*. Also present were eight Chilean warships. The *Topaze*'s report to the Admiralty stated that "Should this squadron sail on a hostile expedition it is most probable that whatever their own fate may be they will do considerable mischief to the enemy."

But all was for naught. The diplomats arranged a truce, and though it would be years before a final peace was signed with all the countries involved, the war was over. *Almirante* Tucker would be discharged and go on to survey the interior of Peru and look for the source of the Amazon. But the ships and guns would face a new war shortly.

The Spanish squadron that had departed to the Philippines meanwhile continued on, with the *Numancia* circumnavigating the world via the Cape of Good Hope, being the first ironclad to do so. With the threat of hostilities still in the wind, the *Numancia* was sent to Rio de Janeiro, arriving there on 18 May 1867. Eventually she returned to Cadiz, Spain on 20 September.

THE CARTAGENA REVOLT

A major factor in the Canton's brief history was sea power.
    —Isidro Valverde

The period of 1868 to 1874 in Spanish history is one of transition and turmoil. Isabella II had been forced out in 1868, but who or what would replace her regime was open to question. A small Republican force failed to change Spain into a Republic, and various factions contested over which royal family house would give Spain her new King. The Second Carlist War was fought from 1872 to 1876 between rival monarchical parties. It was also during this period that the First Cuban War (1868-1878) raged and the *Virginius* affair took place on Halloween of 1873, almost bringing the United States and Spain to blows.

It was at this time on 12 July 1873 that Cartagena, the major Spanish naval base in the Mediterranean, was seized by revolutionaries, who would become known as the Cantonists. The city was "liberal and republican in attitude with a strong antimilitaristic and anticlerical current running through the people." They "aimed to break all ties with the Central Government and to set up a left-oriented federation of communes (the cantons) in Eastern Spain." They were anti-monarchical in attitude, and many viewed them as a modern form of peasant revolt. Some have even described the revolt as being made up largely of "galley slaves and deserters." The fear of communism, coming on the heels of the Paris Commune, was strong.

Out of this revolt came an episode that was in part the fruit of all this Spanish activity, a short lived revolt in Spain seldom covered in English texts that included an ironclad battle and a victory against the odds.

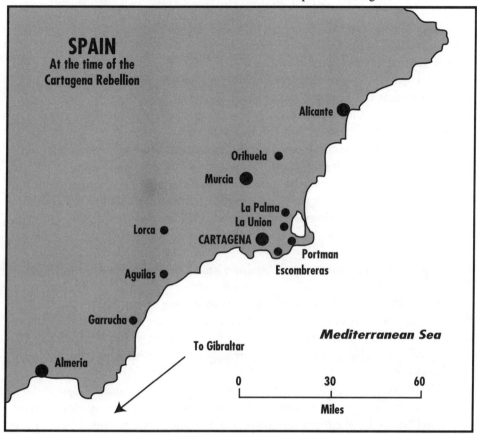

In the ensuing days of the revolt, the port was seized, along with the fortifications, local army troops joined the revolt, and suddenly the Cantonists had control of the ironclad frigates *Vitoria, Numancia, Tetuan,* and the ironclad corvette *Mendez Nunez,* as well as numerous smaller craft. All the officers of the ships fled, and the Cantonist fleet was now officered by merchant seamen. The commander of it was a cavalry general, Juan Contreras.

The *Vitoria* along with the armed steamer *Vigilante* steamed to Alicante, and negotiated their joining the Cantonist camp. This lasted but one afternoon, as upon their departure back to Cartagena, Alicante rejoined the central government.

So the *Vigilante* returned to Alicante, and was now seized by the German ironclad *Friedrich Karl.* The captain of that ship had heard that the Cantonists had been declared pirates, and the citizens of Alicante had called upon the Germans to protect them—which the captain had done. The *Vigilante* would later be returned to the national government.

Spain's national government was in a quandary. She had no effective navy—the Cantonists had seized most of it. So by declaring them pirates, Spain hoped that foreign powers would do her work for her. The next opportunity to do so came about when the *Vitoria* and steam frigate *Almansa* threatened Almeria with bombardment if a ransom was not paid. This was refused, and while steaming towards Malaga, they were attacked. The ironclads *Friedrich Karl* and the British *Swiftsure* (a small central battery ironclad armed with ten 9" and four 6" muzzle-loading rifles, completed in 1872), both lacking the backing of their home governments, seized the two revolutionary ships, inflicting some small damage to the *Almansa* in the process when the *Friedrich Karl* rammed her bowsprit. While the action was later disavowed, it was popular at home with the people of both nations, and the two ships were turned over to the Spanish national government.

The Cantonists considered declaring war on the German Empire in August after this affront. Some of the reasoning was that Germany was not really a naval power and it would rally more of Spain to her side. This motion was defeated by the Cantonist Council.

The National Government by now was advancing by land and had organized a weak naval squadron under Rear-Admiral Miguel Lobo. Appointed on 9 August 1873, he undertook a reconnaissance of the Cartagena coast. The two recently captured Cantonists ships would be turned over on 26 September to the Madrid government.

Meanwhile, the Cantonists fleet of the *Numancia, Mendez Nunez,* and a wooden warship again appeared off Alicante, shadowed by various foreign warships. They skirmished with the city's batteries and suffered some light damage in return.

In October the Cantonist ironclads *Numancia, Tetuan, Mendez Nunez,* and the wooden *Fernando el Catolico* were at sea when Lobo challenged them on 11 October near Cartagena. Lobo began the engagement at about noon, with one ironclad, the flagship *Vitoria*, but supported by three wooden frigates, two small steamers, and two schooners. Lobo's fleet formed a line ahead and maintained a distant slow rate of fire on the Cantonists. Lobo did not want to close in order to avoid sinking the rebel controlled, but central government owned warships. The *Numancia*, recently strengthened by the addition of eight powerful 300 pounder Armstrong guns, and three smaller 180 pounder (20cm) Woolwich guns, attempted to attack Lobo's wooden ships, but "every attempt was foiled by the ironclad *Vitoria.*" The other two Cantonist ironclads retired on Cartagena, eventually to be followed by the *Numancia*. The Cantonists would suffer 13 dead and 49 wounded in this skirmish.

Lobo pursued the Cantonists' squadron and arrived off Cartagena. He then steamed to Gibraltar to coal in a safe port and to rendezvous with the ironclad frigate *Zaragosa,* which had arrived on the scene. For political reasons, Lobo was now replaced by Rear-Admiral Nicolas Chicarro on 18 October.

The only serious loss occurred now when the wooden hulled *Tetuan* entered the dockyard for repairs. According to Jose Lledo Calabuig, who has a published history of the Spanish navy of this period with many photographs, the *Tetuan* was a 12 knot ironclad frigate begun in May of 1861. This 6,200 ton 40 gun warship had a crew of only 600. While in the dockyard (being run by a postman under the new revolutionary government), and with the city now under siege and constant bombardment beginning on 26 November, the *Tetuan* was burned, possibly by a saboteur. By 30 December it was a total loss.

Chicarro was now blockading Cartagena beginning on 23 October. As pointed out by Isidro Valverde, the *Vitoria* had now been joined by a second Spanish ironclad frigate, the *Zaragosa,* as well as three frigates, a sidewheeler, and two schooners. The action culminated on 11 January 1874, when a key fort overlooking the town fell to the central government. The Red Cross helped in negotiating a surrender of the Cantonists and on 12-13 January the city was reoccupied.

One last naval card was played on the night of 12 January, when the *Numancia* stole out of harbor, steamed past Chicarro's squadron, and deployed but failed to stop the Cantonist ship. Pursued by the *Vitoria* and a wooden warship, the *Numancia* was loaded with men and women who did not want to face the justice waiting for them from the central government, and they fled to French Oran, anchoring near there on the 13th. Chirarro took control of the *Numancia* on 18 January, and she was anchored in Cartagena on 20 January 1874. The failed revolt was over.

Later there would be some minor coastal bombardments, led by the ironclad *Vitoria* and the Spanish ironclad monitor *Puigcerda,* of coastal towns controlled by the Carlists during that war, primarily in 1874 and 1875. Several supporting wooden warships would participate in this, recently rearmed with longer range French built artillery. Over a half dozen ports would be attacked and many Carlist civilian and military losses would result, until the end of that civil war in May of 1876.

THE HUASCAR INCIDENT, 1877
by Andrew Smith

Acquaint the commander of the Huascar that I have come to take possession of that ship in the name of Her Majesty the Queen of Great Britain. That I am adopting this course in consequence of the Huascar having committed certain illegal acts

against British subjects, ships, and property. That I am not acting on behalf of the Peruvian Government.
　　　—extract from the orders of Rear-Admiral de Horsey to Lieutenant Rainier, 29 May 1877

On 29 May 1877 two unarmored cruisers of the British Pacific Squadron fought the rebellious Peruvian ironclad *Huascar* in perhaps the most unusual naval action covered by this book. Britain and Peru were not at war, yet the action was fought within Peruvian territorial waters.

On Sunday evening, 6 May 1877, the *Huascar* was anchored at Callao. While her captain was ashore, and with the connivance of one of her officers, Second Lieutenant (Reserve) Bernabe Carrasco, the *Huascar* was boarded by supporters of a political malcontent, Nicolas de Pierola. Pierola had been Treasury Minister under the Balta government (1869-1872), and was later a subject of a Congressional inquiry into financial mismanagement under Balta. He was exonerated, but exiled himself to Chile to plot the seizure of power in Peru. He led failed revolts in 1874 and 1876.

The Pierolistas were backed by seventy armed sailors and marines from the *Apurimac,* now a training ship. Before the alarm could be raised, they had taken over *Huascar,* and sailed her, as her boilers were cold, into the night. Command of the *Huascar* was assumed by Lieutenant-Commander Manuel Maria Carrasco, Bernabe's brother, under the general direction of the senior rebel naval officer, Commander Luis German Astete. The *Huascar's* total complement in rebel hands, as of 29 May 1877, was 167, some of whom were civilians or soldiers, leaving her rather undermanned (her normal completment was about 200). Her technical characteristics were unchanged from 1866.

The rebels' initial objective was to pick up Pierola, who was still in Chile, to carry him to Peru so that he could try to start a revolt ashore. However, the *Huascar* had left Callao with coal for only six days. As she steamed south, she began to interfere with British merchant ships, mostly steamers of the Pacific Steam Navigation Company ("PSN"). She boarded PSN's *Santa Rosa* and *John Elder* on 10 and 11 May respectively, in each case unsuccessfully demanding the surrender of all Peruvian government mail. *Santa Rosa* was anchored at the Peruvian port of Mollendo, but *John Elder* was stopped in international waters. On 12 May the *Huascar* captured the port of Pisagua, where her crew remained until the 14th. While there, she requisitioned 69 tons of coal, the property of British merchants, from the British barque *Imuncina.* A receipt was given, but no payment made. On the 14th, *Huascar* boarded the PSN steamer *Colombia,* seizing mail and taking prisoner two Peruvian colonels. The *Huascar* then sailed for Caldera, Chile.

The Peruvian government, led by President Mariano Ignacio Prado, serving his second term, responded to the rebellion on 8 May with a decree which disclaimed any responsibility on the part of Peru for any acts committed by the *Huascar's* crew, and which offered a reward to any persons, except Peruvian naval personnel who helped to recapture the *Huascar*. In effect this decree treated her crew as pirates. A squadron to recapture the *Huascar* was formed under Captain, and temporary Commodore, Juan Guillermo Moore, captain of the ironclad frigate *Independencia* (in most, but not all Peruvian accounts, his surname is spelled "More"). The *Independencia's* technical characteristics were also as in 1866, except that her boilers were in very poor condition, reportedly reducing her maximum speed to five or six knots. Moore was accompanied by the wooden corvette *Union* (Captain N. Portal), and the monitor *Atahualpa* (Commander G. Miro Quesada). The *Union* was unchanged from 1866. The *Atahualpa* was built for the United States Navy as the *Catawba*, but was completed as the Civil War ended and never commissioned. She was sold to Peru with a sister ship, the USS *Oneota*, which became the Peruvian *Manco Capac* in 1868. Peru had originally intended to use them in the war against Spain, possibly mounting an unlikely expedition from New Orleans against Havana. She had a speed of 6 knots and was armed with two XV-inch Dahlgren smoothbores. Her hull had five inches, and her single turret ten inches, of iron laminated armor (layered one-inch plates). Due to her low speed and poor seaworthiness, the *Atahualpa* was towed by the hired PSN steamer *Limena*.

Moore left Callao on 11 May for Iquique in southern Peru, but had a difficult voyage as the *Atahualpa* was a hindrance. He arrived on the 22nd, joined also by the wooden gunboat *Pilcomayo*. The latter had been launched in 1874, displaced 600 tons, had a speed of 10 knots, and was armed with two 70-pounder and four 40-pounder Armstrong muzzle-loading rifles.

In the meantime, the British Commander-in-Chief Pacific Station, Rear-Admiral Algernon Frederick Rous de Horsey, arrived at Callao from Caldera, Chile on 7 May in his flagship, the large unarmored iron frigate HMS *Shah*, commanded by Captain Frederick George Denham Bedford. She had recently been sent out to replace the ironclad HMS *Repulse*, sent home in February 1877 to be paid off and refitted. Completed in August 1876, she was named in honor of Shah Nasir ud-Din of Persia (reigned 1848-1896). The *Shah* was the second of three big frigates designed to destroy the fast American cruisers of the *Wampanoag* type, themselves laid down in 1863 as commerce raiders. Displacing 6,250 tons, the *Shah* was then the Royal Navy's largest and fastest cruiser. Her horizontal single expansion engines developed a maximum 7,480 indicated horsepower, giving a speed of 16.2 knots. She was ship-rigged and recorded the very fast speed of 13.5 knots under sail alone. She was heavily armed, mostly on the broadside. She mounted fourteen 7" (6.5 ton) Mark III muzzle-loader rifles on the main deck. With the heaviest battering charges, these could fire 115-pound Palliser armor-piercing shot at 1,520 feet per second. At either end of her upper deck, *Shah* carried a 9" (12-ton) Mark V muzzle-loader rifle in a box superstructure, which could be moved over racers to either side and fired through ports in chase or to the broadside. With battering charges, they fired 250-pound Palliser shot or shell at 1,420 feet per second. Both types of gun could also fire common shell. The *Shah's* upper deck also carried eight 64 pounder 71-cwt. muzzle-loader rifles; of 6.3" caliber, these fired common shell only. Common shell was a non-armor-piercing shell, used extensively before the invention of high explosive, which broke up into large pieces when the fuse detonated the charge. *Shah* also carried a Gatling machine-gun.

The *Shah* was also armed with the new Whitehead torpedo, which she could fire at ship speeds of up to 14 knots from pneumatic discharge carriages, through a port on either side of the forward end of the main deck. The *Shah* carried eight 16" torpedoes, probably of the Fiume Standard type. She was unarmored, but her machinery and magazines were below the waterline; her boilers were protected by lateral coal bunkers, although these were only about one-third full on 29 May 1877. With a complement of about 600 officers and men, *Shah* was as expensive to operate as an ironclad, and was sent to the Pacific only because no ironclad could be spared for those waters in 1876, due to the Balkan crisis in Europe.

On arrival at Callao, de Horsey's main concern was that Britain might be drawn into the Russo-Turkish War, which had broken out on 24 April. He had to watch a Russian cruiser squadron lying at San Francisco. The *Shah* was en route to North American waters. He learned of the *Huascar* revolt at Callao, but at first paid little attention, except to warn PSN that hiring out the *Limena* to operate against the rebels was illegal under British law.

An earthquake on 9 May disrupted telegraph lines in southern Peru, but on the 14th de Horsey learned of the boarding of *Santa Rosa* and *John Elder*. The same day several prominent British merchants requested the British *charge d'affaires* at Lima, Mr. James R. Graham, to arrange for a British warship to be sent to Iquique to protect British property from the *Huascar*. Graham agreed to do so; de Horsey cabled the corvette HMS *Amethyst* under Captain Arthur John Chatfield then at Coquimbo, Chile, ordering her to call at Iquique. The *Amethyst* was then the only other British warship on the west coast of South America. She was a wooden ship of 1,970 tons, completed in July 1873, able to make 13 knots under steam or sail, and armed with fourteen 64 pounder 71-cwt. guns. She had a crew of about 225.

On 16 May de Horsey wrote to the *Huascar's* unknown captain, warning him that further interference with British shipping, persons, or property would force him to capture the *Huascar*, British neutrality notwithstanding. Copies of this letter were distributed to PSN steamers.

On 17 May de Horsey heard of the *Huascar's* seizure of coal from the *Imuncina* and of mail and passengers from the *Colombia*. As he later argued, the *Huascar's* illegal actions were intolerable; if left unstopped, no British property on the coast was safe, and no compensation for losses could be obtained from Peru. He felt obliged to deal with the *Huascar*. Coincidentally, the same day de Horsey entertained Prado, the Peruvian president, at lunch aboard the *Shah*, giving rise to Peruvian suspicions that Prado had requested British assistance. In fact, no such approach was ever made.

The *Huascar* arrived at Caldera, Chile, on 16 May. She was seen there, cleared for action, by the *Amethyst*, which called there briefly on 17 May. However, before Pierola could join her, Chile insisted that the *Huascar* leave. She departed for Antofagasta, and then Cobija, on the Bolivian coast. On 18 May de Horsey cabled the *Amethyst* to remain at Iquique (she had arrived on the 20th) and obtain news of the *Huascar*. He himself left Callao in the *Shah* on the evening of the 18th, bound for Iquique, where he arrived on the 23rd. There he learned from the *Imuncina's* master that a Mr. Armstrong, the *Huascar's* British chief engineer, was being forced to serve the rebels against his will.

Pierola finally joined the *Huascar* at Cobija on 22 May. That day the *Huascar* received a copy of de Horsey's letter of 16 May, presumably via the PSN. Pierola drafted a reply, signed by Astete, denying that the *Huascar* had done anything illegal, complaining of British interference in Peru's internal affairs, and warning de Horsey that any attack on the *Huascar* would be resisted as a violation of Peruvian sovereignty. This letter, like a subsequent Pierola manifesto to Peru complaining about Prado's decree and British intervention, was mainly for home consumption. There is no record of the letter coming to British official notice until it was published in June. Pierola paid off and landed the *Huascar's* two British engineers, replacing them with two Frenchmen. However two British stokers agreed to serve on, for a 50 per cent pay increase.

De Horsey spent 24 May at Iquique, coaling the *Shah*. He knew that Pierola was aboard the *Huascar*, and believed that he intended to land at Ilo, Quilca, or Camana, to rally his many supporters in the Arequipa region of Peru. De Horsey therefore decided to cruise along that part of the Peruvian coast, using the *Amethyst* as a despatch vessel to put into Arica and Mollendo, which, with Iquique, were the only local ports where the telegraph functioned, for news. Leaving Iquique just after midnight on the 25th to join the *Amethyst* at Arica, de Horsey spent 26 to 28 May between Camana and Mollendo.

Pierola left Cobija on either 26 or 27 May (accounts differ) to raid Pisagua. His reason for doing so is unknown. The *John Elder*, steaming south, sighted the *Huascar* about ten miles off Pisagua at 03:00, on the 28th. Two hours later, part of the *Huascar's* crew landed at Pisagua, supported by her guns, and drove out the garrison by mid-morning. During the morning Moore was told of the *John Elder's* sighting. Leaving the *Atahualpa* and *Limena* behind at Iquique, Moore sent the

Pilcomayo to intercept the next southbound steamer for news, and he then proceeded to Pisagua with the *Independencia* and *Union.*

At about 16:00 Moore sighted the *Huascar* off Punta Pichalo. Pierola hastily recalled his landing force, and closed with Moore. The ensuing action, sometimes referred to in Peru as the battle of Punta Pichalo, took place about eight miles offshore, between that point and Junin cove. At 17:25 the ironclads opened fire on each other at about 1,500 meters range. The *Union* and the newly arrived *Pilcomayo* joined in. The action lasted about 80 minutes, ending shortly before 19:00, as darkness fell and the *Huascar* escaped out of range northwards. The tactics used are now obscure. According to one account, Moore's ships attempted to surround the *Huascar*; according to another, she steamed around them. At times the range was close enough for both sides to use rifles.

Writing home later, one of *Shah's* officers commented: "Captain Moore's furious engagement was the most bunkum affair possible ... [the] battle of Pisagua was not half as dangerous as a pyrotechnic engagement at Cremorne ..." (Cremorne was a London pleasure garden of the time). In fact, it is quite likely that at least the *Huascar* tried to avoid inflicting serious damage. Her firepower was reduced by defects in her 10" guns. The securing bolt of one gun carriage, and the running-out winch chain of the other, both broke. According to Peruvian press reports, she fired only 5 rounds from her big guns, while the *Independencia* fired 10 rounds from her 150 pounders and 30 from her 70 pounders.

Moore claimed afterwards that both *Huascar's* turret and steering gear had been damaged. In fact, she received only insignificant hits from splinters and rifle bullets, and suffered no casualties. The *Independencia* was hit by a 10" shell, which passed through her funnel and steam escape valve, then exploded, wounding two men and blowing away her gig. Her other boats and port rigging were damaged by rifle fire. The *Union* was also hit by rifle bullets, without suffering casualties. The *Pilcomayo* was unscathed.

As the action ended, the *Union* tried to chase *Huascar,* but was driven off by rifle fire and a shot above her masts. Moore's squadron spent the night off Pisagua, then returned to Iquique in the morning. Pierola decided to continue north for Pacocha, near Ilo.

Unaware of events at Pisagua, de Horsey spent much of the 28th patrolling the coast near Quilca in the *Shah,* under sail to save coal. The *Amethyst* went to Mollendo during the morning for news. She rejoined at 17:00 to report that the *Huascar* had been seen off Pisagua by the *John Elder.* De Horsey then steamed south, but stopped for the night off Punta Carnejo (known today as Punta Islay), near Mollendo, sending the *Amethyst* in again for the latest telegrams. She returned just after daybreak with news of *Huascar's* bombardment of Pisagua the previous day.

The times given in the following narrative are based on those in *Shah's* subsequent action report and/or log. In the *Amethyst's* report and log, like events are timed about 30 minutes earlier. Accordingly, we have added 30 minutes to times taken from the latter sources.

At 06:45, on Tuesday, 29 May, the *Shah* weighed anchor and steamed south at 11 knots with the *Amethyst*. The latter steered close to the coast, with the *Shah* to seaward at maximum flag signalling distance, thus forming a scouting line of two ships. When north-west of Punta Coles, near Ilo, at 12:50, the *Shah* sighted a steamer on her port bow, standing towards her. Twenty minutes later the vessel was observed to alter course to Ilo. At 13:15 she was recognized as the *Huascar*. The *Shah* lit fires in those boilers not required at cruising speed. The *Amethyst*, which sighted the *Huascar* somewhat later, altered course to cut her off from Ilo. At 13:32 the *Shah* went to action stations. The *Huascar* was too slow to run from the *Shah*, and by 14:00 was boxed in off Punta Coles. At 14:10 the *Shah* fired a blank charge to indicate that the *Huascar* should stop to enable them to communicate. The *Huascar* complied at once. De Horsey sent Lieutenant George Rainier, the *Shah's* first lieutenant, over in a cutter to demand the *Huascar's* surrender.

Rainier was taken to the *Huascar's* wardroom, where he was confronted by Pierola, flanked by Astete and Manuel Carrasco, seated at the table surrounded by their officers and civilian supporters. In accordance with his written orders, Rainier demanded that the *Huascar* be surrendered forthwith, because of her recent illegal acts against British ships and subjects. If that were done, de Horsey would not hand over the *Huascar's* crew to the Peruvian government, but instead would land them at some convenient neutral place. If denied, the *Shah* would first fire warning shots, then, if the *Huascar* refused to surrender, she would be fired on and her crew treated as pirates. Using all his oratorical skill, Pierola replied that the Peruvian flag that the *Huascar* flew would only be hauled down when there was no longer a single man aboard able to uphold it. The threat of force was a very grave offense to the sovereignty of Peru, and a breach of international law, for which reparations would be demanded from the British government. If used, force would be met with force, and the responsibility would be de Horsey's.

As Rainier's boat pulled away from the *Huascar* to report to de Horsey, Pierola delivered a short speech to her crew: "Gentlemen, everyone to his post; now the Pierola revolution has ended; now we are only Peruvians to whom the destiny has fallen to defend our flag and that of all America." As the crew cheered for Peru, two previously arrested colonels volunteered to join the fight. The *Huascar* began to steam for Ilo.

At 14:56 the *Shah* fired a blank round at 4,200 yards. The *Huascar* ignored it. The *Shah* began to close, and fired a shot across the *Huascar's* bow at 15:00. This had no effect either, and at 15:06 the *Shah's* port guns opened fire at 1,900 yards. The *Huascar* replied at 15:07 and the *Amethyst* joined in at 15:09.

It is difficult to reconstruct this action, as neither side made any track charts of it. It took place between Punta Coles and Ilo itself, between which lay the port of Pacocha, hence its Peruvian name of the battle of Pacocha. Pacocha is now the center of present day Ilo; old Ilo, 1.5 kilometers to the north, had been reduced to ruins by an earthquake in 1868. It was fought partly within Peruvian territorial waters, in spite of shoals extending up to two miles from shore, which gave the *Huascar* an advantage, as she drew 15 feet maximum, compared with *Amethyst's* 18 and *Shah's* 27 feet. The weather was good, and the sea moderate.

De Horsey later wrote in his report:

> The engagement was partly a following one and partly a revolving one, with occasional attempts on the part of the *Huascar* to ram, which had to be guarded against ... The *Huascar* appeared to be steaming at about 11 knots, and to be beautifully handled, always contriving to keep her turret guns pointing on us, except when in their loading position.

De Horsey chose to use the *Shah's* speed to fight at long range, mainly 1,500 to 2,000 yards, although ranges (estimated by eye) varied from 300 to 3,000 yards. The *Amethyst*, which Captain Chatfield maneuvered independently, kept at 1,500 to 2,500 yards, though her Able Seaman Patrick Riley records a minimum range of 1,000 yards in his memoirs. The rationale for fighting at long range and maximum speed was that it avoided being rammed by the *Huascar*, which was a very maneuverable ship, and exploited superior British gunnery. In theory the *Shah's* 9" and 7" guns could still pierce *Huascar's* thickest (turret) armor at 3,000 yards and 1,200 yards respectively. The *Shah's* and *Amethyst's* 64 pounders were ineffective against armor at any range, as they only fired common shell.

Pierola sensibly left the conduct of the battle to his naval officers; his biographer does not explain where he was during the action. Although Astete was present in the conning tower, the *Huascar* was fought by the Carrasco brothers, Manuel conning the ship and Bernabe commanding the turret. Manuel Carrasco steered what was probably a sinuous course, trying to ram if possible, to keep *Huascar's* turret bearing on her enemies, and to avoid presenting her stern as a target. The *Huascar's* stern was weakly armored. There was no armored transverse bulkhead aft to protect the rear of the engine room.

Maneuvering turned out to be the *Huascar's* best defense. Her attempts at ramming failed, and her gunners fired slowly and failed to score a single hit. Captain Bedford's action report from *Shah* mentions only six or seven shots from *Huascar's* 10" guns. The actual number of rounds fired is not recorded, but was evidently low. Several possible explanations are given for this: poorly trained gunners, inability to see the target due to British shell splashes, and *Huascar's* unaccustomed high-speed maneuvers. Her turret was traversed by hand. It took sixteen men fifteen minutes to turn it through 360 degrees. Some or all of these may be true. Evidently there was also a problem with the friction tubes (primers) used to fire the 10" guns.

The Huascar *as it appears today.* (Chilean Naval Mission)

Either these ran out, and those for the 40 pounders had to be adapted in haste, or they were wet, and often misfired. Further, it is not clear whether or not the gun defects of the 28 May had been repaired. The crews of *Huascar's* 40 pounders were unprotected, and were driven from their guns by British fire in the later stages of the action.

The *Huascar's* gunners made some near misses on the *Shah*, cutting away a few pieces of rigging with shots through it, but caused no other damage, or any British casualties. De Horsey thought this was "... singular and Providential, as her 300-pounder shell entering a ship with a large complement like the *Shah* would have had serious results." The *Huascar* devoted most of her attention to the *Shah*, but also fired at the *Amethyst*. On the latter's upper deck, Able Seaman Riley noted that:

> ...several of the shots that she aimed at us [struck] the water just short enough to ricochet over us. We could plainly see her projectiles, owing to their high trajectory, coming through the air like large blacksmith's anvils.

The *Shah* and *Amethyst* fired steadily throughout the action hitting the *Huascar* frequently. There were interruptions when one fouled the other's range, or the *Huascar* came into line with Ilo or Pacocha. There were also technical problems. At 15:26 the fourth round from *Shah's* forward 9" gun jammed in the bore, perhaps because the previous round broke up on firing, putting the gun out of action for 15 minutes. The crews of both 9" guns had trouble moving their massive weapons from one broadside to the other over the racers. The pivot bolts broke on the carriages of three port and one starboard 7" guns, so that they could only be fired with full, rather than the heavier battering, charges. Fire control was extremely primitive. Ranges were estimated by officer's eye, shouted at the gunners through the noise of battle, sights set accordingly, and guns mostly laid and fired individually. However, the *Shah* also fired several broadsides from her 7" guns, including three by electric firing, mostly aimed by the director sight at *Huascar's* turret, in hope of disabling or jamming it by shock, even if the armor was not penetrated.

By 16:00 the *Huascar* was trying to keep as close inshore as possible. The *Amethyst* followed her in, worrying de Horsey, who signaled to Chatfield "Do not get ashore" at 16:40. Shortly before 17:00, the *Shah* herself began to close in, firing broadsides from her starboard guns. She then turned to run past the *Huascar* in the opposite direction. As she did so around 17:10, the *Huascar* began to close fast to ram, from off the *Shah's* port bow. At 17:13 *Shah's* Gatling gun, mounted at the foretop, opened fire to sweep *Huascar's* deck, supported by riflemen in the tops. This was a tactic also employed by *Amethyst* as opportunity offered; her riflemen fired about 500 rounds in the battle. Tactically, this fire served to snipe at *Huascar's* exposed 40 pounder gunners, and to protect *Shah's* command team from similar fire. Her key officers and helmsmen were exposed on her upper deck and bridge.

At 17:14 the *Shah's* port guns gave the *Huascar* an electrically fired broadside, shooting away her main topmast. She also fired a torpedo, reportedly set to run at nine knots, at 400 yards. Unluckily for the *Shah,* the *Huascar* turned away as the Whitehead was discharged. As the *Huascar* was steaming at 11 knots, the Whitehead could not catch her, and its bubble track was seen to end only halfway to the target. This was the first-ever firing of a Whitehead torpedo in action, and gave rise to a legend in the Royal Navy's Torpedo Branch that *Shah's* gunnery officer had asked for the order to fire to be confirmed in writing, as the Peruvians had shown themselves to be gallant fellows, and did not merit such an appalling fate. In fact, as we shall see, the *Shah's* gunnery officer was also her torpedo expert, and had no such scruples.

This joust with the *Huascar* was too close for comfort, and the *Shah* opened the range from 300 to 2,000 yards as fast as possible. In the meantime, Chatfield had concluded that there was something wrong with *Huascar's* turret, and began to chase her, keeping on her quarter. Riley heard a rumor that Chatfield intended to overhaul and board the *Huascar,* grappling her by dropping an anchor onto her upper deck. However, at 17:25 de Horsey signaled "Recall." Riley remembered Chatfield, normally a reserved man, "... stamping his feet with vexation at losing such a splendid chance." It was the third time that the *Amethyst* had been ordered to pull back.

By 17:30 the light was fading fast. The *Huascar* fired her last recorded shots from her turret at the *Shah* at 17:35, good for line, but short. By dusk, the *Huascar* was close inshore off Pacocha, whose government garrison fired on her with rifles from the beach. At 17:45 de Horsey ordered his ships to cease fire. This was a wise precaution, as Peru later claimed that British shells landed in Pacocha during the battle. British inquiries found that three rounds struck a hillside above the port. Those were probably "overs" from the *Shah*, which ricocheted off the sea.

The action had lasted about 2 hours 40 minutes. The *Shah* fired 32 rounds 9" (2 common shell, 11 Palliser shell, 19 Palliser shot), 149 rounds 7" (4 common shell, 145 Palliser shot), and 56 rounds 64 pounder shell, total 237 rounds. The *Amethyst* fired 190 rounds 64 pounder shell. Total British expenditure was thus 427 rounds, of which 175 were of armor-piercing (Palliser) type.

What had this achieved?

There are two damage reports on the *Huascar*, one compiled by Manuel Carrasco on 30 May, and the other written by the *Shah*'s gunnery officer, Lieutenant Charles Lindsay, after briefly inspecting the *Huascar* at Iquique on 1 June 1877. Neither report gives the total number of hits scored. Lindsay estimated that 25 per cent of rounds fired were hits, but it is not clear if he included the *Amethyst*'s expenditure when working out the percentage. His report lists at least 26 separately distinguishable hits, while Carrasco's mentions at least 16. Probably both men would have had difficulty in assessing the exact number of hits on the *Huascar*'s upperworks, which were riddled with fragments and bullets. A further complication was that a large number of projectiles struck the side armor, but glanced off or exploded ineffectively. Lindsay later estimated that there were 30 to 40 such hits. We may safely conclude that the *Huascar* received at least 50 hits, and quite possibly the 70 to 80 hits claimed by contemporary press reports.

Lindsay's and Carrasco's reports differ in detail, but agree that the *Huascar* was not seriously damaged, and that her armor was pierced only once. Surprisingly, the penetrating hit was a 9" common shell, which struck the *Huascar* two feet above her starboard waterline, fifty feet from the stern. It pierced a 3.5 inch armor plate and burst in the teak backing, sending fragments through the officers' cabins, killing marine bugler Ruperto Bejar and wounding three others. Three Palliser shot gouged the side armor to a depth of two to three inches. The *Huascar*'s turret was hit "direct" (in British parlance, at right-angles to the plate) by a 7" shot, probably fired at 1,700-1,800 yards, three feet from the left gunport and about one-third down from the roof. This penetrated 3 inches into the 5.5 inch armor. Other hits on vertical armor were ineffective, either because they were by common shell, or because they struck obliquely, not direct; the *Huascar* was often an end-on target. Her deck armor was not scored at all.

The remaining damage was extensive, but superficial. There were about twelve hits on the funnel and funnel casing, and a shot through the foremast. The main cross-trees, gaff and rigging were shot away. All the boats were destroyed or rendered useless. A 9" round passed blind through the stern, wrecking the officer's heads and wounding a marine sergeant, who was rehoisting the colors, which had been shot away. A hit on the bridge sent fragments into the conning tower. Astete was slightly wounded in the left hand, and Manuel Carrasco struck harmlessly in the face. Total casualties were one dead and five wounded.

Two later Peruvian accounts state that *Huascar's* battle steering gear, located directly below the conning tower, was put out of action, and that the rudder had to be worked directly with relieving tackle. However, neither Lindsay nor Carrasco mention this.

As darkness fell, de Horsey's problems grew. The *Huascar* was still defiant, but it was impossible to follow her into shoal-strewn water after dark. She might escape, or try a night ramming attack. He therefore ordered Bedford to prepare a torpedo attack on the *Huascar*, using the *Shah's* boats. While this was being organized, the *Shah* and *Amethyst* patrolled respectively north and south of Ilo, about three miles offshore. At 19:40 the *Shah* hoisted out her steam pinnace, armed with an "outrigger" (spar) torpedo, and a whaler, fitted to lower a Whitehead into the water (where it would be started by throwing the air release lever by hand). The boats were manned by volunteers, commanded by Lieutenant Lindsay.

At 21:05 Lindsay's force left the *Shah,* the steam pinnace towing the whaler directly toward the coast north of Ilo. Lindsay then searched southward for six miles toward the town. Off Ilo a single ship was sighted at anchor 1,000 yards off. Lindsay closed to attack it, but soon realized that she was not the *Huascar.* She proved to be the Peruvian steamer *Maria Luisa,* whose master eventually explained that the *Huascar* had gone, he knew not where. Lindsay's boats took until 03:30 on 30 May to return to the *Shah.*

After dark on 29 May Pierola had held a council of war aboard the *Huascar.* Around 19:00 it was decided to break out of Ilo immediately, and go to Iquique to try to persuade Moore to join in a combined attack on the British aggressors. To play the patriotic card suited Pierola's political philosophy, and might further undermine President Prado's popularity. The *Huascar* escaped by steaming in a darkened state, close to the steep shoreline, which was shrouded by fog. De Horsey's own dispositions for the night probably helped. To avoid any risk to the *Amethyst,* he had recalled her to a patrol position three miles northwest of Ilo, where she passed the night steaming slowly around the compass, with the *Shah* further out. This left the bay clear for Lindsay's expedition, but the southwest approaches went unobserved.

After stealing out of Ilo, *Huascar* steamed hard for Iquique, about 175 miles away. She arrived off the port about 14:00 on 30 May, flying a flag of truce. Moore's squadron was anchored, apparently unaware of the battle at Ilo. Pierola sent a delegation to see Moore. They explained the situation, inviting him to lead a joint attack on de Horsey. Moore telegraphed Lima for instructions. Prado replied "Order *Huascar* to surrender and if she does not surrender defeat her." Moore was in a difficult position. De Horsey might arrive at any time, which would create an explosive situation. That evening he negotiated the surrender of the *Huascar* on terms that no legal action would be taken against any of her crew, except Pierola himself, who was to be detained; the rest were free to go. The *Huascar* was formally handed over at 6:00 on 31 May.

Having lost the *Huascar*, on the morning of 30 May de Horsey decided that Pierola would still attempt to land in the Quilca area, and proceeded north accordingly, sending the *Amethyst* into Mollendo during the afternoon for the latest news. She rejoined him at 19:00 with the information that the *Huascar* was at Iquique, preparing a landing. At 19:35 both ships headed southeast at their cruising speed of nine knots. Coal supply was now a serious concern. At 08:45 on 31 May de Horsey increased speed and went ahead in the *Shah*, ordering the *Amethyst* to join him off Iquique. Lindsay was ordered to organize a second torpedo attack for that night. At 17:00 the *Shah* stopped 20 miles from Iquique. The *Amethyst* caught up after dark, and was sent to obtain news from a north-bound steamer due to leave Iquique that night.

The *Shah* then proceeded to within seven miles of Iquique with Lindsay's three boats in tow: the steam pinnace, armed with one or two spar torpedoes, to tow the cutter; the cutter armed with *Shah*'s Gatling gun for covering fire and fitted to lower a Whitehead torpedo; and a whaler also being towed by the steam pinnace, carrying Lindsay himself, to guide the Whitehead once it was in the water. This time the plan was that Lindsay should first board a British merchant ship in the harbor to find out exactly where the *Huascar* was, then lower the Whitehead, use the whaler to tow it, and release it at the *Huascar* from a shoreward position at not more than 80 yards, to ensure a hit. If this failed, the steam pinnace was to attack with the spar torpedo from the opposite side. The Gatling was not to be used unless the *Huascar* opened fire on the attackers.

De Horsey waited for some time for the *Amethyst* to return, but at 21:15 felt that he could wait no longer, lest the attack be revealed after the moon rose. Lindsay's force left *Shah* for Iquique. Two minutes later signal rockets and guns were heard from the northward. De Horsey now worried that the *Amethyst* had run aground, and made for the signals. In fact, Chatfield had learned from the steamer that the *Huascar* had surrendered. De Horsey reversed course at full speed to the south, firing rockets and burning blue lights, the agreed signals to recall Lindsay, who spotted them a mile from the ships at Iquique. Lindsay's boats returned to *Shah* at 00:20 on 1 June, to de Horsey's great relief.

The following morning both British ships put into Iquique, exchanging the usual salutes with Moore. The *Amethyst* had to fire the British reply, as the *Shah*'s guns were still loaded for battle. De Horsey was allowed to send Lindsay and another officer to inspect the *Huascar* while the *Shah* took on some coal. Late that afternoon de Horsey ordered the *Amethyst* to resume duty off Chile, and himself set off for Callao.

News of the action at Ilo broke in Lima and Callao on the evening of 30 May, causing anti-government and anti-British demonstrations for several days. In an attempt to maintain order, Prado repeatedly proclaimed that he would defend Peruvian national honor, and demand satisfaction from Britain for the attack on the *Huascar*. On 1 June the Peruvian cabinet resigned, partly because of the *Huascar* incident. Its successors took vigorous, but ultimately unsuccessful, steps to obtain an apology and compensation from London.

De Horsey arrived off Callao in the *Shah* on 6 June 1877, aware that public opinion was largely pro-Pierola and anti-British, but with little idea of the sense of outrage in Lima and Callao. When the *Shah* was sighted approaching, the shore batteries were manned, and excited crowds lined the waterfront. Further trouble was averted by Mr. Graham, the British *chargé d'affaires,* who intercepted the *Shah* off San Lorenzo island in the PSN steamer *Guayaquil,* briefed de Horsey on the political situation, and advised him not to call at Callao. De Horsey agreed, and set off on the long voyage to Esquimalt. He managed to coal at the small port of Paita in northern Peru without trouble, but remained *persona non grata* in Peru until 1879.

In the meantime, Prado had reneged on Moore's terms for surrender of the *Huascar*, and ordered that all the rebels be held under arrest in Iquique. This decision proved to be extremely unpopular and Moore himself resigned his command in protest. All the prisoners were pardoned by a decree of 5 July 1877. Pierola left for Chile to resume the role of *caudillo* in exile. The others were given a triumphant reception at Callao and Lima on 9 July. Bugler Bejar was given a hero's funeral at Lima on 17 July.

The *Huascar* incident blighted de Horsey's career. When the news reached London, questions were asked in the House of Commons by opposition members, and there followed much correspondence between de Horsey and the Admiralty. The case was referred to the Law Officers for their opinion, on the basis of the papers available in mid-July 1877. They concluded that the *Huascar* had acted piratically, and that de Horsey's action was justified.

Ultimately the Admiralty approved of de Horsey's general conduct, but disapproved of his peremptory demand that the *Huascar* surrender. Their Lordships considered that instead de Horsey should have begun by requiring the release of British subjects detained against their will, compensation for wrongs done, and an undertaking not to commit further illegal acts against British persons and interests in future. This might have avoided resort to force. The Admiralty also disapproved of the night torpedo attacks attempted on the *Huascar*. Not only were these flagrant violations of Peruvian territorial waters, but the method of attack risked killing the *Huascar*'s entire crew (any British detainees included), and was considered disproportionate to the *Huascar*'s previous acts. The tone of de Horsey's later dispatches in response to Admiralty questioning was considered unacceptable by the Second Naval Lord, Rear-Admiral Arthur Hood, then the most influential member of the Board. Hood, one of a distinguished naval family, was later promoted to Admiral and served as First Naval Lord in 1885-1889.

De Horsey was allowed to serve out the remainder of his three-year term in command in the Pacific, but was unemployed for years after hauling down his flag in September 1879. His next and last appointment was the command of the Channel Squadron in 1884-1885.

The incident had little influence on British naval policy, which already took into account the presence of foreign ironclads on distant stations. As a result of this affair, the Admiralty returned to its earlier policy of allocating an armored ship as flagship on the Pacific Station. The central battery ironclad HMS *Triumph*, sister ship of the *Swiftsure*, was recommissioned in May 1878 and sent out. She overlapped the *Shah* on station for some months, relieving her as flagship on 2 December 1878. The *Shah* was then sent home. She was paid off at Portsmouth in October 1879, and was never recommissioned.

THE WAR OF THE PACIFIC

The discipline of the Peruvian navy was very lax, and drills were almost unknown.
—Lieutenant T.B.M. Mason

Children, the odds are against us. Our flag has never been lowered in the presence of the enemy. I hope that it will not be today. As long as I live that flag shall fly in its place, and, if I die, my officers will know how to do their duty.
— Captain Arturo Prat to his crew before the Battle of Iquique

After reading a description of the battle (of Iquique), one is confronted with a bewildering and yet intriguing paradox: why is it that Condell, who triumphed at Iquique, is all but forgotten while Prat, who was defeated, became and still is Chile's favorite hero?
—William F. Sater

The Opening Phase

Chile went to war with the Allied nations of Bolivia and Peru over her northern border that contained the richest nitrate deposits in the world. This territory is

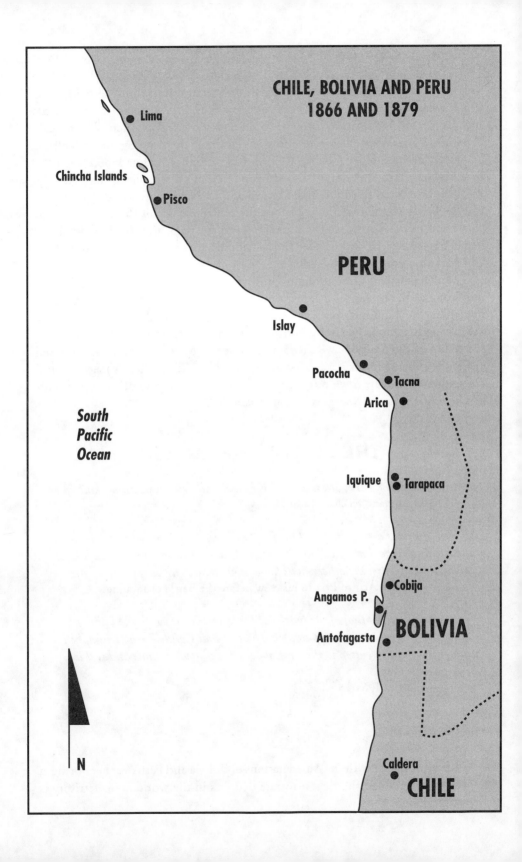

CHILE, BOLIVIA AND PERU
1866 AND 1879

PERU

Lima

Chincha Islands

Pisco

Islay

Pacocha
● Tacna
Arica

South
Pacific
Ocean

Iquique ● Tarapaca

●Cobija
Angamos P.

Antofagasta

BOLIVIA

Caldera

CHILE

N

Warships of Chile and Peru During The War Of The Pacific

Country	Name	Armament	Armor belt	Speed (knots)	Date of Launch	Tonnage
Chile	Almirante Cochrane	6-9", 12 ton M., 1-20 pdrs, 1-9 pdrs, 1-1" Nord	9"	11	1874	3500
Chile	Blanco Encalada	6-9", 12 ton M., 1-20 pdrs, 1-9 pdrs, 2-1" Nord	9"	11	1875	3500
Chile	O'Higgins	3-7-ton M., 2-70 pdrs M., 4-40 pdrs M		10	1866	1670
Chile	Chacabuco	3-7-ton M., 2-70 pdrs M., 4-40 pdrs M		10	1867	1670
Chile	Abtao	3-150 pdrs M., 3-30 pdrs M		6	1864	1050
Chile	Esmeralda	14-40 pdrs M		3	1854	850
Chile	Magellanes	1-7 ton M., 1-64 pdrs M., 1-20 pdrs M		11	1874	772
Chile	Covadonga	2-70 pdrs M		8	...	412
Chile	Tolten	Light guns only		6	1875	240
Chile	Amazonas	1-6" BL		14	1875	1970
Chile	Angamos	1-8" BL		14	1876	1180
Peru	Huascar	2-10" 12.5 ton M., 2-40 pdrs M., 1-12 pdrs M., 1 Gatling	4.5"	11	1865	1200
Peru	Independencia	1-250 pdr M., 3 150 pdrs M., 12-70 pdrs M.	4.5"	12	1864	1500
Peru	Manco Capac	2-XV" SB Dahlgren	5"	6	1866	320
Peru	Atahualpa	2-XV" SB Dahlgren	5"	6	1866	320
Peru	Union	2-100 pdrs M., 2-70 pdrs M., 12-40 pdrs M		12	1864	400
Peru	Talisman	...		...	...	...
Peru	Pilcomayo	2-70 pdrs, M., 4-40 pdrs M (latter BL guns)		10	1864	180
Peru	Chalaco	2-40 pdrs M		11	...	...
Peru	Limena	2-40 pdrs M		12	1865	...
Peru	Oroya	...		...	1873	400

BL = breechloader   pdrs = pounder   M = muzzle loader   Nord = Nordenfelt today the north part of Chile in the Atacama desert. The exact border had been disputed for some years. Bolivia had a small coastal province and exorbitantly raised the duty on the nitrate export firm that was jointly owned by Chilean and British investors. Nitrate was important for fertilizer, as well as in ammunition, and Chile's eventual control of it due to the war would give her a world monopoly on nitrate. The dispute mushroomed to a point where on 14 February 1879, a Chilean naval expedition occupied the Bolivian coastal provincial capital of Antofagasta.

Why Bolivia chose this moment to raise duties and precipitate this crisis is hard to say. However, the Bolivian dictator Hilarion Daza needed money and was aware that Chile was embroiled with Argentina in a border dispute over Patagonia and Tierra del Fuego. That dispute had seen the mobilization of Argentina's fleet (which included two new small coast defense ironclads) and the dispatch of Chile's two ironclads towards Cape Horn.

Peru's involvement was due to a "secret" alliance well known to Chile. Peru's president was again Prado, who had been replaced earlier and after a series of revolving presidents and coups, had recently returned to power. With the occupation of Antofagasta, Bolivia declared war, and when Peru refused to declare her neutrality, general war between the two allied nations and Chile resulted by 4 April 1879.

All three contestants in this conflict were ill prepared for the war. Chile is sometimes said to be "The Prussia of the Pacific," but that overstates the case. Her army officer corps was small and lacked training, and her army was tiny. Chile expanded her regular army in the course of the war to 55,000 men, and had a small and virtually worthless National Guard of 6,687 men. Chile was numerically outnumbered in overall population by a factor of 2 to 1, while at the start of the war the combined Bolivian and Peruvian armies were almost twice the size of Chile's. It should be noted that Peru had a ratio of almost 1:3 officers to men. Peru's army increased in size to 40,000 and while Bolivia's army did have a theoretical size of over 50,000, it lacked modern arms for but a fraction of that total.

The population of Chile was actually in a net decline in this decade as Chileans left home to find work in the neighboring nations. So economically, in population, and with her army, Chile was on paper not the powerhouse of the region. Her strongest suit was that her government had been stable with regular elections, and had not been faced with forced changes of presidents or dictators such as in Peru or Bolivia. The majority of the population of all three nations was essentially Indian or mixed race, with a ruling class and officer corps of largely "white" background that reflected the old Spanish ruling class during the colonial period. Still, the class and race division was less rigid in Chile than in the Allied nations, which had an immense indigenous Indian underclass that did not even speak the "national" language of Spanish.

Chile's decisive weapon would be her ironclad navy. After the war with Spain and the humiliating bombardment of Valparaiso, she had purchased two new ironclads from Great Britain. The *Almirante Cochrane* and *Blanco Encalada* were sister ships of 3,560 tons, authorized in 1871, launched in the mid-1870's and designed by Sir Edward J. Reed, who also designed many of the British so-called "central battery" ironclads.

The central battery ironclad had its main armament located in an armored casemate in the central part of the ship. Some of the guns would usually be at each point or corner of the box so as to provide some gunfire fore and aft. However, it must be recalled that even if a gun could physically be lined up parallel to the ship, the resulting blast would cause structural damage to the ship, thus the *theoretical* "circle of fire" and reality were not the same. Still, at a distance from the firing central battery ship and with a small adjustment of the helm combined with the traversing of guns, a warship could cover every point with fire. This type of ship would compete for a few years with turreted ironclads, before fading away in the mid-1880's. They were a smaller and more maneuverable warship than traditional broadside ironclads like the *Warrior* or *Gloire*, almost always twin screwed, and with heavier armor protecting fewer but larger guns. This meant that they displaced less water, required fewer crew, and were less expensive than an older broadside style ironclad design.

The Chilean ironclads were armed with six British built Armstrong 12 ton 9" muzzle-loader rifles, three or four small guns and a 1" Nordenfeldt machine-gun on the *Cochrane*, with two on the *Encalada*. The central battery was protected by a maximum of 8 inches of wrought iron backed by 14 inches of teak wood. They both had seven watertight compartments and the central battery ship had introduced a double bottom that added structural strength to the ship and some minimal protection from torpedoes. At normal speeds they could steam for about seven days before needing to coal.

Their machine-guns offered an opportunity to defeat any attempt at boarding, and kill crews around any open top or exposed gun batteries. At close range they could also be used to fire at enemy gunports, while, especially at night in conjunction with the recently invented electric searchlight, they could defend against torpedo boat attacks—be it spar torpedoes, or the new "automobile torpedo" powered by a small motor, or with a "Lay torpedo" which was wire guided.

The Nordenfeldt consisted of ten 1" barrels in a horizontal line. "The projectiles, of which more than two hundred can be fired in one minute, are of steel, and are capable of penetrating at a distance of one thousand yards iron plates of a greater thickness than any with which torpedo-boats have as yet been armored."

The French used the Hotchkiss, similar to a Gatling gun, with the barrels revolving around in a circle. The Chilean fleet was commanded by Admiral Juan Williams Rebolledo, the former commander of the *Esmeralda* in the war with Spain, and a man with presidential aspirations. Some have argued that he actually feared combat in this war, that he deliberately kept from cleaning the bottoms of his ironclads so as to avoid catching the Peruvian ironclads, and that his abortive raid on Callao in May 1879 was designed to fail. This is a difficult charge to prove. Considering his previous personal bravery in the war with Spain, and that it is well known that he was not an easy man to work with, leads one to suspect that he was too old for the post and was simply past his prime. At the outbreak of war the Chilean navy had 145 officers and 1,563 men, as well as a small Marine Corps.

Another point that needs to be remembered is that Chile's moves in the war were pressured throughout by a somewhat hostile public. Chileans were upset with what was perceived to be Chilean President Anibal Pinto's retreat on the territorial question with Argentina. Further, they described the Allied enemies as "a horde of inferior Indians and blacks, men of impure heritage, unknown parentage, and questionable sexual orientation, who would collapse once confronted with a show of strength. Consequently, when (Pinto) could not provide instant victory, the press became hostile, accusing the government of failing to act decisively." Of course, as so often in any nation with a partial or fully free press, there is a conflict over release of information that may be valuable to the enemy. It would cause President Pinto at one point to exclaim that "to know what is happening in Chile, the Peruvian government only has to subscribe to our newspapers!"

In turn there was a conflict between the military and civilian leaders. In Chile this was summed up as the conflict between the "Cucalones" and the "Militares." "Cucalones" is a term that was derived from a Peruvian newspaper correspondent named Antonio Cucalon, who was lost overboard while at sea on one of the *Huascar's* operations against Chile. He became, as William F. Sater has written, "synonymous with the amateur military strategists who filled Santiago's cafes, criticizing the direction of the various military or naval campaigns." Hence this political struggle was always in the background, but similar power struggles also would affect the course of the war for Peru and Bolivia—most vividly brought home for Peru when President Prado abandoned his post in the midst of war and failure in December of 1879, to be succeeded legally by a man quickly replaced by Nicolas de Pierola in a military coup. Daza, too, would not see the end of the war, being replaced by General Narciso Campero in a coup while in the field leading the Bolivian army.

Turning to the Allied navies, we find that the Bolivians had no navy, though in the early 1870's there had been discussions about purchasing two ironclads similar to the *Cochrane,* but this was rejected as there was no money. The loss of Bolivia's coast has always been sorely felt, and though one of the poorest nations on the planet, she still has a "navy" for the eventual day she regains an outlet to the sea.

Peru, however, had a relatively large navy, but one of inferior quality. Her seagoing units were commanded by Captain, later Rear-Admiral, Don Miguel Grau, while Rear-Admiral de la Haza commanded the navy from his headquarters at Callao. Grau would become Peru's greatest naval hero in this war and for all time. Even to this day once a year at the Peruvian naval academy it is announced at muster that Grau is present in spirit. Her crews were largely foreign-born, and included Chileans.

Her two main ironclads were the *Huascar* and the *Independencia,* built to fight Spain. The *Independencia* had received an increase in her armament. She now sported an 8" 250 pounder muzzle-loader in a forward pivot and a 150 pounder Parrott aft. Otherwise, they were as in 1866 except they were a bit slower and the *Huascar* had added a Gatling gun to her armament.

In addition to them, Peru had bought two American monitors completed in Cincinnati in 1865, and renamed them the *Atahualpa* and *Manco Capac* after Inca kings. They were *Canonicus* class monitors displacing 2,100 tons, bought on 2 April of 1868, and sister ships to the *Tecumseh* of the Battle of Mobile fame. Their effectiveness as ironclads was strictly limited to a role as coastal defense warships, though the Chileans feared their defensive strength, rightly thinking that they were better armored than their European built comrades.

One of the early reinforcements built in the United States were two small "Herreshoff" torpedo boats armed with spar torpedoes. One, the *Republica,* would use in lieu of the spar torpedoes, the Lay torpedo. This was patented in 1873 by John Louis Lay. It used a cable to guide it and had to run on the surface at a speed of 12.5 knots with a 90 pound warhead of dynamite. The *Republica* had a speed of only nine knots and would prove ineffective. She would be sunk by the *O'Higgins* after an abortive night raid against the Chilean ironclads off Callao on 3 January 1881. The other one would be captured by an armed steamer "whilst coaling at a small neutral Ecuadorian port" while being delivered to Peru in December of 1879. She was renamed the *Guacolda* and would operate off Callao for most of the war before being wrecked in 1881.

Peru also built a small 48 foot long submarine, designed by a locomotive engineer Frederico Blume, and tried to employ it against Chile's ironclads. An attempt by this submarine using Lay torpedoes would fail as Chile moved her ironclads out to sea at night—this small and primitive submarine simply could not maneuver quickly or far enough to matter. In addition Peru tried to purchase an ironclad from Italy, but also failed in this endeavor.

The war opened with Williams, the Chilean fleet commander, steaming north on 5 April to blockade the Peruvian port of Iquique. Williams' squadron consisted of the *Cochrane* (flagship), *Encalada, O'Higgins, Chacabuco,* and *Esmeralda.* He had been urged to attack the Peruvian fleet at Callao, but had decided it was too well defended to attack. Iquique is one of the driest ports in the world, requiring a desalination plant to supply water to the town. It was also the busiest port in the region due to having the richest and easiest to mine nitrate deposits. Up to one thousand ships a year docked at the port. Williams argued that, by blockading Iquique, the Peruvians would have to come south and do battle, with their main source of revenue cut off.

A skirmish, with the glorified name of the "Battle of Chipana," took place on 12 April between the little steam corvette *Magellanes* commanded by Captain Juan J. Latorre, and the *Union* and *Pilcomayo.* The *Magellanes* managed to race by the Peruvian ships, resting in a quiet cove, and they quickly raised steam and pursued her. During a two hour chase the nominally faster *Union* damaged one of her boilers, as it had not been properly maintained, and had to return to Callao for docking and repair. Damage was negligible but Chipana was hailed in both countries as a victory—by the Chileans for seeing the little British built *Magellanes* escaping superior forces and by the Peruvians because they chased off the Chileans.

Meanwhile, several weeks of fruitless Chilean blockade of Iquique, protected by only four 9 pounder fieldpieces, as well as some small local naval raids of the southern Peruvian coast, had led to pressure to "do something." Williams decided to head to Callao and attempt to deliver a *coup de main.* He left the weak *Esmeralda,* now joined by the captured Spanish gunboat *Covadonga,* to carry on the blockade. Williams had devised a daring plan.

On 16 May the strongest elements of the Chilean fleet slipped off in ones and twos to rendezvous 40 miles off the port of Pisagua. This force consisted of her two ironclads, the corvettes *Chacabuco* and *O'Higgins,* the *Matias Cousino* acting as collier, the little *Magellanes,* and the old *Abtao* loaded down with black powder and crewed by a skeleton force.

The plan called for steaming north, beyond view of the shore, and having the *Abtao* slip in among the Peruvian ironclads at anchor at Callao. She would then drop anchor and "the *Abtao's* crew would first fire a broadside at the enemy, then after setting its ship afire, the Chileans would evacuate. As they rowed their lifeboats to their rescue vessel, they were instructed to shout that the *Abtao* was about to explode."

The other Chilean warships would then open fire and the steam launches from the ironclads and the *Chacabuco* would enter the harbor and attack with spar torpedoes. The main targets were to be the seagoing Peruvian ironclads. The two corvettes would then fire on the city or shore batteries, preferably the former, and then cover the withdrawal of the fleet with the little *Magellanes* acting as the rescue ship.

However, on the voyage north the squadron was beset with problems. Several ships suffered engine problems, slowing the squadron, and at one point the *Matias Cousino* became lost, but managed to rejoin the fleet. When they finally arrived off Callao in the early morning of 21 May 1879, the crews were "animated with festive enthusiasm" with the chance of approaching battle. Delay followed delay, and as dawn approached Williams decided to withdraw behind San Lorenzo island. Dawn revealed only one of the monitors (the other was present but not sighted), the *Union* and the *Pilcomayo*, along with foreign shipping in the port, but not Chile's two main adversaries, the *Huascar* and the *Independencia*. Later an Italian merchant ship leaving port was hailed and told the Chileans that the main quarry had flown with "three or four transports." Fearing where the enemy's squadron might have steamed to, Williams called off the attack and headed south.

So what had occurred? On 16 May President Prado, accompanied by his staff and reinforcements, had left Callao southward bound via a "circuitous route" for Arica, a port north of Iquique. Prado was escorted by the *Huascar, Independencia* and the two monitors, protecting his three small lightly armed transports. Within 24 hours, the monitors were both laboring and slowing down the expedition and they returned, at Grau's urging, to Callao. Williams' fleet had passed there in the night without either sighting the other. Williams had not deployed a search line of two or three of his wooden ships during his voyage north which had further limited the chance of encountering the encumbered and inferior Peruvian squadron.

Prado, on arriving at Arica and learning that Iquique was blockaded only by two old wooden warships, ordered the *Huascar* and *Independencia* south to attack the *Esmeralda* and the *Covadonga*. With Grau in command they sped south, only touching briefly at Pisagua to confirm that the Chilean ironclads were still absent off Iquique.

The *Esmeralda*, now under the command of Arturo Prat, had the reputation of being the most "wretched ship of the fleet." It, along with the *Covadonga*, had the fleet's worst officers transferred to them before the rest of the fleet under Williams headed north. The *Covadonga* was commanded by the Chilean-Peruvian Captain Carlos Condell, who was known to be quite lucky. Prat was unpopular with Williams, who disapproved of "literate sailors"—Prat had earned a law degree between wars and while still serving in the navy. This "sin" was compounded by his successful defense of two officers charged with insubordination.

Before heading north, Williams had asked Prat what he intended to do if the *Huascar* appeared off Iquique. Prat had replied that he would board her. Neither thought that such an opportunity would occur. But now, on the morning of 21

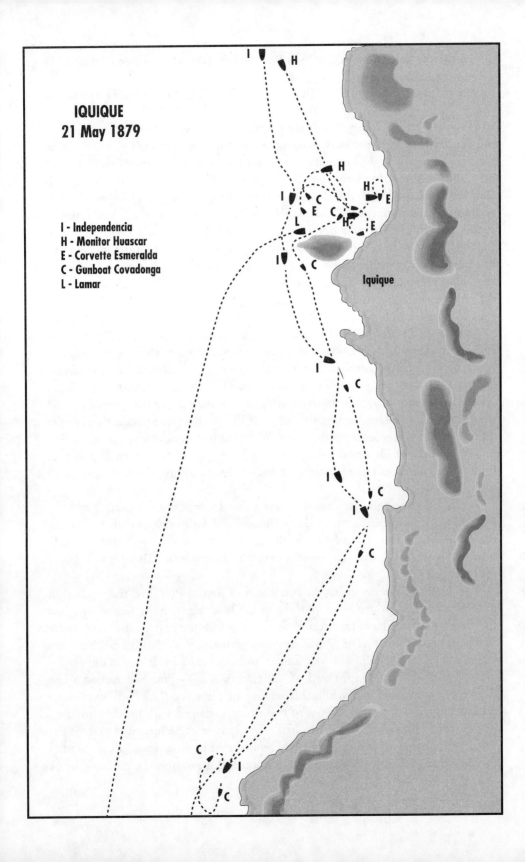

IQUIQUE
21 May 1879

I - Independencia
H - Monitor Huascar
E - Corvette Esmeralda
C - Gunboat Covadonga
L - Lamar

Iquique

Armored turret of the Huascar. (Chilean Naval Mission)

May 1879, the *Huascar* under Grau and the *Independencia* under Commander Juan G. Moore hove in sight, and Prat would have his date with glory.

A Chilean transport slipped out of the harbor by flying a United States flag. Next the two Chilean warships piped hands to breakfast and fell back into shallow waters of the harbor. Prat now ordered the *Covadonga* to follow in his wake and to keep to the shallow waters where the deeper draft Peruvian ironclads could not follow. Prat then issued Nelson's signal at Trafalgar, asking all Chileans to "do their duty."

As Grau approached, a small boat was launched from shore and informed him that the *Esmeralda* was protected by stationary torpedoes, which was not true. This made Grau somewhat circumspect at the start of the action, but he would become more aggressive when the *Esmeralda* was forced to come out further in the bay.

At 08:00 the action opened with a shot from the *Huascar.* The *Huascar* engaged the *Esmeralda* while the *Independencia* fought the *Covadonga.* Peruvian gunnery "was execrable," which lends credibility to a later statement that Peru had not provided for gunnery practice for several *years* before the war. The *Esmeralda* also tried to stay between the Peruvian town of Iquique and the *Huascar* which made her fire much more deliberate, if still inaccurate—some damage was done to the town. The Peruvians were aided by the local light field battery, which began peppering the *Esmeralda* at 500 yards range and approximately 30 threatening small boats began swarming with troops along the harbor front.

The Chilean gunnery was much better, but the hits from the *Esmeralda's* 40 pounders simply bounced off the *Huascar's* armor. Her rifle fire was heavy enough to make the *Huascar* think she carried a machine-gun, but the small arms fire was even less effective than the cannons. She did damage the forward tripod mast of the *Huascar* and one shot incredibly entered her gunport, bounced around in the turret, but injured no one. This points out, as so much of this battle shows, the effect of luck. What if that shot had been an exploding shell? Or later, what if the *Independencia's* helmsman was not hit at a critical stage? In the battle of ironclads the lucky hit or the plan of one individual—usually the captain—could affect the fate of a nation or a war.

The first hour of the battle was fought at ranges of 800 to 2,000 yards and little was accomplished. The *Covadonga* had been hit once by the *Huascar* with little damage resulting, while the *Independencia* with many more guns failed to hit at all. Condell in his official report noted that small arms fire from shore was affecting his ship and that she was close to a reef. The *Independencia* was also trying to run his ship down. He went on to write,

> I considered that our position was not desirable; from this location we could not help the *Esmeralda*, which was fighting desperately. A shot from the *Huascar's* 300 pounder gun had pierced my ship, shattering the wooden foremast at its base. I managed to leave the port, directing all my fire at the *Independencia*, which at a distance of 200 meters was firing its own guns.

At this point the *Covadonga* headed south, keeping close to shore. The *Esmeralda*, largely due to the shore fire, now headed out towards the *Huascar* in the middle of the bay. At about 10:30 one of the two boilers on the *Esmeralda* exploded, which reduced her speed to barely three knots. About now the *Huascar* hit her for the only time (out of forty rounds fired in the course of the action), though it killed every one of the *Esmeralda's* engineers when it exploded in the engine room, bringing her to a near standstill. The *Huascar* now attempted to ram her. Coming at a virtually motionless ship, Grau stopped his engines too soon and though touching, did no damage.

It was now at about 11:00 that Prat earned his immortal fame. He shouted "Men, board the enemy ship!" and leapt on board the *Huascar* with a sergeant of marines (Scheina states that a sailor also was with Prat). As Sater has written,

> The two men, virtually powerless, stood exposed on the *Huascar's* decks while their enemies crouched behind armored (bulwarks). For a few moments they remained motionless, perhaps searching for some weak spot to attack, in order to avenge their dead shipmates. Turning, they rushed headlong at the ship' armored

bridge only to be cut down by rifle fire. Both men were mortally wounded and lay, like broken rag dolls, at their enemy's feet.

Prat did kill a Peruvian signals officer with his pistol. Grau, as he reversed engines, called on Prat to surrender, who would not, and was forced to have him shot down.

When Grau rammed their ship a second time, the *Esmeralda's* crew was now inspired to follow their Captain, to attempt to board yet again. This time a full dozen men rushed the *Huascar's* deck, but failed to seize her. Finally, rammed yet a third time, the hulk of the *Esmeralda* sank at 13:30, having never lowered her flag, giving up 63 prisoners and suffering 149 dead. Every year on 21 May the town of Iquique celebrates the stand of the *Esmeralda* that still lies under the waters of that harbor as a reminder of the war. The *Huascar's* forward watertight compartment filled due to damage on the final ramming, she suffered a few crew losses due to small arms fire, but, she received no significant gunnery damage. Grau later stated that his crew was demoralized at this time from the Chilean fire and the ineffectiveness of his own, and that a larger, luckier, and more determined boarding party might have succeeded.

Prat became the national hero of Chile, a sort of Nathan Hale combined with George Washington. A Peruvian paper would write in 1879 that "The Chileans have lost their minds. They have become idolaters of a new religion which is called Prat. There everything is Prat. The names, the ships, the battalions, the societies, the statutes: even the scapularies. This is real Pratomania." Even babies were named for him. To give an idea of how popular he became, as late as the 1930s over 200 columns of stories would appear in six of the major Chilean papers every year devoted to reminding their readers of Prat's sacrifice and bravery. Captain, shortly Rear-Admiral, Grau would write a letter to his widow Carmela Carvajal de Prat and included with it what valuables that could be collected on 2 June. In it he wrote that "Captain Prat had died a victim to his excessive intrepidity, in the defense and for the glory of the flag of his country. I sincerely deplore this unlucky occurrence during our duel."

As the *Covadonga* steamed south, keeping close to the shoals, her larger ironclad adversary under Captain Moore dogged her every step. She was also subjected to some minor coastal fire in her flight south. But the *Independencia's* gunfire was poorer than the *Huascar's*, even with the range usually between about 300 to 200 yards and occasionally down to 125 yards. With more guns, though usually only able to employ her forward 250 pounder pivot gun, she scored but one hit, which raked the little *Covadonga* and exited the forward part of the ship. The *Covadonga* hit the *Independencia* repeatedly, and her small arms fire also convinced Moore that she had a Gatling gun on board—which she did not. She also succeeded in dismounting the *Independencia's* main pivot gun.

Like Grau, Moore also tried to ram the retreating *Covadonga,* making two abortive attempts during this run to the south when he charged a third time. The *Covadonga* "was within a hundred yards of the beach, and had just touched a reef" near Punta Grueso when the *Independencia* charged at about 11:45. A rifle shot from one of the *Covadonga's* sharpshooters at the instant when the helmsman of the *Independencia* was ordered to turn to the starboard, hit home at this critical moment. The helmsman was at the fully exposed ordinary wheel—as on a warship of Lord Nelson's day. His fall caused the *Independencia* to run hard aground and she even fell over on her starboard side and took on water.

Condell, then smartly wheeled the *Covadonga* about, and sped past the crippled *Independencia* to come up under her stern, from where she could not fire back. Condell plied her with shot and shell from the two guns that could be brought to bear, starting a fire aft, and forced her to run up a white flag. The *Huascar* at this time appeared from Iquique bay after helping to rescue some of the crew from the *Esmeralda,* and the *Covadonga* now made off to the south, briefly chased by the *Huascar.*

The *Independencia* was a total loss, except for two 150 pounders salvaged and used on land. Moore would be placed under arrest and would later die defending Arica. The *Independencia* had four dead and eleven wounded. The *Huascar* suffered one dead, the signals officer, and seven wounded in the battle. The *Covadonga's* losses were minor.

The *Huascar* now steamed south, throwing a few shells at the *Covadonga* that lay well protected at Antofagasta on 27 May, and was hit by a Chilean 150 pounder on shore. The round hit sideways near the waterline, but still penetrated her armor. While giving a scare, it caused only minor damage.

Next Grau cut the telegraphic cable between Antofagasta and Valparaiso, and turned north. At dawn on 3 June he sighted two warships and closed to within five miles. Instead of two wooden corvettes, they turned out to be the *Blanco Encalada* and *Magellanes.* The Chileans gave chase, and almost caught the *Huascar,* which was burning some very poor and smoky coal and at first could only manage nine knots. Shots were exchanged in this 18 hour chase but Grau escaped to Callao.

Upon returning on 7 June the *Huascar* repaired her leaky bow and added some armor protection to her Gatling gun in her main mast. Grau also had removed the damaged tripod foremast. He also recruited some new and more skilled crew from idle foreign shipping lying at Callao due to the blockade of Iquique. Grau was fêted by the authorities and populace and was promoted for his victory by being made Admiral, though he asked and was allowed to remain on board the *Huascar.*

Grau's career was now to reach its apex. His ship, with other Peruvian vessels, would range up and down the Pacific Littoral, paralyzing Chilean military activity.

As long as the Peruvian fleet was a threat, the Chilean army could not be too aggressive.

Grau's Raids and the Battle of Angamos

The Huascar now became the sole hope of Peru. While her gallant commander out-manoeuvred the immensely superior forces of the enemy, and kept his ship on the seas under the Peruvian flag, the Chilians did not dare to undertake any important expedition. The coasts were safe from serious attack. For more than four months this feat was achieved, and Peru was safe-guarded by her heroic son.
—Clements R. Markham

By the beginning of July the *Huascar* had completed her refitting and once again was at sea. Grau was under orders to raid the enemy's shipping and coasts, and *not* to seek combat with an equal or superior force.

On the night of 9-10 July Grau encountered the transport *Matias Cousino* and forced her surrender at Iquique. While endeavoring to take possession of her, another vessel loomed up, first thought to be the *Cochrane,* but in fact the little *Magellanes.* Latorre was determined to fight his stronger adversary and a night skirmish resulted. The *Huascar* attempted to ram twice, but her gunnery was still poor, and failed to hit on all counts. This did allow the *Magellanes* to hit her once with a 7" projectile that inflicted some damage to the *Huascar.* The *Huascar* was now thoroughly roused by this sting, and tried two more times to ram—and failed again. Now the *Cochrane* arrived on the scene and it was time for the *Huascar* to depart, which after a short running fight she succeeded in doing, running north to Arica. Three men were wounded in the action on board the *Magellanes.* The *Huascar* fired six times from her large guns, missing with all shells, though she did pepper the *Magellanes* with small arms and Gatling fire. Only one 7" 115-pound projectile was fired from the *Magellanes* and had inflicted damage, all the other smaller guns from the *Magellanes* failed to do any damage.

Next the *Huascar,* with the *Union,* headed south from Arica on 17 July. Small Chilean landing boats were destroyed at several points on the coast. Two transports were taken "loaded with coal and copper." The *Huascar's* most notable success now occurred with the capture of the *Rimac* with 300 soldiers on board, and she was added to the Peruvian Navy's list.

The loss of the *Rimac* brought about riots in Santiago which were only broken up by mounted police using sabers on the crowd. Several civilians and police were hospitalized from the riot. This was the trigger for congressional inquiries that brought about a change in the parliamentary government and would lead indirectly to a new Chilean admiral, and a new direction in the war.

The new Minister of War, the dynamic Don Rafael Sotomayor, first ordered the lifting of the blockade of Iquique. Next he began moving his ships into port to have their bottoms cleaned by divers and general maintenance performed so as to improve the speed and strength of the ships. Rear-Admiral Williams was replaced by Commodore Galvarino Riveros. Then, with other staff changes including the sending of Captain Latorre to the *Cochrane*, a plan was prepared to destroy the raiding *Huascar*.

Sotomayor and Riveros decided to establish two squadrons. One would be the faster ships under Latorre in the *Cochrane*, with the *O'Higgins* and the *Loa*, that would remain about 30 miles off the coast. Close to the coast would be Riveros on the *Blanco* accompanied by the *Covadonga* and *Matias Cousino*. When they heard where the *Huascar* was raiding they would intercept her and catch her between two fires, forcing an action with her. That would be exactly what happened.

Meanwhile, the Peruvians now decided to once again transfer one of the monitors south to Arica, and so the best one, the *Manco Capac*, left Callao on 3 August, escorting two armed transports carrying troops and supplies. The *Huascar* was cruising in the south near Antofagasta providing long range protection. The convoy successfully arrived on 7 August. The *Huascar* at this time almost captured the hired transport *Lamar*, but it was hauled in too close to shore for the *Huascar* to succeed.

This was followed by the dispatch of the *Union* to the far south in the hope of seizing two transports arriving from Europe with arms and ammunition. Grau had learned of this by examining the papers on board the captured *Rimac*. Arriving at Punta Arenas on 18 August, the local Chilean governor hoodwinked the *Union* into going on an abortive chase, which allowed the two transports to arrive safely at Valparaiso. This safe arrival would allow the dispatch of 3,000 trained and now freshly equipped Chilean troops north on 20 September in a convoy of 12 ship transports and warships to Antofagasta.

But before then another event had occurred at that port. Grau had taken on board two Lay torpedoes and an operator. On the night of 27 August he appeared off Antofagasta, and approached the anchored *Abtao*. Quietly steaming to within 200 yards of her, the operator now deployed the torpedo.

> One of the torpedoes was then launched from the deck, and had proceeded some distance on its course, when it began to turn to port, making a half-circle in that direction, and coming back towards the vessel. Efforts were made to stop it, but nothing but a reduction in speed was effected. Lieutenant Diez Conseco, appreci- ating the danger to which all were exposed, jumped overboard, and caused the torpedo to deviate from its dangerous course.

Grau, later, on returning to Iquiqui, landed the torpedoes and had them buried in the local cemetery. Later the Chileans would unearth them.

Before burying them, he attacked Antofagasta the next morning. Also present was the little *Magellanes*, the older *Abtao*, and a Chilean armed transport. Grau attacked from over 3,000 yards out and succeeded in hitting the *Abtao* twice with his 300 pounder. Each shell damaged her and killed a total of nine and wounded thirteen officers and men. The *Huascar* was hit once with a 150 pound shell which killed one and wounded one "and went overboard without exploding." The two Chilean ships took advantage of the neutral shipping at the port by moving near them, and Grau did not press the attack for fear of involving neutral major powers in the war against Peru.

Grau next steamed south, continuing minor depredations on the coast against small craft, and returning to Arica. Grau wanted to refit the *Huascar* at Callao, but President Prado decided against it.

It was now that the refitted Chilean fleet headed north to see if they could find and finish off this lone seagoing Peruvian ironclad that had caused so much mischief. On 1 October the fleet headed towards the southern Peruvian naval base of Arica. In tow were two steam launches of the Chilean ironclads outfitted with spar torpedoes.

The plan called for them to enter Arica at night and attempt to attack the *Huascar*. However, the plan went awry. First, the launches were too far out to sea and arrived off the port not at night, but in full daylight. Additionally, the *Huascar* had escaped and was not in port. Riveros did learn from local fishermen that the *Union* and the *Huascar* had headed for Iquiqui on 30 September, escorting the *Rimac* with reinforcements, and then south for her fourth raid. Riveros considered attacking the *Manco Capac* at Arica, but decided that the risk of damage to his ships from shore batteries and the monitor, overshadowed the fact that Grau was at sea yet again. He ordered the fleet south.

On 5 October, the Peruvian pair quietly entered the fortified Chilean port of Coquimbo, passing the United States naval steam sloop *Pensacola,* with the only sound heard from the pair being "a whispered order, in English, to 'Go ahead, slow'." The shore batteries never opened fire, but, nor was there any shipping in the port. The two now stood off the port to the south on the 6th and intercepted two mail steamers. Grau now knew the enemy fleet was north of him, and that Antofagasta, from which he had been ordered to remain at least 70 miles, was now uncovered.

Grau had also learned that the *Cochrane* had suffered an engine breakdown, so he stood north and with just the *Huascar* expected Antofagasta in the early morning of 8 October—nothing was present. Grau rejoined the *Union* and now headed north when at a little after 03:00 smoke was spotted to the north. The day was "fine and clear." Three ships, soon identified as warships, were steaming south. This was the squadron made up of the *Blanco* with Riveros' flag, the *Covadonga,* and the *Matias Cousino* that had orders to skirt along the coast while the other squadron stood out to sea—and the *Cochrane* had repaired her engine.

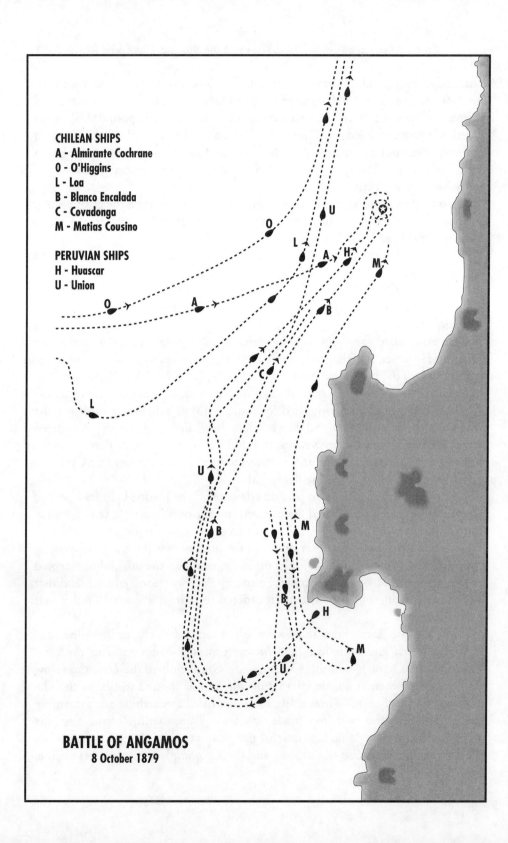

CHILEAN SHIPS
A - Almirante Cochrane
0 - O'Higgins
L - Loa
B - Blanco Encalada
C - Covadonga
M - Matias Cousino

PERUVIAN SHIPS
H - Huascar
U - Union

BATTLE OF ANGAMOS
8 October 1879

With her hull cleaned and with the *Huascar's* fouled, she probably had at least a knot on the Peruvian ironclad.

The Chilean fleet was in telegraphic communications with their government and so was supplied with information about the raiding Peruvians. They had been ordered to operate in the vicinity of Point Angamos, which is where the *Huascar* and the *Union* were sighted.

Riveros chased the Peruvians, who were making about ten and three quarters knots, while the Chileans lumbered along at about seven and a half. Riveros knew he could not catch them, but possibly one or both of the Peruvians would suffer an engine breakdown. A stern chase may be a long chase, but one never knows what chance might bring.

Grau, after seeing the distance between his ships and the Chileans lengthening, decided about 05:40 to slow his speed and head north again, further out to sea now, and he actually lay down to rest. At 07:15 new smoke was seen and at 07:30 the *Cochrane, O'Higgins,* and *Loa* were identified.

Grau ordered the *Union* to make for Arica independently. So at 07:45 the *Union* was off, being pursued by the *O'Higgins* and *Loa.* The pursuit would go into the evening, but the *Union* made good her escape.

Grau determined that he could not escape to the south with his home port to the north and would have to race past the approaching ironclads, especially the *Cochrane.* However, Grau had neither the position nor the speed to succeed. By 09:10 the *Blanco* was still distant, but the *Cochrane* was going to cross the *Huascar's* bow. At about 09:25 the range had dropped to 3,000 yards and the *Huascar* opened fire, hitting the *Cochrane* with a ricocheting shell that failed to explode and did little damage.

At 2,000 yards range distant, with the *Blanco Encalada* still about six miles away, the *Cochrane* now was ready to open fire. As Mason later wrote, "one of her first shots penetrated the *Huascar's* armor on the port side, and, exploding, entered the turret chamber, where it set fire to the light wood-work, killed and wounded twelve men ... " and temporarily jammed the turret. The accuracy of the Chileans was better *and* they had more guns—a difficult situation for the *Huascar* to overcome.

At 09:40 the *Huascar* tried to ram, which the *Cochrane,* with sea room and her twin screws, easily evaded. It was five minutes later when Grau's life was ended when a shell entered the small conning tower and exploded, most likely, when the shell had transfixed Grau's body at about waist level. Only his foot was later recovered. A man below him was killed by the concussion alone. But the *Huascar* did not give up. This morning she would fight on, going through four different commanders.

It would be about 10:10 when the *Encalada* arrived to join the battle. But it was the *Cochrane* that continued to worry her opponent the greatest. She

The preserved Huascar *at anchor in Santiago Harbor, today flying the Chilean flag.* (Chilean Naval Mission)

attempted to ram, which failed but by five yards, but one of her projectiles carried away the steering ropes. A second attempt failed, though again she fired into the *Huascar* at 200 yards range. A third attempt was thwarted by the *Encalada's* presence that came close to ramming the *Cochrane*, causing her to increase the range to about 1,200 yards and loop away from her adversary, but the *Encalada* continued the attack against the *Huascar*.

The *Huascar* was being riddled by this point. "On account of the number of shots which had traversed the smokestack, driving down soot, *debris*, and smoke into the fire-room, it was impossible to see the gauges. The water fell too low in one of the boilers, which allowed the tubes to be burned through and caused a great escape of steam," leading the Chileans to think they had hit one of her boilers. It was about this time that yet another shot penetrated her turret and "killed or mortally wounded every man in it." When the body of the turret commander who died, "was found and identified, all the upper part of the head was gone, the lower jaw only remaining, four wounds on the right leg, a cut across the stomach, and six body wounds; the right shoulder and arm had disappeared entirely."

Surrender was the only course left and her flag was hauled down. The *Huascar* tried to scuttle herself. When she was boarded she had four feet of water in the hold, but was saved by the Chileans, pistols in hand, to become a prize.

What they captured in this 90 minute action was a scene of horror and destruction. On board were 32 dead and 48 wounded out of a crew of about 200. As Mason later wrote,

> There was hardly a square yard of her upper works that did not bear marks of having been struck with some species of projectile. Her smoke-stack and conning-tower were nearly destroyed, her boats gone, and davits either entirely carried away or bent out of all shape... Below, the scene was much more terrible. Everywhere was death and destruction caused by the enemy's large shells. Eighteen bodies were taken out of the cabin, and the turret was full of remains of the two sets of guns' crews.
>
> The light wood-work, ladders, and bulkheads were all destroyed ... She had her steering-gear disabled three distinct times by the enemy's fire, was set on fire in eight different places, had her turret jammed, her right turret gun disabled, and her light guns and Gatling unmanned... The armor in this case was only a great disadvantage to her. It served to explode the enemy's projectiles, which it in no case stopped when they struck at any but the smallest angles. The backing and inner skin only served to increase the number of fragments, which were driven into the interior of the vessel with deadly effect.

The two Chilean ironclads had fired seventy-six 9" Palliser shells (armor piercing shells)—forty-five from the *Almirante Cochrane* and the remainder from the *Encalada*. The *Huascar* fired 40 Palliser shells in reply. The *Huascar* may have hit the *Cochrane* three times, though clearly some, maybe only one, of those three hits were due to the fire of the *Encalada,* and all did little damage. The *Huascar* however was struck herself twenty times with her armor being penetrated thirteen times, two of which penetrated her turret. Two other shots glanced off her turret.

As the firing was mostly from a range of 500 yards, ending at 150 yards, on a smooth sea, many at the time considered the guns "were unskillfully handled, the firing, in fact, being mostly at random." This point can be debated as even late in the American Civil War, one was more apt to miss rather than hit, even at close range—due not just to the skill or lack of skill of the gun crew, but also the state and quality of the shells and powder charges; nor should the sea condition be forgotten. Even a calm day, or night, can disturb ship's gunnery.

The small guns and machine-guns on board were heavily employed, though being so light and with no crews exposed outside of armored positions, they had little overall affect. Riveros was made Rear-Admiral for the action, and Commander Latorre was made Captain. The only Chilean losses were on the *Cochrane,* which lost 12 men killed or wounded.

Grau's loss was mourned everywhere, and he received a full burial service in Santiago. Peruvians, with news of his death, rushed to subscribe funds for a

European ironclad, to be named the *Almirante Grau,* but it was not to be in this war.

The Ascendancy of Chile

Both navies had difficult tasks. The Chileans had to maintain a tedious blockade against an enemy that showed no signs of giving up. The Peruvian navy, most of its major warships having been lost, had to attack the enemy with cunning.
—Robert L. Scheina

The loss of the *Huascar* to the Chileans was quickly followed by the loss of the little *Pilcomayo.* It also meant that the Chilean seaborne offensive could now get under way. Pisagua and Iquique were captured with the support of the Chilean fleet in November.

The next operation was to be against Arica, which had received some clandestine reinforcements. On 27 February 1880 Arica was attacked by the *Huascar* and *Magellanes* under Captain Manuel Thompson of the *Huascar.* The *Magellanes* had to draw off due to the plunging fire from the coastal batteries, but the *Huascar* continued the attack, though hit and losing several men killed and wounded. It was now that the *Manco Capac,* accompanied by a small torpedo boat, ventured forth to do battle. Both ironclads fired away at ranges as short as 200 yards, but the *Huascar* refused to try ramming in the presence of the enemy torpedo boat. After a lengthy gunnery exchange, the *Huascar* withdrew.

Thompson died in this battle and was replaced by Condell who had fought so well against the *Covadonga.* Thompson's death would bring about the bombardment of the port that lasted from the end of February to 3 March. Arica was soon cut off as an invasion force captured the rest of the province and now turned on the fortress at Arica itself. It was strongly defended, having on its flanks a 200 meter high mountain, the El Morro, with gun positions and fortifications, as well as the *Manco Capac.*

A bombardment by the army failed to bring about a capitulation. So a bloody night attack on El Morro now succeeded, which brought about the surrender of the city. The fall of the port saw Captain Moore dying in its defense and the scuttling of the *Manco Capac.*

The Peruvians next resorted to stealth to help bring about a naval victory. On 3 July they artfully let a small sailing vessel loaded with provisions fall into the hands of the *Loa.* As the sailing ship was being unloaded, a bag of maize was lifted that caused an explosion, which caved in the side of the *Loa* and sank her. The loss of life was heavy.

The loss of the *Loa* became a political question as her captain, Juan Pena, was thought to be a favorite of President Pinto's who had made other errors of judgment in the past. It was claimed that if he had lived he would have been court martialed. But the next loss would ignite the anger of the Chilean public.

The prize ship from 1865, the gunboat *Covadonga,* was lost when she sank an "abandoned" launch near the small Peruvian port of Chancay. Moored to the small launch was a rescue boat, clean, sharp, and the captain, Pablo Ferrari, ordered her to be hoisted on board. As soon as the lines were taut the rescue boat exploded and sank the beloved *Covadonga.* Ferrari died with much of the crew.

The orders were to bring fire and brimstone to the Peruvian towns. One newspaper wrote that instead of an idle blockade of Callao where ships were "consumed by torpedoes and tedium," Peruvians should be punished so hard as to "spill tears of blood." Riveros ordered the bombardment of three Peruvian towns, but clearly the war was not going to end.

In September of 1880 the Chileans organized a 3,000 man naval raiding brigade under naval captain Patricio Lynch. This brigade raided at least ten seaport towns north of Callao on the Peruvian coast with the goal of destroying "private property, seizing merchandise, and damaging public works—such as piers, rail-roads, and custom-houses," all of which they could legitimately, and sometimes illegitimately, do. This was just one more way to bring pressure on Peru to surrender, on the eve of a peace conference to be brokered on board the steam sloop USS *Lackawanna* at Arica. This conference failed and the war was to continue.

Patricio "Red Prince" Lynch was half Peruvian and half English. He would end the war in charge of many of the land operations being established in the interior of Peru. Ironically, as Chile was raiding and bombarding Peru's coast, it was the same Chile in 1879 and 1880 that was shipping vast amounts of wheat to Ecuador, which was then shipped on to Peru. There was a feeling that business was business, and profits were profits, and if the Chilean wheat was not sold, then the price of wheat would become depressed.

The bombardment of Callao concerns us next. Callao had been heavily fortified in the war with Spain in 1866, and additional work had since been performed. It was perceived that the only way to bring about peace was for Chile to directly assault Callao and in turn, nearby Lima. The army would be moved by sea to attack Callao and Lima.

But Chile did not want to engage land fortifications at close range. She had purchased an Irish cattle-ship, the *Belle of Cork,* renamed her the *Angamos,* and armed her with the latest Armstrong breech-loading 8" 11.5 ton gun mounted on a revolving carriage. It was used in the bombardment of Arica in 1880, firing at ranges of 6,000 to 8,000 yards.

With the fall of Arica, the *Angamos* moved north where she sniped at Callao and the ships present in the port. She placed a shot in the boiler of the *Union,* sank a torpedo hulk, and on 3 September, sank a Peruvian tug which ventured too far out of the mole.

The Chilean fleet off Callao was now joined in October by the newly rearmed *Huascar* that had also received a pair of the new 8" guns. She joined the *Angamos* in firing at Callao at ranges of up to four miles; the shot from the port's fortifications fell a mile short. Shortly after this the Chilean fleet, minus two blockading warships, headed south to escort the Chilean army north in transports for the final assault on Callao and Lima.

This operation was repeated several times until 11 December 1880. The Peruvian monitor *Atahualpa*, escorted by a tug, ventured out to do battle with the Chilean squadron. It was during this action that a discharge from the gun on the *Angamos* caused it to accidentally slip from its carriage and fall overboard. In the process it killed the gun captain and a visiting lieutenant, as well as wounding several men. The tactical significance here is the use of heavy *long range* guns. Combat now clearly had an almost sharpshooting quality to it that had seldom been seen in the past—and would continue to develop into the next century. A ship with little in the way of protection could now fire at ranges longer than the enemy could reply at.

The end of the naval war was near. The Chilean army landed at Pisco, a few miles south of Callao, and began marching north. Lynch's Brigade would fight well alongside the army to which it was attached. On 13 and 15 January 1881 the battles of Chorillos and Miraflores were fought. The Chileans were successful in both battles and Callao and Lima fell. During the battle of Miraflores, the Chilean fleet, which enfiladed the Peruvian line, gave gunfire assistance that helped stem a local Peruvian success on the sea flank. The war would drag on until 1883, but Peruvian ability to resist had collapsed and eventually Peru, Bolivia, and Chile came to a peaceful agreement. Bolivia would lose her coast, and Chile would end up with Peruvian territory to Tacna in the north. This has led to an uneasy relationship between all three powers, persisting to this day.

THE CHILEAN CIVIL WAR

Now, two very important facts must be borne in mind. Chile, being a very long, narrow strip of land may be regarded as practically all coast-line; consequently the command of the sea is all-important, and Congress commenced with an enormous advantage. Secondly, Iquique is the capital of Tarapaca, the largest and richest of the provinces conquered from Peru in the last war, and is the port whence by far the largest portion of that valuable commodity, nitrate of soda, is shipped; and when it

is stated that the export duties upon nitrate yield some $30,000,000 per annum,
the value of the northern capital as a basis for operations will be at once understood.
 —Maurice H. Hervey, Special Correspondent of *The Times*

Another lesson suggested by the operations is the immense value of speed in
torpedo-craft, especially when they are employed in work where surprise is an
essential element in their success.
 —W. Laird Clowes

The civil war which broke out in January 1891 over Presidential versus Congressional powers, was very unusual. It was fought between the party of President Balmaceda, known as the Balmacedists, and the Congressists, or the Party of the Chilean Congress. The Balmacedists were the leftists of the day and were talking of reforming the extremely lucrative nitrate industry of northern Chile. President Balmaceda was concerned that too much wealth was flowing out of Chile, and was controlled by foreign capital, primarily British. They had also offended the powerful Catholic church by reducing its powers, with, among other laws, the introduction of civil marriages.

The Congressists represented for the most part the conservative, nitrate, and clerical interests of the nation. The Congress controlled the Navy, while the President's party controlled the Army, so it was to be another war between the elephant and the whale. It gained a great deal of notoriety in Europe, especially Great Britain, as it demonstrated that a navy could defeat an army.

Another factor in this war that was quite similar to the War of the Pacific was the extended coastline and the value of sea communications. The Congressists' control of the arid northern portion of Chile made them very dependent on seapower, since water and food could only arrive to supply their forces and the populace by maintaining control of the sealanes. Coloring this mix was the fact that all the towns and cities had their supporters for each of the factions.

Eventually the Congressists gained a foothold on the coast in the north at Iquique, largely through naval demonstrations. Having thus gained control of the nitrate industry, they now had a great deal of financial leverage. This, combined with the control of the seas, would allow the Congressists to build an army *supplied with modern arms,* with which they defeated the Balmacedists.

The Balmacedists were forced to await naval reinforcements from Europe to turn the tide, unless they could destroy the Congress Navy—especially its three ironclads, the *Blanco Encalada, Almirante Cochrane,* and *Huascar.* On the way from Europe were two torpedo gunboats, the *Almirante Lynch* and the *Almirante Condell.* Two protected cruisers were being completed in France that were fast and also armed with torpedoes, which the President hoped would counterbalance the advantages of the navy. At home the Balmacedists had one 15 knot passenger ship, the 2,363 ton *Imperial,* seven coastal torpedo boats, and some minor small craft. The Congressists had a monopoly on ironclads, and the 18 knot protected cruiser *Esmeralda.* The *Esmeralda* was a 2,950 ton British Elswick-built ship (by now the new name for the older Armstrong Company which built both guns and ships) armed with one 10" gun forward and another aft. She had a curved steel deck ½ inch to 2 inches thick covering her vitals, and had the distinction of being the prototype of her type, the protected cruiser, which would quickly replace the construction of unarmored cruisers. All sorts of small merchant ships, steam and sail, were hired by the Congressists and given machine guns and small guns.

While the fleet was at Valparaiso, there was a regular exchange of small arms fire between the fleet and the forts. Eventually the fleet steamed north, leaving the *Encalada* in port with some minor craft. On 16 January three forts in the harbor, which was crowded with foreign shipping and warships, fired a single round each from large coast defense guns at her, and two struck. One hit was from a 10" muzzle-loading rifle throwing a 450 pound shell with 130 pounds of powder. It hit a portion of the ship fully armored with 8 inches of plate and at 600 yards failed to penetrate, though it did send an armor bolt head clear through into the interior and disabled one of her 8" guns.

The second hit was from 1,200 yards, from a German Krupp built 8.2" 10 ton gun firing a 250 pound capped (Palliser) shell. It passed through the captain's quarters, taking the pillow literally from under his sleeping head but not hurting him in the least and exploded on a 5 inch steel bulkhead designed to protect "… the battery from fire from astern." Nine crewmen were killed and three were wounded. That night the *Encalada* departed north with the remainder of the Congressists' forces.

The arrival of the *Lynch* and the *Condell* created quite a stir. Twin screwed, when in good order capable of 18-19 knots at sea, armed with small guns and machine guns, and five 14" Whitehead torpedoes, they also carried powerful searchlights. Their protection was their small size, speed, and coal bunkers protecting their vitals. "In resolute, daring hands, what havoc might they not inflict if they go amongst the enemy's ships during a dark night!" Some felt that the torpedo gunboat was too big and too slow for attacking enemy ironclads at sea. It was recognized that there needed to be a large seagoing torpedo boat, with guns to also combat torpedo craft, and with good speed for attacks at sea. In a few short years experiments would be proceeding to perfect the first "Torpedo Boat Destroyer" or the Destroyer.

In company with the *Imperial,* acting as a mother ship, the torpedo gunboats proceeded several times to search the bays and anchorages frequented by the Congressists in the hopes of catching their ironclads—while avoiding the numerous neutral merchant and warships.

Once the *Esmeralda* chased the *Imperial.* On 12 March at daybreak the *Imperial* sighted the *Esmeralda,* and the chase began. Fortunately for the *Imperial,* the *Esmeralda* had a fouled bottom, and could maintain the chase but could not close the distance. That evening the *Imperial* was almost caught when she had to slow to rake out her furnaces of the accumulated ash. During this pause several shots passed over her. But with this task accomplished the *Imperial* was off again. The *Esmeralda* tried to use her searchlight, but on that moonless night, the *Imperial* altered course and escaped.

On 23 April the *Encalada* was quietly at anchor in the small harbor of Caldera Bay. Also present was a small Congressist schooner which took no substantial part in the action. The *Condell* and *Lynch* quietly slipped up on her early in the morning, at about 04:00. It was a cloudy morning and though the moon was up, the clouds periodically obscured it. Apparently the alarm was raised when the torpedo gunboats were about 2,000 yards distant. With the *Condell* leading the way, she fired three torpedoes, all of which missed. Fire however, was also concentrated on her, and this allowed the *Lynch* to approach. She fired two torpedoes *while stationary,* one of which hit square amidships and exploded. British Captain St. Clair later reported from interviews with the survivors that some "officers who were on the main deck on the port side describe the shock as having been severely felt there. They say that one of the 8-inch guns on the starboard side was thrown off its trunnions, and that men were killed on that side. On the upper deck and after bridge the shock was felt only slightly."

The *Encalada* did not have time to shut her watertight doors. She was hit near the boilers and so her engines were quickly stopped. Pumps were now useless and the ship could not be beached. So within five minutes she heeled over and sank after being hit by a 14" torpedo with a running speed of 23 knots, set for a depth of six meters, and a charge of 58 pounds of gun cotton.

The entire action, from the discharge of the first torpedo to the last, was only seven minutes long. Of the official crew, 102 men were saved while 182 were lost. Torpedo enthusiasts hailed the action, but it was noted at that time that inadequate measures of protection had been taken by the *Encalada,* including the absence of torpedo netting, which was now in vogue. This was thick material in nets placed around the ship similar to a hooped skirt around a lady. It could be cut and it had to be deployed to be effective, and when in place delayed a ship from getting under way in an emergency, as it had to be hauled up and stored.

The *Encalada* was armed with six of the new quick-firing Hotchkiss 6 pounders which could fire 25-30 rounds a minute. It was partly due to this attack that progress in developing better and larger quick-firers was furthered. The British 4.7" quick-firer by Armstrong/Elswick had been tested in 1886/7 and had been introduced into the service in 1889. In a gunnery trial between it and the older style 5", the 4.7" gun discharged ten rounds at sea in 47 seconds while the 5" took five minutes and seven seconds to get off ten shells. Quick-firing guns would become both larger and more in demand over the next decade.

After this loss, the Congressists were careful to move out to sea at night, and even though there was some additional stalking on the part of both sides, no other significant naval actions occurred. One small skirmish involved the *Cochrane* chasing the *Condell* while the telegraph on shore wired ahead for the *Huascar* and the *Magellanes* to try and head her off. When the *Condell* discovered the trap, her captain did not steam directly off, but actually let the enemy ships get within range and fire a few shots. He in turn replied with his small Hotchkiss against the wooden *Magellanes,* as well as burning some of the Congressists' coal in the chase. At just over 3,000 meters the *Huascar* began to fire fairly accurately, when the *Condell's* captain remarked that, "No use wasting powder upon an ironclad. I'd fight that wooden tub all day, but I can't stand the *blindado* (ironclad)." Within two more hours the *Condell* was out of range and the action over, though a few shells had landed within 30 yards.

One ruse attempted by the Balmacedists in June 1891 involved the steaming of the *Imperial* "ablaze with lights on purpose to attract the notice of hostile cruisers." The two torpedo gunboats lurked nearby in the darkness hoping that a Congressist warship would come to investigate, but nothing came of this.

The Civil War culminated in a surprise assault from the sea with a landing of over 9,000 men just north of Valparaiso on 20 August. The Congressist fleet convoyed the transports south while keeping the *Huascar* at Iquique to protect that port. The Balmacedists had two small torpedo boats near by, but chose not to attack the transports shielded by the rebel squadron. The Balmacedists had deployed their 32,516 troops at several points up and down the coast as well as Santiago, while the Congressists with their smaller army chose where they wanted to land, and forced a decisive battle before the Balmacedists could concentrate all their forces.

When Valparaiso was attacked by the Congressists, the Balmacedists attempted to hold the port, but they were defeated, largely due to the well trained and equipped Congressist force, supported by the guns of the *O'Higgins, Magellanes, Esmeralda,* and one armed transport, which fired on the advance post of the Balmacedists. This occurred on 21 August and the Balmacedists lost approximately 4,500 men, of which almost half were unwounded prisoners who joined, or were impressed, by the Congressists, and all for a Congressist loss of about 1,100.

President Balmaceda called for reinforcements, even dispatching the *Condell* and *Imperial* twice to the north to bring back reinforcements, but not enough could arrive in time from their isolated coastal positions. The only check the Congressists suffered occurred now, on the 23rd, when they advanced south to a suburb of Valparaiso guarded by the coastal fort, Fort Callao. It "replied with vigor" and with the *Cochrane, Esmeralda,* and *O'Higgins* not coming closer than 7,000 yards, the position could not be easily forced.

The Congressists' army now marched inland so as to take Valparaiso from the rear, when it met the main Balmacedist force. So on 28 August the battle of La Placilla was fought, which left the two top Balmacedist generals and their cause dead on the field. By that evening Valparaiso had been occupied and the *Almirante Cochrane* was riding quietly at anchor in Valparaiso, the port she had quitted in January with the outbreak of war.

With the victory of the Congressists, the Civil War was all but over. President Balmaceda fled to the Argentine legation and later shot himself. Other supporters of his saw their homes pillaged or their lives taken if they did not flee in time. The Civil War had cost £10,000,000 and 10,000 lives. The Chilean admiral, Jorje Montt, would become the new president and would grant a pardon to all parties the following year. The *Lynch* was surrendered in port with several of her officers seeking asylum on board the United States protected cruiser *Baltimore.* The *Condell* and *Imperial* interned themselves at Callao.

Callao Defenses

Until its capture Callao was the most powerfully protected port on the west coast of South America in the 19th century. It was heavily reinforced with Dahlgren style guns after the Spanish attack of 1866. Not all sources agree on her armaments, but we have relied on T.B.M. Mason's account prepared for the then recently formed United States Naval Intelligence section, William Laird Clowes account, and Peruvian and Chilean secondary and primary sources. While the heavy guns at the site were the most important, it should be noted that some of the older smoothbores were brought over by the Spanish *over* 100 years previous to the events of 1866 and 1879-81.

Starting at the sandspit, there is the battery Dos de Mayo. Mason would write of this battery that "it had but lately been finished, and consisted of an immense pit in the rubble and gravel, the inside face being revetted with sand-bags. The gun-platforms were on heavy crib-work resting on piles, the platforms themselves being of stone." According to Mason there were two XX" Rodmans present firing a 1,000 pound shell with "extreme" powder charges, but that it was inferior gunpowder. Clowes states in one place that there was one Dahlgren and one Rodman, and in another that they were both Rodmans, but Mason points out that the *carriages* were different—one was United States naval style and the other army style which may account for the discrepancy. The Peruvians often referred to the battery as "la bateria de canones Rodman ... ." The Chileans at the time of the bombardment of Callao referred to them as Dahlgrens, but in post war works called them Rodmans. What makes this point particularly interesting lies in the fact that according to Professor Spencer C. Tucker in *Encyclopedia of the Confederacy* at least one XX" Dahlgren was sold to the Peruvians on 15 December 1865, but it did not carry the usual Registry number and was known as "Beelzebub." Both Rodmans and Dahlgren guns were cast at the Fort Pitt Foundry. Our best supposition is that there was one of each type of gun and that the Peruvians referred to them as Rodmans because at least one was a Rodman and they had several other smaller Dahlgrens, but no other Rodmans. Being located at the tip of the sandspit, the two guns could traverse around 7/8th of the horizon.

The XX" Rodman was developed in 1864 and weighed 116,497 pounds. With an elevation of 25 degrees it could throw a 1,100 pound roundshot with a 200 pound powder charge close to 4.5 miles. Greville Bathe notes that in 1871 the three most powerful guns in service were the XX" Rodmans, the Woolwich 12" muzzle-loader rifled gun weighing 35 tons, and the 11" Krupp breech-loader rifle. Bathe wrote that at a range of 500 yards,

A Blakely in the Callao defenses.

the energy of the XX inch Rodman was found to be 50 per cent greater than the Woolwich or the Krupp gun. However, the elongated shot of the rifled guns afforded a far greater degree of penetration at ranges of two thousand yards than the round shot of the Rodman guns, results which may be likened to a blow struck by a pickaxe and a sledgehammer of equal weight.

The next two batteries each mounted two XV" Dahlgrens. Battery Pierola faced Callao Bay while Battery Tarapaca (named for the Allies' only land victory of the war) faced south. They were similar in construction to Dos de Mayo.

Next came the Torre del Merced still mounting two 10" Armstrong guns, next to Fort Santa Rosa, an old brick fort. It contained two 11" Blakelys. The Callao Castle, located in the town, contained two towers, each armed with two 11" Blakelys. These all faced Callao harbor and the two towers were named Manco Capac and Independencia. Some Chilean sources say that one of these towers housed four 300 pounder French guns, but this appears to be in error. Six smaller batteries were ranged through this section of the defense. They were named (in parenthesis is the number of 32 pounder smoothbore guns present—it should be noted that a British Admiralty report based on a warship observation at the time indicates that additional 32 pounders were present) Maipu (2), Provisional (5), Zepita (8), Abtao (6), Pichincha (4), and Independencia (6).

Next along the harbor's sea pier, or mole, was a series of sandbagged batteries mounting five XV" and two XI" Dahlgrens, plus two 32 pounder smoothbores. To the right of the city was Fort Ayacucho, an old brick and mortar fort like Santa Rosa, and armed with one 11" rifled muzzle-loader Blakely and one XV" Dahlgren. Heading north was another turret, named Junin armed with two 10" Armstrong rifled muzzle-loaders. Finally the sandbagged battery Rimac was armed with four XV" Dahlgrens.

Peru had done much to provide for the defense of Callao, but the Chileans commanded the sea and were able to import newer and longer range guns in the course of the War of the Pacific. These new guns would allow them to snipe at the ships in the harbor and not suffer return Peruvian fire. This advantage would wear down the defenses of Callao and cause the attrition of the naval forces inside. With the port's fall all the major guns would be removed to Chile.

Plans for the Chilean–American War

During the Civil War in Chile, relations between Chile and the United States of America had not been the best for a variety of reasons, and these poor relations dated back to the earlier War of the Pacific, when the United States sided more with Peru and Bolivia than with Chile, and in the current conflict more with the Presidential party than with the Congressional party. The upshot of this was that during the Chilean Civil War the U.S. Marshal in Southern California seized and held the gunrunning steamship *Itata* of the Chilean line that was being loaded in San Diego with arms and ammunition for the insurgents. The *Itata's* crew made the Marshal prisoner, and headed south with him on board.

Needless to say the Justice Department and the Navy were upset over this turn of events and the most powerful United States cruiser on station was sent off in hot pursuit. Meanwhile, the insurgents, made up of most of the navy of Chile, sent the cruiser *Esmeralda* to Acapulco Bay to meet the *Itata.* Steaming up was the USS *Charleston* whose captain cleared for action. "The insurgent captain followed suit, and all hands braced themselves for the roar of gunfire." It never came as the *Itata* passed well out to sea on her way to Valparaiso, but was eventually seized by the United States Navy. After the Chilean Civil War she was ruled to be a legal Chilean vessel and was released to Chile.

The second near chance for war occurred after 36 sailors on the *Baltimore* were beaten and two killed while on liberty in Valparaiso on 16 October 1891 in a "saloon, in a rather disreputable quarter of the city." It should be noted that in an interview previous to the incident that the officers of the Baltimore were clearly of the opinion that the Congress party was in the wrong. The officers "... regarded the alleged causes of the revolution as mere flimsy pretexts, and believed that the whole affair had been worked up by agitators on behalf of the European nitrate syndicates." The U.S. warships had also been a haven for the defeated Balmacedists after the war and for this, and other reasons, were "absolutely detested in Chile." The Baltimore's captain was Winfield Scott Schley who would later be second in command off Santiago in 1898, and would end that war under a dark cloud.

While waiting for the Chilean government to offer compensation and apologies for this event, the United States prepared for war. During the ensuing crisis Argentina, long at odds with Chile over their border, indicated that they would support the United States in a war with Chile, though the nature of that support was never solidified.

The only published primary source of the warplans for the United States come from W. E. Curtiss *From the Andes to the Ocean* (Chicago, 1900) a travel book of the day. General Benjamin F. Tracy, then Secretary of the Navy, commented about United States preparations for war with Chile, and Curtiss was able to quote him extensively in his book. These preparations were undertaken after the incident and "Stand down" did not occur until the now victorious insurgents apologized for the incident and paid an indemnity. The plans for war were worked up from December 1891 to January 1892.

> ... our preparations for an emergency began. These were carried on so quietly that it never has been known just how far we went. The reason that we were able to keep what we were doing from the public was that all the preparations on the part of the Government were controlled by one person, who carried on all his transactions with principals and not with agents. In this way the Government was saved a considerable amount in commissions.
>
> As soon as the (Diplomatic) note was sent the Chairmen of the Committees on Naval Affairs of the Senate and House were invited to a conference with the Secretary of the Navy. Whatever that official did after that was with approval of those gentlemen. The first order issued was to make every available ship in the navy ready for immediate service.
>
> Next, all available coal on the Pacific Coast was bought by the Government, and the largest steamer owned by Collis P. Huntington was chartered to carry it to Montevideo. There were 5,000 tons of coal. Two cargoes were purchased in London and two more cargoes in New York, all to be delivered at Montevideo. Then the American line, or what is now the American Line, steamer "*Ohio*" was chartered for a repair ship. She was sent to Boston and work was immediately begun on her to put her in shape for service.
>
> These arrangements made, Captain Alfred Thayer Mahan was invited to consult with the Secretary of the Navy. Before the consultations were over a plan had been completely mapped out. According to this plan, the first order to be issued was to concentrate the fleet. A point of concentration was agreed on, and this was to be telegraphed to the three fleet commanders with the orders sent to them to begin operations. Admiral (Bancroft) Gherardi (who had served with Farragut at Mobile Bay) was to be in command of the united fleets.
>
> According to the plan laid out, after the fleets had concentrated, they were to proceed to Chile, drive the Chilean men-of-war under the guns of the forts at Valparaiso, and then attack the whole coast line of Chile. The coal mines in the southern part of that country were to be seized, thus cutting off the coal supply for the warships of the enemy, and all other details were looked after. Then came Chile's note of apology and her offer of $75,000 indemnity, which was accepted. This was distributed among the sailors who had been injured and among the families of the dead.

Major combatants in such an event would have been cruisers for the most part, though Chile had the 15-year-old small battleship, the *Almirante Cochrane*. Chile had two cruisers completing in France in 1892, the *Presidente Errazuriz* class and a 2nd class battleship the *Capitan Prat*, though the latter was not completed until 1893.

The United States at this time could field no battleships or even the large reconstructed monitors of the *Puritan* or *Monterey* type, though the *Miantono-*

moh was completing for sea. Her major combatants would have been the *San Francisco, Charleston, Baltimore, Philadelphia, Newark, Chicago, Boston,* and *Atlanta* with some small modern gunboats. In some ways this war would have been fought in much the same manner as a 19th century equivalent of the Falklands War, with a distant theater of operations and no common frontier.

CHAPTER VIII

Ironclads at War Around the World

In 1855 it needed the keen eye of a seaman to distinguish between a British and foreign ship; in 1865 their differences were obvious; by 1875 they could not be confused.
—Oscar Parkes

...the advocates of the armor-plating system retort that ironclads of the most powerful type are absolutely indispensable to a modern fleet, which without them (they) would be powerless to act against a hostile squadron or to come within range of a fort; that the risk resulting from torpedoes would have to be run were it even far greater than it is, and that precautions are available to minimize this risk... armored ships are essential.
—Maurice H. Hervey

It is our position that the course of history is propelled along by many forces. Economic needs, real or perceived, often shape the past and the future. So do particular *individuals* both as supreme leaders of nations, such as the dictator Lopez, or warriors, like Farragut, who might help end a war quickly, or a more timorous leader who may slow down the process.

The introduction of this supreme technological weapon of the industrial age, the ironclad, also had its impact. It helped in industrializing nations, rethinking and reshaping social practices, and changing and altering the very fabric of life.

One aspect of this industrialization was the growth of armament companies. Firms like Armstrong, Ansaldo, Krupp, and others were growing, and while some failed in the late 19th century, many prospered. Some of the profit realized by these companies was in the growing foreign arms market. One of the areas to receive war goods as the American Civil War was winding down was the southern tip of South America where a vicious though ultimately one sided war was being fought.

THE DESPOT LOPEZ AND THE WAR OF THE TRIPLE ALLIANCE

When the war broke out the population of Paraguay was 1,337,439; when hostilities ceased it consisted of 28,746 men, 106,254 women above 15 years of age, and 86,079 children.
—11th edition Encyclopedia Britannica

In some ways more crucial to Paraguayan survival in a protracted struggle than its army was its navy, which would have to keep the rivers open, transport men and supplies, and maintain contact with the outside would.
—John Hoyt Williams

There are several good English accounts of this war available in the academic literature, though nothing of a more "popular" nature has appeared. Unfortunately, even when well researched, the accounts vary widely. For example, the surrender at Uruguayana on 18 September 1865 by Paraguay to the Allies, has surrendered troop totals running from 4,200 to 5,500 to 6,000 depending on the account one consults. And this, one would think, should be a firm number. Another recent example is an article in *MHQ* by Dolores Moyano Martin in which at the battle of Riachuelo she gives the Brazilians "the latest 120- and 150-pounder Whitworths." The largest Whitworths on board that day were 70-pounder Whitworths. Of all the chapters in Wilson's original *Ironclads in Action*, his chapter on this war was probably the most inaccurate though most entertaining reading, as he unfairly painted the Brazilians as utter cowards.

Paraguay in 1864 was a landlocked nation fed by the Parana and Paraguay Rivers that ultimately fed the Rio de la Plata. It was well off in rich soils and a great many crops could be grown, but she was dependent on her rivers for transportation, especially in light of virtual wilderness and/or vast distances that covered much of her border with Brazil and Argentina. The bulk of her population was primarily of Guarani Indian background intermixed with Europeans and was run by the Creoles, though, like Chile, she was fairly united as a nation. Nationalism was strong in Paraguay as was her desire to remain an independent nation.

The local military had gained some expertise at fighting as there was a constant threat of Indian attacks by both river Indians and Indians in the north of Paraguay. As late as 1747 her capital at Asuncion had been "ravaged by a large daylight raid." Paraguay had originally been established as a Jesuit state and was fairly rich. This Jesuit background also tended to unify Paraguay—and make her dependent on a strong leader that has been part of her political landscape up until modern times.

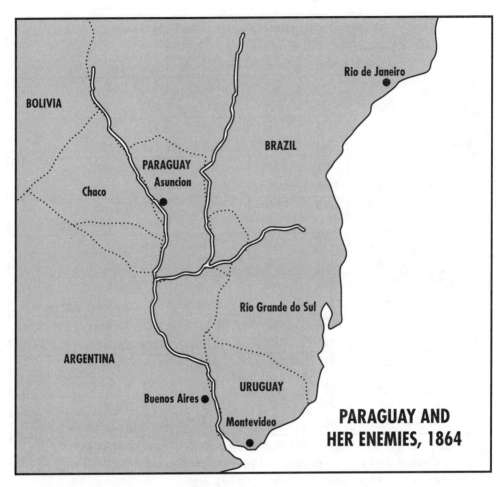

PARAGUAY AND HER ENEMIES, 1864

She enjoyed her independence in part by lying between Argentina and Portuguese-speaking Brazil. Argentina at the time of her revolt from Spain in the early 1800's had coveted Paraguay, but a strong local movement had secured Paraguay's separate independence—though at the expense of dictatorial rule by one *El Supremo*—Jose Gaspar de Francia. Portuguese Brazil was looked upon as an alien nation so there was little hope of uniting with her. Neither of these two larger powers wanted to see the other in sole possession of Paraguay.

Francia would be succeeded by Carlos Antonio Lopez, and then in September of 1862, with Carlos' death, his son would come to rule Paraguay. Francisco Solano Lopez was short and wore a full beard. An intelligent man, he enjoyed appearing in full dress uniform in public. He spoke both his nation's native Spanish and Guarani, as well as French, German, English, and Portuguese. His father had given him many and varied duties early in his life and so he had a good

Brazilian Ironclad Fleet in the War of the Triple Alliance					
Ship	Country of Origin	Year	Tonnage	Engine Power	Armament
Cabral	England	1865	858	240 hp	2-5.8", 2-68 pdrs
Colombo	England	1865	858	240 hp	4-7"
Herval	England	1866	1353	200 hp	4-7"
Mariz e Barros	England	1866	1197	200 hp	2-68 pdrs, 2-7"
Brazil	France	1864	1,518	250 hp	4-68 pdrs, 4-7"
Rio de Janeiro	Brazil	1866	casemated		mined
Tamadaré	Brazil	1865	980	273 hp	1-68 pdr, 2-5.8", first armored ship built in Brazil
Barroso	Brazil	1865	1,354	130 hp	2-68 pdr, 2-7", 3 32 pdrs*
Bahia	England	1865	1008	140 hp	2-7", 2-2 pdrs
Lima Barros	England	1866	1,705	300 hp	4-7" in two turrets
Silvado	France	1866		100 hp	4-7" in two turrets, 2-32 pdrs
Alagoas	Brazil	1867	342	30 hp	1-5.8", in a turret
Ceara	Brazil	1867	342	30 hp	1-5.8", in a turret
Para	Brazil	1867	342	30 hp	1-5.8", in a turret
Rio Grande	Brazil	1867	342	30 hp	1-5.8", in a turret
Santa Catarina	Brazil	1867	342	30 hp	1-5.8", in a turret
Piaui	Brazil	1867	342	30 hp	1-120 Whitworth pdr in turret

Brazil relied heavily on Whitworth guns. All 5.8", 7", and probably the 120 pdr are Whitworths. The 7" is sometimes called a 150 pdr and the 5.* a 70 pdr. Also note that Conway gives higher HP figures These figures for HP are from Meister's 1972 article in Marine Rundschau

background for running his nation. Both father and son had invested heavily into the military machine. Lopez once said of himself "I am Paraguay," which is also why in the coming war the alliance against him insisted on his removal from power.

The nation that this dictator ruled was one that had enjoyed economic growth over the past few decades and was financially sound. She had a loyal standing army and small navy. She also had long term border disputes with three of her neighbors—Uruguay, Argentina, and Brazil. Her population was almost the size of Argentina's, though Brazil numbered almost 7,000,000 free and 2,000,000 more slaves.

Brazil was a constitutional monarchy under Pedro II, and had resolved many of the earlier regional differences she suffered from, including a civil war in the province next to Paraguay. By 1864 she was the strongest power in South America. Her navy consisted of "45 armed ships, 33 steam (at least five being paddle-wheeled) and 12 sailing" warships. They were armed, according to Jurg Meister, with 239 guns and she had 609 officers and 3,627 sailors. The first ironclad to arrive would be the *Brasil* in December of 1865. She had been funded by a popular subscription in 1862 and was an eight gun casemated warship. By the end of the war she would have 16 ironclads out of a total of 94 warships manned by 6,474 men.

Argentina also had earlier suffered from factionalism and by the 1860's was still recovering. In the war, she would field a much smaller army, and a navy that was primarily made up of transports. While Argentina would not acquire ironclads in this war, her president did give the elderly Brazilian Admiral the Marques Lisboa Joaquim Tamandare a two volume report by Gideon Welles on American Civil War naval operations (it was reported that he did not read it but his secretary, Artur Silveira da Mota "seized it and studied it earnestly"). Uruguay's contribution would be negligible though her fiery Colorado leader would help unite the Triple Alliance.

Lopez's motives are not clearly known as he was quite secretive and never fully announced his intentions. Also Lopez did not realize the enemy's potential strength. He wanted to take his fairly modern army and increase his nation's territory down to the Rio de la Plata and possibly incorporate Uruguay into Paraguay. Paraguay would then at minimum be a recognized regional power.

Uruguay, created as a buffer nation in 1828 when Great Britain mediated the Cisplatine War of 1825-28 fought between Brazil and Argentina over that land, was a pawn between those two powerful neighbors. Usually these two powers supported one or the other of the two major political parties (Blanco and Colorado) in Uruguay but by 1864 they both supported the Colorado—which was out of power. The Blancos kept Lopez aware of what was transpiring and asked for his support. Finally, Brazil, slighted over various points, massed an army and invaded Uruguay on 14 September 1864. Her navy drove ashore a Uruguayan wooden warship. By February of 1865 the Blancos were out of power and with the exception of some minor guerrilla activity by the Blancos, Uruguay was in the camp of Paraguay's enemies.

This culminated on 11 November when a Brazilian steamer with funds, arms, and a small number of Brazilian troops took on coal at Asuncion while heading up river to Brazilian Mato Grosso. As it steamed off, Lopez, soon to take on the title of *El Mariscal* (The Marshal), ordered the warship *Tacuari* to seize her which it did on 13 November. The Brazilian flag would shortly appear in Lopez's palace as a rug. War was now certain.

The Paraguayan army probably numbered 14,000 men, though some modern authorities give her an army much larger than the three allies fielded. She had a small officer corps, in part to keep dissent against Lopez from appearing. Her standing army was fairly well supplied with modern arms. She had a small European run domestic munitions manufacturing capability, which in the course of the war would produce some artillery including three 150 pounder Whitworth style rifles. But beyond this she had no way of obtaining new guns and munitions except by capture or breaking the river blockade and importing them. She had a river fortress at Humaita, below Asuncion. This had been built by the elder Lopez as an overrated "Sevastapol of the Americas."

Her navy consisted of one war built steamer, the eight gun *Tacuari,* and nine river steamers. Lopez purchased or requisitioned at the outbreak of war six other steamers. Eventually by the end of the war her navy would have 23 steamers, three steam barges and five sailing ships carrying a total of at least 99 guns. As Williams has written, "foreign technicians labored almost around the clock to ready this hybrid Paraguayan fleet for action, and many British machinists were recruited to serve aboard on active duty." All but two were 200 or less tons and a typical crew was 50 men. There were also a handful of sailing vessels and small gunboats present with most of the gunboats stationed at Humaita. Paraguayan domestic war munitions production would be inadequate to meet all the war needs, but did produce a fair number of rifles and guns—including some quite large cannon.

Lopez had ordered a large amount of war materials in Europe and ended up not taking delivery of much of it. In the latter part of the war he would be forced to arm his troops with bow and arrow, and even wood spears and shards of glass. But, according to Hugh Lyon in *Conway's All the World's Fighting Ships 1860-1905,* he also had ordered a large number of ironclads at the time of the outbreak of war. One, the turreted *Nemesis,* was started in France. Part way through construction payments were halted and so France resold it to Brazil where it was renamed the *Silvado.* She was 1150 tons, 190 feet long, and armed with four 70 pounder 5.8" Whitworths.

Lopez also ordered two ironclads from Lairds in Great Britain. One, the *Bellona* was a 1,330 ton 12 knot twin turreted ship while the *Minerva* was about 1,008 tons and had a single turret. Each turret housed two guns and the main armor plating was 4.5 inches thick. Both ships would end as the Brazilian *Lima Barros* and *Bahia* respectively and would never fly the Paraguayan flag. Their main armament was 7" Whitworth rifles. This was a typical Laird design and would remind one of the similar Dutch designs or the Peruvian *Huascar.*

Finally, he also had ordered the *Medusa* and *Triton.* These small casemated warships were armed with four guns each and had a speed of nine knots. Like most of the ironclads for this war, they were armored with 4.5 inches of wrought iron, and would end up as Brazilian ships. These two would become the *Herval* and *Mariz E. Barros* respectively. It should be noted that modern sources, including scholarly studies, vary wildly in guesstimating the size and conduct of Paraguay's military policy. For example, the number of ironclads ordered in Europe by Lopez vary from five, four, two, to none in four different fairly reliable sources.

Lopez opened the war against Brazil by launching a drive north into the Mato Grosso that enjoyed quick success. Much war booty would later be shipped down to help the Paraguayan defense. Lopez next decided to drive south-east towards Uruguay. The easiest route lay across Argentine territory and after formally asking and being denied the right to transit, he declared war and entered anyway. Expecting factionalism to divide Argentina, he was surprised to find a new enemy on his flank. But Lopez would prove to be a poor war leader, even if he had a people who fought bravely throughout for Paraguay and his regime, and to keep the "alien" Brazilians from conquering their country.

By 1 May an agreement was signed by Brazil, Argentina, and the new government of Uruguay to fight Paraguay—hence the name of "The War of the Triple Alliance" as it is best known. Both sides were mobilized, with Brazil ordering many new ironclad warships from foreign yards as well as domestic shipyards. Lopez ordered his main army to Corrientes, Argentina. Loren Scott Patterson quotes a German historian of this phase of the war,

> The campaign in Corrientes was a war of movement with no major or decisive battles... The Argentines, who bore the brunt of all the fighting in this theater (at this early stage), conducted delaying operations skillfully, buying time for the concentration of the Allied army. It was up to Lopez to force the fight and in this he failed.

Brazil played her best card, and sent her wooden fleet up river loaded with troops. This ability to move up the river effectively flanked Paraguay's military movements. One early raid actually temporarily recaptured Corrientes, forced Paraguay to halt her easterly advance down river—an advance that had carried her to the border of Uruguay.

Lopez, who had now come down to take personal command, ordered his entire fleet to attack the Brazilian squadron anchored nearby. So would transpire the Battle of Riachuelo on Sunday, 11 June 1865. Lopez recognized that the defeat of the Brazilian fleet would be key in bringing victory and allowing the Paraguayan advance to continue. While it did not include any ironclads, we want to give an account of this action as it appears incorrectly in other sources of the battle.

Lopez's admiral was the elderly Rear-Admiral Pedro Ignacio Meza. In a meeting with him and other senior officers, it was determined that the best assault would be an early morning surprise attack between 03:00 and 04:00. The plan called for nine wooden warships, all but one being paddlewheeled, to steam downstream, towing six *"chatas"* (a small 35 or 40 ton rounded barge with no motive power

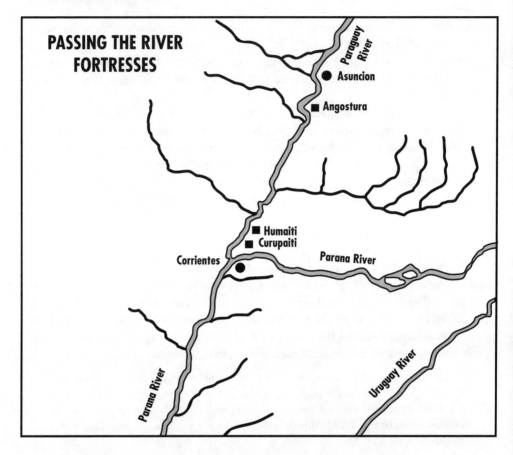

PASSING THE RIVER FORTRESSES

carrying one large caliber gun, usually a 68 pounder though two carried an 80 pounder), and advance through the Brazilian fleet firing often and quickly, then reform below the enemy, advance up stream and have each ship board one enemy ship. The Paraguayan ship's crews were fleshed out by 500 infantry. A fundamental error existed from the start by not *directly* attacking the Brazilian ships as by steaming by them they only would alert them and possibly cause some damage. The *chata* would capture the imagination of Europe, and as pointed out by Martin, "were described as some ingenious new war device."

The actual attack was carried out by eight warships and six *chatas* with a fleet speed of about ten knots and a river speed of about two knots. Being almost exclusively paddlewheeled, it was discovered that the screw Brazilian warships were more maneuverable and it was difficult to board *from* a paddlewheeled warship (only the Brazilian flagship *Amazonas* was paddlewheeled). Additionally most of the machinery of the Paraguayan ships was above water and more vulnerable to hits. The Brazilian fleet had in addition to the flagship four screw corvettes and four screw gunboats. None of the warships were ironclads. The nine ship Brazilian squadron mounted 59 guns to the Paraguayan 44.

The Brazilian fleet was nominally under the command of Tamandare but he was in the rear organizing the logistics required for the campaign. The Brazilian river squadron was under the second in command Rear-Admiral Barroso de Silva, who had taken measures to avoid being surprised. It was arranged in a long line on the southern side of the river, away and out of range of some hidden (and unknown to the Brazilians) Paraguayan shore batteries on the opposite shore. The Paraguayans were delayed in their run downstream and ended up attacking at about 09:00 just as Mass was about to be performed on the Brazilian ships. Alarm was given and General Quarters was sounded. Surprise had been lost.

In the course of running by the Brazilian fleet, the Paraguayan fleet suffered the most damage with one ship temporarily disabled. Brazilian losses were minor. Meza now decided to change his plan of attack. As pointed out by Patterson, "it was not healthy to alter a plan of the Marshal/President, even though Lopez was safe at Humaita and uninformed as to how the battle was unfolding. Meza had plenty of reason for a change. There was no surprise, he was out-gunned, and possibly by this time he discovered that someone had forgotten to bring the grappling iron(s)!"

Meza decided to anchor below the Brazilian fleet near some of the hidden Paraguayan shore batteries. The *chatas* were cast loose and anchored near the shore. This was completed by about 10:00. Both fleets were now effectively cut off from their bases. Barroso raised two signals, one reading "Brazil expects that everyone will do their duty" and "attack and destroy the enemy at the closest possible range." The Brazilian fleet steamed down on the enemy at about 10:50 roughly in line ahead.

The third ship in line was the flagship, *Amazonas*. Barroso pulled out of line so he could act independently, but the ships behind him, instead of following the two lead ships, followed the *Amazonas*. By the time this was rectified, the first two Brazilian ships were among the Paraguayan fleet. The second ship, the eight gun *Jequitinhonha*, tried to regain position with the *Amazonas*, and failing this, advanced on the Paraguayan fleet and ran firmly aground on a sandbar. She would end up being destroyed by the enemy shore batteries in the ensuing battle.

The lead ship *Belmonte*, now alone, steamed past the entire enemy fleet and beached herself to prevent her sinking at 11:55. She lost 9 dead, 23 wounded, and had been hit 37 times.

The *Amazonas* had meanwhile closed to about 50-100 yards from the enemy fleet and proceeded to pour it on. Meza ran up a signal for his fleet to board, but they could not due to the intense fire. After a heavy exchange, the Brazilian fleet found itself below the Paraguayan fleet and trying to find deep enough water to turn around and steam back up river. The six gun *Parnayba*, which was the tail ship, noted that the *Jequitinhonha* was hard aground and saw three Paraguayan ships attempting to board her (an attempt she would beat off).

So the little *Parnayba* made a turn in the narrow river at that point and grounded, damaging her steering. As she steamed up to aid the *Jequitinhonha* a shot disabled her rudder and she was adrift, under fire, in the midst of the hostile fleet. An attempt to board was now made, in which the *Parnayba* rammed and sank a Paraguayan ship, the *Paraguari*, but she was eventually boarded. They gained control of the deck, which is when they discovered she could not steer. The Brazilian crew remained below and preparations were made to blow up the powder magazine.

By now Barroso had found a place in the river to turn, which he did, and he raced up river to continue the fight. As pointed out by P. L. Scott, "Admiral Barroso had never even considered abandoning the fight." Barroso charged with two ships following, directly towards the battle around the *Parnayba*. With grape shot from the *Amazonas* killing and maiming many of the Paraguayan boarders, the "sailors and marines come from the holds and fought successfully for the main deck."

The *Amazonas* next rammed two Paraguayan ships, disabling them, and then completed the defeat of the Paraguayan navy by sinking or capturing the *chatas*. It was now, with the Paraguayan fleet retiring, that they tried to capture the stranded *Jequitinhonha*. Meza was wounded during this attempt. Only five Paraguayan warships made it back up the river and the Brazilian pursuit was half hearted.

The elderly Meza would die from his wounds, but not before he received the following message from Lopez, "Tell Meza that as soon as he recovers, he will be shot for cowardice and for not carrying out my orders to not abandon the battle under any circumstances." Approximately 200 Paraguayans died, while Brazil lost 104 dead, 40 missing, and 148 wounded and the *Jequitinhonha*.

After the battle of Riachuelo, combined with three engagements shortly thereafter with Paraguayan shore batteries that resulted in no ship losses but some casualties, a decision was arrived at by Admiral Tamandare. He wanted the Allied fleet to not advance past enemy shore positions and "thus (be) out of communications." This would heavily influence the naval conduct of the war for some time to come.

However, with this defeat, combined with the destruction of about 18,000 Paraguayan troops, including 5,545 who surrendered at Uruguayana, Lopez's offensive into Brazil and Argentina was over. He was now conducting a defensive, and very bloody war. Beginning in 1866 he was asking for slaves to be released from plantations to fight in his armies and navy. By late 1866 volunteer units of 10 to 14 year old children were being enrolled into military units. By April of 1867 active recruitment of 12 to 15 year old boys was in full swing, and even some women fought, though most ran the home front. Lopez's consort, Irish born

Eliza Lynch, formed a woman's corps and, once, dressed as a Colonel, "actually led a cavalry charge!"

The Brazilian troops would bare the brunt of the Allied offensive and would make great use of slaves offered their freedom if they would fight in the war. The advance up the rivers would be slow and would last until Lopez's death in 1870, in part due to the fanatical courage of the Paraguayans. The Brazilians were surprised by the ferocity of these bloody attacks, which even if resulting almost always in Allied victories, would still be costly to both sides. Combined with disease, overall casualties would soar.

Supporting the Allied advance would be the Brazilian ironclad fleet that offers another example of the influence of the American Civil War on naval and river warfare. The main obstacle was to reduce or neutralize Humaita, which guarded the Paraguay River and the hinterland behind it which had "extensive swamps and marshes." The goal was the capture of Asuncion and the deposing of Lopez. To achieve this, Humaita (Indian for "the stone is now black") must either be forced to surrender or passed by a strong naval force that could be supplied.

By 1866 Corrientes had fallen to the Allies and preparations were underway for the next advance. The *Brasil* and *Tamandare* first engaged Paraguayan positions below Humaita, known variously as the Flat or Passo de la Patria. A series of small skirmishes now took place as more ironclads arrived. The Paraguayans would occasionally send down a *chata* or a gunboat to test the Brazilian ships. It was soon realized that a 68 pounder could not penetrate the Brazilian ironclads.

However, on 27 March one of these engagements involved the *Bahia* and the casemated *Tamandare* and *Barroso*. The official Brazilian record stated

> The ironclads *Bahia* and *Tamandare* approached the Flat to silence it. The Flat continued to fire on the ironclads and two balls entering the square box of the *Tamandare* placed thirty-four men *hors de combat*, ten being killed (including her Captain) and twenty-four wounded, the greater number severely. The *Bahia* took position near the fort, and her first shots broke the Paraguayan cannon. The ironclad *Barroso*, which likewise went to destroy the Flat, had six men severely wounded, all in her square box. The monitor *Bahia* ... had no casualties reported except the wounding of the Commodore while outside the turret. These two vessels were struck respectively by twenty and thirty-nine 68-pounder balls at short range.

A series of maneuvers now transpired that forced this position. One such move involved the ferrying of over 42,000 men, 90 guns, and accompanying horses and supplies up river to turn a Paraguayan position. On September 1 and 2, 1866, a bombardment of fortifications at Curuzu brought about the worst Allied loss to date, that of the new ironclad *Rio de Janeiro*. She was hit by gunfire and pierced twice before exploding at least one and probably two mines, rapidly filling and sinking in the river. Her captain was lost, and as reported by Meister, along with

52 other men and officers while 61 survived. The fort was stormed by the army on 3 September.

On the 4th, the next fort was being bombarded at Fort Curupaiti, with the *Lima Barros* receiving 40 hits and the *Brasil* being hit 38 times. A later land assault on 22 September with the support of the fleet was bloodily repulsed and indirectly led to the relief of Tamandare by Vice-Admiral Joaquim Jose Ignacio. Ignacio, along with Tamandare, would prove that they were willing to fight but were not overly aggressive. None of the Brazilian commanders would prove to be fiery Farraguts in the course of the war.

The war now was focused on Humaita and Curupaiti. These back to back forts on the same side of the river employed thousands of men in defense, over 178 cannon, and some locally manufactured Congreve style rockets. However, these cannon were often antiquated and many did not bear on the river. Also present were three chains extending across the river, backed by minefields (including some electrically controlled ones).

The forts would be bombarded a number of times, though Ignacio had to be directly ordered to do so. It was on 29 December 1866 that the Brazilian fleet again bombarded Curupaiti with no result. Attacks were repeated on 2 and 8 February 1867, as well as 29 May and 24 June 1867. The captain of the *Silvado* was killed in the attack of 2 February.

Finally, on 15 August 1867, Ignacio passed the lower fort at Curupaiti with a mixed wooden and ironclad squadron, consisting of nine monitors and other ironclads, along with one *chata*, seven wooden ships and two mortar vessels, taking about two hours. Done in the daylight, the Brazilian squadron expended 665 shot and shell and were hit 256 times, losing 10 dead and 22 wounded. During the action the *Tamandare* had her engine disabled and was towed through by the *Silvado*. The operation was repeated on 9 September, and again on 13 February 1868. A tenuous land supply line was established between the two enemy forts. They were preparing for the "Big Game"—the passing of Humaita.

Before then, the Paraguayans tried to harass the Brazilian ironclads by mounting a large rifled gun on 26 September 1867, but were forced to withdraw it from the fire of the *Tamandare* and *Bahia*. Additionally, they moved about 18 guns from Fort Curupaiti to Humaita, so the Brazilians would have to pass them twice. All this time land operations were in progress and Humaita was finally cut off from a land link with Asuncion.

The decision was finally made to force the passage on the night of 18/19 February. The fort would be passed by six ironclads. Three larger ships would be closest to the fort with three diminutive monitors lashed to their sides. These small monitors had a single gun on a 342 ton vessel propelled by a 30 hp engine. The three larger ships were, in order of advance, the *Barroso* the *Bahia,* and the *Tamandare.* Lashed to them were the *Rio Grande,* the *Alagoas,* and the *Para.* The lead ship was commanded by the former secretary, to Admiral Tamandare, Captain Mota, who after reading of Farragut, wanted to emulate him. The overall command was given to Rear-Admiral D.C. de Carvalho on the *Bahia.*

Before the advance began in earnest, several ironclads proceeded up river and opened fire on the Paraguayan defenses. Others were stationed just below Humaita and fired at the enemy as well. The squadron slated to run by the forts began steaming into position at 23:00 on the 18th.

As the passage of the forts was in progress, with rockets signaling the attack, the river bank came alive with gunfire from 98 cannon, including one that fired "projectiles weighing 420 pounds." Aim was aided by huge bonfires lit on the shore and the moon was also up to help the firing. The chains, booms, and minefields did not help this night as the river was particularly high, a reason why the Brazilians chose to make the attempt.

The lead pair managed to steam quickly pass the fort and the *Barroso* was only hit twice. Part way past, the lashings of the *Alagoas* to the *Bahia* broke, and the *Alagoas* began to drift down river. Ignoring an order to retire, she pushed on. Twice the river current carried her back down the river, the first time carrying her all the way back to the supporting Brazilian squadron where she collided with the *Herval!* She did not finally pass out of enemy gun range until 06:30. She was hit that night approximately 180 times. Her 4.5 inch armor with 15 inches teak backing (with an additional half inch of "skin" plates) was pierced 12 times and her 6 inch turret backed by 10 inches of teak, also with an additional half inch skin, was pierced twice. The "turret was very badly damaged; nearly all the bolts being broken, and the wood-backing being badly crushed in several places."

Meanwhile, her consort the *Bahia* was having a difficult time of it. Carvalho wanted to retire at one point and actually collided with the *Para*, which sprung a leak. By 04:50 they were safely past with the *Tamandare* suffering 120 hits.

Pushing further up river in the coming days, these ships engaged various forts, culminating on 24 February 1868 with the *Barroso, Bahia,* and *Rio Grande* arriving off Asuncion. They proceeded to bombard the naval arsenal and Presidential Palace, though Lopez had already evacuated key elements from the city. With this success, the naval war would begin coming to a close, and the days for Lopez would be numbered.

Humaita was now fully surrounded and under siege and Lopez had retreated north with a large force. But the Paraguayans next tried a surprise attack. On 2 March 1868, 200 men of the *Cuerpo de Bogabantes* (Canoe Paddlers Corps) on 24 disguised canoes (made to appear as floating masses of hyacinths) came down on two picket ironclads, the *Lima Barros* and *Cabral.* A Brazilian, Midshipman Jose Roque da Silva, as described in an article by Ricardo Bonalume Neto, decided to investigate the rather regular and large masses of vegetation floating down river. He quickly saw they were swarming with men. While raising the alarm, the *Lima*

Barros was boarded and her captain was on deck. He was a small man and "was able to wiggle his way into his vessel's interior through a porthole." The division commander on board was not so lucky and died sword in hand on that same deck. In the ensuing action the ironclads buttoned up and grapeshot from arriving ships killed or dispersed over 150 men, for the loss of 8 dead and 52 wounded.

Later on 22 March, two of the remaining wooden gunboats of the Paraguayan navy were sunk by four ironclads while lying under the guns of a Paraguayan fort. This was accomplished by the Brazilians with little in the way of loss. The last of the Paraguayan wooden ships would be burned, after being disarmed, as the Brazilians approached them on 18 August 1869.

Another paddler attack was chanced on 9 July with 240 men. The *Barroso* and the little *Rio Grande* were attacked. The *Barroso* was boarded but the *Rio Grande* helped clear her deck and the attackers were beaten off. Paraguayan losses were heavy and 24 prisoners were taken. The Brazilians lost 1 dead and 12 wounded.

The end was now near. The garrison escaped from Humaita on 24 July 1868, with the Allies entering it on the 25th. Inside they found 144 iron, 36 bronze, and eight other guns. Pursued, the now desperate garrison of 1,324 men and women was forced to surrender on 5 August. Lopez had the commander's wife executed for this surrender that he viewed as treason. The previous commander of Humaita, the blind Colonel Paulino Alen had earlier tried to commit suicide. He had been evacuated from the fort, and some accounts say he was now executed, though he still suffered from his wounds.

The remainder of the war can be summed up as a continuing advance on Asuncion and pursuit of Lopez. The Brazilian fleet several times passed up and down the river, sometimes to the Paraguayan capital. Engaged by forts several times, their ironclads would be hit, but not damaged. This culminated in the ferrying of the Brazilian army on 4 December 1868 to the rear of Lopez's army. A series of battles were fought, climaxing in the Paraguayan defeat on 20-27 December at Ita-Ibaty. In that month of fighting over 7,000 Allied and over 10,000 Paraguayans had died. On 1 January 1869 Asuncion was entered by the Brazilians.

As pointed out by Meister,

> Lopez retreated from the rivers, controlled by the Brazilian fleet ... Lopez wanted to prolong the war until there was dissension among the allies or he could find safety in Bolivia. He forced the civilian population to follow his retreat into the wilderness, causing the death of hundreds of thousands of women, children, and old men. Thousands were executed on mere suspicion of disagreeing with his scorched earth policy...

Lopez would finally be killed in a small action on 1 March 1870 and the war would end shortly after that. Considered by some the first of the modern "total wars," it spoke highly of the determination of the Paraguayan people to fight on,

Brazil maintained an up-to-date naval arm long after the War of the Triple Alliance, as this rare shot of the Marechal Floriano *in the 1880s clearly shows.* (Vittorio Tagliabue)

but it did not speak well of the leader they had followed, too many unto death. Polygamy was temporarily adopted after the war to help repopulate it.

The war itself had been conducted by the Allies as a river war, reminiscent of the American Civil War. "It showed the superiority of armor over the penetration capabilities of the cannon shell, allowing the Brazilian armored ship and monitors to pass, relatively unpunished, even the strongest Paraguayan barriers." This failure of the gun to deliver decisive blows against enemy ships encouraged the use of ramming early in the war when a Paraguayan navy existed, as well as the novel concept of boarding in this now modern age.

Ironically, Lopez died sword in hand while trying to escape the destruction of his last meager "army" with the cry of "I die for my fatherland" on his lips, though he more than any man almost literally destroyed it. He is an honored hero today in his home country "and the war of 1864-1870 is the Paraguayan national epic."

THE STONEWALL AND JAPAN'S CIVIL WAR

Fictional quarrels and acts of violence were becoming more frequent. There were many minor and several major political assassinations.... . The more important of the (Shogun's) disgeneraled captains thought and plotted measures of resistance.
—Edwin A. Falk

Japan was an ancient Far Eastern nation that had only been recently opened up to the West. It created turmoil, as in China and Siam, that boiled over into war in the 1860's until the final strengthening of the Emperor and his hold on power over the old Shogunate and forces opposed to change.

In 1863 the British Rear-Admiral A. L. Kuper of the British Royal Navy's East Indies and China Station was ordered to Japan to "take measures of reprisal" against a Japanese lord's fort at Kagoshima armed with smoothbore muzzle-loading guns. It would be successful but the British squadron would consist of only wooden warships.

In the following year, Kuper returned with an international squadron to bombard the forts at the Straits of Shimonoseki. What was interesting about the two bombardments was that there were numerous Armstrong breech-loaders on board the British warships and the rate of failure was excessive. With 28 gun "accidents" on five warships, it was one of the nails in the coffin that would drive the Admiralty to shift back to muzzle-loaders for the following decade. This would make the British Navy and the United States Navy the only major powers not to fully embrace the breech-loader in the 1860's. Both the British rifles, and the French steam frigate *Semiramis* armed with French designed rifled muzzle-loaders, plied their shells at a range from which the forts at Shimonoseki could not reply. Shortly thereafter the European powers and the United States had firmly and finally opened up Japan, and a new Emperor, willing to learn from the West, the Emperor Meiji, was coming to power.

So the forces of change were on the loose in Japan. The power of the Emperor was waxing as the Shogun's was waning. The Shogun was eventually ousted from his position but a conservative rump decided to carry on the fight by fleeing to the most northern island, Hokkaido, with its capital at Hakodate.

There a Republic was set up, their nation being known as the Republic of Yezo, offering the followers of the Shogun a last stand. Its naval force was commanded by the young Captain Enemoto Kamajiro, who had received a naval education in the Netherlands. He had cobbled together a small squadron of wooden warships—six warships and seven transports with about 2,000 men, and headed north. Between storms and other events, the fleet had been reduced to four warships. But it was still a formidable fleet and could be unstoppable if they could seize or sink the *Kotetsu*.

This was the former Confederate ironclad the *Stonewall*. Originally built in France for the Confederacy, her destination had been discovered by Union agents and so she was sold to Denmark to help in her war of 1864. Ironically, her sister ship was sold to the Prussians and served in that navy as the *Prinz Adalbert*. Arriving too late for that war, the *Stonewall* was repurchased by the Confederacy in early 1865. She ended up surrendering to the Union with the close of the war in Havana and was bought by the Shogun for Japan after the American Civil War.

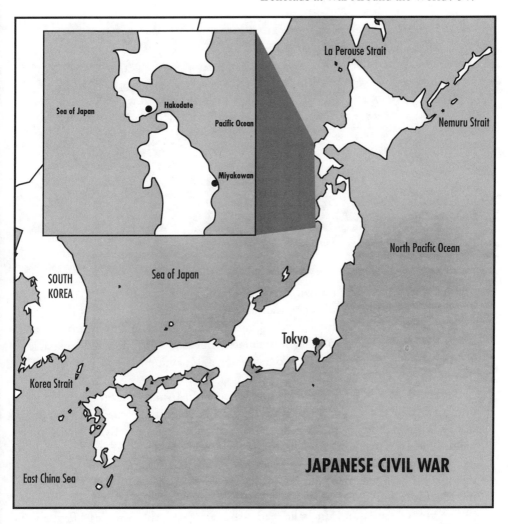

La Perouse Strait

Nemuru Strait

Sea of Japan

Hakodate

Pacific Ocean

Miyakowan

North Pacific Ocean

SOUTH
KOREA

Sea of Japan

Tokyo

Korea Strait

JAPANESE CIVIL WAR

East China Sea

She was known as the *Kotetsu* (which is Japanese for Armored One) until 1871 (sometimes shown as 1881) when she was renamed the *Adzuma*. Though bought by the Shogun, she had been obtained by the Japanese Imperial forces. Japan also obtained the 1,429 ton broadside ironclad *Ryujo* which arrived in 1870 after the Civil War was over. The *Ryujo* was a Scottish constructed ironclad speculatively built for the Confederacy.

The civil war would be the last stand of the Shogun's forces and mark the restoration of the power of the Emperor of Japan. The Satsuma and Tyohsyu (often known to the English speaking world as Choshu) clans had allied to restore the Emperor and were known as the Kangun. The Satsuma would go on to control the Imperial navy while the Tyohsyu would control the army.

Contemporary Japanese woodcut of the Hakodate battle.

The Yezo forces were known as the Enomoto force (Rikugun Bugyounami). Their marshal, Toshirzo Hizikata, wanted to regain the *Kotetsu*. To do this he first tried a surprise attack, which was suggested by the captain of the *Kaiten*, Koga Genroku. Koga wanted to move immediately but Enomoto hesitated to attack. Therefore the operation started two days later, and would be irreparably affected by running into bad weather.

The battle would be fought at the small port of Miyakowan, on the Japanese northeast coast of Honshu. Hizikata ordered three ships, the *Kaiten, Banryu*, and *Takao* from Hakodate and attacked the Kangun forces at Miyakowan. The paddlewheel steamer *Kaiten* would hold off the other Imperial Japanese warships in the port while the other two boarded the *Kotetsu*, captured her, and then steamed off with her. The voyage south was broken up by bad weather and only the *Kaiten* arrived off the port to launch the attack.

She arrived easily and unchallenged—she was flying the American flag, and was aided in this as she had her appearance altered by storm damage. Entering the harbor, she ran up the Japanese flag and began to approach the *Kotetsu,* and rammed her port side. The *Kaiten* had a lower freeboard that made it difficult to climb on board the *Kotetsu* and by now the *Kotetsu* was thoroughly roused. In the struggle, the *Kotetsu* opened up with a Gatling gun that inflicted numerous casualties, including killing Koga Genroku, on the *Kaiten*. Koga Genroku was hit first in the leg and the arm before a shot through his head killed him instantly. By now the Imperial fleet was thoroughly awake and small arms fire was peppering the *Kaiten*. Liberty crews were rowing quickly to regain the *Kotetsu* and the other Imperial warships. Repulsed, the *Kaiten* retreated towards Hakodate.

During the retreat the *Takao*, with a damaged engine, and the *Banryu* rejoined her as the Imperial fleet chased them. The *Takao's* engine failed her again and she was run ashore and lost. The other two warships arrived safely at Hakodate.

If this attack had succeeded, it might have handed the Enomoto naval superiority which would have kept the Kangun from invading Hakodate. If this had been achieved, the northern island of Japan might have become the Republic of Hokkaido. But it was not to be.

Enomoto's force was still a fleet in existence, but now faced two new dangers. After a long hard march, the Imperial army joined the Imperial fleet at the northern end of the island of Honshu. The second problem was that the island of Hokkaido offered little in the way of supplies beyond food, so if the land army made it across the straits and onto Hokkaido, the Republic's army could fight for only a short time before ammunition and other supplies would be exhausted.

After some jousting and several ineffectual Imperial bombardments of Hako-date, five Imperial warships, with the *Kotetsu* leading, advanced to do battle. The ensuing action fought on 11 May 1869 saw the last two warships of the Republic, *Kaiten* and the *Banryu* come out and engage the Imperial fleet as it bombarded the forts.

The *Kaiten* would be sunk in the action while the *Banryn* would find herself without ammunition and with her engines giving her trouble at the end of the battle, so she beached herself so her crew could join the fight on land. One Imperial ship blew up and sank. Hakodate would be abandoned after a bombardment led by the *Kotetsu*, and the Emperor Meiji's generals persuaded the remnants of the Republic of Yezo's forces to surrender shortly thereafter, instead of making a futile gesture of continued fighting.

Enomoto would survive the rebellion and was also persuaded not to commit *seppuku*. After a short prison term he went on to help the Emperor and in the 1880's actually held the naval portfolio in the government—something akin to if Rear-Admiral Franklin Buchanan had ended up heading the Department of the Navy in 1886 under Grover Cleveland.

RUSSO–TURKISH WAR

In one way or another, as much by "suicide" as by anything else, the Russian Navy had become nearly non-existent when the Crimean War ended.
  —F.T. Jane

All our causes (objectives) will end in a fiasco if our fleet is lost.
  —**Peter the Great to Menshikov, December 21, 1716**

A Long Term Russian Aim

The Balkans were rarely quiet in the 19th century because there was the so called "Eastern Question," a contest between the Great Powers interested in the worsening internal situation of the "Sick Man of Europe"—the Turkish Empire, and the fate of her domain after her probable collapse.

The Crimean War was one example of the fact that any conflict in the area was not a limited crisis. Russia was the Empire that aspired to reaching the warm waters of the Mediterranean and Turkey's weakness improved her chances of reaching this goal of controlling the straits between the Aegean and Black seas. But at the same time Austria-Hungary had many interests in the Balkans, an area partly ruled for centuries by Turks, and did not want a Russian advance into the Balkans. England and France both were important investors in Turkey and felt uncomfortable with any change in the *status quo;* after 1869 they both had an interest in protecting their trade through the Suez Canal and a Russian navy in the Mediterranean was perceived as a strong threat. Moreover they did not want to divide possible spoils of the Ottoman Empire with Russia.

After the Crimean War, the worst situation for Russian naval planners was to face a Franco-British alliance. But in 1870, with French attention focused on the Franco-Prussian war, Russia had a new chance to follow her traditional southern goals, having also new reasons for her traditional interest in Constantinople (a holy city for Orthodox Russia) and the increasing wheat trade through the Straits. Thus she denounced the Paris Treaty that had forced her at the conclusion of the Crimean War to limit herself to only five police patrol boats on the Black Sea. With the London Congress of 1871, Russia was again allowed to have a fleet limited to the east of the Bosphorus.

Another area of penetration of Russian influence under the flag of Pan-Slavism was the Balkans, where she also confronted Austria-Hungary's interests. The opportunity for war against Turkey arose with the uprising of the Slavic populace in Bosnia, Serbia, and Bulgaria, countries under Turkish rule in the Balkans in July 1875. Turkish reaction was strong and massacres of Christians, coupled with the repudiation of financial debts against the European powers, helped the Russian Pan-Slavists support the uprising. Russia wanted to intervene, but first had to come to terms with the other major European powers. Agreements were reached first with Prussia and then with Austria-Hungary on a basis of noninter-vention in the conflict on Turkey's side by Prussia and Austria-Hungary, a policy which would later obtain for the latter the administration of Bosnia-Herzegovina. But the initiatives of the Russian and Austro-Hungarian empires to urge the Sultan to modify the administration of the Ottoman provinces in the Balkans was not favorably seen by the Disraeli government in London. Meanwhile the Turks were winning the war against the Serbs and the massacres that followed her victories also horrified public opinion in London. As a result, an international conference was proposed by the British in Constantinople in December 1876.

In November the Russian army mobilized six army corps (VII to XII) which were concentrated on the southern front, along the Rumanian border to influence the coming conference.

At this point the diplomatic situation was favorable for Russia, although many shortcomings of her army were apparent. Recent enforcement of conscription had resulted in lack of trained men and officers. However, when the Turks refused the Powers' proposals in April 1877, the pressure of the Pan-Slavists on the tsar caused a declaration of war on 24 April 1877. Russia began her long march to the south for the sixth time in the century.

A Comparison of the Opposing Navies

Although the Russo-Turkish war was mainly fought on land in Bulgaria and partly in the Caucasus, the naval dimensions had great importance. After the Crimean War, Russia was forced to abandon the militarization of the Black Sea and especially her naval arm, since she was allowed no fortresses or warships in that sea. The Crimean war had proven that the Russian navy was unequal to the task of contesting the major powers' navies and that she was plagued by great organization problems. But the treaty obligation was the consequence of the importance of a Russian naval force in the waters near Constantinople, which could directly attack that city without long land campaigns in the Balkans or in the Caucasus, thus capturing the heart of the Ottoman Empire. After this defeat, the Russian Admiralty responded with a new policy for the navy, affecting not only her shipbuilding policy, but also the updating of the technological level of the navy and especially regarding naval personnel education. In this process a key role was played by General-Admiral Konstantin Nikolaevich. In the fifteen years after the defeat, the General-Admiral was able to overcome financial and bureaucratic problems, introducing ironclads and steam propulsion in the reorganized navy. Having had the opportunity to travel abroad and to see the organization of the European navies, he was impressed as many other Russian naval officers had been by the French ironclad steam batteries. He reported, upon his return, his impressions after having "just seen with his own eyes the gigantic fleets and naval methods of our former enemies." In 1858 he brought to the Tsar's attention the French project for the *Gloire* ironclad as a new weapon for the war at sea, and the following year the ministry ordered trials with armor plates.

Particularly interesting was his care for the cadet corps, where education was improved with the replacement of unfit instructors. He also oversaw the development of the naval magazine *Morskoi sbornik,* which reached a good quality level, encouraging open discussion on various naval matters and paying attention to developments abroad, and which helped to exploit the human resources of the nation. *Morskoi sbornik's* new course was started in 1853. The magazine was written to be read by the public, not censored in any form (pressure on the press would increase in the mid-1860s), and rejecting the habit of silence concerning the inefficiency and corruption of the naval organization. As an example of the progressive thought in the magazine, in 1860 R. Musselius, a naval officer, published an article on the first ironclad foreseeing the competition between armor and gun, and the great improvement in the coming years of naval armaments.

In the years following the defeat of the Crimean War, the navy was under financial restraint, due to the alarming state of the public treasury. This has to be seen in the perspective of replacing a wooden sailing navy with a steam powered one and crewing it with technically competent sailors. Nevertheless naval expenditure began to increase constantly, from 18 million rubles after the Crimean War to 27 million at the outset of the war with Turkey.

Helped by such leading figures as Admiral G.I. Butakov, well known for his tactical writings, Admiral I.F. Likhacev, the creator of the Pacific fleet, and the famous Vice-Admiral A.A. Popov, Konstantin succeeded in raising the level of the Russian navy to world power status, with results which were clearly visible in the following war against the Ottoman Empire.

During the years between the end of the Crimean War and 1870, the Russian navy introduced the bulk of a modern fleet and to do so Konstantin had to overcome the many problems which faced Russian construction, that is the extreme shortage of non-specialized workers (forced labor was employed), and the corruption and the inefficiency of the public administration, which resulted from a lack of adequate public funding.

The first Russian seagoing ironclad, the frigate *Pervenetz,* was delayed until 1861 because of the poor financial status of Russia, and then ordered from the Thames Iron Works in London. She was completed in 1864 and displaced 3,277 tons, powered by a 1,067 horsepower boiler built by Maudslay and did not exceed nine knots. Her iron hull was protected with 4.5 inches of wrought iron on her belt and battery. Her armament originally consisted of smoothbore 68 pounders, and was later replaced with six 8", nine 6", and four 9" guns.

Later shipbuilding began to exploit the private yards in St. Petersburg in order to gain independence from foreign suppliers. This was important because the rebuilding of a fleet to keep pace with the western powers demanded that the fleet not be limited by dependence for guns, machinery, or plates on Great Britain or France. Nevertheless the Navy Ministry had to reach agreements with foreign companies, the first being that with Carr & MacPherson for the building of a 270 ton gunboat in the Baltic and then with the British shipbuilder Mitchell for a yard to be built at St. Petersburg.

In the following years two broadside ironclads, the *Sevastopol* and *Petropavlovsk*, were transformed from wooden ships in the Baltic, protected with 4.5 inches of armor and mounting 21 guns of 9 tons each. These ships displaced 6,210 tons and could develop 11 knots; two sister ships of the *Pervenetz* were also laid down, the *Netron Menya*, in 1863 in the Mitchell yard, and *Kreml* in 1864, which was built in the Neva yards by the Semjannikov & Poletika company beginning in 1863. Of the many ironclads laid down before the war only *Petropavlovsk, Sevastopol, Kniaz Pojarski, General-Admiral, Petr Veliki*, and *Gerzog Edinburgski* were ready for sea duty, but none would be employed in the war against Turkey, remaining instead in the Baltic for the most part.

The influence of the American Civil War was visible also in the monitor policy. After Vice-Admiral Stepan S. Lesovskii returned from New York, ten Ericsson style monitors were built in the Baltic, mainly to counter a possible Franco-British attack like that which occurred in the Baltic during the previous war. Of these monitors, two were ordered in state yards, two were ordered from Belgian yards, and the others from a private builder. The ten monitors of the *Bronenosetz* class were all laid down in 1863 and completed by 1866, but none in the Black Sea.

A special effort also was made for gun production by Major Obuchov, who developed a founding process for guns, establishing a private enterprise that later became a state enterprise.

After the building of the *Petr Veliki*, Russia abandoned ironclad "battleship" construction for ten years, and instead, began in 1873 to build armored cruisers like *General-Admiral*, followed by the sister ship *Gerzog Edinburgski*. These two ships had a greater radius of action than many other Russian ironclads, and were somewhat unique for ironclads in that the gun batteries were not armored, although they did carry an armored belt.

This marked a shift in shipbuilding policy toward armored cruisers which the Russians were the first to build. It is interesting to note that this policy was pursued by Grand Duke Konstantin (to which the *General-Admiral* was dedicated) who felt he had achieved a minimum defense posture in the Gulf of Finland with the existing core of ironclad ships. Later bitter criticism was directed at his ironclad and cruiser building policy by officers and even by Grand Duke Alexander Alexandrevich, with the assumption that the money should be spent on a cruiser navy for conducting a *guerre de course*. It must be remembered, though, that the Russian conservatives of the time never fully trusted Konstantin *because* he was a reformer.

Taken by surprise when the war began, the Russian navy had 25,076 men, being larger than her Ottoman opponent, which had 23,000, but her fleet was dispersed around the world. More than half of her ships—137 out of 223—were in the Baltic and the others between the Atlantic and Pacific, while the little Mediterranean squadron was unable to force the Straits and thus remained

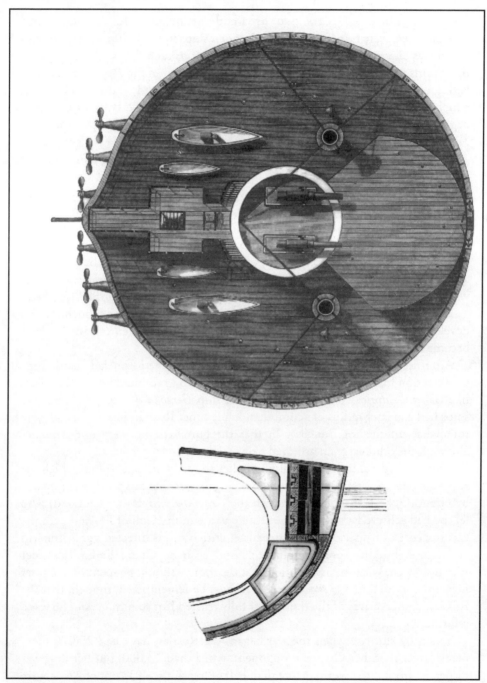

Russian Novgorod *circular monitor.*

inactive. The *Petropavlovsk* remained at the Italian port of La Spezia during the entire war. The only other Russian battleships available were in the Baltic. The 27 ships stationed in the Far East were the result of the new Russian approach to the Pacific theater, where they thought it necessary to gain control of the three accesses to the Sea of Japan. The tsar did not favor such a strategic view, at one point compelling his seamen to give up the island of Tsushima, where a naval station had been placed on Grand Duke Konstantin's initiative.

Summing up Russian naval policy, it suffered from the disadvantage of having ships so scattered that they were unable to support each other in a short period of time, but on the other hand a naval presence had strengthened all theaters where the Russian empire had interests. The Russian naval strategy was to withdraw the small Mediterranean squadron in order to avoid having to confront the British navy, in case of complications with Britain, and the redeployment of those ships around the world for a possible *guerre de course*. It is interesting that both Great Britain and Russia made emergency purchases of warships in preparation for possible war. Great Britain would purchase, among other vessels, one large ironclad being completed for the Ottoman Empire, while Russia would purchase from U.S. yards four steam powered "clipper" style cruisers like the CSS *Alabama* for raiding.

In the Black Sea the Russians had two more ironclads, the *Novgorod* and *Vice Admiral Popov*, circular monitors with a radius of 101 and 120 feet respectively, which were propelled by six screws—later four screws; but both were interesting failures in shipbuilding, as they were really able only to be used for harbor defense because of their low speed and their tendency to spin unnaturally in a cross current. They were intended for the protection of the mouth of the Dnepr and the Kertch straits. During trials one of them was propelled from the Dnepr river to the sea, where it began to continuously spin. Unfortunately for General-Admiral Konstantin, they were one of his adversaries' favorite topics of criticism.

Coastal defenses were strengthened not only in the Black Sea, but also in the Kronstadt and Sveaborg area, whose approaches were also defensively mined at the outbreak of war. Some small ships were sent to the Black Sea theater of operations via rail transportation, and nineteen steam merchant ships were bought for naval operations. The Russians thus had 29 steam propelled warships, but 20 were old and fit only for coastal operations.

Russia opened a School of Mines in 1875 and studied the American Civil War's results with mines (at the time called torpedoes) closely. Russia also equipped vessels for the laying of mines.

The Russians also adopted larger steam vessels for the carrying of launches armed with torpedoes. Much credit for this should be given to Lieutenant Stepan Osipovich Makarov, for his determination to prepare for the employment of the torpedo boats. A naval writer and protege of Vice-Admiral Popov, he later was well known for his tragic end in the Russo-Japanese war. His proposal to prepare a steamer for transportation of torpedo boats was preferred to Captain-Lieutenant N. M. Baranov's one which argued for the arming of merchant steamers with heavy artillery and the reinforcement of their decks to counter the Turkish ironclads. Makarov was put in command of the armed merchant steamer *Grand Duke Konstantin,* a 1,480 ton ship equipped with four sets of davits for lowering the torpedo boats near the objective shortly before the action and then hoisting them in after the action. Until that point the boats, very small, weighing about 6 tons, were transported by the support ship since they had poor seagoing capability. This allowed the crews to enter the battle rested and in better physical condition and give a better performance. Makarov also developed a system to directly deliver hot water from the *Grand Duke Konstantin* to the boilers of the boats, allowing for them to be launched almost ready for action. Finally, the support ship burned Welsh coal to reduce the smoke and the chances of the Turks in spotting them. Makarov was aware that this kind of action was well suited to Russian sailors with their taste for a guerrilla warfare, their ability to improvise and their personal initiative. The boats towed torpedoes on rafts or had them on spars, and did not initially make use of "automobile torpedoes."

Spar torpedoes were used with success in the American Civil War and other navies learned the lesson, introducing among their ships small boats able to bring an explosive charge against the side of an enemy ship. From the end of 1866 Robert Whitehead began to propose to the Austro-Hungarian navy first, and then to many other European navies, the use of his torpedo. By 1876 it was a rather reliable weapon developing 18 knots and reaching some 600 yards with an explosive charge of 12 kilos. The weapon needed a means of delivery, which would be a fast, small, specially equipped boat. In 1877 Britain commissioned the *Lightning,* her first torpedo boat, built by the British firm Thornycroft, displacing 27 tons and reaching 18 knots. Starting the project in 1873, Thornycroft also supplied the Norwegian and French navies with similar boats beginning in 1875.

Before the Whitehead, torpedo boats had been equipped with spars, like those supplied by the British firm Yarrow, to the Argentine and US navies, developing only eight and half knots, or the first supplied by Thornycroft to the Norwegian navy. The first Norwegian spar torpedo boat, which is considered to be the first true torpedo boat, was the conversion by Thornycroft of the *Miranda* into the *Rap.* The *Rap* was a 15 ton and 57 foot long slender craft developing barely more than 14 knots and armed with two spar torpedoes. Other navies, including Denmark, Sweden, Austria-Hungary and Russia, ordered examples of this boat.

The armament of spar torpedoes consisted of an explosive charge mounted on long spars, which could be brought in contact with the enemy ship—*possibly* without being punished in the process. Other nations, including Great Britain,

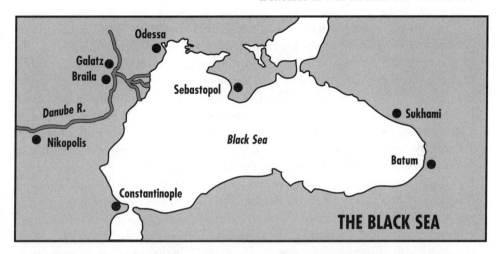

THE BLACK SEA

Peru, and Sweden, made use of this weapon, first developed in the American Civil War and now to be used in combat again in the Turkish war.

The fact that the Navy Ministry under General-Admiral Konstantin had planned the building of an ironclad fleet as the bulk of the navy does not mean that this new naval instrument was forgotten; on the contrary, the war value of the torpedo gained his attention and torpedo boat construction was planned in great numbers—110 entered service by the end of 1878. The Russian navy had tested spar torpedoes and various boats before, and ordered these new torpedo boats from several yards. Orders were given to Baird in St. Petersburg and Schichau in Germany, but also civilian yachts were requisitioned like those supplied by Thornycroft, the *Shutka* and *Sulin,* the first of which found good employment in the war. With the coming of the war, the same fate befell many little steamers and yachts that were in many cases transported from the Baltic Sea to the Black Sea. The navy also ordered 100 more torpedo boats from domestic and foreign shipyards. The Turkish defenses of their navy soon became one of protecting their ships with timber booms and boats connected with ropes because of this threat.

In the theater of operation the Russian navy was still playing her traditional role of support for the army in the Balkans, transporting troops and protecting flanks. First she began to take defensive measures, carrying out minelaying operations at the mouth of the Danube and in defense of the ports. These moves were particularly important in the general strategy of the Russian naval operations, which were then supported by an active defense using small boats.

The strategic situation at the outset of the war was greatly improved from the times of the Crimean War, since new rail lines directly connected Moscow to St. Petersburg and these cities to the Black Sea. Also the Caucasus was served by a rail link with the heart of the Empire. This facilitated the main Russian effort on land, avoiding her weak position at sea.

The Turkish navy consequently had command of the Black Sea and could have revenged its 1853 defeat at Sinope, if she had had a Russian squadron to fire upon and an aggressive strategy. The Ottoman Empire had devoted a good deal of its budget to increasing its navy. As a result, the navy had 13 ironclads, good warships built in the 1864-1874 period. The Ottoman navy had eight ironclads in the Black Sea ironclad squadron, under Mustafa Pasha: that is *Asar-i Tevfik, Orhaniye, Asar-i Sevket, Necm-i Sevket, Iclaliye, Feth-i Bülend, Muin-i Zafer* and *Avnillah.* These ships were supported by a wooden squadron composed of nine ships. Turkish ironclads were built abroad in French (*Societe de Forges et Chantiers de la Mediterranee* or *SA des Chantiers et Ateliers de la Gironde* in Bordeaux), British (Napier & Son, Thames Iron Works, and Samuda & Son) or in some cases in Austrian (*Stabilimento tecnico* in Trieste) yards. The *Hamidiye,* a central battery ironclad, was built at Istanbul by Tersane-i Amire. These ironclads were generally protected with armor plates in some cases up to 12 inches thick, as was the case of the midship plates of the *Mesudiye.*

The Black Sea fleet began intensive training with the support of British navy officers in the service of the Sultan, while ships were assembled at Buyukdere. One foreign officer was Hobart Pasha, the successful blockade runner. Hobart Pasha received an appointment as Rear-Admiral to the Turkish navy in 1868 while visiting Constantinople. He had not received the endorsement of the British Admiralty at the time (they were quite upset at his appointment as they preferred that plum to go to one they owed a favor to). It grew out of a conversation he had with the Vizier in which Hobart Pasha suggested that the current insurrection on Crete could be resolved quickly by proper enforcement of the blockade laws. As a former blockade runner during the American Civil War, he quickly ended the insurrection. He was reported to have examined torpedoes during a visit to Devonshire, England, a couple of year before the war. Hobart Pasha would command the Turkish fleet in the Black Sea.

The wooden squadron of the Black Sea fleet also proved helpful but was mainly employed for transport. Under command of Liva Ahmet Pasha, it comprised the following ships: *Edirne, Hüdaveandigar, Asir, Ismail, Mecidiye, Ismir, Mubir-i Surur, Muzaffer* and *Sinop.* These ships and the ironclad *Asar-i Sevket* were sent to Batum in May 1877 under the command of Ferik Hasan.

The larger Turkish warships could not control the upper course of the Danube, because of the limited depth of the river waters, which were left to monitors and minor vessels, totalling 46 units of various sizes. Two were seagoing monitors, the *Lufti-u-Celil* and *Hifz-ur-Rahman,* which were sent to control the river when the war broke out, and five were small monitors of the *Feth-ul Islam* class and the slightly larger *Seyfi* and *Hizber,* of the *Hizber* class. The first class of monitors were built in France, displaced 335 tons and were equipped with 290 horsepower engines which allowed for eight knots of speed. Armament consisted of two 6" and six 3" muzzle-loader rifles. The *Hizber* and *Seyfi* were built in Istanbul, the former of 404 tons and the latter of 513, both very slow, having only reached eight knots on their trials. Both vessels were armed with two 120mm rifles and all of these river monitors were less protected than the seagoing ironclads. Nevertheless this force, supported by 18 unarmored wooden gunboats, could have heavily influenced the land operations in Romania, hindering the passage of the river to Russian troops and hitting relatively easily the important rail line which passed near the Danube between Braila and Galatz.

Turkish strategy was limited to patrolling off the Straits and controlling the Danube, a defensive attitude that was a strategy of failure in light of the fact that they did not try to effectively blockade the Russian ports. However, in this limited role the Turkish navy compelled the Russians to maintain strong land forces to guard the long coasts of the Black Sea against a possible invasion and denied them operations along the coasts of the Black Sea. On the other hand, Russian ships steamed unpunished between the ports of the Black Sea.

In the Mediterranean the Ottoman Empire had another fleet under the command of Ferik Giritli Huseyin Pasha with a squadron of five ironclads available, the *Mesudiye*, of almost 9,000 tons, which had a sister ship seized by the British and which became the *Superb*, and *Aziziye*, *Osmaniye*, *Mahmudiye* and *Mukaddeme-i Haiyr*, under command of Miralay Faik Bey. The wooden squadron commanded by Liva Hasan Pasha had the *Selimiye*, *Mansure*, *Utarit*, *Eser-i Cedid*, *Sehir*, *Taif*, *Fevaid* and *Talia*.

The Bosphorus had its own squadron with six wooden ships, among them the ship-of-the-line *Fethiye* with 95 guns. It should be noted that, since the ironclads of the Turks were recently built, the guns mounted were generally good ones, all Armstrongs, while the influence of the British sea experience was visible from the British officers serving in the Ottoman fleet.

Opening Naval Operations

By April 1877 the Russian army had assembled the bulk of 257,000 men in Romania along the border with Bulgaria southwest of Bucharest, and launched an offensive passing the Pruth river and approaching the Danube. On the same day as the declaration of war, the Russians seized the strategic rail bridge over the Seret river at Barbus by surprise. Other forces, about 70,000 men, were maintained in the Caucasus and along the Black Sea coasts, while the same number garrisoned the Austro-Hungarian Empire's border. It is interesting that the Turkish superiority at sea compelled the Russians to avoid the more comfortable line of operation along the coast, which could be more easily supplied.

The Turks alerted their Mediterranean fleet and the wooden squadron patrolled the Albanian coast without finding Russian ships, while the ironclad squadron remained at Suda on Crete. From that point the Turkish warships limited their activity in the Mediterranean to patrol service.

The Turks numbered 135,000 men north of the Balkans and another 120,000 in Asia Minor. The Ottomans remained on the defensive for both political and strategic reasons, as they were inferior on land.

Although reacting very cautiously to the massive Russian deployment of mines and the threat of torpedo attacks, the Turks carried out a well mounted operation on the port of Sochum on 14 May 1877, attacking with *Muin-i Zafer, Necm-i Sevket, Feth-i Bülend, Mukaddeme-i Hayir, Avnillah* and *Iclaliye.* Using Russian refugees equipped and armed by Turks and distributing arms to the population, they organized a local revolt and compelled the Russians to surrender the position after a couple of days.

The Danube mouth was difficult to enter, as it was blockaded by mines laid down by the Russians. On 4 May the *Hifz-ul Islam* tried to force Russian opposition but coastal batteries broke up the attack. On 11 May the Turkish ironclad *Lufti-u-Celil* blew up near Ismail while exchanging shots with a Russian coastal battery of 25 pounder rifles and one 6" mortar. It sank with 160 dead but some 20 survivors were rescued by *Feth-ul Islam*. There is still some degree of uncertainty concerning this loss, although it was probably a lucky shot of the Russians that took her to the deep. Eyewitnesses suddenly saw a big cloud of black smoke that interweaved with the steam, which favored the opinion that the boiler was hit.

A Russian action was successful on 12 May when Lieutenant N. Dubasov in the *Machinsky* channel of the Danube exchanged fire with a Turkish squadron under Arif-Pasha, which had to retreat. On the same day Lieutenant Makarov had sent four torpedo boats to Batum but their advance was disturbed by a Turkish ship off the port and failed in their mission.

On the 25th, another torpedo attack was launched with much more success, being preceded by a Russian reconnaissance. This notable action with spar torpedoes was carried out by four Russian boats *(Tsarevna, Xenia, Tsarevitch* and *Djigit)* against the port of Mauin on the Danube at about midnight in very favorable weather—heavy rain and a dark night. The torpedo boats steamed towards the enemy ports in a straight line starting from Braila on the Danube. This was recorded as the first massed torpedo boat attack in history. Perhaps it should be remembered that at this stage of torpedo development the weapon was very different from later Whitehead torpedoes launched by tubes; they either had to be towed underwater to the target or they needed to be brought into contact with the enemy on a spar, a somewhat dangerous operation for friend and foe alike.

While the other two boats were supporting the action, the *Tsarevitch* and *Xenia* remained in reserve picking up failed spar torpedoes. They succeeded in approaching at five knots, since visibility was very bad, making little noise at low speed so as not to alert the Turks. The Turkish river monitor *Seyfi* was sighted at about 135 yards, and the torpedo boats ordered full speed against the target. First the *Tsarevitch* hit the monitor on her stern while the Turks lit up the port, and the small boats came under rifle fire. The subsequent explosion caused pieces of iron and wood to fly about. The amount of water that came on board Dubasov's boat was so great that he thought they were sinking. Then Chestakov, commander of *Xenia,* on Dubasov's orders, hit the target near the turret, stopping that gun's fire. Although the musketry still continued it was with little effect.

The *Seyfi* sank, but only after one of her shots hit and damaged the *Djigit's* stern. Dubasov retired as day was breaking and ineffective wild fire came from the other two Turkish ships. This attack caused the Turkish Danube flotilla to withdraw further upriver.

In the meantime on the Danube the Russian ships were able to successfully assist the land armies in the passage of the Danube between Svistov and Nikopolis, losing some units in the Kama. This river crossing begun on 23 June with boats and continued from 1 July on one 1,300 yard long bridge at Nikopolis, while another was under construction. The river crossing was cleverly carried out by the Russians, who placed two minefields to protect the flanks of the passage point, blocking at the same time any Ottoman movement north of Revi, where the downriver minefield was laid. On the other hand the Turks did not try to impede the river crossing, preferring instead to bring reserves ahead to the Danube and hit the attacking enemy when he was approaching to besiege Shumla and Ruschuk, the latter bombarded by the small river monitors *Hizber* and *Semendire.*

The minefield laid down cut off the Turkish small monitors *Iskodra* and *Podgorice* which were captured with the seizure of Nikopolis on 17 July and were incorporated in the Russian navy. Eight thousand Turks were captured.

Aggressive Russian strategy was again demonstrated by the sailing from Odessa of the armed merchant steamer *Grand Duke Konstantin* and a similar ship, the *Vladimir,* to the Danube's mouth under the command of Makarov. Both ships were armed and carried torpedo boats, the former with four 4 pounders and four howitzers, besides four torpedo boats. The *Grand Duke Konstantin* had already carried out a dangerous mining mission on 28 April at Batum under Turkish fire. Now the boats were at sea to attack the Ottoman ironclads believed to be near Sulina. On 10 June six boats were released in two groups of three each. The first wave had Lieutenant Poutschine in boat No.1 and Lieutenant Rojdestvenski in No.2, both armed with spar torpedoes. The other boat, *Tchesma,* had Lieutenant Zatzarennyi who also commanded the action, and towed a torpedo. The Russian advanced slowly to keep their engines' noise at the minimum and discovered the Ottoman ships at anchor at Sulina as foreseen. *Tchesma* approached the small Austro-Hungarian built central battery ironclad *Iclaliye* but his action was impeded by the guard-boats connected with ropes underwater which caused the torpedo to blow up prematurely. The explosion "threw up a huge column of water" that filled the fore part of the boat which was also damaged against the boom placed to protect the *Iclaliye*. The torpedo boat was barely able to escape with her boiler at minimum pressure, under Turkish fire, and pursued slowly by the *Iclaliye*. The first boat was badly injured by the shock against the protecting boom and afterwards received a critical hit which sank her. This attack was a failure since the Russians lost one ship without inflicting any sort of loss on the Ottomans, who had been surprised by the daring Russian sailors; the Russians also left six survivors in Ottoman hands.

By the end of the year the Danube was under Russian control, but meanwhile the Turks had managed to defend themselves more actively. On 20 June a monitor attacked some Russian boats that were laying down mines and repelled one torpedo attempt, with a lucky bullet that cut the "wire that fired the charge." On 23 June 1877 the Russians from behind an island ambushed the same monitor off Nikopolis with two boats that were waiting for it. The two boats which began the attack were the *Mina* under command of Sublieutenant Arens and the *Choutka* under Midshipman Niloff, but the monitor, which was under the command of an Englishman, put up a tenacious defense with nets and a boom with attached explosives, which drove off the Russians. The torpedo boats were almost crushed or run ashore on the river bank by the monitor. The *Choutka* barely escaped and was probably saved by the fact that her sides were armored with boiler parts.

At the same time the fight on the Black Sea was largely of attrition, and ship against ship fighting seldom occurred. At the end of August, the Russians had suppressed the uprising around Suchum, whose spread was regarded as highly dangerous, and the Turkish forces abandoned the city, employing the squadron of Ferik Ahmet to withdraw the troops and Russian refugees from that port to Batum and Trabzon. At the same time the ships *Feth-i Bulend, Mukaddeme-i Hayir, Mubir-i Surur, Sureyya, Asir* and *Talia* transported troops to Varna. The first two were ironclads, the *Mubir-i Surur* was a screw frigate, and the last three were yachts and dispatch ships.

In the meantime operations in the Caucasus were under another brother of the Tsar, Grand Duke Michael, whose forces were too weak (65,000) to attack the 70,000 Turks under the command of Mukhtar Pasha. He therefore waited until August for reinforcement before commencing operations. After a first victorious clash at Aladja Dagh, the Russians drove toward Kars and Erzeroum. The fortress of Kars was seized on 18 November.

The Vesta Engagement and the Turkish Surrender

One of the few gunnery actions in the war is reported on 11 July 1877 (according to other sources on the 23rd) and was surrounded at the time by some degree of uncertainty. The Russian armed steamer *Vesta,* which was under command of the same Captain-Lieutenant Baranov, spotted smoke while steaming 35 miles off the Romanian coast. Captain Baranov was sharply critical of the navy's decision to follow Makarov's proposal and the Grand Duke's ironclad building policy, especially the circular ironclad failure. By 08:00 she could see that it was the Turkish ironclad *Feth-i Bülend* (at the time Baranov identified the enemy ship as the *Asar-i Sevket,* which led to incorrect accounts by F.T. Jane and H.W. Wilson) near Sunne with which she sustained an exchange of gunfire.

Originally ordered for Egypt with the name *Kahira,* this casemate ironclad was commissioned in 1870 with a displacement of 2,762 tons. The *Vesta* was 1880 tons and developed a speed of 12-13 knots with her 130 hp engine. She was judged to be superior to her opponent, who could only manage 11 knots, but the Turkish ironclad proved to have 2 and a half knots of advantage. The *Vesta* tried to disengage to avoid a dangerous encounter for which she was not fit, but was pursued for four and a half hours by the Turk. The Russians found the enemy was capable of overhauling them, and fire was exchanged at about 3,000 yards. The *Vesta's* armament was five 6" mortars (and possibly four rifled guns) against four 11" (222mm) muzzle-loaders of the Turkish ironclad that, however, could not fire directly ahead.

Because of this, the ironclad would turn away from her pursuer to fire broadsides and tried to ram the Russian ship. Both sides had suffered some damage but the Russian ship was beginning to suffer substantial damage (rudder and gun damage in particular) and had lost two artillerymen. Lieutenant Pureleschine wanted to launch two boats to try to attack with torpedoes, but Captain Baranov refused to give orders for such an action in the heavy and open sea. The desperate move of boarding the Turkish ship was also considered but a retreat was favored because the Turks had supposedly been hit by a couple of lucky blows on the *Feth-i Bülend's* smokestack and main armament, fired by the mortar of Lieutenant Zinovi P. Rozhestvensky, who would later command the Russian fleet in the defeat of Tsushima in 1905.

Baranov, who became a hero and was awarded with the St. George's Cross IVth degree for bravery for this action, reported that the enemy had lost speed and he was about to finish them off, when smoke from two more ships was spotted, compelling him to leave the battle waters. This account also proved Baranov's own theory, but he was then refuted by British officers in the service of the Ottoman navy. First the ship was identified as the *Feth-i Bülend* and not the *Asar-i Sevket,* and second the fighting was described as a long range exchange—about 4,000 yards—and that the Turkish ironclad had reported no damage at all. It had not pursued more vigorously as it was transporting 20 pieces of artillery for the Turkish army.

Baranov probably exaggerated in writing down his battle report because this would help him in his struggle against Makarov, the Ministry and the Grand Duke's policy. Baranov was a strong proponent of the theory about "the effectiveness of light cruisers against ironclads ... ," as Jacob W. Kipp has pointed out. The philosophy of this action envisioned a fast cruiser armed with powerful guns literally pounding a slower ironclad into submission by fighting it at long range. This concept was not shared by Baranov alone. A senior United States naval officer once remarked that "Give me a fifteen-knot wooden vessel armed with four heavy guns of long range, and I'll laugh at your lumbering iron-clads."

For one year no officers of the *Vesta* countered his statements, so he was allowed to become a popular hero and the *Vesta* engagement became a legend. Later his theories would again attract public attention for the possibility of conducting a *guerre de course* with armed steamers. However, when one year after the action, Lieutenant Rozhestvensky wrote "Ironclads or Cruiser-Merchantmen," an article that defended the ironclad, Baranov wanted to court martial him. It is interesting to note that the army supported Baranov and his faction advocating submarines and cruisers for raiding commerce—this would mean less money for the navy and more for the army! When the dust settled, Baranov had been repudiated.

At the same time, on the Balkan front the Russians launched two major attacks on the Plevna fortress on 20 and 30 July, but both failed. At this point they decided to reconsider the offer of Romanian help and with their aid the Russians launched another bloody general attack on Plevna on 11 September. This too failed with 15,000 Russian and 3,000 Romanian losses.

The Romanian navy also committed herself on Russia's side with three gunboats, the *Stefan cel Mare, Romania* and *Fulgerul,* plus some barges. Before they declared war on 9 May, the Romanians withdrew these boats upriver on the Pruth to avoid destruction, while after that date the boats were put at the Russian navy's disposal, adding one vessel, the *Rindunica,* which later fought with the Russian name *Tsarevitch* under Lieutenant Dubasov.

Minor actions were again the main Russian navy activity, exploiting the Turkish ironclads' fear of the "devil's" weapon. Another torpedo action took place on the night of 24 August, when Makarov counterattacked the movement of Turkish ships that occupied the port of Sukhum Kalu. This time towed torpedoes were employed by four boats as follows: *Tchesma* (Lieutenant Zatzarennyi), *Sinop* (Lieutenant Pifarefsky), *Torpedoist* (Sublieutenant Hirst) and the *Navarin* (Lieutenant Vishnevetski). The approach towards the enemy ships that comprised, besides some minor vessels, the ironclad *Asar-i Tevfik,* was easier then foreseen because a conspicuous fire was burning on the beach, while an eclipse of the moon helped the attackers.

However, the attack went badly because of the gunfire from the beach and the Turkish ships, combined with difficulties discovered by the Russians in managing the towed torpedoes; the *Sinop* succeeded in exploding her device but only against a boat protecting the enemy ironclad, while other torpedoes were released inaccurately. The attackers were damaged, the *Sinop* by the Turkish guard boat, and in the fighting her commander was wounded; the *Tchesma* was damaged by the effects of her torpedo explosion and it was lucky that the ships were able to retreat. During this maneuver, the *Torpedoist* lost its way and was rescued by Lieutenant Zatzarennyi who had to search for the boat. Although the Russians received the impression during the action that the Turkish ironclad had been sunk, in reality *Asar-i Tevfik* was very lightly damaged and later repaired at Batum; the whole action was a complete failure. However, Makarov was fortunate that he was not sighted by a Turkish warship during the rescue of his boats, and he reached Odessa safely.

On 8 October 1877 (but we must note that other sources give a different date, as Wilson gives 9 November) the *Sunne,* a seagoing gunboat commissioned in August 1859, was sunk by a Russian mine at the mouth of the Danube. Survivors were picked up by the paddle steamer *Kartal,* with 27 dead.

Makarov's mother ship was ordered off for transport duty and some time passed without torpedo attacks by the Russians. However, in November the Russians again launched an attack force with the task of attacking the Turkish forces on the Danube at Sulina.

This force comprised the gunboats *Voron* with three 16cm mortars and two 9 pounder guns, *Outka,* with the same armament but 4 pounders instead of 9 pounders, *Lebedi,* armed as the *Outka* but with one 3 pounder, a mortar barge with two 16cm mortars towed by gunboats, and a couple of tugs armed with one mortar and two 4 pounders guns. (According to some source there were three tugs). Seven torpedo boats completed the expeditionary force, which carried some ninety torpedoes and mines, and seventy-five rockets. It is interesting that some of the torpedo boats were armed with two each of the new Whitehead model "automobile torpedoes." The Turkish force consisted of the three ironclads *Muin-i Zafer* (flagship of Mustafa Pasha), *Asar-i Sevket, Hifz-ur Rahman,* and the old wooden paddle frigate *Mecidiye.* They were at anchor between two breakwaters at the Danube's mouth, which had three approaches, well protected by obstacles (chains stretched across the breakwaters) and guns both toward sea and stream. Upstream protection was assured not only by a strong battery, but also by the ironclad *Mukaddeme-i Haiyr* and the old gunboat *Sulina.*

The operations were opened cautiously by the Russians who lacked real strength to attack the opponents. They steamed upstream at Kilia at the mouth of the Danube, where shallow water caused the loss of one gunboat. Then they come down on 8 November, approaching the first of the two chains that protected the Turkish ships upstream and laid down several mines while being fired upon by the Turks without losses. As always the Ottoman gunners were not very accurate and the Russians proved to be cool opponents, continuing their work under the wild fire. The alerted Turks immediately opened fire on the following day as one Russian armed steamer was sent to spy on the Turkish situation. The steamer then retreated and was pursued by the gunboat *Sulina* which crossed the newly laid mines, and was quickly sunk in a powerful explosion. The *Mukkaddeme-i Hayir* had also raised steam to attack the Russian ship, but did not join in the unlucky gunboat's pursuit. The Turkish ironclads opened fire and shelled the Russian gunboats, which in the meantime had appeared, although without causing much damage.

The next day the Russian gunboats approached again and began at almost 5,000 yards to fire their mortars, hitting the boiler of the turret ship *Hifz-ur Rahman,* and putting her out of action. Although the exchange of fire continued until the *Mukkaddeme-i Hayir* ran out of ammunition, there were no significant results since both opponents' fire was quite inaccurate.

While land operations continued with the isolation of Plevna and its capture on 10 December, the Russians also resumed their torpedo operations in the Black Sea. On 27 December Makarov attacked again in favorable dark and rainy weather at Batum with the same four torpedo boats lowered there by the *Grand Duke Konstantin.* This time he had received some Whitehead torpedoes and the *Tchesma* and *Sinop* were equipped with this weapon, a considerable improvement after the difficulties the Russians had experienced in the handling of towed torpedoes. The darkness and the fact that Hobart Pasha ordered no lights to be shown did not make it easy for Makarov to find his way and only after some time spent in the area was the profile of Turkish ships spotted. The Russians attacked with *Tchesma* and *Sinop* on the largest ship sighted but the launched torpedoes caused no damage at all, since the first of the *Tchesma* exploded against a boom, and the second launched by *Sinop* did not explode at all. The four torpedo boats retired under inaccurate rifle fire, and the *Tchesma* and *Sinop* were about to attack their support ship, thinking her to be an enemy vessel.

On 9 January 1878 the Turkish government asked for an armistice with Russia. Makarov did not remain quiet for long. On 25 January, the immortal *Tchesma* and *Sinop* attacked Batum again, this time alone, but both armed with Whitehead torpedoes. They were lowered about midnight and approached the enemy coast with difficulty caused by snow blanketing the shoreline. According to the Turkish version they missed an armorclad but hit and sank the 163 ton gunboat *Intibah* which lost 23 sailors.

On 31 January 1878 the Ottomans obtained the armistice and surrendered Batum to the Russians. The Russians were compelled to accept, because the British were displaying their naval power, threatening to enter the Black Sea. The

Russians had won the war more on land than on sea, but the role played by the little Russian navy was remarkable. It had allowed the Danube crossing and impeded any Turkish action against the vital rail line passing near the Danube. At the same time it maintained a relative level of freedom of action in the Black Sea, otherwise under Turkish control.

The Peace from San Stefano to the Congress of Berlin

(in 1890) the list of the Russian Navy was impressive enough on paper, but its ships had no homogeneity as to speed, size, range, protection, or anything else … The Russians were at their worst in exactly the areas on which the French Navy was working the hardest after 1890: tactics, speed, mobilization, organization, and the use of light craft and cruisers.
   —Professor Theodore Ropp

Negotiations began on the 19th with the British siding with the Turks. The problems were the same that had brought on the Crimean War, the question of the Straits, and the British pushed heavily on that question during discussions. The occupation of Constantinople—the city was within Russian sight—would cause British naval intervention in the Black Sea, where Turkish wooden ships from the Mediterranean were also assembling *(Asar-i Nusret, Fethiye, Medar-i Zafer, Zafer, Izzeddin, Kandiya* and *Hania)*. This was made clear to the Russians when Admiral Sir Geoffrey Hornby, British representative at Constantinople, anchored his powerful squadron in the Sea of Marmora and influenced the negotiations of the Turks.

To do this the British squadron of five ironclads had forced the Dardanelles with guns loaded and ships cleared for action "entering the Straits at daybreak in the teeth of (a) blinding snowstorm and gale from the eastward," but without any Turkish reaction. If British ships were to try to force the Straits to the Black Sea, which would also put the Danube under threat and the long Russian lines of communication, Vice-Admiral A.A. Popov had planned to mine the upper entrance of the Straits to block the British advance and to allow the seizure of Constantinople. The plan was abandoned because in a few hours the British squadron would have reached the Black Sea and a quick mining attempt would have to be accomplished under the fire of the powerful Turkish coastal batteries.

The chance to see how this would have worked was not given, since the Tsar decided to stop his advance and to sit down at a peace conference. This was because the British presence was coupled with the menace of Austro-Hungarian hostility in the Balkans. The conference produced the peace treaty signed on 3 March 1878, called the Treaty of San Stefano, which created Bulgaria and confirmed Romania's independence from Turkish rule, with heavy economic conditions imposed on Turkey.

The Congress of Berlin between Britain, Turkey, Russia, Austria-Hungary, Germany, France and Italy, superseded the San Stefano treaty limiting the Russian acquisition to Bessarabia, given up by the allied Romania, and the cities of Ardahief, Kars and Batum. Britain obtained Cyprus for her support and Austria-Hungary the administration of Bosnia-Herzegovina, although sovereignty remained with Turkey. The principle that the Straits passage was closed to foreign warships was confirmed.

During negotiations, tension ran high and the British made it clear to the Russians that any move on Constantinople would be considered a threat to British interests. Russian circles in Moscow organized a volunteer league to collect money for buying raiders to be used against British merchant shipping. Four vessels out of the twenty proposed for the so-called "Volunteer Fleet" were bought in the United States at Cramp & Sons of Philadelphia, where they were designed with great bunker capacity for long range operations. They were not however armed there.

To conclude, the importance of the British ironclads, coupled with the prospect of Austro-Hungarian intervention on the British side, was evident when the Russians were forced to accept the conference in Berlin to settle the Eastern questions. There in June the terms of the peace that victorious Russia had obtained in March were limited in their favorability, and they had to accept practically no advantages on the Straits question. The Ottoman Empire again lost some pieces, but Russia had gained little. Only in March 1915 did the British promise the possession of the Straits to the Russians once the war was won in order to gain more Russian support in the war against the Central Powers.

Operations had showed that the lack of a first class navy had frustrated the Russian victory on land and more successful operations at sea. The use of weak forces armed with new weapons like torpedoes and mines was also a consequence of the experience of the American Civil War. It must be remembered that the Russians were deeply interested in United States developments during that war and that in 1863 they dispatched the S.S. Lesovskij mission with the shipbuilding engineer Artseulov to visit the Union navy both for diplomatic reasons and to learn how monitors could be built. The Russians were enthusiasts of the monitors, after their experience in the Crimean War. When they heard of Lieutenant Cushing's operations against the Confederates they grasped how to deal with coastal operations by using mines extensively, which paralyzed the Turks and allowed the Russian boats an almost absolute freedom of movement. During these operations the Russian navy showed a remarkable aggressive spirit and a good organization in carrying out her actions, a result of a new personnel policy established before the war.

All major navies now began to build torpedo boats. The new exploding device gained much attention, with the only previous employment of a Whitehead being

Torpedo boats of the late ironclad era, showing clearly the ancestry of the modern destroyer. (Vittorio Tagliabue)

The Russian armored cruiser Admiral Nakhimov, *completed in 1888.* (Vittorio Tagliabue)

by HMS *Shah* against the *Huascar.* Moreover a new school of thought was about to be created in France under Admiral Aube, the *Jeune Ecole,* which theorized about the effectiveness of less costly weapons with which navies without the industrial resources of powerful nations could fight successfully at sea. This school would never take root in Russia, although with the coming to power of Alexander III the advocates of the armed steamers raiding enemy traffic succeeded in firing the General-Admiral, Grand Duke Konstantin in July 1881. He also suffered from the fact that several new vessels had huge cost overruns and costly problems with their engines,and with criticism of the circular battleships. It was the problem of the circular battleships, and another experimental failure with the Imperial Yacht *Livadiia* that was oblong in design, that cost Tsar Alexander II's brother General-Admiral Konstantin Nikolaevich, who had been in charge of the Navy since after the Crimean War, his job. These problems, combined with the death of Alexander II and the coming to the throne of the conservative Alexander III, led to Konstantin Nikolaevich being turned out of office, along with many of his men during 1881-1882. Building policies retained after his departure contained a large degree of continuity with the past.

The post war Russian naval policy was a consequence of the lesson that without a naval force in the Black Sea, she had been forced to retreat in the face of a British squadron in the Sea of Marmora. At first the Russian navy ministry recognized the need for a fleet in the Black Sea, but opposition by Britain did not allow new construction for at least five years.

On the other hand the successes scored by the torpedo boats resulted in increasing orders to yards by all the navies, showing general growing interest in torpedoes. The Russians demonstrated that torpedoes were suitable weapons, that the crews had good chances of survival in well prepared operations. Also, such action needed to be carried out by several boats and in poor visibility conditions. This last experience led to the order of 85 more boats in spring 1878, for which Russia had a total of 110 boats entered into service in 1878, completing her program for coastal torpedo boats. These boats were to be built according to specifications that foresaw 24.4 tons of displacement, 220 hp engines allowing for 13 knots and were assigned a name, but later from 2 September 1885 they received a number in lieu of a name. Their poor seagoing qualities and the strain which the crews had to undergo limited their employment to coastal defense or with a support ship. In 1877, the Russian navy also ordered the larger 160 tons *Vzruiv* at the Baird yard, which reached 17 knots with her 800 hp engine, and was completed the following year with two spar torpedoes and one underwater forward one. At the Schichau yard at Elbing in Germany the *Karabin,* built according to British Yarrow design, which displaced 11 tons, reached 16 knots, was served by eight sailors and equipped with two spar torpedoes. Building of larger torpedo boats continued with the 43 ton *Batum* in a British yard. This last boat showed her seagoing qualities by steaming 4,805 miles at an average speed of 11 knots from London to Nicolaiev. According to the Russians she reached 22 knots in trials (without the load of equipment). During the voyage she mounted two Whitehead tubes at Fiume.

Armament began to shift from torpedo spars to Whitehead tubes, although spars survived for some twenty years with some improvement in construction, such as the use of steel instead of wood or in the use of smaller charges, since they could be employed to open the way for larger vessels protected by booms and obstacles. This new weapon required new countermeasures, which led to the introduction of machine guns and light guns for the defense of the bulk of fleet, which remained the ironclads.

The nations of the world began, according to Harald Fock, to classify torpedo boats into various classes, based on their projected capabilities and uses. The Russians, from their war experience, were probably the first to see the need to differentiate their torpedoboats, but this is an area that should be further pursued. The British would classify torpedo boats as sea-going, 1st class, 2nd class, and 3rd class, which would become the benchmark for this type of small warship.

As recounted above, the ironclad program was abandoned for some time, but the new Tsar did not understand much of naval matters, after relieving Grand Duke Konstantin of his post at the navy ministry he did not change the shipbuilding policy. The international situation after the Congress of Berlin saw Great Britain as the main enemy of the Russian Bear because of her tendency to go south towards the Mediterranean and also into Asia. This from a naval point of view also favored a friendly approach in relations with France. In Toulon in 1880, the first ship for the Black Sea after the war was laid down, the cruiser *Pamiat Merkuria.* Three battleships of 10,000 tons followed in 1883, *Ekaterina II, Tchesma* and *Sinop,* built in the Black Sea and completed between 1889 and 1890.

Ironically Alexander III appointed a naval administration that by June of 1882 confirmed a naval policy that was anti-*guerre de course* and pro-battleships. His twenty year plan called for a fleet of 16 battleships, 13 cruisers, 11 gunboats, and 100 torpedo boats. Unfortunately an 1885 law establishing a rigid seniority system went along with it, followed by a Russification program that would drive Baltic Germans and Finns out of the service, and the curtailing of ocean cruises which had helped promote the initiative, "independence and self reliance" that had been so key in the Russo-Turkish War—and would be lacking in the Russo-Japanese War of 1904-05.

The Ottoman Empire would continue her decline, while her navy would be starved in the coming years. Part of this starvation was due to a change at the helm. The Sultan at the start of the crisis had been kicked out and just before the outbreak of war had been replaced by Sultan Abd-ul-Hamid. The navy had directly supported this change in power, but Hamid would starve it of funds in the coming years until his passing in 1904.

THE BOMBARDMENT OF SFAX AND ALEXANDRIA

If we have learned anything in the past century, it is that technology confers power.
—Daniel R. Headrick in *The Invisible Weapon*

By 1880 France saw the need to destroy the decaying Barbary State of Tunis. It was no longer a part of the Ottoman Empire. In fact a French squadron under Vice-Admiral Bouet-Willaumez had stared down an Ottoman squadron in 1864 intent on reasserting the power of the Porte during troubles there, and thus assuring the continuing sovereignty of Tunis. By seizing Tunisia, France would protect her traders, guard her eastern boundary of Algeria, and gain Italy's enmity as many Italians saw Tunisia as a natural colony for Italy.

Tunisians had raided the Algerian border for years, and the government of the Bey of Tunis had been incapable of stopping them. The French answer was an invasion from Algeria that advanced on Tunis. The land invasion went easily and the navy assisted in landing troops at Bone, Bizerta, and elsewhere. The Bey was forced to accept the French protectorate.

Local Arab elements in the south rebelled and were determined to resist the French. The port of Sfax, in southern Tunisia near the border with Libya, would become the focal point of this resistance. It was there that a French squadron was dispatched.

The operations opened with two small 3,500 ton French ironclads supported by French gunboats bombarding the ancient and poorly gunned fort and batteries located at Sfax. This first attack took place on 5-7 July 1881 and was conducted at ranges of about 5,000 yards. Feeble return fire reached but did not harm any French ship. The town, over the next few days, was "shelled ... from time to time."

On 14-15 July, Vice-Admiral Garnault, with a larger squadron, now undertook the reduction and capture of Sfax. He anchored his nine large ironclads up to a distance of 6,500 meters from the fortifications (some were closer) and employed his large pivot guns, while the smaller gunboats operated at a range of about 2,200 meters against the defenses. The port was bombarded for two days.

On the morning of the 16th, the squadron covered a naval brigade, consisting of six battalions of French infantry, and supporting steam launches and boats, many armed with Gatling guns, in an assault. The ships launched a fierce bombardment to cover the attack.

The French protected cruiser Cassard.

The defending Arabs had made trenches using bales of hay. The shell fire ignited many of the bales, and "the east wind drove the smoke back on the town, and the trenches had to be abandoned by their defenders." The attack moved ahead quickly and the French seized the town after house to house fighting. The town was captured, losses to the French were minor and no damage was inflicted on their ships. Arab losses are unknown.

The French navy assisted the movement of troops in southern Tunisia and the seizing of other Arab held towns through September. Tunisia was now part of the French Republic.

We now turn to a larger, but equally successful British bombardment of an Islamic North African port. The most famous British naval action after the Crimean War was the bombardment of Alexandria.

By 1880 the British had finally, and reluctantly, adopted breech-loading guns. This adoption took place in part due to experiments with slow burning powder, an area the Russians were leaders in. As it ignites, large grain slow burning powder gives more force through the entire acceleration of the shell as it passes down the gun tube. Thus a longer tube allows the shell to be propelled with greater force. Muzzle-loaders never exceeded 1,600 feet a second for driving a shot out of the tube, while by the 1890s 2,000 was common for a breech-loader and the French, who specialized in developing high initial velocities, hit 3,200 feet per second with some of their guns. Additionally, a longer gun is much more easily handled when reloading if it is a breech-loader. Combining a higher rate of fire and greater safety of the gun crew, the breech-loader was the gun of the future. In terms of safety, they protect the crews better, and a muzzle loading accident that occurred on the British battleship *Thunderer* could not have occurred with a breech-loader. On that occasion in 1879, the crew of one of the *Thunderer's* turrets accidentally loaded two charges causing the gun to fatally burst and knocking the turret out—the gun breech on a breech-loader would not allow that to happen. But the attack on Alexandria would occur with ships that still had the older muzzle-loaders, and the ships present would be anything but homogeneous.

In 1882 the Egyptian crisis had erupted. Egypt, with its valuable Suez Canal, was bankrupt. An "Egypt for Egyptians" party, led by the Egyptian brigadier Arabi Pasha seized effective control of Egypt, forcing the Khedive from power. The British were intent on restoring the Khedive to power, recovering their financial investments in this now bankrupt country and protecting the valuable Suez Canal.

By June and July of 1882 the crisis had come to a boil at Alexandria, where a large international fleet had gathered. Unrest onshore, including the massacre of Christians and Europeans, and a call to drive foreigners out of Egypt, had brought a number of refugees to seek shelter on board various ships and warships. Arabi was busily strengthening the port's fortifications, and the squadron was alert for the placement of minefields, or attacks by spar torpedoes.

Vice-Admiral Sir F. Beauchamp Seymour, Flag Officer of the Mediterranean Station, delivered an ultimatum for the strengthening of the forts to cease, which was not done. The object of this attack, in the words of Seymour, on 10 July 1882, was "the destruction of the earthworks and dismantling of the batteries on the sea front of Alexandria." The attack was to take place on 11 July.

In an excellent article by Colin S. White in *The Mariner's Mirror,* he points out that many future famous British naval officers were on board various warships that day. "Jacky" Fisher who would introduce HMS *Dreadnought* to the world was there, as was Doveton Sturdee who would command at the Battle of the Falklands, Percy Scott of gunnery fame, and Prince Louis of Battenburg—head of the later Mountbatten family.

As pointed out by Parkes, "Alexandria at that time ranked as a first-class fortress mounting (nearly) 250 guns, but of those only (42) were modern rifles equal to those in the ships. The remainder being smooth-bores of little effect against armor." Of the rifles, the largest were five Armstrong 10" guns (one of which saw no action that day), the others being smaller. The fortifications stretched along a lengthy sea front. The Egyptians fired with poor accuracy and employed mostly shot, though some shells were fired. Of the numerous smoothbores present, White estimates that only about half were fired during the battle.

The bombardment was fought from ranges of 1,000 to 3,700 yards. Gunfire opened at 07:00 and continued until 17:30 in the afternoon. The eight ironclads and five gunboats removed some, but not all, of their masts, and the ironclads were allowed to anchor and set their own ranges, as Seymour did not expect the

Egyptian fire to be effective. The ironclads tended to anchor in the course of the day as the bombardment continued.

Most of the British ironclads were of the central battery type, mounting for the most part 9", 10", and 11" guns, and although the *Inflexible* with four 81 ton 16" rifled muzzle-loaders contributed her slow fire to the battle, there were many differences between the ships. White later wrote that,

> No two of the eight capital ships were alike: some were ship rigged, some brig rigged; some carried 10- and 16-inch guns in turrets; some had single screws, some twin screws and their engines and boilers were a bewildering mixture of experimental designs which must have made the provision of spare gear a nightmare.... For our purposes it is sufficient simply to note that, between them, the eight ironclads mounted seventy-seven rifled guns although, since five of them were broadside ships, only forty-three of these guns could be brought to bear at once.

An additional factor, one used especially against the smoothbore guns mounted on the exposed parapet, were the numerous Gatling and Nordenfelt machine guns present on the British warships. They were effective, but would have been more so if the range had been shorter.

The weather was clear, with an onshore breeze. The shell explosions (armor piercing shells were not employed) caused smoke to rise "a hundred feet high before dispersing" and this somewhat obscured the targets.

The Egyptians fired back immediately but their fire was for the most part ineffective. Their hits tossed "showers of splinters when they struck the unarmored parts, . . . falling idly into the sea where they encountered armor."

By the end of the day the Egyptians were driven from their guns and there was no reply to the accurate British fire by the time the "Cease Fire" was signaled at 17:30 by Seymour. Egyptian casualties are not known, but there were about 150 killed and 400 wounded out of probably about 2,000 engaged. During the bombardment the British warships fired a total of 3,198 rounds, of which 1,731 rounds were 7" or above, indicating a rate of fire that was both slow and deliberate. Six were killed and 27 wounded on board the British fleet.

However, there was much to be concerned with, even with the seizure of Alexandria that followed. Firstly, half the British shells were either duds, or split in half, due to the poor fuses. Secondly, for all the gunfire, only 10 of the 42 modern guns were disabled and one neutral observer stated the next day that the forts could still have been defended by a well-trained land force. Thirdly, the British were almost out of ammunition. The ships also suffered some damage, either blast damage from their own gunfire or concussion. The central battery ironclad *Alexandra* was hit the most, 60 times, 24 of which were on her unarmored portions. What is interesting to note here is that while not totally armored, she suffered little damage from those 24 hits. One wonders whether, if they had been powerful shells she might have suffered more damage or had caught fire.

The central battery ironclad *Superb,* sistership to the Turkish *Mesudiye,* received the single worst hit, a hole ten feet long and four feet wide just above the waterline, and two other hull hits. One positive aspect from the action was that the "resistance of armor proved to be better in action than estimated from proving ground results." Essentially, all the range and penetration tables of the period were prepared for hits *under ideal conditions* and perfect shell hit angles, that, under war conditions are seldom achieved.

There is another illustration of the growing power and influence of technology in this action. The telegraph submarine cable connecting Alexandria with Malta and Cyprus was pulled up and communications were established. "Thus hour by hour intelligence was telegraphed from Alexandria to London, and almost before the event had happened, the news of it was received in London." Just a few short years before when Spain fought her war with the American Union, it had taken upwards of a month for the Spanish Admiral to communicate from South America to Madrid. The rapid movement of news would continue to gather speed as the century unfolded.

Finally, during the bombardment it had been sort of a gunnery free for all. The captain of the *Superb,* which had an armored conning tower,

> had noted that he had a clearer view of the action than the individual gun captains stationed at each firing gun. As pointed out by White, the captain suggested that an electric telegraph should be installed between the tower and the guns so that the bearing and elevation could be passed down. Other captains of ships not fitted with conning towers suggested that a similar connection should be made between the fighting tops and the guns ... Thus, in a sense, the Bombardment of Alexandria may be said to mark the first practical step towards the concept of "Director Control" (for gunnery).

A short military campaign would follow that would restore the Khedive and drive Arabi from power. Egypt was effectively a British possession until the end of World War II.

THE FRANCO-CHINESE WAR
OF 1884-85

Despite these significant advances in naval material and training, the political organization of the empire showed no formal adjustment to the needs of a modern navy. These new ships, whether bought or built at Shanghai and Foochow, were not organized into a single national fleet.
　　—John L. Rawlinson

A note to the readers: we have endeavored to note the older Chinese names in parenthesis after the modern form.

In the period after the first two Opium Wars and the final end of the Taiping Rebellion, one of the several factions at the Emperor's court prevailed upon the Chinese government to begin a modest naval modernization process. This movement was led by Li Hongzhang (Li Hung-chang). Ironically, one of his rivals, Zuo Zongtang (Tso Tsung-t'ang), had earlier entered into an agreement with both the French and the British to establish naval schools at the Fuzhou (Foochow) naval complex on the Min river. The French were instrumental in helping the Chinese establish a naval yard where warships could be constructed. The first one launched there in 1869 was a wooden sloop. By 1874 fourteen more ships had been built there. Mostly small and all wooden hulled, they did establish a small fleet that was helpful in suppressing piracy and superseding the earlier fleet of junks that had proved worthless in the Opium Wars. A smaller yard was established near Shanghai which also produced some warships, including a small river ironclad and another yard existed at the river port of Nanjing (Nanking)—for the Nanyang fleet.

Li began the development of Northern China's fleet by establishing the Tianjin (Tientsin) arsenal near Beiyang (Peking). Li, in part due to his strength at court, oversaw much of the overall Chinese naval effort in this period, but favored his power base at Tianjin.

Li advocated purchasing warships overseas to augment the fleet. One of the more unique designs, was the building of the so-called Rendel gunboats at the Armstrong yard. Displacing about 400 tons and being 118 to 120 feet long, 11 were built beginning in 1875. What was unique about these 9-10 knot warships was that they mounted a particularly heavy gun—11" or 12" muzzle-loaders. As an aside, this interest in inexpensive heavily armed gunboats was a phenomena that was not limited to just China. Germany, Sweden, Italy, and even Great Britain also built several ships of this type, though usually with smaller guns, and sometimes protected by armor.

The 12" 38–ton Elswick gun could penetrate 19.5 inches of iron backed by 10 inches of teak at point blank range. Several of these gunboats also had the unique capability of being double enders—they could steam in either direction. All 11 gunboats cost a total of $1,000,000 in a time when a small battleship cost about $1,500,000.

Factionalism was so strong in China at this time, that these, and other warships being built in foreign yards, became pawns at court. There were in affect, four fleets. Hongzhang had his Northern fleet, then there was the Fuzhou fleet of Zongtang. There was a small Shanghai navy, or Nanyang fleet, and there was a small southern fleet in Kwangtung province led by the ruler of Canton. An

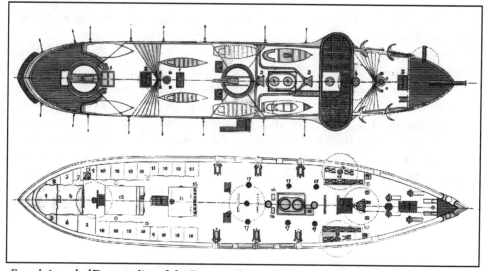

French ironclad Duguesclin *of the Franco-Chinese War era, showing two decks.*

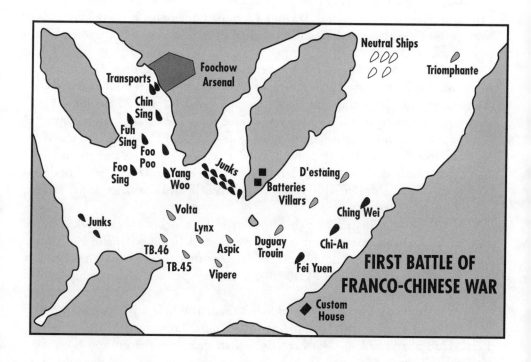

American Captain Robert Shufeldt spent some time in China on the eve of the war with France, and quoted in Rawlinson's book, remarked,

> The absence of naval rank and consequently of esprit de corps—of maritime experience and knowledge of the outside world among the officers—incongruous crews from different provinces, wanting in that pluck and dash which national feeling and a national flag can create—deep seated and ineradicable financial corruption—all these combine to neutralize the qualities of the ships and render them valueless as a fighting force.

The training of the Chinese crews was poor and indifferent at best. There would be stories in this war of sentries sleeping in boats, captains leaving their ships to visit fleshpots, "near mutiny," and this level of professionalism varied from fleet to fleet. The two best trained fleets at the time were the Fuzhou and Northern fleets.

One of the first threats to China's growing fleet came from a Japanese naval expedition in 1874 to Taiwan (Formosa) to punish some natives who had massacred a shipwreck's crew from the Ryukyu, or Liuchiu, Islands in 1871. The local king sent tribute to both Japan and China. China's response was fitful and certainly not a unified effort, but eventually it was settled peaceably—with the Ryukyu Islands formally acknowledged as belonging to Japan. What is important to note here is that Japan was seen as a threat to China (a future threat that would be realized in two wars), and that the Chinese still lacked a unified naval command. There was no single governmental naval minister administering the entire navy—it was all done by regional officials and the interplay of factions at court.

The problems facing China were substantial, and now the second most powerful maritime power on the planet was about to go to war with her.

France had been establishing a colonial empire from the 1830's onwards. One area of rich colonial growth was in what is now known as Vietnam. The French, beginning in 1858, had begun annexing the so-called Annam Kingdom. It was in 1884 when she decided to annex the region around Hanoi, which lay directly on the border of China, that France and China came to blows. A border skirmish was fought in early 1884, but war had not been declared.

The naval war broke out with a surprise naval attack by the French. Rear-Admiral Amede A. P. Courbet had the *Triomphante* as his flagship, a second class "Foreign Station" central battery style ironclad. Completed in 1879, she had a maximum of 6 inches of iron armor and was armed with six 9.4" rifles, one 7.6" rifle mounted in her hull and firing directly ahead, and six 5.5" secondary battery rifles. With his squadron was a large wooden cruiser, two smaller ones, three gunboats, and two spar torpedo boats capable of 16 knots and with the torpedoes "containing a bursting charge of 28 lbs. of gun-cotton." The French crew totalled

1,830 men. Rawlinson incorrectly states that "all" the French ships were "armor-clad."

Before the declaration of war, the French wooden warships ascended the river to Fuzhou and anchored *amid* the Chinese fleet there. The *Triomphante* was at the mouth of the river lightening her load so she could cross the bar and also ascend the river. Meanwhile another French squadron deployed off the river mouth, and it also included several ironclads, similar in design to the *Triomphante*. With the outbreak of war they would bombard the mouth of the Min river.

Meanwhile, the local Chinese commander, Chang P'ei-lun (who would direct the Chinese fleet from a nearby mountain top) had 11 modern ships, none larger than a 1,400 ton wooden cruiser. The rest were steam sloops, and he had two American built Rendel style gunboats armed with one 8" rifle each. He also had 12 war junks, seven launches armed with spar torpedoes, and even "three or four rowboats" carrying the same weapon.

Chang P'ei-lun had advocated for weeks before the French attack that the Chinese fleet needed reinforcements and that they could attack first. Both were sound ideas, but the paralysis at the Chinese court was such that only honeyed promises emanated from there, and the results would be disaster. The French were waiting for the arrival of the *Triomphante*.

On 22 August 1884 Courbet, after a conference with his captains, ordered his fleet to begin firing on the Chinese when the ebbing of the river ended and the *Triomphante* hove in sight, at about 14:00 on the 23rd. The Chinese had an inkling of the attack, but simply did not react quickly enough for this Pearl Harbor style strike.

The attack would be known as the battle of Ma-wei, but was simply a slaughter. The Chinese only hit the French ships twice, and only five of the Chinese steam warships got underway. As Swanson has noted, "in less than thirty minutes the firing ended and twenty-two Chinese warships were at the bottom of the river. Thirty-nine Chinese naval officers and two thousand Fujianese sailors and soldiers were dead."

There were several interesting aspects to the action. One of the French torpedo boats had successfully torpedoed the Chinese flagship, while the other was less successful, being shot up by rifle and pistol fire, and being partially disabled. At another point, one of the Chinese Rendel style gunboats came out from behind a point and fired her 8" gun, which missed. The French then "concentrated upon this luckless craft, and the torrent of descending and exploding shells was so great that it literally stopped her way. For two minutes she remained almost stationary, a helpless target; then, with a crash, her magazine exploded, and she dived headlong to the bottom." Another aspect was the effective fire of the French machine-guns and their small Hotchkiss cannon usually mounted in their fighting tops (mastheads). They peppered the Chinese at short range with particularly deadly effect, and if not killing directly, causing splinters to fly about maiming and killing more.

After the battle of Ma-wei it was found that some of the Chinese shells were filled with charcoal or coal—hence the name "Manchu-shot," a derogatory term for corruption. Local officials simply did not buy gunpowder and had pocketed the money. They also grossly exaggerated the effects of their own fire, claiming at one point that they had killed Courbet.

The Northern Fleet was called upon to send help south against the French, but Li Hongzhang refused. This would also result in the war taking place off the south and central portions of the Chinese coast.

Courbet next proceeded to reduce the Fuzhou arsenal to ruins. Courbet now descended the river, while the French squadron bombarded the forts at the mouth of the river. As Courbet steamed down, he took each Chinese fort and battery in reverse, that is, the Chinese guns pointed *down* river, not *up*. It was almost a triumphant cruise down the river. At night the French had the advantage of newly introduced "photo-electric apparati," or searchlights, to keep small craft from approaching too close. This is probably the first use of this device in naval combat and predates the often claimed first use of searchlights in the Spanish-American War. On 28 August the French squadron emerged from the river, having destroyed all the Chinese fortifications in their way.

In September and early October, Courbet attempted to seize Keelung on northern Taiwan. For various reasons, including disease and difficult terrain, the French could not capture the port. He next established a blockade of Taiwan on 23 October, and it would be maintained until 23 April 1885.

The Chinese decided they must try to relieve the beleaguered island and so gathered together a second squadron. This was the Nanyang fleet under the command of Li Ch'eng-mo. He had two modern German built cruisers armed with 8" guns as well as 11 smaller but relatively modern warships. Other ships from other fleets were ordered to help, but in the end, no others arrived. In the case of Li Hongzhang, it was partly due to Japanese diplomatic moves in Korea and their support of the French. Li Hongzhang was afraid to weaken the Northern fleet in light of the Japanese threat.

Finally a fleet of five warships under Admiral An-K'ang Wu went to sea in January. They travelled only by day and never left the sight of the coast. Wu did dispatch a merchant ship to test the blockade but was still milling about on the Chinese coast directly across from Taiwan, south of Ningbo (Ningpo), when the French arrived. With nine ships, they blockaded the Chinese in a complex anchorage at Shih-p'u.

Events are confused, but Wu left his two slowest ships at Shih-p'u where the French attacked them at night with torpedo boats. On the night of 13-14 February, Courbet ordered that two 30 foot launches armed with spar torpedoes attack the two Chinese ships. The torpedo boats successfully passed through numerous fishing junks working that night, possibly using one that was bribed, to quietly approach one of the Chinese warships. It successfully exploded its torpedo, sinking the ship, while the other Chinese ship scuttled itself.

Wu was now joined by two Kwangtung fleet ships. Wu and Courbet's ships would occasionally fire at each other over the next few weeks, but nothing more decisive would occur as the war was ending.

Eventually peace was brought about with the end of hostilities on 15 April 1885. By 1893 France would have control of all of what would be known as French Indochina, but in the northern part of Vietnam she was locked in a decade of guerrilla warfare. This resistance was described in a 1911 history as "opposed to an intangible enemy, appearing by night, vanishing by day, and practicing brigandage rather than war." It ironically reminds one of the future Indochina Wars that would follow in the post World War II period.

The French ironclads may not have been decisive in this war, but they did give the French a powerful edge over the Chinese. The Chinese would shortly take possession of two powerful German built battleships, which would change the naval equation in the Far East.

The Chinese Navy would continue to purchase and build warships in the next few years, with most modern warships going to the Northern Fleet of Li's. The Chinese would also establish, shortly after the death of Zuo Zongtang in 1885, the *Shuishi Yamen,* or Navy Office. Unfortunately, it was rife with political intrigue and the modernization of China would have to wait until the following century.

THE END OF THE IRONCLAD

In earlier days progress in the instruments of war was so slow that a nation could easily be a century or two out of date in its equipment without certainty of defeat. To-day progress is so bewilderingly rapid that the failure to keep up with the scientific developments of a single year might very conceivably ruin a great empire.
—G.W. Steevens in *Naval Policy*

So now we come to the end. We have seen the growth of ironclads from primitive steam batteries with 4 inches of iron plate, to battleships of moderate speed with immense guns, and armor plate of a thickness unimagined back in 1855. There have been only two significant battles between seagoing ironclads, one the Battle of Lissa and the other the Battle of Angamos.

Many thought that the ironclad was still the queen of the seas. The torpedo was still a new and in many ways untried weapon—many felt that its successes had not been against first class opponents. As late as 1887 Hobart Pasha was

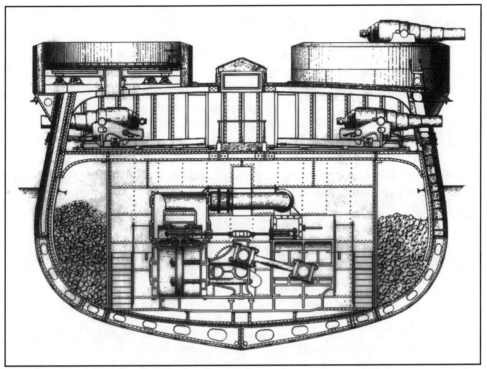

Cross section of ironclad of the 1870s and 1880s with open barbettes instead of turrets. Note how coal is banked for extra protection.

writing of them that "A shark somewhat reminds me of the torpedo of the present day, and in my humble opinion is much more dangerous."

The theory that a large unarmored ship with a powerful gun(s) defeating an ironclad had also failed. The experiences of the *Shah* and the *Vesta* seemed to indicate that an ironclad remained superior.

Technological changes were moving forward quickly as well. The quality of armor was about to evolve to its more modern form, through developments at Krupp. Smokeless powder, introduced in 1884, allowed high muzzle velocities; the French introduced high explosive shells at the end of the 1880s; and by 1890 the German navy was thinking seriously about training their officers and men in sophisticated fire procedure.

But war clouds were now looming, clouds that would bring forth storms to fully test this weapon.

In the Far East one of the major imperialist wars was about to break out between Japan and China. The new United States navy would soon cross swords with the dying colonial empire of Spain. The diplomatic and colonial struggle between the

Dual Alliance of France and Russia was about to break at Fashoda and later in Russia's war with Japan.

So, soon, as the name "ironclad" was becoming a historical term, and the new term of "battleship" was becoming the new definition of naval power, major wars were about to occur. The fine delineation of types combined with bursting worldwide naval budgets, and shortly the world would see regular publications such as Brassey's and Weyer's be joined by Jane's *Fighting Ships,* and more. This would bring the ironclad into the modern era.

The ironclad had shown itself to be the revolutionary weapon system which affected the course of history and technology, and was about to play itself out even more as the approach to the Dreadnought era began.

Naval Defence Act of 1889

The protection of commerce and food supplies was the piece de resistance of all arguments for building an unchallengeable fleet.
—Arthur Marder

A ship grows old as quickly as a racehorse does.
—F.T. Jane

Great Britain with her Empire was the strongest world power in the 19th century, and her navy was the most numerous and powerful. However, it was rudderless for much of the 1870s and the 1880s as it lacked a goal, especially after the fall of the Emperor Napoleon III. In the 1870s, France, her old rival, rebuilding a nation after a disastrous war, built little in the way of new ships, unlike in the 1860s. However, by the 1880s France was once again building a modern fleet.

Also, Great Britain's ships were a collection of individual experiments for the most part. She had warships that had low and high freeboards, were central battery, turreted fore and aft as well as in echelon, etc. The value, or lack of value, of these ships was also questioned. Would the newly introduced high explosive shell, first used by the French in 1888, render many of the older ships worthless in action by destroying large portions of the unarmored sides of many of the ironclads? Masts were not done away with in new warships until the late 1870's—when it was realized that by substituting more coal bunkerage for the weight saved by masts and sails a ship could actually steam further with the improved and more efficient engines of the day.

Additionally, the value of the ironclad was in question against the power of giant guns and the threat of the torpedo. Was the *Jeune Ecole* correct and had the day of the large battleship passed?

In 1884 a series of articles in *Pall Mall Gazette* entitled "The Truth about the Navy" by W. T. Stead, and other articles that followed it, fired the public. Questions about the strength and capability of the British Royal Navy began to be asked in Parliament, as well as by the press and public. The following years did see some ship building increases, but even the Admiralty was wondering about the value and need for more battleships. As Arthur Marder pointed out, "the enormously destructive power of the torpedo and the apparent impossibility for even battleships to withstand its attack led many to believe that the heavily armored and armed warship was doomed, and that in the future only small fast ships, armed with light guns and strongly fortified bows for ramming should be constructed."

What changed the equation was the naval scare of 1888. It was suddenly realized that if the French and Russian fleets were to act together (and in a few

The French **Admiral Duperre,** *built when ironclads' steam engines were still supplemented by sails.*

short years these two powers would conclude the "Dual Alliance"), that the British fleet might not match in strength those two *combined* powers. Back then, as during so much of the Cold War, there was a constant numbers game of comparing the available and building battleships of various powers, and the numbers purported to be correct often varied depending on the point that the speaker or the writer wanted to prove. Still, by any calculation, the British Navy did lack the required overall numbers of powerful ironclads that could steam and fight together in the event of a world war in which she faced *more* than one Great Power.

Nor was it just a question of ships. The British Royal Navy lacked a proper mobilization scheme. Her Intelligence Service was rudimentary "nor did a naval 'plan of campaign' exist." Additionally, in the British naval maneuvers in 1888, the "French" fleet operating out of Ireland had wreaked havoc on "British" ports and shipping, seizing Liverpool and laying contributions against other ports. These maneuvers had been closely followed by the press.

These events, and others, all culminated in two important decisions. The Conservative government of Lord Salisbury established the "Two-Power Stand-ard." This stated that Britain's naval strength would be predicated on being equal to the next two most powerful world navies, i.e., the French and Russian navies.

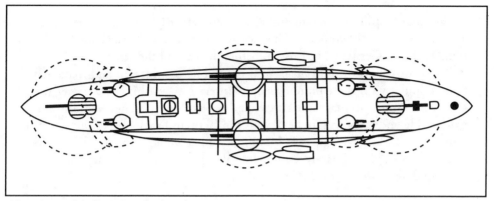

Clowes' wonder ship, the Mary Rose, made famous in his adventure novel.

This standard would remain in force until the destruction of the Russian navy in the Russo-Japanese War and the rise of the German navy in the next century.

To implement this decision the Naval Defence Act was passed. It called for the expenditure of £21,500,000 sterling above the normal naval budget over several years. Seventy new warships were to be built, of which ten were to be battleships.

Eight of the 10 were of the *Royal Sovereign* class. These high freeboard and powerful ships were of 14,150 tons, over 380 feet long, could steam at 18 knots, and were armed with four 13.5" breechloading rifles in barbettes fore and aft (one, the *Hood,* was given turrets). Armor plate was of the new compound type that was a combination of iron and steel, and the thickness of the plate varied from a maximum of 18 inches on a portion of the belt to 17 inches on the barbette, and a curved 3 inches deck. Two inches of compound armor were equal to about 3 inches of wrought iron. In size they were about 40% larger than contemporary foreign warships, with much of the additional weight being taken up by large coal bunkerage—so they could remain at sea for longer periods of time for blockade duty. Now here was a *class* of battleships that could act together as a squadron. The era of individual examples of various warship types was over. The *Royal Sovereign* class would be "the standard type of English battleship for ten years."

Another aspect of the Naval Defence Act was the speeding up of construction. Several British battleships laid down in the early or mid-80's had taken up to seven years to build. The new and powerful *Royal Sovereign* class would be built in four. The rapid construction of new warships would become a hallmark of the British navy from this point on.

Combining with the Naval Defence Act and the earlier maneuvers that brought all this to a head, were new publications and the education of the public, the government, and the Navy. The United States Navy's Captain Alfred Thayer Mahan's *Influence of Seapower 1660-1783* appeared in 1890 and British Admiral P. H. Colomb's *Naval Warfare* first appeared in 1891. Such works as these had an impact that would be far ranging. Kaiser Wilhelm II had a translated copy of Mahan's book on the desk of all his captains and *Naval Warfare* ended up being translated into German and Russian before the turn of the century.

These works also would break into the public mainstream and make navies more popular with the common people. Interest in warships and navies would grow with numerous magazine articles and books. Navy Leagues would spring up world wide and grow in numbers, with the German League becoming the most numerous. Additionally, the relative military quiet would be broken by a series of wars that would ultimately culminate, along with revolutionary changes in warship design, with World War One.

Italian Shipbuilding Policy

"... the most powerful gun, the toughest plates, the highest speed and the mightiest ram..."
—Simone Pacoret di Saint Bon

When in 1861 the Italian Royal Navy, the *Regia Marina,* was formed, it was the result of the union of four different navies: the Sardinian, the Tuscan, the Neapolitan and the few vessels collected by Garibaldi in Sicily. The most important elements were the Sardinian and the Neapolitan, they brought into the shotgun marriage of the navies an internal rivalry because of differences in education and culture. Each claimed the other had the upper hand in the distribution of appointments.

From the beginning, when she had only 77,031 tons and 745 guns, the new navy was intended to be one of the strongest in the Mediterranean, and had to face the Spanish and the French ones in the west, and the Turkish and Greek ones in the east. The British were considered friendly. The first navy minister was Cavour, who saw clearly the need for a domestic industry to build a major navy. He said in 1860 before the Parliament that the lack of a steel industry "... is a severe lack for the Government ... the Government wish greatly to favor the development of such industry." He also asked the American industrialist Ward to introduce his plants in Italy. Large ship building plans were conceived, although a certain degree of uncertainty existed in those years, especially with the rapid military technology changes sweeping the Industrializing world. An example was the fact that in 1862 the Italian navy ordered wooden warships, but, shortly afterwards during the time when Carlo Pellion di Persano was in charge, the navy addressed its efforts toward an ironclad fleet. Also the type of guns was a matter of discussion in those years. In the *Studio per la compilazione di un piano organico per la Marina italiana* of 1863, a compilation which should resolve problems concerning the creation of a new and modern navy, it was said about artillery,

> Tests carried out in recent times, and especially in England, to establish the penetration power and the effectiveness of shots on the armor plates, seem to incline toward the solution of spherical shots and smoothbore guns. The friction in the rifled guns is much more than in the smooth ones, and consequently the muzzle velocity is lower in rifled guns; and the effect at short range is lower.

Nevertheless the navy continued to buy many wrought iron rifled guns from Sweden, thanks to the insistence of Cavalli and at the direction of the navy minister Menabrea (who, on the other hand, favored wooden warships). Rifled guns were deployed into the coastal fortresses of Gaeta and Messina. Later, hoops were ordered from France. Hooping (or banding), to raise the resistance to larger charges, was mainly executed in domestic plants, namely Ansaldo at Genoa.

Armor plates were ordered in Sweden, Great Britain, and France, but also from the Ansaldo company. At the end of 1865, the Admirals' Council with the gunnery training school, decided to adopt the 20, 22, and 25 centimeter Armstrong guns, and the navy began to order Armstrong steel guns. However, orders were sent too late and most of the guns were still on the way when Persano went into battle at Lissa on 20 July 1866.

Until the war against Austria in 1866 and the defeat at Lissa, the naval construction policy was beyond the state's capabilities, and so ships were ordered from United States, French, and British yards. In fact, only one of Persano's armorclads was of Italian construction in the 1866 campaign, while ten ironclads were commissioned in France, London and the United States between 1863 and 1866. After the 1866 war the navy continued its policy of replacing the old 16cm wrought iron rifled guns with the new Armstrong made steel rifled ones.

The Lissa disaster had among other consequences caused a limitation of the navy budget in the following years. The navy obtained only about 15% of the entire defense budget in the 1870's. But pressure in the country for a large navy, especially because of the worsening relations with France after the seizure of Rome and the fall of the Emperor Napoleon III, suggested a new building plan. Literary and expert articles and pamphlets of the time always pointed out that Italy could be invaded by sea, and that the Mediterranean should be an Italian lake. From this point of view the issue was how to build a Navy. Two of the principal architects of the Italian naval building plan were Simone Pacoret di Saint Bon and Benedetto Brin, the latter being a naval engineer and ship designer, and later navy minister. Saint Bon's plan was to sell the old ships and build new and updated ones. This concept always remained in the background, although it was not always successfully applied.

One example was the navy ministry in the years 1881-1883, when Rear-Admiral Ferdinando Acton was minister. He reasoned that Italy had long coasts to defend and needed many small and fast boats to meet such a requirement, along with coastal defenses. This was a reflection of French Admiral Aube's ideas of the *Jeune Ecole*. In those years the traditional Italian large ship program lost ground in favor of coastal defenses and torpedo boats, which entered the service in large numbers in 1883 and thereafter. But there were many points against Acton, for instance the fact that politically Italy wanted to engage in some African adventures, and also the British Royal Navy with its traditional large ship policies played a strong influence in the new Italian navy. Moreover, the influence of the political idea of building a domestic steel industry was also a vital issue.

Eventually Acton lost the battle against Brin and Saint Bon fought in the press over the question of building big ships or many minor vessels. The Brin concept

The Italian battleship Dandolo, *showing the armored crow's nests of the later ironclad period.*

of "great speed, to master the (enemy's) offensive and to be able to avoid those of the new insidious ships (such as torpedo boats), ... guns not inferior to the enemy ones, ... the plates not to be pierced by the enemy ..." ended up being the winning one and Acton was forced to resign in 1883.

In 1884 the new steel company *Societa degli altiforni fonderie ed acciaierie di Terni,* or Terni, was founded and fed with navy armor plate orders, while for guns, the Navy had to still rely upon Armstrong deliveries. Armor plates were of wrought steel or compound (generally produced by Terni) and changed in 1894, when the Harvey patented armor plate system was introduced.

Links with major foreign suppliers were established. Armstrong and Vickers formed joint ventures with Italian companies, and later also French and German companies invested in Italian iron and armament plants, like Schneider at Genoa and Schwarzkopf in Venice for torpedo manufacture. Armstrong supplied guns both from Elswick and from the new plants in Pozzuoli.

As a consequence of the evolving might of the private armament industries, at the beginning of the 20th century the relations between these companies and the navy would be the subject matter of a Parliamentary Commission inquiring into

The Italian cruiser Sardegna. (Vittorio Tagliabue)

Ruggero di Lauria. (Vittorio Tagliabue)

the expense of the Navy Ministry. This was because of the state of monopoly in which Terni was allowed to operate, a state of affairs common to many European states, where the arms industry was rarely operating in a true open market. It was the beginning of the modern "industrial-military complex." The Commission made it clear that Terni had produced armor plates at much higher prices than foreign producers, and that Terni delayed the adoption of the Krupp patent only in order to save money, hoping to continue to supply the navy with the Harvey style armor plates—a now inferior style of plate with the perfection of Krupp type armor at the turn of the century. The same happened with Armstrong that quoted prices which were much higher than those contracted to the British Royal Navy, also taking into account the percentage allowed for contract.

Coming to the shipbuilding policy, the steps firmly taken by Saint Bon and Brin resulted in a wave of new ship construction. They started with the 1873 Naval Law, approved in 1875, which planned the construction of *Duilio* and *Dandolo* battleships (on Brin's design). These new vessels were designed to exhibit speed, in addition to being well-armed with limited areas protected by thick armor. Their armor was of French steel, which was used because of experiments undertaken at La Spezia in 1876 in which the "first decisive victory of steel over iron" occurred. The maximum armor thickness was built around the waterline, protected amidships with 22 inches thick armor plates, while their two turrets had 17.6 inches. The rest of the hull protection relied mainly on the 83 watertight compartments, and in the high speed (15 knots) they were supposed to sustain (15.04 knots was obtained in the trials). The deck was only of 2 inches of armor. Their armament consisted of four new monster 17.7" (450mm) muzzle-loader guns of 100 tons produced by Armstrong for the first time. Brin and the navy in general were somewhat concerned with these guns and their reliability.

Discussions about the new big ships raged in Italy and abroad. Interestingly enough, after the launch of the *Duilio*, which displaced 12,265 tons, modifications were made on the following large warships in order to increase range of action and carrying capacity, which was clearly intended to aid in shipping army troops overseas.

Public opinion in Italy and abroad criticized the new design and the possibility that these ships could capsize; Sir E.J. Reed, famous chief constructor of the Royal Navy from 1863 to 1870, foresaw such possibility in the London *Times*. The launch in 1876 proved beyond a doubt their seagoing capabilities and this fear was dispelled. Nevertheless, the *Duilio* had an accident on board when one of the big 100 ton guns exploded. The inquiry concluded that one small flaw, probably between the breech and the gun's barrel, had caused the accident. The commission suggested lowering the powder charge from the ordinary 551 pounds to 440 for normal use and 507 in extraordinary conditions of need, such as a duel with an enemy ironclad:

Thus holding fire until 2,000 meters range with a maximum angle of 30 degrees, the ships protected with plates 35cm thick, that is the most powerful today available, would be pierced thanks to the power supplied by the 200 kg powder charge, (firing) hardened cast iron piercing shots.

The large sums needed for the building plan were distributed over many years of expenditure and the selling of old ships, thus gaining money and saving on maintenance.

A basic concept in Italian naval strategy from the outset was that the Italian navy should be comparable with the combined Spanish and Austrian navies, while no comparison could be considered with the powerful French navy, and the British Royal Navy was always considered neutral—if not an ally. In such a contest with France, Italy had few hopes for success, except with British intervention, which was possible, but unlikely. This was one of the reasons why between 1880 and 1895 ten large battleships entered service: *Duilio, Dandolo, Italia, Lepanto, Ruggero di Lauria, Francesco Morosini, Andrea Doria, Re Umberto, Sardegna*, and *Sicilia*. They enabled the Italian navy to be for a while the third largest navy in the world, after England and France, but, still, in 1886 France had 44 capital ships against 21 Italian ones. On average, the Italian ships were larger than the comparable French ones.

After the yards launched the *Duilio* class, some improvements were made to the *Italia* and *Lepanto*, which were much less protected than the former ships—almost fast cruisers. These ships too were built in domestic yards, but the plates were supplied partly by the British manufacturer Cammel, French Schneider and partly by Terni. The Brin concept in this design was that contemporary armor plates were unable to resist the largest guns mounted on ironclads and thus he planned these ships accordingly giving them a speed of 17–18 knots. Interestingly enough, the *Italia* class was armed with powerful 102 ton guns like the *Duilio*, but they were Armstrong of lesser caliber (431mm) and breech-loaders. Protection relied mainly on watertight compartments enclosed between two armored decks, one below and one above the waterline, while the funnel bases and main gun positions were protected with thick armor. Each of these large ships (over 15,000 tons when fully loaded) could carry 10,000 men, giving them an important strategic role.

The following *Ruggero di Lauria* class of three ships *(Andrea Doria, Francesco Morosini*, and *Ruggero di Lauria)* were completed between 1888 and 1891, having required from seven to nine years for construction. They could be considered a return to *Duilio* building concepts, and the result of the fact that under Acton's term as navy minister the displacement of the major ships was limited to 10,000 tons, while many advocated torpedo boats and ships designed to carry torpedo boats for action against enemy ports, instead of big ironclads. The last class laid down in the period considered here was the *Re Umberto*, again designed by Brin.

The class consisted of three ships *(Sardegna* and *Sicilia* were the other two) displacing 13,300 to 13,800 tons, with the main armament of four 343mm guns placed on fore and aft barbettes. Protection was widened and armor thickness reduced to some extent to have a belt of 4 inches, barbettes of 14 inches thick and numerous watertight compartments which were still favored. Speed was raised between 18.6 and 20 knots.

One of the main problems with Italian shipbuilding was the long time required to build a ship. Seven years passed between 1873, when *Duilio* was laid down, and 1880, when she entered service. The British 11,880 ton *Inflexible,* similar to *Duilio,* took the same time, from February 1874 to October 1881, but for the *Dandolo* it took nine years and eleven for *Sicilia.* The contemporary and smaller British *Devastation* was built between November 1869 and April 1873. British shipbuilding would develop more quickly, funding would be more rapid, and the two would combine for shorter yard time: for example the battleship *Repulse* was laid down in 1890 and completed in 1894. This was partly because the production of steel plates was often delayed in Terni's new plants, and often guns were produced well beyond the contract terms.

The policies of the Navy Law of 1873 were later continued by the 1887 one, which became active in a changed international situation, since from 1882 on Italy had entered the Triple Alliance with Austria-Hungary and Germany. The new law foresaw an expenditure of 85 million lire over nine years for the increase in the number of battleships, but also for a goal of 190 torpedo boats.

The development of the Italian Navy between 1861 and 1891 is reflected in the following figures, in millions of dollars ($1 = 5.20 lire 1907 rate), for expenditure in significant years:

YEAR	1861	1865	1866	1870	1873	1875	1880
in $	9.76	11.4	11.9	4.82	6.59	6.94	8.67

YEAR	1883	1885/6	1890/1
in $	12.1	16.1	21.7

In the 1890's the Navy had to accept restrictions on the budget because of the poor condition of the national economy, lowering her expense from $23.65 million in 1889/90 to the lowest point of 18.4 in 1894/5. It is clear that the Italian Royal Navy was truly formed in the 1880s, when the number of sailors with the colors went from 12,980 to 21,420.

Again, as before Lissa, the mighty expense of shipbuilding prevented the proper training of the personnel and the complete maintenance of the ships, although from 1870 to the First World War the officer corps and the crews improved considerably in forming a new united navy.

Glossary of Selected Terms

Barbette: the gun turned on a platform, while the protection offered by the barbette wall remained in place. This meant that the machinery moved less weight. In this period the French preferred open topped barbettes that allowed for entry of shells into the compartment at longer ranges (a sort of lob shot just over the barbette wall), but the French always designed their warships until World War I for close range battles. Additionally, the barbette would be the raised platform that a turret sat on and would be protecting the ammunition supply trunks. The pure barbette tended to sit higher on a ship (less overall weight) and so was more easily worked in foul weather and allowed for plunging fire at close range that could propel a shell deep into the vitals of an enemy ship and possibly through its bottom.

Beam: width of a ship—from side to side. It tended to increase in later ironclads from older broadside ships for two reasons. First, shorter and broader ships were more maneuverable—easier to ram, and second, as the size and weight of guns increased one had to compensate for the shifting of a ship's list when the guns on a broadside were run or run out. In other words, they were more stable for larger guns—running guns out would cause the stable gun platform to move and the broader the beam the more stable the platform.

Belt: the belt armor was the ship's side armor. Early coastal Ironclads would have the armor extending the entire length and height of the ship's side, though even the *Gloire* and other early seagoing ironclads had to leave some areas, usually each end above the waterline, unarmored or lightly armored. As the size and power of guns increased and the quality of armor also increased, there would be a constant redesign of the height, length, and thickness of the armor belt of a ship. The introduction of the rapid fire light gun with the high explosive shell (the French were first with Melinite in 1890) severely upset this balance as unarmored ends could now be riddled with shells causing fires and leakage.

Belted Cruiser: early name for armored cruiser, used primarily by the British for their early armored cruisers or for pre-*Dupuy de Lome* period armored cruisers

(1888). Usually not much faster than a battleship of that period, but with great range. The first armored cruiser is considered to have been the Russian *General-Admiral.*

Built up gun: quite common in the early period of the ironclads, it is literally a breech, reinforced, usually with hot iron bands, giving many guns their distinctive "pop" bottle look, such as with the Armstrong, Dahlgren, or later French ordnance. It would allow for heavier powder charges and less likelihood of the gun exploding. Also called banded or hooped gun.

Bolt: a large caliber elongated and flat nosed solid shot. First developed for Whitworth guns in 1858. Often chilled during manufacture to harden them.

Breech-loader: a gun loaded from the breech. Allows for a longer gun tube that improves range and velocity of the shell.

Cable: 120 fathoms in length, usually chain or hemp.

Casemate: an enclosed gun position on a fort or on a ship, roofed, and protected with stone, brick, or armor.

Compound Armor: a combination of layers of wrought iron and layers of steel, which makes the overall armored position stronger than if armored with just one or the other plate by a ratio of 2:3. It was developed and used extensively in the 1880's.

Conning Tower: the armored fighting position for the commander of the ship or the admiral. Located near the bridge (often one deck lower), it was more confined than the bridge, but was usually, but not always, as heavily armored as the turrets or barbettes. A second fighting position was aft, and usually less well armored. Some fighting doctrine saw the admiral in the rear Conning Tower and the Captain forward and the flagship at the head of the fleet.

Cruiser: a general term for a non-battleship, but more properly a ship that took over the role of the old frigate or sloop. Often unarmored or lightly armored, usually faster than a battleship and often used on detached service or for scouting.

Displacement: this is always a tricky item, as it is the ship's weight. Almost always given in tons, the measurement can vary. Additionally, it must be noted if it is "full load" (all the crew and supplies on board at the start of the voyage), "normal" (that is how this book tries to list it), or "light load" (which would be with no supplies or men on board).

Fort: a fort is formally defined as having full height walls on all sides. Thus Fort Wagner at Charleston is a misnomer—she was really a battery as on her rear side (the backside on the Charleston side) was a simple breastwork.

Foul: to collide or entangle.

Guerre de Course: war of chase, it was the French concept of making war on the enemy's trade, and in the late 19th century was envisioned as the way to bring down Great Britain by the *Jeune Ecole* in France. Mahan's writings were strongly against this school of thought.

Helm: the tiller or steering area. Usually on large ships later in this era there would be two or more positions to steer from, i.e., the bridge, conning tower, and aft conning tower.

Lee: Downwind or side of a ship away from the action or wind.

Lozenge: literally four equal sides. This was the French style of disposing the main armament with one main gun forward, one aft, and one on either broadside. This gave more all around fire and would also allow for more heavy guns to fire forward or aft, instead of the standard two in a more traditional ship. To get this extra forward or aft fire would require the ship to yaw back and forth, as to fire a heavy gun directly in line with the deck forward or aft would cause severe damage to the firing ship from the affects of the gun blast.

Muzzle-loader: old style of gun that is loaded from the muzzle end of the gun tube.

Pennant: a flag, either giving the rank of the officer on board, or else a signal to a particular ship or shore position.

Pivot guns: a type of gun mounting, usually fore and aft, which allows the firing gun to be fired either ahead or aft, respectively, as well as on either broadside. Usually the largest gun on board, it allowed for taking advantage of long range fire and increasing the affect of one's broadside. It also meant that when trained on a target it would not cause the ship to yaw to one side or the other.

Points: 32 points on the circle. There would be eight points, for example, from north to east, which would translate into—north, north by east, north-northeast, northeast by north, northeast, northeast by east, east-northeast, east by north, east. Using the like naming, for east to south; from south to west; and from west to north.

Port: or left side of a ship.

Protected Cruiser: a type of cruiser with a curved armored deck. The first one designed in this fashion was from the Armstrong yard and was the Chilean *Esmeralda,* built in the 1880's. The armored deck offered protection to the vitals of the ship which was defined as the magazines, boilers, and engines. Being curved, it gave more protection as the usual angle that a shell hit meant that more armor needed to be penetrated, as shells seldom hit perpendicularly.

Racers: the tracks used for shifting guns from one gunport to another. Used extensively on central battery type ships.

Rake: a raking shot is one that passes lengthwise along a ship and is most damaging. The *Virginia* fired such a shell against the *Congress* which killed or wounded most of an entire line of powder boys supplying the guns.

Secondary battery: as the main armament of ships grew in the size of the gun, only with fewer of them, a secondary battery of smaller guns, usually on the broadside, sometimes in small turrets or sponsons, were gradually introduced. Often unarmored, with the development of the quick-firing gun and high explosive powders, these batteries would become more protected. Their primary use was to fire on small enemy warships or unarmored sections of larger warships.

Single Screw: a single screw propeller allowed for the engine and vulnerable high pressure boiler to be farther below the waterline than with a paddle steamer. Additionally, the screw being hidden contrasted with the exposed paddle of an older steam warship.

Sponson: a gun platform projecting from the side of a vessel. Quite popular with late Ironclad cruisers, the sponson had some disadvantages in that heavy seas could splash heavily on them and affect the ship's gunnery, as well as speed. Their chief advantage was that they allowed for a wider arc of fire.

Springs: or ropes (cables) used when a ship is anchored, usually with one at each end of the ship. By hauling in and letting out in combination, one might turn a ship.

Starboard: or right side of a ship.

Turret: See Barbette. The turret was more protected than a barbette, but was more likely to be jammed from shell fire. The entire structure turned on a spindle. There were two main designs for a turret, one by the Swedish inventor John Ericsson and the other by British naval Captain Cowper Coles.

Twin or Triple Screw: by having two or three screw propellers (see Single Screw) a warship could turn quicker and in a smaller turning radius. This was done by having one screw in reverse while the other was going forward. This was seen as an advantage primarily in ramming or any other close range tactical situation.

Wake: the track left by a ship through the water and being directly "in the wake" of a ship, would be directly astern.

Watertight compartment: with the advent of underwater warfare (though actual experiments to see how much force it would take to blow a big enough hole in the side of a ship, would not take place until late in the 19th century) and the use of metal instead of wood for hulls, iron ships could be compartmentalized. These watertight compartments could be used to help keep a ship from sinking if underwater damage occurred. They were walled off sections of the ship, usually only from side to side, with doors and water pump arrangements so that various compartments could be isolated and pumped full of water. Later lengthwise compartmentalization would be introduced. As compartmentalization increased, it allowed for a list to be corrected by counterflooding a compartment on one side or the other, and so prevent a damaged ship from capsizing.

Selected Bibliography

(Readers must note that this does not include all sources used in writing this book, especially many foreign language secondary sources, but are either important sources or ones that readers may obtain easily for further study on their own).

Unpublished Sources

Archives des Ministere des Affaires Etrangeres - Paris.

Rapport de la bataille de Hampton Roads, Capitaine Gautier aux Gouvernement Francais adresse au Baron Henri Mercier de líOstende qui etait le Ministre de la Marine Francaise a Washington, dated March 9 1862, AMAE CP, E-U 126.

Archivio centrale dello stato, Rome.

ACS, Carteggi di personalita Benedetto Brin

Cass.2, fasc.2, doc.57: "Rapporto dei danni riportati dai bastimenti dell'Armata nell'attacco alle fortificazioni di Lissa e nella battaglia contro la squadra austriaca," 28.7.1866, signed De Luca.

Cass.2, fasc.6, doc.32: Giornale uffiziale della 2nd dal 16 al 21 luglio 1866

doc. 33: Giornale Uffiziale della 3rd squadra dell'Armata díoperazione dal 15 luglio a tutto il 20 luglio 1866.

ACS, Carteggi di personalita, Persano Carlo di Pellion

Cass.2, busta 2, fasc.5, Relazione sul combattimento navale fuori líisola di Lissa, dated 23 July 1866.

Papers held by National Maritime Museum, Greenwich, London.

Album 23, PR 1959/223, Captain F. G. D. Bedford's album "Record of the proceedings of HMS Shah . . . August 1876 (to) April 1878."

Public Record Office, London.

Class ADM 1 (Admiralty and Secretariat Papers)

      ADM 1/6414 From Admirals Y: Pacific (1877)

      ADM 1/6424 From Foreign Office Sept.-Dec. 1877)

      ADM 1/6429 From Captains (A-K) (1877)

Class ADM 50 (Admirals' Journals)

      ADM 50/314 Admirals' Journals: Pacific (1876-1878)

Class ADM 53 (Logs of H.M. Ships)

        ADM 53/10881 Log of HMS Amethyst (1876-1877)

        ADM 53/11121 Log of HMS Shah (1876-1877)

Class FO 61 (Foreign Office General Correspondence: Peru)

        FO 61/299 Peru: general correspondence (January-May 1877

        FO 61/300 Peru: general correspondence (June-December 1877)

        FO 61/302 Peru: Consuls at Callao, etc (January-December 1877)

        FO 61/305 Peru: diplomatic drafts and dispatches (January-May 1878)

Published Sources

Attlmayr, Ferdinand von, *Der Krieg Osterreichs in der Adria im Jahre 1866*, (Pola, 1896). Important Austrian study of the Lissa campaign.

Barsali, M., *Giovanni Cavalli*, in: Dizionario bibliografico degli italiani.

Baxter, James P. III, *The Introduction of the Ironclad Warship*, (Cambridge, Harvard U. Press, 1933). Superb early study of how it all came together at Hampton Roads from a global perspective.

Bathe, Greville, *Ship of Destiny*, (Philadelphia, Allen, Lane, and Scott, 1951). Short sweet story of the *Merrimac(k)* and *Virginia*.

Bergeron, Arthur W., Jr., *Confederate Mobile*, (Jackson, University Press of Mississippi, 1991). Very good discussion of Mobile if written in a somewhat flat style.

Bourne, Kenneth, *Britain and the Balance of Power in North America 1815-1908*, (Berkeley, University of California Press, 1967). Good detail on warplans and British policy of defending Canada in the event of war with the USA.

Brodie, Bernard, *Sea Power in the Machine Age*, (Princeton University Press, 1943). An early classic review of the impact of industrialization on naval power, with minor errors of detail.

Brooke, George M. Jr., *John M. Brooke, Naval Scientist and Educator*, (Charlottesville, University Press of Virginia, 1980). Has some good detail but deserves a larger study.

Brown, D.K., *Before the Ironclad*, (London, Conway Maritime Press, Ltd., 1990). Discusses in much detail and with great illustrations the 1815-1860 development of *British* warships. Pro British point of view.

Browning, Robert, *From Cape Charles to Cape Fear: The North Atlantic Blockading Squadron during the Civil War*, (Tuscaloosa, U. of Alabama Press, 1993). Scholarly account - quite good on the blockade marred by errors on tactical detail.

Buloz, L., Lissa, in: *Revue des deux Mondes*, 1st November 1866, pp. 295-328.

Burton, E. Milby, *The Siege of Charleston 1861-1865*, (Columbia, University of South Carolina Press, 1990).
>First appearing in 1970, a good study, though slanted towards the Confederacy, this siege needs a fresh look.

Busk, Hans, *The Navies of the World*, (Annapolis, Naval Institute Press, 1973).
>First appearing in 1859, it is of limited value.

C.1833, Peru No. 1 (1877) *Correspondence relating to the engagement between Her Majesty's Shiops "Shah" and "Amethyst" and the "Huascar"*.

Callwell, C. E., *Gli effetti del dominio del mare sulle operazioni militari da Waterloo in poi*, (Turin, Casanova, 1898).
>This is the Italian translation of *The Effects of the Maritime Command on Land Campaigns* which was well known in Italy, perhaps more than Mahan.

Carr, William, *The Origins of the Wars of German Unification*, London-New York, Longman, 1991.

Cavalli, Jean (Giovanni), *Memoire sur divers perfectionaments militaires*, Paris, 1856 and as *Memoria sui diversi perfezionamenti Militari*, (Torino, Stamperia Reale, 1856).
>Cavalli's contributions are outlined in his own work

Century Magazine, various issues,

Clowes, William Laird, *Four Modern Naval Campaigns*, (London, Unit Library, 1902).
>Good account of Lissa, the Pacific War and the Brazilian and Chilean Civil Wars, but with some errors.)

Civil War Times Illustrated, various issues, Gettyburg, Pa.

Cogar, William B. editor, *New Interpretations in Naval History, Selected Papers from the . . . Naval History Symposium*, (Annapolis, Naval Institute Press, various).
>An excellent article by Tucker on the "Peacemaker" appears as well as material by Still and others on the USN *Monitor*.

Coker P.C. III, *Charleston's Maritime Heritage*, 1670-1865. (Charleston, CokerCraft Press, 1987).
>A beautifully illustrated and well researched coffee table maritime history.

Colomb, P.H., *Naval Warfare*, (Annapolis, Naval Institue Press, 1990).
>First appearing in 1891, this is a good series of essays on strategy and history.

Commissione d'inchiesta sulla Regia marina. Relazioni speciali in 3 vols., (Rome, 1906, UNIPD: Pubbl.Uff.751/1-3).

Coski, John M., *Capital Navy*, (Campbell, 1996).
>A comprehensive study of Richmond and the James River squadron in the American Civil War and makes use of many original items. Definitive on the subject.

Cranfield, Eugene B., *Notes on Naval Ordnance of the American Civil War, 1861-1865*, (Washington D.C., GPO, 1969).
>A small pamphlet with lots of data - only wish it was longer.

Daly, R.W., *How the Merrimac Won*, (New York City, Thomas Y. Crowell, 1957).
Argues that the *Virginia* prolonged the war by years with McClellan's failure in the Peninsular Campaign. Lively account with some small errors of detail, and tends to ignore evidence against his thesis, as well as making giant leaps of faith.

Davis, William C., *Duel Between the First Ironclads*, (New York City, Doubleday, 1975).
Prolific writer on the war, some small errors (*Congress* is given as a steamer for example) but quite readable.

Davis, William C., *The Last Conquistadores*, (University of Georgia Press, 1950).
Only full length treatment of the troubles between Spain and Peru.

Delafield, Majors Richard & Alfred Mordecai & Captain George B. McClellan, *Report on the Art of War in Europe 1854, 1855, and 1856: Military Commission to Europe, 1854-1856*, 1 or 3 volumes Washington, GPO, 1857-60.
Incredible American source of material on the siege of Sevastopol and European military developments. Ultimately wrong in concluding that forts were stronger than ships. Commissioned by the then Secretary of War Jefferson Davis!

Der deutsch-danische Krieg 1864, hrsg. vom Groben Generalstab, Abt. feur Kriegsgeschichte, (2 Bde, Text, 2 Bde, Karten, Berlin, 1866/67).

Deutsche Marine Institut & MGFA (ed.), *Die deutsche Flotte im Spannungsfeld der Politik 1848-1985*, (Herford-Bonn, Mittler & Sohn, 1985).
A collection of papers from a historical meeting. One by Michael Steurmer on the Navy 1880 - 1914.

Dockum, Admiral Carl Edvard van, *Livserindringer*, (Kjobenhavn, Ernst Bojesens Kunstvorlag, 1893).

Dijk, A. van, *Voor Pampus*, (Amsterdam, De Bataafsche Leeuw, 1987).
A well illustrated oversize book with English synopsis on the Dutch ironclad transition to 1864 - well done but short.

Dufour, Charles L., *The Night the War was Lost*, (Lincoln, U. of Nebraska, 1960, 1988, 1990).
Argues that the fall of New Orleans was the turning point in the war.

Elliott, Robert G., *Ironclad of the Roanoke*, (Shippensburg, Pa., White Mane Publishing Company, 1994).
New comprehensive history of the CSS *Albemarle*. Many fine illustrations in it, accurate, and a labor of love.

Falk, Edwin A., *Togo and the Rise of Japanese Sea Power*, (New York, Longmans, Green and Co., 1936).
One of the very few historians who tackled the Civil War of 1868-1869 and did a good job of it. Worked with Japanese source material which should be done more often.

Fischer, Friedrich von, *Der Krieg in Schleswig und Jutland im Jahre 1864*, (Wien, 1870).

Fleischer, Josef, *Geschichte der k.k. Kriegsmarine wahrend des Krieges im Jahre 1866* (Geschichte der k.k. Kriegsmarine 3/3), (Wien, 1906).

Fock, Harald, *Schwarze Gesellen Torpedoboote bis 1914*, (Herdorf, Koehler, 1970?).
Well illustrated history of the torpedo boat to 1914.

Fowler, William M., Jr., *Under Two Flags: The American Navy in the Civil War*, (New York, W.W. Norton and Co., 1990)
Fowler is an academic who has written a popular and general study of the naval war. He tends to make broad statements.

Gamio, Captain Jose Valdizan, *Historia naval del Peru*, vol IV. Orden *Republicano*, (Lima, Direccion General de Interese Maritimos, 1987.
Used for *Shah* section.

Gibbons, Tony, *The Complete Encyclopedia of Battleships*, (New York, Crown Books, 1983).
Lovely coffee table picture book with insightful commentary.. It is extensive, but not "complete." He also has an equally attractive *Warships and Battles of the U.S. Civil War*. However his co-authored work *The Civil War Military Machine* with Ian Drury is replete with errors of detail. Maps with the *Virginia* coming from the wrong direction, Fort Wagner at Charleston in the wrong spot, 11" Brooke rifles never built, etc., etc.

Greene, S. D. , Ramsay, H. Ashton, and Worden, J. L., *The Monitor and the Merrimac*, (N.Y. Harper Bros., 1912).
An oft quoted short firsthand account, with some small errors.

Greenhill, Basil and Giffard, Ann, *The British Assault on Finland 1854-1855*, (London, Conway Maritime Press Ltd., 1988).
Unusual topic very well done with much travel to the battlefields, and has good insights.

Hamilton, C.I., *Anglo French Naval Rivalry 1840-1870*, (Oxford, Clarendon Press, 1993).
Excellent and detailed study by a South African historian.

Hearn, Chester G., *The Capture of New Orleans, 1862*, (Baton Rouge, Louisiana State University Press, 1995).
A very good study of the campaign, much better than his earlier book on Mobile.

Hendrick, Burton J., *Statesmen of the Lost Cause*, (New York, The Literary Guild of America, 1939).
A series of biographies on Jefferson Davis and his Cabinet, with a good study on Secretary of the Navy Mallory.

Herrick, Walter R. Jr., *The American Naval Revolution*, (Baton Rouge, Louisiana State University Press, 1966).
Takes the US Navy from the doldrums of the early 1880's to the Spanish American War. Excellent academic study.

Hervey, Maurice H., *Dark Days in Chile*, (London, Edward Arnold,1892)
A correspondent who covered the 1891 Civil War and had difficulty getting his dispatches printed as he was in favor of the President's Party, an unpopular position in Great Britain.

Hodges, Peter, *The Big Gun*, (London, Conway Maritime Press, 1981).
  If you like big guns you will want to look at this.

Hogg, Ian V., "The Royal Navy, La Royale, and the Militiariazation of Naval Warfare, 1840-1870", in (*Journal of Strategic Studies*, vol. 6, (1983), pp 182-212).

Hooker, Terry D., *The Pacific War 1879-84*, (Cottingham, El Dorado Books, 1993).
  Poorly written handbook with much in the way of excellent material on the war, but largely from Chilean sources - a publication of the South and Central American Historians Society.

Hucul, W.C., *The Evolution of Russian and Soviet Sea-Power 1853-1953*, (1953, U. of California dissertation).
  Interesting but of limited value, but does research in Russian.

Krebs, H. W., *Gefechtsentfernung 3,000 Schritte*, in: (Atlantische Welt, 8/1968, n.3, p.13).

C. Jacobi, *Gerzogenen Geschuetzo der Amerikaner bei der Belagerung von Charleston*, (Stokker, Berlin, 1866)
  A pamphlet on artillery, mostly land artillery, and its use in the siege of Charleston.

La Campagna del 1866 nei documenti militari austriaci. Le operazion navali, (edited by Angelo Filippuzzi, Padua, 1966).
  A selection of Austrian documents published in German including Tegetthoff's complete report of 27 November, 1866 on the Battle of Lissa.

Lambert, Andrew, *Battleships in Transition*, (London, Conway Maritime Press, 1984).
  Excellent, though short, book on the creation and use of the the British steam battlefleet.

Lambert, Andrew, *The Crimean War*, (Manchester, Manchester University Press, 1991).
  A must read for understanding the strategy of the war, though suffers from the publisher editing the original text down which makes for short, choppy sentences.

Luraghi, Raimondo, *Marinai del Sud*, (Milan, Rizzoli, 1993).
  A 600+ page look by an Italian historian on the exploits of the Confederate Navy. Well researched, looks at the big picture, and uses wonderfully poetic language, it has just been published in an English edition from the Naval Institute Press as *A History of the Confederte Navy*. Our translations are from the Italian edition.

Mahan, Alfred T., *The Gulf and Inland Waters*, (N.Y., Charles Scribner's Sons, 1881-83).

Magazines. We made much use of academic publications, also the esoteric *The Mariner's Mirror*, as well as *Journal of Military History, Military History, Military History Quarterly* (MHQ), and *Command* magazines. Sometimes the best small little details will appear in an academic study and where possible we have tried to note the authors in our text. We apologize if we have missed any.

Marder, Arthur, *The Anatomy of British Sea Power, A History of British Naval Policy in the Pre-Dreadnought Era, 1880-1905*, (London, Frank Cass & Co., 1940 & 1973).
  A brilliantly written classic. Reading this book in his youth brought the American co-author into a fascinating period of interest.

Marine & Technique au XIXe Siecle, (Paris, Service Historique de la Marine and Institut d'Histoire des Conflits Contemporains, 1989).

    An overview of some of the technological and naval advances in the 19th century in a series of essays, mostly in French, but some in English.

Marshal, Ian, *Armored Ships* (London, Conway Maritime Press, 1990).

    Great pictures, accurate text. His *Ironclads* is equally good.

Mason, Lt. Theodorus B.M. (USN), *The War on the Pacific Coast of South America between Chile and the Allied Republics of Peru and Bolivia.* (Washington D.C., GPO 1883).

    Prepared by the Office of Naval Intelligence, Bureau of Navigation, and while short, quite detailed.

Melo, Resendo, *Historia de la Marina del Peru*, Vol I (Callao: Museo Naval del Peru, reprinted 1980, first printed in 1907). Used in *Shah* section.

Paloczi-Horvath, George, *From Monitor to Missile Boat* (London, Conway Maritime Press, 1996).

    Solid addition to the topic though not definitive, only wish it was longer. Good illustration selection.

Parker, Foxhall, *The Battle of Mobile Bay* (Boston, A. Williams & Co., 1878).

    A short and accurate account by a Union officer who served there.

Parker, Captain W. H., *Recollections of a Naval Officer 1841-1865*, (Annapolis, Naval Institute Press, 1883, 1985).

    Interesting, humorous, and sometimes bizarre, views from a Confederate officer.

Patterson, Loren Scott, *The War of the Triple Alliance: Paraguayan Offensive Phase*, (Ann Arbor, UMI, 1975).

    Interesting, well researched, weakly written account of the start of the war.

Rawlinson, John L., *China's Struggle for Naval Development 1839-1895*, (Cambridge, Harvard University Press, 1967).

    Revealing and well researched story of conservatives trying to handle the modern Western World facing the dying Chinese Empire - needs maps.

Roberts, William Howard, *U.S.S. New Ironsides: The Seagoing Ironclad in the Union Navy*, (Ann Arbor, UMI, 1992).

    A solid thesis about the most fought ironclad ever built and an ideal candidate for being in the "Anatomy of a Ship" series.

Ropp, Theodore, *The Development of a Modern Navy, French Naval Policy 1871-1904*, (Annapolis, Naval Institute Press, 1987).

    Brilliant, but a bit dated - excellent use of foreign source material.

Saibene, Marc, *Les Cuirassés Redoutable, Déastation, Courbet*, (Bourg-en-Bresse, Marines, 1994).

    Beautiful though thin book on post Franco-Prussian War French battleships.

Sandler, Stanley, *The Emergence of the Modern Capital Ship*, (Cranbury, N.J., University of Delaware Press, 1979).

    Excellent book, though focused on British naval development to HMS *Devastation*. In many ways picks up where Baxter in his *The Introduction of the Ironclad Warship* leaves off.

Santi-Mazzini, Giovanni, *La Technologia Militare Marittima di 1776 al 1916*, volume I, Munitions and Naval artillery. (Italy, PHAROS, 1994 - ISBN 88-86375-05-0).

An elongated book (*Janes Fighting Ships* size) in Italian that is one of the most beautifully produced books we have ever seen. It is 504 pages, with an illustration (over 800) on virtually every page, using no secondary sources - only primary ones.

Sater, William, *The Heroic Image in Chile*, (Berkeley, UCB, 1973).

A story of the impact of Arturo Prat and the role of the hero in Chile's history. Also *Chile and the War of the Pacific*, U. of Nebraska, 1986. The latter gives more an overview of Chile during the war and little on the war operations.

Scheina, Robert L., *Latin America, A Naval History 1810-1987* (Annapolis, USNI, 1987).

Only modern study in English, cries out for an expanded version.

Soley, James Russell, *The Blockade and the Cruisers*, (New York, Charles Scribner's Sons, 1881-83)

Classic, well written account with some errors of detail and pro-North viewpoint.

Spencer, Warren F., *The Confederate Navy in Europe*, (Alabama, U. of Alabama, 1983).

Largely concerned with the diplomatic machinations of buying a navy, little on the hardware. Also of value is his *United States and France: Civil War Diplomacy* co-authored with Lynn M. Case.

Steinmetz, Hans-Otto, *Im Schatten der Armee und grossen Politik. Ein Betrachtung der Einsatz der deutsch-preussisch Marine im Krieg*, in: (Marine Rundschau, 1973, pp.212-299).

Still, William N., Jr., *Iron Afloat*, (Columbia, S.C., University of South Carolina Press, 1971/1985).

Starting point, very dependable, but more detail is out there now. Also did an excellent *Confederate Shipbuilding* in 1969 (U. of Georgia) which shows clearly the decline of the Confederacy after 1862 for building a fleet of ironclads, but not due to lack of materials and facilities, but due to lack of proper exploitation.

Swanson, Bruce, *Eighth Voyage of the Dragon*, (Annapolis, Naval Institute Press, 1982).

Not too detailed history of the Chinese Navy.

Tucker, Spencer, *Arming the Fleet*, (Annapolis, Naval Institute Press, 1989).

Quite detailed with a lot of nuts and bolts on the guns of the American Civil War period.

Turner, Maxine, *Navy Gray*, (Tuscaloosa, University of Alabama, 1988).

This has been her lifelong work and has received a great deal of help from the Confederate Naval Museum at Columbus Georgia. Her book examines a tiny slice of naval history and does demand that you are familiar with the entire history of that navy.

Violette, Aurele Joseph, *Russian Naval Reform 1855-1870*, (Ann Arbor, UMI, 1971)

A thesis aimed at manning reforms and not ship building reforms. Very little else in English on the topic.

Williams, John Hoyt, *The Rise and Fall of the Paraguayan Republic 1800-1870*. (Austin, U. of Texas, 1979).

Wallin, Franklin W., *The French Navy During the Second Empire* (1953, U. of California dissertation).

Dated, but holds some insights.

Warship, various. This British publication originally appeared as a quarterly but now is published jointly by Conway Maritime Press and the Naval Institute as a hardbound yearly.

Filled with essays by top writers in the field, virtually every issue contained an article drawn on for *Ironclads at War.*

Warship International, various. This publication has appeared over the years and is simply excellent and a labor of love.

Great articles on individual ships or classes, with an occasional more esoteric brew. If you want to know about a warship, you can probably find some reference to it somewhere in the back issues of this quarterly.

Werlich, David P., *Admiral of the Amazon: John Randolph Tucker* (Charlottesville, University of Virginia, 1990).

Unique biography of a Confederate who fought for Peru after the American Civil War.

Wilson, H.W., *Ironclads in Action 1855-1896*, 2 volumes (London, Sampson Low & Co., 1896).

A classic which can be often read, but loaded with minor errors. It was followed after World War I with a less detailed *Battleships in Action.*

Wise, Stephen R., *Lifeline of the Confederacy, Blockade Running During the Civil War,* (Columbia, South Carolina University Press, 1988/91).

Not strictly on our topic but an excellent study that gives real insight into the Confederacy's struggle. His recent *Gate of Hell* (Columbia, South Carolina University Press, 1994) is an excellent and balanced study of the year 1863 at Charleston.

General Index

Index of Ships